CMMI® and Six Sigma

The SEI Series in Software Engineering represents a collaboration between the Software Engineering Institute of Carnegie Mellon University and Addison-Wesley to develop and publish a body of work on selected topics in software engineering. The common goal of the SEI and Addison-Wesley is to provide the most current software engineering information in a form that is easily usable by practitioners and students.

For more information point your browser to www.awprofessional.com/seiseries

Dennis M. Ahern, et al., *CMMI® SCAMPI Distilled.* ISBN: 0-321-22876-6

Dennis M. Ahern, et al., *CMMI® Distilled, Second Edition.* ISBN: 0-321-18613-3

Christopher Alberts and Audrey Dorofee, *Managing Information Security Risks.* ISBN: 0-321-11886-3

Len Bass, et al., *Software Architecture in Practice, Second Edition.* ISBN: 0-321-15495-9

Marilyn Bush and Donna Dunaway, *CMMI® Assessments.* ISBN: 0-321-17935-8

Carnegie Mellon University, Software Engineering Institute, *The Capability Maturity Model.* ISBN: 0-201-54664-7

Mary Beth Chrissis, et al., *CMMI®, Second Edition.* ISBN: 0-321-27967-0

Paul Clements, et al., *Documenting Software Architectures.* ISBN: 0-201-70372-6

Paul Clements, et al., *Evaluating Software Architectures.* ISBN: 0-201-70482-X

Paul Clements and Linda Northrop, *Software Product Lines.* ISBN: 0-201-70332-7

Bill Curtis, et al., *The People Capability Maturity Model®.* ISBN: 0-201-60445-0

William A. Florac and Anita D. Carleton, *Measuring the Software Process.* ISBN: 0-201-60444-2

Suzanne Garcia and Richard Turner, *CMMI® Survival Guide.* ISBN: 0-321-42277-5

Hassan Gomaa, *Software Design Methods for Concurrent and Real-Time Systems.* ISBN: 0-201-52577-1

Elaine M. Hall, *Managing Risk.* ISBN: 0-201-25592-8

Hubert F. Hofmann, et al., *CMMI® for Outsourcing.* ISBN: 0-321-47717-0

Watts S. Humphrey, *Managing Technical People.* ISBN: 0-201-54597-7

Watts S. Humphrey, *Introduction to the Personal Software Process℠.* ISBN: 0-201-54809-7

Watts S. Humphrey, *Managing the Software Process.* ISBN: 0-201-18095-2

Watts S. Humphrey, *A Discipline for Software Engineering.* ISBN: 0-201-54610-8

Watts S. Humphrey, *Introduction to the Team Software Process℠.* ISBN: 0-201-47719-X

Watts S. Humphrey, *Winning with Software.* ISBN: 0-201-77639-1

Watts S. Humphrey, *PSP℠: A Self-Improvement Process for Software Engineers.* ISBN: 0-321-30549-3

Watts S. Humphrey, *TSP℠—Leading a Development Team.* ISBN: 0-321-34962-8

Watts S. Humphrey, *TSP℠—Coaching Development Teams.* ISBN: 0-201-73113-4

Daniel J. Paulish, *Architecture-Centric Software Project Management.* ISBN: 0-201-73409-5

Robert C. Seacord, *Secure Coding in C and C++.* ISBN: 0-321-33572-4

Richard D. Stutzke, *Estimating Software-Intensive Systems.* ISBN: 0-201-70312-2

Sami Zahran, *Software Process Improvement.* ISBN: 0-201-17782-X

CMMI® and Six Sigma

Partners in Process Improvement

Jeannine M. Siviy
M. Lynn Penn
Robert W. Stoddard

Upper Saddle River, NJ • Boston • Indianapolis • San Francisco
New York • Toronto • Montreal • London • Munich • Paris • Madrid
Capetown • Sydney • Tokyo • Singapore • Mexico City

The SEI Series in Software Engineering

Library of Congress Cataloging-in-Publication Data
Siviy, Jeannine M.
CMMI and Six Sigma : partners in process improvement / Jeannine M. Siviy, M. Lynn Penn, and Robert W. Stoddard.
p. cm. — (The SEI series in software engineering)
Includes bibliographical references and index.
ISBN 978-0-321-51608-4 (hardcover : alk. paper)
1. Software engineering. 2. Computer software—Quality control. 3. Capability maturity model (Computer software)
4. Six sigma (Quality control standard) I. Penn, M. Lynn. II. Stoddard, Robert W., 1959- III. Title.

QA76.758S549 2007
005.1—dc22 2007038174

ISBN-13: 978-0-321-51608-4
ISBN-10: 0-321-51608-7

Text printed in the United States on recycled paper at Courier in Westford, Massachusetts.
First printing, December 2007

To my mom, Ann,
and to my brother and his family, George, Paula, Gregory,
Christopher, and Andrew,
who all inspire me with their strength of conviction,
passion for all pursuits, and perseverance through life's challenges.
And in memory of my father, George.
—j.m.s.

To my family, Steve and Christie, you have truly been
my inspiration and support.
To my parents, my mother, Kit, and
in memory of my dad, Jim, who shaped my early learning.
To other family members who sacrificed my companionship—
our daughter, Gina, and her family, Vaughn, Trevor, and Allie,
and my sister, Karen, and her family, Rich and JD.
—m.l.p.

To Dr. Mikel Harry, for providing me the inspiration, during his 1993
visit to Texas Instruments, to begin a career pursuit of Six Sigma; to
Mr. Clyde (Skip) Creveling, for providing such a fervent zeal, during his
2004 visit to Motorola, for the implementation and dramatic results
of Design for Six Sigma, including Marketing for Six Sigma; and to
Jimmy C. Jobe, my former manager at Texas Instruments, without whose
support and funding I would not have been afforded the opportunity to join
in such a life-changing and exciting topic.
Also, to my wife, Heather, for her patience during the nights and weekends
committed to authoring material for this text!
—r.w.s.

Contents

List of Figures

List of Tables

Foreword

by Forrest W. Breyfogle

When working with clients, I introduce basic Six Sigma concepts via the themes of Smarter Six Sigma Solutions and Integrated Enterprise Excellence (S^4/IEE)—a system developed through more than 15 years of experience working with Six Sigma practitioners. A successful Six Sigma–based business strategy includes a suite of cross-functional and vertically aligned metrics that lead to significant improvements in customer satisfaction and bottom-line benefits as well as an infrastructure to support the strategy. After discussing what I call satellite-level and 30,000-foot-level metrics, I typically proceed through a discussion about drilling down from the satellite level through strategic plans to high-priority projects at the 30,000-foot level. From this S^4/IEE-based and vertically aligned project portfolio, detailed Six Sigma projects and operational plans may be effectively launched and managed. I close my introductory material with a discussion about how Six Sigma relates to "other improvement initiatives."

My list of comparisons typically focuses on "other *manufacturing* improvement initiatives" since, for many years, this has been the main focus of Six Sigma. But, in recent years, I have worked with an increasing number of software and systems engineering and IT organizations that are implementing Six Sigma. In this book, I have found answers to key questions and misconceptions about the relationship between Six Sigma and the Capability Maturity Model Integration (CMMI), a domain-specific *engineering* improvement initiative. Among my key takeaways is that the relationship between Six Sigma and CMMI exemplifies one of the principles of S^4/IEE: CMMI provides process infrastructure that is needed to support a successful Six Sigma strategy.

Of course, there are many other dimensions in the relationship between these two significant improvement approaches. This book elaborates on those, shares insights about relationships with other domain initiatives, and provides several different illustrations of the general application of Six Sigma frameworks and methods to the IT, software, and systems engineering domains. It is an adept balance of breadth and depth of informative material—deep enough to be useful for novice and expert Six Sigma practitioners working in or interacting with this domain, as well as for engineers and CMMI practitioners who find themselves facing the world of Six Sigma; broad enough for managers trying to effectively straddle (or resolve conflicts across) both worlds.

I began pondering the application of Six Sigma to software several years ago, when I first met Jeannine at the II Symposium on Six Sigma, sponsored by the Centro de Investigacion en Matematicas. I am pleased that through her efforts and those of her colleagues, the SEI has engaged in substantive work in connecting the worlds of software process improvement and enterprise process improvement.

Forrest W. Breyfogle III
CEO
Smarter Solutions, Inc.
www.SmarterSolutions.com

Foreword

by Jack Ferguson

Finally, a book that bridges the software and hardware process toolset. To date, there have been hardware and software engineers who for one reason or another have not communicated their process methods. And so, myths formed that convinced the hardware community that CMMI was *only* for software and likewise convinced the software community that Six Sigma was *only* for hardware.

It is both refreshing and thought provoking to dispel these myths. This book not only dispels the myths but also goes beyond to demonstrate through real case studies and illustrations that the tools when used by either discipline indeed complement each other. The ability of these two process tools to accelerate process improvement is something that few have discussed.

This book provides an excellent strategy in combining CMMI and Six Sigma methodologies for process improvement. My background is within the software community and CMMI adoption. My use and familiarization with Six Sigma is limited. Yet the arguments and mappings presented here are straightforward and understandable, even by me.

The explanation of CMMI and Six Sigma cooperating to provide organizations with an expeditious way to deploy process is intriguing and convincing. Frequently, we find organizations competing for process initiatives, each initiative needing separate funding and resources. This book gives organizational management the data to stop these turf wars.

I have worked with Jeannine and Lynn for many years and with Bob for the last few months. Their knowledge of and dedication to the adoption of both

CMMI and Six Sigma practices is founded in real business cases. This is not theory but application of the relevance of partnering these two methodologies.

Jack Ferguson
Manager, SEI Appraisal Program
Software Engineering Institute
www.sei.cmu.edu

Preface

Why Did We Write This Book?

Over the past several years, we have fielded an increasing number of questions about how to apply Six Sigma in software and, more specifically, how to apply it in the context of the SEI Capability Maturity Model Integration (CMMI). Often, the questions revolve around perceived competition between the two initiatives. Other frequently asked questions have related to case studies, examples of statistical tools in use, tailored training, and measurement infrastructure. Questions have come from organizations already implementing CMMI or Six Sigma as well as those implementing both and also those not yet implementing either. They have come from the defense industry, government agencies, commercial industry, consultants, and academia.

Until now, our primary approach for widespread sharing of information has been conference presentations, tutorials, and panels. The original intent of this book is to be a companion guide to such speaking engagements—primarily Jeannine's and Lynn's—to capture the commentary that is never evident from viewing slides downloaded from the Internet and to further explain the underlying research and practice.

Our text focuses on the synergistic, rather than competitive, implementation of CMMI and Six Sigma, with "synergy" translating to "better, faster, cheaper" achievement of mission success. Topics range from value proposition to tactics. We point out how *not* taking advantage of what both initiatives have to offer runs the risk of an organization sinking time and energy into inventing something that already exists. Along the way, we try to debunk a few myths about Six Sigma applications in software.

While this book concentrates on the interoperability of Six Sigma and CMMI, we recognize that organizations rarely implement only these two initiatives. Accordingly, we have included a discussion of the more general case of multimodel process improvement—an area of emerging research. We offer an overall process for multimodel process improvement, noting strategies and practices that transcend the models, and enable organizations to make informed decisions about how to effectively knit them together into a unified, single internal process standard. With the increasing pervasiveness of software in our society, we believe that the pressure from senior management to optimize the software portion of the business is going to escalate and that the interest in "better, faster, cheaper" and obsessively mission-focused software process improvement will grow considerably in coming years. The strategies and tactics we offer for an integrated approach to process improvement serve this purpose and mitigate the risks of "programs of the month," competing initiatives, resource conflicts, funding conflicts, and other issues that plague process improvement groups.

All this having been said, there is no such thing as a "silver bullet" answer. What we offer in this book is a framework for reasoning about the task at hand and information to help readers formulate their own strategies and tactical plans.

Who Is the Audience for This Book?

We wrote this book primarily for people in process improvement roles, as well as the managers and technical staff with whom they frequently interact.

For process improvement personnel—including engineering process improvement group leads and members; measurement working group members; Six Sigma Black Belts, Master Black Belts, and Champions—the book supports strategic and tactical decision making about initiative adoption and joint, synergistic implementation. It also provides information, in the form of both facts and ideas, that can be used to gain sponsorship and buy-in for joint initiative implementation.

For technical management—including program, project, engineering, and line managers—the book also serves decision making. For this group, however, the value is more strategic. The book provides an independent view about joint initiative implementation strategies that can be used as a reference when internal proposals are put forward. It can enable technical management to more confidently sponsor and support such proposals because there is data to support how the achievement of mission and performance improves with these proposals. For senior technical personnel, who are charged with completing projects and delivering, this book provides insight into how joint initiative implementation can help them accomplish the mission. Additionally, it provides insight into the rationale behind the several different joint implementation approaches—which may enable these personnel to better partner with improvement groups to select the most effective and efficient joint implementation design for their particular organizational culture.

How to Navigate This Book

The book is structured as follows.

- Chapters 1 through 3 present the foundational set of problem statements that have motivated most of our work. These chapters also provide a high-level explanation of CMMI and Six Sigma. Our presumption is that the majority of our readers have awareness of these technologies. We present enough explanation to allow you to understand the rest of the book even if you have no prior knowledge of CMMI and Six Sigma; however, this book will not make you an expert, and we strongly advise that you seek other references and training courses prior to any implementation. If you have an intimate knowledge of these technologies, Chapters 2 and 3 will scope and clarify their use in the remainder of this book.
- Chapters 4 and 5 describe the motivation for further considering the synergistic and mutually enabling aspects of Six Sigma and software improvement technologies. To do so, these chapters summarize the results of research as well as case studies.
- Chapters 6 through 8 discuss the strategic and tactical aspects of jointly implementing CMMI and Six Sigma, with a primary focus on the establishment of process infrastructure. This portion of the book closes with current thinking and emerging research regarding integrated approaches to multimodel process improvement.
- Chapter 9 illustrates several projects that may be part of a managed improvement project portfolio (a change from the majority of chapters in the book, which discuss leveraging CMMI and Six Sigma for the implementation of process infrastructure). The examples focus on project and product performance and also connect to issues of process infrastructure. They cover the gamut of Six Sigma framework usage—from Define, Measure, Analyze, Improve, Control (DMAIC) to Lean to Design for Six Sigma (DFSS).
- Chapter 10 summarizes key points from the whole book (for those who like to read the ending first!).

- The appendices contain additional details behind the main chapters of the book. The appendices also offer supplementary information on measurement practices, transition practices, and organizational change management. While not the main focus of this book, measurement, transition, and change management are critical to success, and we include in the appendices the principles and practices that we most often use.
- Following the appendices are the lists of references, additional resources, and acronyms.

Acknowledgments

Many people, and their conversations and presentations, contributed to the writing of this book. While references are incorporated throughout, we would like to acknowledge and thank several people and organizations here.

We would like to thank the SEI Director's Office for funding an independent research and development project in 2004 to investigate Six Sigma's role as an enabler and accelerator of CMMI and other best practice adoptions. The project and its results were a strong motivator to write this book. We thank Eileen Forrester for her involvement as a coresearcher with Jeannine on this project, and we thank all participants (most of whom wish to remain anonymous to all but Jeannine and Eileen) for their contributions.

We would also like to thank those who have participated in SEI-facilitated Six Sigma panels over the last few years and whose experiences and presentations have enriched our thought process and ongoing research: Rick Hefner, Northrop Grumman Mission Systems; Gregg Beardsley, L-3 Com; Jim Serazio, Raytheon IT; Dave Hallowell, Six Sigma Advantage; and Tony Hutchings, JP Morgan Chase. Separate from the panels, Rick Hefner has delivered several presentations that we refer to *frequently*, and we would like to acknowledge the staying power of his contribution to this topic.

Thank you to Lockheed Martin Integrated Systems & Solutions (IS&S) for granting permission to Lynn to coauthor this book and for allowing her to share the company's concepts of integrated process development, upon which our key points about strategy are based. Thank you also to Greg Niemann, of Lockheed Martin, for contributing a DFSS example for us to include in Chapter 9. Thank you to Motorola for granting permission to Bob to include his Motorola experience in this book.

Thank you to Mike Phillips, Dave Zubrow, Pat Kirwan, Mike Konrad, and Jay Douglass for reviewing this text on behalf of the SEI and for their continued support and encouragement of our effort to address the connections between CMMI, Six Sigma, and measurement best practices. Thank you also to several reviewers from software or engineering organizations other than SEI who have taken time out of their busy personal schedules to preview our text and help ensure that we haven't become so engrossed in our work that we are no longer understandable: Steve Penn, Paula Siviy, Jeanne Elliott, Stefan Ferber, and Larry McCarthy.

There are always some people behind the scenes who help bring a book to fruition. We would like to acknowledge the SEI Library Staff for their support with literature surveys and ongoing searching of journals for keyword hits on six sigma + software. Thank you to Lisa Marino for her support in preparing diagrams for our 2007 presentations and tutorials—the updates are reflected herein. And thank you to Cheryl Jones for updating our description of Practical Software and Systems Measurement to include the most current information.

And, of course, all three of us extend special thanks to our respective families who have held down the fort, dog-sat, and otherwise tolerated our traveling, our staying late at work, and our working countless hours at the computer. Without their support, this book would never be a reality.

Jeannine M. Siviy
Deputy Director, Dynamic Systems Program
Senior Member of the Technical Staff
Six Sigma Black Belt
Software Engineering Institute
jmsiviy@sei.cmu.edu

M. Lynn Penn
Director of Quality Systems and Process Management
Six Sigma Black Belt
Lockheed Martin IS&S
mary.lynn.penn@lmco.com

Robert W. Stoddard
Senior Member of the Technical Staff
Six Sigma Master Black Belt
Software Engineering Institute
rws@sei.cmu.edu

Chapter 1

Introduction

Why do organizations pursue process improvement? Sometimes the journey begins with a product issue in the field. Once the issue is resolved, the organization will investigate how to prevent similar issues in the future. Thus begins a process improvement effort. The journey may also be launched based on business issues and "burning platforms": lost market share, lost contracts, or, on the positive side, new business opportunities. These motivations may be described as *performance-driven improvement*. In contrast, there is *compliance-driven improvement*, which is motivated by regulations and mandates. Maturity-model-based level 3 requirements to win contracts and conformance to the Sarbanes-Oxley Act are examples of driving forces behind compliance-driven improvement. While the pursuit of regulatory compliance is often a requirement for an organization, it does not guarantee process performance. This book focuses on performance-driven improvement, which is a more effective and lasting approach and, if done thoughtfully, can simultaneously yield compliance with models and standards.

Once an organization decides to improve its processes, it faces the sometimes daunting task of how to proceed, both strategically and tactically. Success relies on senior management commitment, beginning with the establishment of resources to develop an approach. Most groups charged with the task of implementing process improvement are savvy enough to recognize that they

> **Motivations for Process Improvement**
>
> There are varying motivations for process improvement:
>
> - Product problems
> - Burning platforms, such as lost market share, lost contracts, or new business opportunities
> - Regulatory compliance
>
> Efforts made to handle product problems, burning platforms, and subsequent process improvement are types of performance-driven improvement. Changes made to comply with regulations and mandates reflect compliance-driven improvement. Compliance can be achieved via performance-driven improvement; however, performance is not necessarily achieved as a result of compliance-driven improvement.

can leverage models, standards, and best practices, such as those shown in Figure 1–1.[1]

Many organizations implement several of these standards and models and also invent a few things on their own. A goal of this book is to help you

Figure 1–1: *Many choices for process improvement*

[1]For acronyms in the figure and throughout the text, see the Acronyms section at the end of the book.

deploy and use the models, standards, and practices effectively and thereby achieve your business performance goals. We will focus mostly on the Software Engineering Institute (SEI) Capability Maturity Model Integration (CMMI) and Six Sigma. We'll explore questions such as the following.

1. How do I leverage Six Sigma with software process improvement initiatives already under way in my organization?
2. Should I pick Six Sigma or the CMMI? Or how do I convince my management that it's not an either/or decision?
3. What evidence is there that Six Sigma works in software and systems engineering?
4. How do I train software engineers when Six Sigma training is typically geared for manufacturing?
5. What are some examples of Six Sigma projects in software? In IT?
6. Isn't Six Sigma only about advanced statistics?

When combined, the CMMI and Six Sigma provide a strong foundation for performance-driven improvement. Six Sigma brings a business focus that is often lacking in CMMI implementations; it can also help mitigate the risks and pitfalls of an improvement effort driven by a dictate to achieve "maturity level x." The CMMI brings a process infrastructure that provides a foundation for Six Sigma efforts and enables an enterprise to relate its engineering processes to its business processes.

In this book, we will discuss strategies and tactics for jointly implementing the CMMI and Six Sigma to achieve business and process performance goals.

CMMI and Six Sigma Synergy

Together, the CMMI and Six Sigma provide a strong foundation for performance-driven improvement. Six Sigma's business focus can help mitigate the risks and pitfalls of pursuing improvements driven by a dictate to achieve a specific maturity level. It also provides tactical improvement frameworks and analytical methods that enable achievement of CMMI objectives. Six Sigma gives the organization a snapshot of the enterprise's current performance that enables it to determine a vision and roadmap toward future performance. The CMMI's process infrastructure offers a foundation for Six Sigma efforts and helps an enterprise's engineering processes relate to its business processes.

Design relationships between the CMMI and Six Sigma will be described to inform their effective integration into the organization's process design. But organizations rarely implement only these two initiatives. The strategies, tactics, and relationships for the joint implementation of the CMMI and Six Sigma will be extended to the general case of multimodel improvement. This will enable an organization to integrate a broader collection of models, standards, and practices (even if it includes none of those that we are discussing). Following the discussions about establishing process infrastructure, we will present examples of improvement projects and discuss long-term sustainment of process improvement efforts, which continue long after the initial process infrastructure is implemented.

We offer in this book an approach that will appeal to those charged with implementing process improvement because this approach enables the organization to appropriately leverage both enterprise (e.g., Six Sigma) and domain-specific (e.g., CMMI) initiatives. And it will appeal to senior managers (and therefore will enable effective organizational change management) because it is efficient, effective, and focused on the bottom line. It's a win-win proposition.

Chapter 2

CMMI Overview

The CMMI is a model, a collection of process and product development best practices, and a framework for process infrastructure. It represents industry best practices and can be used as a roadmap for process implementation and improvement. It is nonprescriptive, in that it explains what processes should be established but does not require specific process designs or implementation methods.

Over the past several years, there have been numerous Capability Maturity Models. Software engineering, systems engineering, integrated teams, risk management, and acquisition have had their own models. Some of these domains, such as systems engineering, have had multiple models. Furthermore, each model had its own terminology and formal appraisal methods. This decreased the efficiency and increased the costs of implementation, thereby increasing the challenges of adoption.

In response to these challenges, a team comprising representatives from multinational, cross-industry organizations and the U.S. government was formed to create a *single* model that integrated the various models into one that covered multiple disciplines. This model would have a single appraisal method and one set of terminology. The result is the Capability Maturity Model Integration.

The CMMI project work is sponsored by the U.S. Department of Defense (DoD), specifically, the Office of the Under Secretary of Defense, Acquisition,

Technology, and Logistics (OUSD/AT&L). Industry sponsorship is provided by the Systems Engineering Committee of the National Defense Industrial Association (NDIA).

2.1 CMMI at a Glance

The CMMI is structured by process areas (PAs), each of which describes goals and practices for a particular process, such as Requirements Management or Project Monitoring and Control. The model also has two representations, which group the process areas in different ways. In the staged representation of the CMMI, the PAs are arranged as a set of building blocks,

Table 2–1: *Process Areas in the Continuous Representation*

Category	Process Areas
Process Management	Organizational Process Focus (OPF) Organizational Process Definition (OPD) Organizational Training (OT) Organizational Process Performance (OPP) Organizational Innovation and Deployment (OID)
Project Management	Project Planning (PP) Project Monitoring and Control (PMC) Supplier Agreement Management (SAM) Integrated Project Management (IPM) Risk Management (RSKM) Quantitative Project Management (QPM)
Engineering	Requirements Management (REQM) Requirements Development (RD) Technical Solution (TS) Product Integration (PI) Verification (VER) Validation (VAL)
Support	Configuration Management (CM) Process and Product Quality Assurance (PPQA) Measurement and Analysis (MA) Decision Analysis and Resolution (DAR) Causal Analysis and Resolution (CAR)

which serve as a recommendation for the order in which to implement processes. Each group of PAs corresponds to a maturity level. In the continuous representation of the CMMI, the PAs are arranged according to four thematic categories: Process Management, Project Management, Engineering, and Support. Table 2–1 and Figure 2–1 show the process areas grouped according to the representations.

Each process area has an associated set of specific goals and specific practices. The goals are the PA requirements. Every goal within a PA must be satisfied in order to get credit for PA compliance. Within each goal are practices, the expected activities through which the organization satisfies the goal. Practices are expected. An organization may perform alternative practices to satisfy the goal.

The following sections, organized using the continuous representation, introduce the process areas. The paragraphs describe the purpose, spirit, and relevance of the individual PAs to an organization. However, the goals and practices of each PA are not summarized here, as this is intended to be a simple, concise introduction.

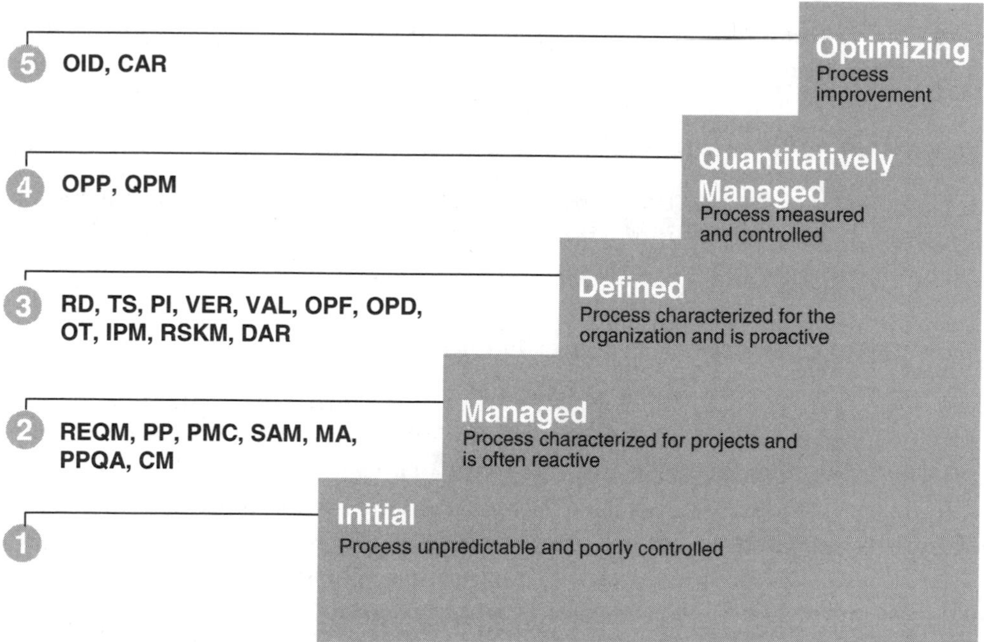

Figure 2–1: *Process areas in the staged representation*

2.1.1 Process Management

The Process Management PAs provide the infrastructure for institutionalization and consistent execution of processes. These process areas illustrate the organization's commitment to process improvement and are the enablers for the organization's process journey. They provide the requisite process resources, process assets, resource training, process performance information, and organizational structure. In CMMI version 1.2, there are five Process Management PAs, as described next.

Organizational Process Focus (OPF)

There is usually a point of contact or group within the organization that is responsible for establishing, maintaining, and improving the organizational process. This person or group monitors the process and drives process improvement within the organization, based on a thorough understanding of its strengths and weaknesses.

Organizational Process Definition (OPD)

The organization establishes a usable set of process assets and work environment standards. These become the underlying foundation for process execution and understanding, including (ultimately) quantitative performance characterizations.

Organizational Training (OT)

Within the organization are specific processes, skills, and knowledge associated with various tasks and activities. Everyone in the organization must be trained to do their jobs.

Organizational Process Performance (OPP)

The organization establishes its process expectations and a quantitative understanding of process performance. It maintains a database of process performance data from which it builds baselines and models that are used at the organization and project levels for quantitative management. The organization needs to plan this activity, similar to project planning. Resources must be identified to support the process infrastructure. The database must be established so projects can use the information in managing process performance against the organization's or project's tailored processes.

Organizational Innovation and Deployment (OID)

As processes mature, the organization compares the performance history and objectives to the business's quality and performance objectives to identify needed improvements. It identifies, evaluates, selects, and deploys improvements in a managed fashion to realize needed performance.

2.1.2 Project Management

A critical factor in any business is the successful management of product development, from concept to sustainment. The Project Management PAs provide the basis for establishing and conducting the projects through which products are created. These management techniques apply to all businesses and disciplines. They are the basic tenets that guide all good management teams. The six management process areas described here are common to commercial, government, production, and service organizations. Executives can identify with these practices and how they relate to organizational and project management. Executives expect this type of management at all levels of their organizations.

Project Planning (PP)

When being conceived or proposed, every project must start with a viable plan that defines the activities needed to complete its mission. The plan begins with an estimate of the time and cost of doing the job. This is necessary whether there is an external customer or an internal stakeholder. The plan must be maintained throughout the project period of performance. Typically, a plan contains a breakdown of the work into tasks or activities. Each task should be scheduled and have an estimated cost. Each task should be allocated resources (people, workspaces, tools, and so on).

Project Monitoring and Control (PMC)

After the plan is generated, it is very important that management track progress against it. Routine status checks should be conducted against schedule, budget, and other critical areas to ensure the plan is under control. Corrective actions should be taken, tracked, and closed when significant deviations from the plan occur.

Supplier Agreement Management (SAM)

It is often more cost effective to acquire something externally than to build it internally. As a result, projects and organizations frequently use suppliers and subcontractors to obtain components of products. This relationship must be managed within the project to avoid schedule slips and identify team dependencies. Precise agreements must be made with suppliers and subcontractors. These supplier and subcontract agreements must be managed in order to avoid surprises, mitigate risks, and meet schedule dependencies. Just as the internal team members must be integrated, so must the suppliers be integrated, status checked, and managed.

Integrated Project Management (IPM)

Project structure plays a part in the successful development of products. The basic activities within the Project Planning and Project Monitoring and Control PAs are elaborated on within this PA to ensure the inclusion, involvement, and commitment of *all* relevant project stakeholders. The team and its tasks and activities must be truly integrated.

Risk Management (RSKM)

As a project progresses, potential issues—or risks—to the project's success are identified. These may include risks related to cost, schedule, quality, or functionality; they may be technical, supplier related, or customer related. In general, they span anything that could prevent the project from achieving its objectives. These risks must be monitored, and depending on their likelihood, their potential severity, and the risk tolerance of the organization, a mitigation plan must be implemented. Risks can come from anyone on the project.

Quantitative Project Management (QPM)

As an organization gains proficiency with data-driven decision making, its management style and overall culture will change. It begins to use data to manage its programs' and projects' defined processes. It manages these processes according to quantitative process objectives that are linked to overall project and business performance. This reliance on data and the ability to predict versus react based on recognizing trends is a sign of true management maturity.

2.1.3 Engineering

In addition to effective project management, which ensures that work is properly planned, resourced, and tracked, a key to successfully delivering products to customers is sound engineering design and execution. The Engineering PAs of the CMMI ensure that engineering processes are established.

In the engineering discipline, there are clearly three legs of equal importance. They are process, technology, and people. Without the right processes, engineers would spend too much of their time defining how things should get done. Once the process is established, each engineer's skills can focus on the product architecture and necessary technologies to further enable the production of a quality product. This includes defining the product based on customer and stakeholder requirements, designing the product, building or acquiring the pieces, integrating the elements, testing, and deploying the product. The six Engineering PAs are described in the following paragraphs.

Requirements Management (REQM)

As the requirements are allocated and a product's components are defined, the requirements need to be managed. Any inconsistencies between these requirements, the project plans, and the work products must be identified and resolved.

Requirements Development (RD)

Each project is associated with a product and an intended customer. That customer has defined uses, specific needs, functionality, and capabilities expected from the product. These can be identified, analyzed, and documented as requirements. These requirements correspond to Six Sigma's "voice of the customer." Requirements, once identified, should be finalized via an agreement between customer and project management. As the requirements mature, they are then allocated to various components of the product, generally dependent on capabilities or functions to be delivered.

Technical Solution (TS)

This PA includes the design, development, and implementation of solutions to requirements. These can include products, product components, and processes. The engineers need to decide how the components will be produced, answering such questions as these: "Will it be developed in house?" "Will it be developed by a subcontractor?" "Will it be bought off the shelf?" These decisions often involve trade studies or other appropriate analyses.

Product Integration (PI)

As a product's components or pieces become available, they must be assembled into the finished product. The integrated product is checked to assure that it functions as intended and that all requirements have been met, via different levels of testing and acceptance. The product is then delivered to the customer.

Verification (VER)

Throughout the product development, from requirements to design to development to testing, the various elements (work products) must be analyzed to check compliance against specified requirements. Organizations often use peer reviews or inspections, throughout the lifecycle, to satisfy VER. Verification answers the question, "Was the product built right?"

Validation (VAL)

A PA that is often confused with VER is VAL. This activity analyzes work products to ensure the product or product components will fulfill their intended uses when placed in the product environment. Some organizations mistakenly assume that VAL applies only to satisfying the end user and is done only prior to product delivery. However, validation should be done throughout the lifecycle as the product is released to the next stakeholder. Validation answers the question, "Was the right product built?"

2.1.4 Support

Within any project, there is a group of activities that complement the management, production, and development efforts. The project infrastructure relies on these activities throughout the lifecycle to ensure that the production effort succeeds. These activities are embodied in the five Support PAs.

The Support functions further emphasize the need for good management techniques in assuring a quality product. They build on the Project Management and Engineering tasks with additional commitments to project success. These processes respond to both the voice of the customer and the voice of the business.

Configuration Management (CM)

The integrity of all work products—whether documentation, training, software, or hardware—must be maintained. This is done via monitoring and managing versions and changes in artifacts.

Process and Product Quality Assurance (PPQA)

Both technical staff and managers must be assured that every product and activity meet certain standards. This is a key aspect of building in quality to both processes and products. Audits are an example of an activity often used to provide assurance.

Measurement and Analysis (MA)

Monitoring and controlling plans, processes, and product performance is important. This is accomplished via the organization's measurement and analysis processes, which include measurement definition, storage, routine reporting, and analysis. Measurements should be identified to support management's information needs. Data is not collected for the sake of being collected. It must be *analyzed* and used to inform decisions, improvement projects, and so on.

Decision Analysis and Resolution (DAR)

Management is expected to make informed decisions, using formal methods and established evaluation criteria. A project team must have clear understandings about who makes various decisions, at what level they are made, and how they are made. Decisions should be evaluated for adequacy and relevance. Alternative solutions should always be addressed, analyzed against established criteria, and prioritized for selection.

Causal Analysis and Resolution (CAR)

Sources of problems must be identified to inform decisions about corrective and preventive measures. Likewise, causal analysis should be done to provide understanding of key drivers of good performance. In short, causal analysis involves both analyzing problems to prevent reoccurrence and analyzing strengths to improve the process. Processes or subprocesses that have measurements under statistical process control are the most effective targets for performing causal analysis. The quantitative information lends itself to analysis and resolution.

2.1.5 Generic Practices

In addition to the specific goals and specific practices mentioned previously, some generic goals and practices are used for all PAs. They form the basis for institutionalizing the processes within the organization. The underlying premise is to mature a process from being performed (generic goal 1) to managed (generic goal 2) to defined (generic goal 3) to quantitatively managed (generic goal 4) to optimized (generic goal 5). Of these, the distinction between managed and defined is possibly the least intuitive from the labels alone. *Managed* assumes a project-centric structure, while *defined* assumes an organizational infrastructure where process is repeatable from project to project. Managed often does not have the ability to draw on best practices or lessons learned from other projects; it has to rely on its own definitions.

The generic practices associated with establishing a managed process include the following:

- Establishing an organizational policy
- Planning for the process
- Providing resources (including people and tools)
- Assigning responsibility for performing the process
- Training those performing the process
- Controlling changes to the process and its work products (e.g., managing configurations)
- Identifying and involving stakeholders who are affected by the process
- Monitoring and controlling the process
- Evaluating the process for compliance
- Reviewing status with higher-level management

The generic practices that provide for the maturing of the individual process areas from defined to optimized are as follows:

- Establishing a defined process
- Collecting improvement information
- Establishing quantitative objectives
- Stabilizing subprocess performance
- Ensuring continuous process improvement
- Analyzing and correcting root causes of process problems

The generic goals and practices can be interpreted for any process and, as such, they are not limited for use with the CMMI.

We refer you to the model as well as books listed in Additional Resources at the end of the book for further understanding about both PAs and generic practices.

2.2 Adoption and Deployment

The CMMI adoption decision typically resides with middle or senior management, depending on the organization. It is easiest to adopt the CMMI if the organization has a significant problem that the CMMI clearly addresses. Whether the problems fall in the category of compliance-driven improvement or performance-driven improvement, as discussed in Chapter 1, an organization may choose to first adopt a piece of the CMMI before attempting to implement the whole model. In either case, an estimate of return on investment (ROI) may be a necessary part of finalizing the adoption decision.

Once an adoption decision has been made, even if only for an initial pilot, an implementation path must be identified. Successful implementation requires management sponsorship and resources charged with improving the engineering process. Often, the latter takes the form of an engineering process group. It is the responsibility of the engineering process group to create a roadmap and implement the process areas described earlier. It is the group's added responsibility to conduct the CMMI adoption as a project or program. A management steering group is often created as well to monitor the activities of the engineering process group.

In the simplest sense, CMMI-based process improvement is deployed using the following approach.

- Baseline the current state of the organization, relative to the model.
- Identify gaps between the baseline and the desired state.
- Develop an action plan to close the gaps.

The baseline and gap analysis may be conducted informally or formally. If a formal analysis is desired, these activities are done as part of an appraisal led by an SEI authorized lead appraiser. In addition to the baseline and gap analysis, formal appraisals yield a maturity rating.

In formal analysis, the appraisal team uses the formal appraisal method published by the SEI. This appraisal method is the Standard CMMI Appraisal Method for Process Improvement (SCAMPI). SCAMPI has three classes of appraisals. These classes, which vary in duration and rigor, are designated as SCAMPI A, SCAMPI B, and SCAMPI C. SCAMPI A is the most rigorous and is the *only* appraisal class that can denote a maturity level or capability level. SCAMPI B and SCAMPI C are less rigorous and may be tailored depending on the organization's desired outcome.

To implement the needed improvements indicated by the gap analysis, the management sponsors and engineering process group may also create process action teams (PATs), technology working groups (TWGs), measurement working groups (MWGs), or other teams charged with the responsibility to implement specific changes.

Various levels of training are pursued to support this approach. Members of the engineering process group typically take basic and intermediate CMMI training. Members may also pursue instructor training and lead appraiser training, noting that these functions may also be obtained as a contracted service. The entire organization participates in a training program that matches the organization's deployment strategy.

2.3 Benefits

CMMI-adopting organizations measure benefits in different ways. The SEI maintains statistics and reports from those organizations that volunteer to share information. Table 2–2 shows improvement statistics for a sample of 25 organizations, by frequently used measurement categories—including return on investment (ROI). The Web page at www.sei.cmu.edu/cmmi/results/results-by-category.html has links to specific improvements, such as these:

- "Costs dropped 48 percent from a baseline prior to SW-CMM maturity level 2 as the organization moved toward CMMI maturity level 3."
- "$2.1 million in savings in hardware engineering processes in an organization moving towards CMMI maturity level 3."
- "Reduced cost of poor quality from over 45 percent to under 30 percent over a three year period as the organization moved from SW-CMM maturity level 5 towards CMMI maturity level 5."

Table 2–2: *CMMI Results*

Performance Category	Median Improvement	Number of Data Points	Low Improvement	High Improvement
Cost	34%	29	3%	87%
Schedule	50%	22	2%	95%
Productivity	61%	20	11%	329%
Quality	48%	34	2%	132%
Customer satisfaction	14%	7	–4%	55%
ROI	4.0:1	22	1.7:1	27.7:1

2.4 CMMI Adoption Myths

We want to address two CMMI adoption myths: (1) The CMMI applies only to software development, and (2) it is useful only for large DoD software development contractors.

Adoption of the CMMI is often associated with only software. This is a legacy perception, from the usage of the Software CMM. By design, the CMMI encompasses multiple disciplines, extending in particular to the hardware and systems engineering arenas. With the release of CMMI version 1.2, the hardware discipline is explicitly mentioned in the model itself, via additional examples and amplifications.

Through designed extensions, and also due to its successful contribution to improved performance, the adoption of the CMMI has expanded well beyond the DoD contractor community to which it is so often connected. Through the use of what are called constellations, it can also be adopted by acquisition and service organizations. Financial organizations and international commercial organizations have embraced the CMMI and are starting to report benefits and transition experiences. Research within the CMMI community will continue as the model itself evolves.

2.5 Summary

The CMMI is a set of best practices that provides the infrastructure for process improvement within any organization across disciplines. Its adoption must be a systematic, planned approach. Senior management's commitment to CMMI adoption is critical. The adoption decision must be made with the interest of benefiting the organization, both internally by addressing mission and process performance needs and externally by addressing customer requirements and satisfaction.

Once the adoption decision is made, a gap analysis is conducted as the basis for creating a process implementation and improvement roadmap. Progress is measured by appraisals. Success may be measured by ROI, bottom-line benefits, customer satisfaction, new business opportunities, product quality, and organizational performance.

Chapter 3

Six Sigma Overview

Six Sigma has come a long way since it was invented in the 1980s at Motorola. In today's world, Six Sigma is a holistic approach to business improvement and includes philosophy, multiple performance measurements, multiple improvement frameworks, and a toolkit, all of which are intended to complement and enhance existing engineering, service, and manufacturing processes. Because of its many dimensions, Six Sigma can serve as both an enterprise governance model and a tactical improvement engine.

When first invented at Motorola, Six Sigma focused on product defects and a shift from the control-chart-oriented *three-sigma* paradigm to a *six-sigma* paradigm. This supported the senior management mandate for tenfold improvement per year and also was close to the *zero defects* mantra of the time. Yet it allowed for the reality of an occasional problem. Through the early 1990s, Six Sigma, the metric, evolved to Six Sigma, the holistic and systemic product and process improvement initiative. During these early years, its philosophy, metrics, and DMAIC improvement framework were codified due to the effort of the Six Sigma Research Institute, an oft-unrecognized consortium of innovators and early adopters including Motorola, Allied Signal, Texas Instruments, Eastman Kodak, and others. A practitioner (Black Belt) certification process was established, with a balanced focus on classroom training, skills demonstration, and successful completion of an improvement project. General Electric realized and publicized significant bottom-line benefits of Six Sigma during the 1990s. That company's public statements as well as the movement of its employees throughout industry have led to an increased popularity of Six Sigma.

With its increased adoption, Six Sigma has evolved beyond its early codification to include more frameworks and methods. Organizations have extended the data-driven improvement initiative to the rest of their business lifecycle and supply chain. Service and transactional Six Sigma have been cited as the second wave. And engineering applications (and possibly applied research and development) of Six Sigma have been cited as the third wave [Hefner 04]. Included in this third wave are software and systems engineering and information technology.

How Is Six Sigma Different Than TQM or Other Quality Improvement Programs?

In past years, there have been many instances and evolutions of quality improvement programs. Scrutiny of the programs shows much similarity and also clear distinctions between such programs and Six Sigma. Similarities include common tools and methods, concepts of continuous improvement, and even analogous steps in the improvement framework—which makes sense given common roots in the work of Juran, Deming, Crosby, and others. Differences have been articulated as follows.

- Six Sigma speaks the language of business. It specifically addresses the concept of making the business as profitable as possible.
- In Six Sigma, quality is not pursued independently from business goals. Time and resources are not spent improving something that is not a lever for improving customer satisfaction.
- Six Sigma focuses on achieving tangible results.
- Six Sigma does not include specific integration of ISO 9000:2000 or Malcolm Baldrige National Quality Award criteria.
- Six Sigma uses an infrastructure of highly trained employees from many sectors of the company (not just the quality department). These employees are typically viewed as internal change agents.
- Six Sigma raises the expectation from three-sigma to six-sigma performance. Yet it does not promote zero defects, which many people dismiss as impossible.

Sources: [Pyzdek 01b, Marash 01, Harry 00]

3.1 Six Sigma at a Glance

Six Sigma is multifaceted. Its name implies a single, absolute metric. In practice, however, it encompasses a philosophy, multiple measurements, multiple improvement frameworks, and a toolkit.

What Is Six Sigma?

Six Sigma is a multifaceted approach to business improvement that includes the following:

- A philosophy
- A collection of performance measures
- Multiple improvement frameworks
- An analytical toolkit

The Six Sigma philosophy is to improve customer satisfaction by eliminating and preventing defects and, as a result, to increase business profitability.

Frequently used measures of defects include defect rate (parts per million, ppm), sigma level, defects per unit (DPU), defects per million opportunities (DPMO), and yield. Practically speaking, practitioners also use other types of measures, such as cycle time, cost, product performance, and bottom-line savings.

A commonly used framework is DMAIC: Define-Measure-Analyze-Improve-Control. A variant of Six Sigma called Design for Six Sigma may be implemented using a number of frameworks, each of which has been codified by a particular company or service provider. DMADV—Define-Measure-Analyze-Design-Validate—is one of the more popular DFSS frameworks.

Six Sigma's philosophy is to increase customer satisfaction by decreasing the number of defects and thereby increasing business profits. Six Sigma defines defects in terms of the customer's viewpoint. Six Sigma defects are any product, service, or process variation that prevents meeting the needs of the customer and/or adds cost, whether or not the variation is detected.

Note the contrast between this definition and the ones listed below.

- CMMI:
    - Defect density is the "number of defects per unit of product size (e.g., problem reports per thousand lines of code)" [CMMI DEV v1.2, 539].
- Personal Software Process (PSP):
    - "Software engineers make **errors** or **mistakes** that result in program **defects** or **faults**" [Humphrey 1995, 12].
    - "[Y]ou should record data on every defect you find during compile and test. A defect is counted every time you make a program change" [Humphrey 1995, 38].
- ISO 9000:2000:
    - Defects are the "nonfulfillment of a requirement related to an intended or specified use" [ISO 9000:2000, 3.6.3].
    - "The distinction between the concepts defect and **nonconformity** (3.6.2) is important as it has legal connotations, particularly those associated with product liability issues. Consequently the term 'defect' should be used with extreme caution" [ISO 9000:2000, 3.6.3].
- Software reliability engineering:
    - "A *failure* is a departure of system behavior in execution from user needs; it is a user-oriented concept. A fault is the defect that causes or can potentially cause the failure when executed, a developer-oriented concept" [Musa 04, 154].
    - "A *fault* in software is the defect in the program that, when executed under particular conditions, causes a failure. . . . A fault is a property of the program rather than a property of its execution or behavior. It is what we are really referring to in general when we use the term defect or 'bug'" [Musa 04, 208].
    - "An *error* is an incorrect or missing action by a person or persons that causes a fault in a program" [Musa 04, 215].

The breadth of the Six Sigma defect definition allows it to be used across an enterprise. When applying this definition within software or systems engineering, it is important to always identify defects in customer and/or business terms—not in engineering terms. Few customers of software-intensive systems speak about defects per line of code, a frequently used engineering measure. Rather, they are likely to express their issues as the number of problems or failures that occurred per transaction or operation. The use of Six Sigma can help clarify the relationship between these defect measures.

Once a specific operational definition of defect is determined, it can then be successfully measured and monitored. Common Six Sigma metrics include defect rate (such as parts per million, ppm), sigma level, process capability indices,

A Customer View of Software-Intensive System Defects

The following are real-life examples of how defects might be characterized from a customer viewpoint [StickyMinds.com 02].

- A 32-step "workaround" was required to move information to a new version of financial software.
- The wrong statement ending balance was given when reconciling a mutual fund account using financial software.
- Bank ATMs debited accounts but didn't give cash.
- University students were unable to enroll due to lingering problems in a multimillion-dollar software system.
- A new air traffic control system was out of action for more than seven hours, resulting in canceled flights and extended delays.
- A carrier plane veered right without warning due to a computer glitch, resulting in an emergency landing.
- Money from payroll direct deposits was missing from bank accounts.

defects per unit, defects per mission opportunities, and yield (the portion of product that is accepted). In practice, however, many Six Sigma project efforts focus on other types of measures, such as bottom-line savings or cycle time.

What Do We Mean by Sigma? (A Statistical View)

Conceptually, the *sigma level* of a process or product is where its customer-driven specifications intersect with its distribution. A centered six-sigma process has a normal distribution with mean at the desired performance level and specifications placed six standard deviations to either side of the mean. The portions of the distribution that are beyond the specifications contain 0.002 ppm of the data (0.001 on each side). Work done at Motorola, Six Sigma's birthplace, in the 1980s showed that most manufacturing processes experience a shift (due to drift over time from such things as mechanical wear and tear) of 1.5 standard deviations so that the mean no longer equals the target. When this happens in a six-sigma process, a larger portion of the distribution extends beyond the specification limits: 3.4 ppm.

Figure 3–1 depicts a 1.5-sigma-shifted distribution with six-sigma (6σ) annotations. Does this shift exist in the software process? While it would take time to build sufficient data repositories to verify this assumption within the software and systems sector, it is reasonable to presume that there are factors that would contribute to such a shift. Possible examples are declining procedural adherence over time, learning curve, and constantly changing tools and technologies (hardware and software).

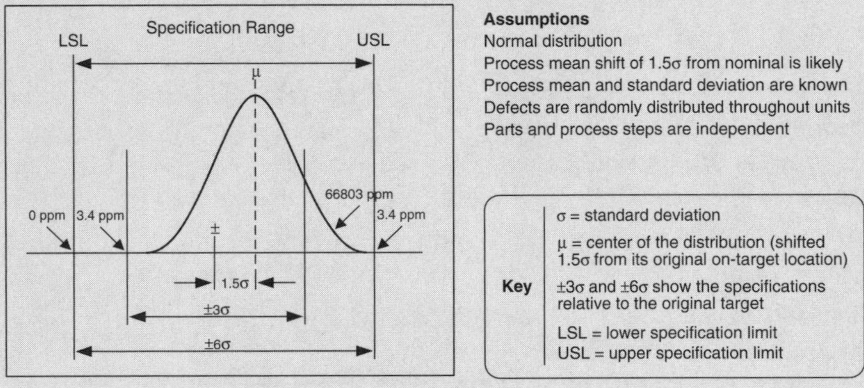

Figure 3–1: *Mean-shifted normal distribution*

What Do We Mean by Sigma? (A Layperson's View)

It is possible to navigate the world of Six Sigma without an in-depth statistical understanding of sigma measurement and its underlying assumptions. Six sigma is nearly zero defects—99.9997% good or 3.4 defects per million opportunities to be exact, noting an underlying assumption that process performance shifts over time. Four sigma is 99.4% good or 6,210 DPMO. That sounds nearly as good as 99.9997%, but it may represent an undesirable level of error. For instance, four sigma is illustrated by the following situations.

- 52 hours/year of downtime for any always-available utility or infrastructure (such as water, electricity, Internet).
- 1,080 hospital prescription errors per year, based on a rate of 9,000 patients admitted and an average rate of 5 prescriptions per patient [Revere 03].

- 1 misspelled word in 30 pages of text. For contrast, two sigma is 25 misspelled words per page, and six sigma is 1 misspelled word in all the books of a small library [Cusimano 06].

If a business decides it needs a sigma measurement (and not every business does), it must determine how that measurement will be calculated and what performance level is needed. As an example of a sigma calculation, the prescription error analysis just cited involved partitioning medication errors in a particular hospital system into prescription errors, dispensing errors, and administration errors—each of which had a different rate of opportunity for the same number of patients (i.e., prescriptions are *dispensed* daily whereas they are *administered* several times per day). Actual sigma rates for these types of errors were 4.7, 5.4, and 5.5. The analysis further examined the rate at which each of these types of errors resulted in patient death, arguably the definition that patients are most concerned about. All were better than six-sigma levels of performance: 2.2 DPMO, 0.35 DPMO, and 0.11 DPMO, respectively.

What sigma level is right? Taking a restaurant business as an example, the immediate consequences of billing errors are the extra time and aggravation for the customer to get a correction. From the business's perspective, the consequences of billing errors can be translated to monetary value in terms of direct labor costs to remedy the error. If the errors and time delays occur frequently, there is the cost of lost business because waiting customers cannot be seated (i.e., the restaurant is forced to run slower than capacity) and possibly because dissatisfied customers may not return. Now, as a contrast to billing errors, consider errors where the meal that a customer ordered is not the one delivered to the table. This is a much more aggravating situation with likely greater costs. In addition to the direct labor needed to correct the situation, the incorrect meal must be disposed of. Depending on the situation and type of restaurant, the meal may be offered at no charge. Despite such measures to resolve the problem, customers may still be quite dissatisfied (much more so than with a billing error). It takes longer to fix an incorrect food order, plus it may be necessary to mollify a customer whose meal is now out of sync with others at the table and so forth. Taking all of these things into account, a restaurant may be more motivated to have higher sigma levels of performance for correct orders than for correct bills.

So, in the general case, sometimes six-sigma levels of performance are desired. But sometimes, the lesser controls of four sigma (or lower) provide an adequate balance of customer and business needs. Product domains involving human safety, health, and money are those most likely to strive for better than six-sigma performance. And, as just described, some have already reached that level!

The quest to achieve the desired level of performance is based on the key underlying paradigm of statistical thinking [ASA 01, ASQ 00].

- Everything is a process.
- All processes have inherent variability.
- Data is used to understand variation and to drive decisions to improve the processes.

Figures 3–2 and 3–3 show two views of this paradigm in practice. Figure 3–2 distinguishes two commonly encountered situations—an off-target process

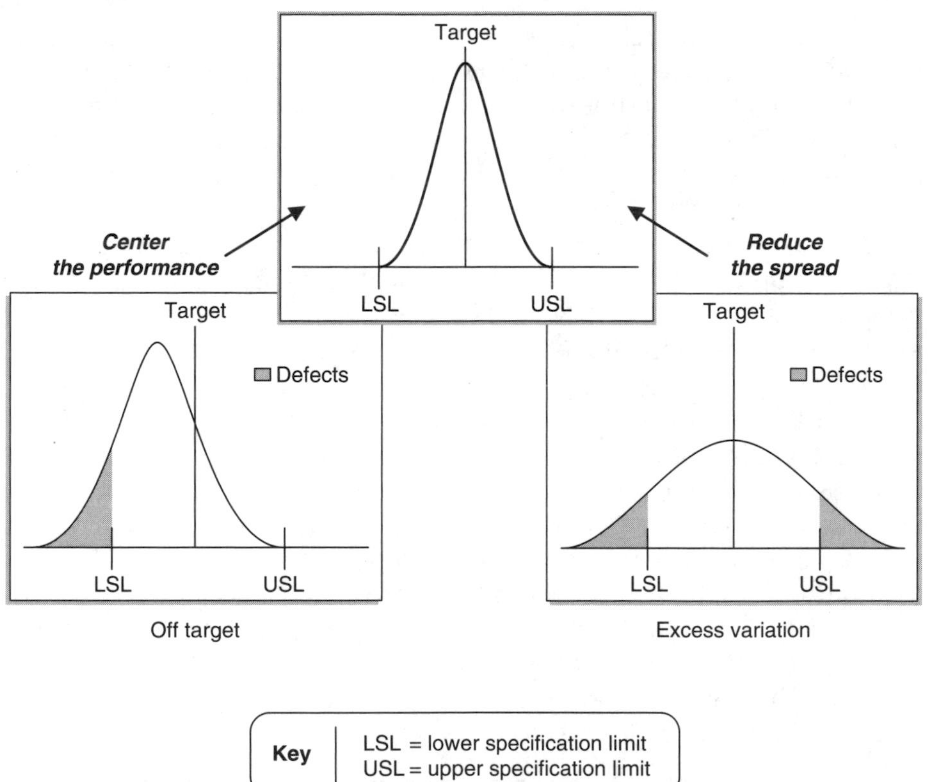

Figure 3–2: *Statistical thinking*

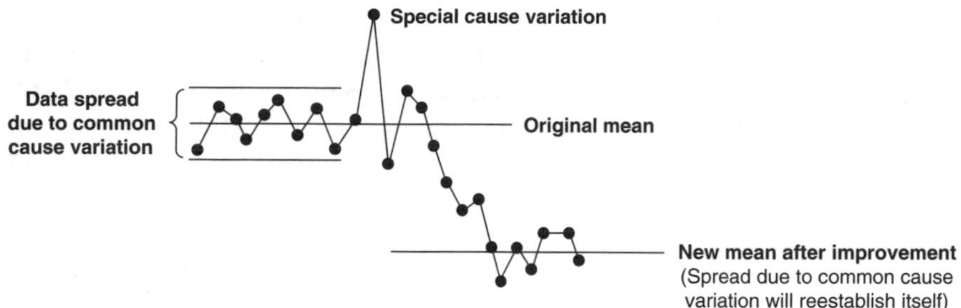

Figure 3–3: *Common and special cause variations*

and a highly variable process. Centering a process to be on target and shrinking its variation both reduce how much of the process is normally outside of specifications. (Note that, by definition, specifications are in customer terms. For processes that a customer does not see, engineering specifications can be set. This might be accomplished by establishing traceability to those processes and products for which there are customer specifications or by establishing alignment to business objectives and performance expectations.) Figure 3–3 is a different view of these concepts, using the terms *common cause variation* (for the inherent variability of the process) and *mean* (or average). It also shows *special cause variation*, a departure from inherent variability caused by a process anomaly. Practically speaking, process improvement efforts usually must address all of these issues: special cause variation, excessive inherent variation, and off-target processes. Ideally, they are addressed in that order, but pragmatically, they are addressed iteratively and sometimes simultaneously (which carries risk and makes for messy data analysis).

The paradigm of statistical thinking is embodied in Six Sigma's methodologies or frameworks, which are used as the basis for executing improvement projects. The following frameworks currently prevail.

- DMAIC is used to improve and optimize existing processes and products. An example of a DMAIC roadmap (some people may consider this format to be a thought map) is shown in Figure 3–4 in Section 3.1.1 [Hallowell and Siviy 05].
- DFSS (Design for Six Sigma) is used to design new products and processes and also to redesign existing processes and products that have been optimized but still do not meet performance goals. This latter case is believed to frequently be needed when moving from a five-sigma level of performance to a six-sigma level. DMADV is one of several DFSS frameworks.
- Lean is now frequently combined with Six Sigma. With roots in the automotive industry, Lean focuses on eliminating non-value-added process

steps and leverages methods specifically aimed at improving speed and cycle time. The tactical aspects of Lean may be implemented within the existing DMAIC or DFSS frameworks. However, Lean is being increasingly implemented as an enterprise governance model, within which organizations are being asked to explain how Six Sigma fits—not all that unlike the questions about how the CMMI fits with Six Sigma.

The improvements depicted in Figures 3–2 and 3–3 are realized through the execution of these frameworks. It is often necessary to iterate through the framework phases.

As organizations institutionalize Six Sigma and the frameworks of their choosing, their general data-driven journey might be described by the following phases and realizations:

- Discovery about their goals and processes/products
- Characterization of the performance of existing processes/products
- Identification of critical control factors and characterization of causal relationships
- Improvement of processes/products or creation of new processes/products with the desired performance
- Sustainment and prediction of performance

This is accomplished one improvement project at a time, preferably as part of an overall managed project portfolio. For each defined project, a Six Sigma improvement team is responsible for identifying relevant metrics. The team evaluates the data for trends, patterns, causal relationships, root causes, and so on. If needed, special experiments and modeling may be done to confirm hypothesized relationships or to understand the extent of leverage of factors; however, many improvement projects may be accomplished with the most basic statistical and nonstatistical tools.

Each framework is further described in the following subsections.

3.1.1 DMAIC Overview

DMAIC refers to the data-driven quality strategy for improving processes and relates to five interconnected phases: Define, Measure, Analyze, Improve, and Control. The purpose of the Define step, in basic terms, is to identify customers and their requirements, to establish project boundaries, and to map the processes of interest. Measure is about developing a data collection plan, collecting the data, evaluating its quality, and creating a baseline. In Analyze, gaps between baseline performance and targets are identified, root sources of variation understood, and improvement opportunities prioritized. In Improve, solutions are developed and implemented. And in Control, monitoring mechanisms are created to prevent regressing to previous performance.

Figure 3–4 shows a DMAIC roadmap, which describes the key activities needed to achieve the purpose of each step. While the roadmap is depicted as a linear sequence of events, this is rarely how the process works. Multiple iterations through Define, Measure, Analyze, and Improve are to be expected. Appendix A contains a list of guidance questions for each activity.

Supporting the DMAIC improvement journey, the Six Sigma toolkit includes a comprehensive suite of proven statistical and nonstatistical methods from previous evolutions of quality and business improvement initiatives. An organization may elect to adapt, add, or focus on specific methods of the toolkit based on the improved ability to deliver on customer needs and business benefit. Additionally, the toolkit should be adapted for domain. Figure 3–5 shows a DMAIC toolkit adapted for use by an engineering process group that is using Goal-Question-Indicator-Metric (GQIM) and Practical Software and Systems Measurement (PSM) methods to support its CMMI implementation. Other possible adjustments would be to elaborate on modeling to include Bayesian modeling or to make explicit parametric versus nonparametric methods.

Appendix F briefly describes a selection of Six Sigma tools.

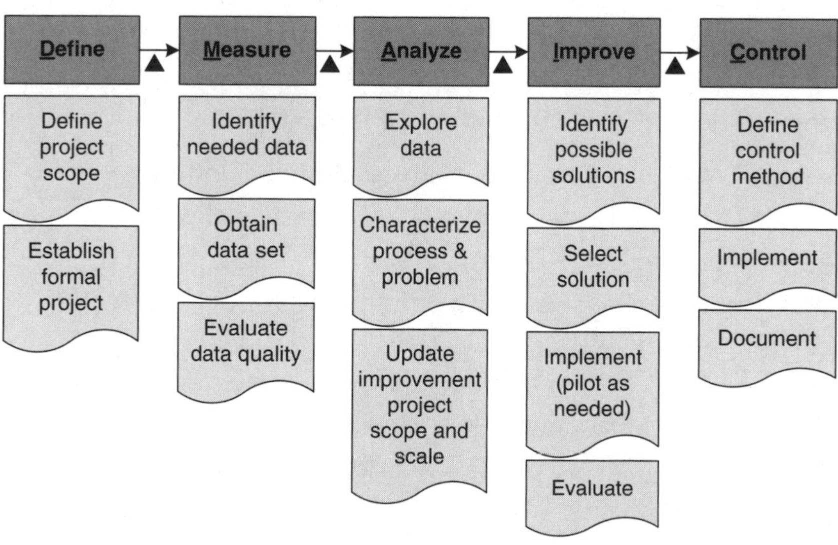

Figure 3–4: *DMAIC roadmap*

Define	Measure	Analyze	Improve	Control
Benchmark	GQ(I)M and Indicator Templates	Cause & Effect Diagrams/ Matrix	Design of Experiments	*Statistical Controls*
Contract/ Charter	Data Collection Methods	Failure Modes & Effects Analysis	Modeling	Control Charts
Kano Model	Measurement System Evaluation	Statistical Inference	ANOVA	Time Series Methods
Voice of the Customer		Reliability Analysis	Tolerancing	*Nonstatistical Controls*
Voice of the Business		Root Cause Analysis, Incl. 5 Whys	Robust Design	Procedural Adherence
Quality Function Deployment		Hypothesis Test	Systems Thinking	Performance Mgmt.
			Decision & Risk Analysis	Preventive Measures
			PSM Perform Analysis Model	

Seven Basic Tools (*Histogram, Scatter Plot, Run Chart, Flow Chart, Brainstorming, Pareto Chart, Cause-&-Effect Diagram*), Control Charts (Diagnostic purposes), Baselining, Process Flow Mapping, Project Management, "Management by Fact," Sampling Techniques, Surveying Methods, Defect Metrics

Figure 3–5: *Tailored DMAIC toolkit*

3.1.2 DFSS Overview

Design for Six Sigma is the arm of Six Sigma used to design or redesign products and processes.

There are numerous demonstrated and emerging DFSS-related frameworks, including but not limited to the following [Houston 03]:

- DMAD(O)V: Define-Measure-Analyze-Design-(Optimize)-Validate
- ID(D)OV: Identify-Design-(Develop)-Optimize-Validate
- CDOV: Concept-Design-Optimize-Verify [Creveling et al. 03]
- I2DOV for technology development: Invent/Innovate-Develop-Optimize-Verify [Creveling et al. 03]
- DCCDI: Define-Customer-Concept-Design-Implement [Tennant 02]
- DMEDI: Define-Measure-Explore-Develop-Implement

DMADV is one of the more commonly used DFSS frameworks. It consists of five interconnected phases:

- Define the project goals and customer (internal and external) deliverables
- Measure and determine customer needs and specifications
- Analyze the process options to meet the customer needs

- Design . . . the process to meet the customer needs
- Verify the design performance and ability to meet customer needs [Simon 07]

By definition, the steps of DMADV (and the other DFSS roadmaps) share a synergy with the core process of engineering a product. Yet DFSS is not intended to replace but rather to enhance or supplement the new product development process, with a systematic integration of analytical tools and methods. It shares a common spirit with the Design for Manufacturing, robust design, and Taguchi Design initiatives. Some have also noted common roots with systems engineering, as it has evolved under Department of Defense direction [Huber 2002].

What is common across these different initiatives is attentiveness to customer requirements and the methodical, analytical translation of those requirements into robust product design. While the steps and acronyms vary, the DFSS frameworks bring to the table particular emphasis on the design-oriented analytical toolkit and a team trained to use it: quality function deployment, design failure modes and effects analysis, design of experiments, modeling and simulation, statistical optimization, and so on.

3.1.3 Lean Overview

Lean History and Fundamentals

To understand how Lean and Six Sigma work together, it is first useful to examine the roots, principles, and methods of Lean. Lean is rooted in the automotive industry and became widely known as a result of the Toyota Production System. This system, based on work by Taiichi Ohno, Eli Toyoda, and Shigeo Shingo in the 1940s and 1950s and officially named in the 1970s, focused on improving manufacturing operations via the central role of inventory and work in process. It built on foundational production strategies set in motion by Ransom Olds and furthered by Henry Ford; on the addition of customer choice to the assembly line by General Motors; and on the quality methods of Ishikawa, Deming, and Juran.

Lean has been adopted by many organizations as a means to manufacturing competitiveness. Its results have led to research efforts such as the Lean Aerospace Initiative at MIT, which was created in 1993 to investigate applying the Toyota Production System to the military aircraft industry. As with Six Sigma, Lean has evolved beyond its manufacturing roots and is now used across the enterprise.

Lean focuses on eliminating all waste in order to create value, typically with minimal capital investment. Its principles are to articulate *value* for a product, identify the *value stream*, make the value *flow*, establish a customer *pull* system, and pursue *perfection* [Womack and Jones 96]. From an implementation viewpoint, this involves reducing cost through the reduction of time, effort, and material while improving quality and providing customers with made-to-order products. [George 03].

Accordingly, the characteristics of an organization that has effectively implemented Lean include such things as zero inventory, products built just in time per customer demands, smaller batch sizes, reduced process and changeover times, and so on.

In addition to sharing several tools (e.g., brainstorming, the seven basic tools) with Six Sigma, Lean also has its own collection of techniques. Among the most common are value stream mapping, cycle time and throughput analysis, process dynamics analysis, pull systems (kanban), setup reduction methods, mistake-proofing (poka yoke), 5S housekeeping (sort, set in order, shine, standardize, sustain), and total productive maintenance (i.e., optimizing scheduled downtime). Of these, value stream mapping, cycle time analysis, and process dynamics analysis arguably have broad applicability across manufacturing, service, and engineering processes. Following are several key terms and definitions.

- Work in process (WIP): all work and tasks officially in the process and not yet complete
- Lead time: work in process divided by average completion rate (Little's Law)
- Queue time: work waiting to be worked on (all queue time counts as a delay, regardless of the underlying cause)
- Value-added activities: those activities for which your customers would be willing to pay if given the option (i.e., were it a known part of the purchase price)
- Process efficiency: valued-added process time divided by total process time

Kaizen Events are a primary tactic of Lean implementation and involve decomposing processes, studying the parts, and making improvements. Kaizen Events bring the right people together to understand the process and make immediate improvements to the process. They enable evaluation of opportunities to reduce cycle time, cost, and inventory and to eliminate all waste. Key Kaizen steps are as follows.

- Have top management kick off the event.
- Determine the team's objectives and goals.

- Provide training in Lean and Six Sigma.
- Map the process as it currently exists.
- Identify waste in the process.
- Use root cause analysis to evaluate issues.
- Brainstorm solutions.
- Evaluate the solutions against the objectives.
- Report to the sponsor.
- Implement validated solutions to improve the process.
- Standardize by mapping the to-be-improved process.
- Report to the sponsor.
- Deploy and monitor actual performance.

Lean and Six Sigma

Some organizations have chosen to expand their Six Sigma toolkit to include Lean. Others embed Six Sigma as a tool of Lean. Some cite Lean as the catalyst for enabling Six Sigma's application beyond its manufacturing roots. Regardless of deployment specifics, each initiative is generally recognized as having a particular contribution to a joint deployment. Six Sigma contributes culture and infrastructure, a focus on customers and what is *critical to quality*, and methods for defect elimination and variation reduction. Lean contributes a focus on eliminating non-value-added steps and methods specifically aimed at improving speed and cycle time.

When a six-sigma defect is defined as being related to cycle time or speed, Six Sigma and Lean explicitly intersect. Yet this intersection is present even when Six Sigma is focused on other types of defects. If we consider that DMAIC is focused on defects per opportunity, and Lean is focused on time and the number of process steps or parts, then a reduction in the number of process steps corresponds to a reduction in the number of opportunities and should result in fewer defects. Table 3–1 illustrates how defects decrease and performance variance improves as the number of process steps decreases. For a given number of process steps, the table shows the "percentage good" for the sigma level at which each process step operates. When Lean is applied to a process, the number of steps typically decreases. This reduces the probability of the occurrence of defects and results in an increased "percentage good," as long as the sigma level of the process steps remains the same. Combining Lean principles with Six Sigma affords the best results, due to both the reduction in steps and the improvement sigma level. As an example, if a 20-step process, operating at four sigma, is "leaned out" to 10 steps,

Table 3–1: *Lean and Six Sigma: Relationships between Process Steps, Defect Opportunities, and Variance**

Number of Parts (Steps)	$\pm 3\sigma$ (%)	$\pm 4\sigma$ (%)	$\pm 5\sigma$ (%)	$\pm 6\sigma$ (%)
1	93.32	99.38	99.98	100.00
7	61.63	95.733	99.839	99.9976
10	50.08	93.96	99.768	99.9966
21	25.08	88.29	99.536	99.9932
40	6.29	77.94	99.074	99.9864
60	1.58	68.81	98.614	99.9796
80	0.40	60.75	98.156	99.9728
100	0.10	53.64	97.70	99.996
150	—	39.38	96.61	99.949
200	—	28.77	95.45	99.932
300	—	15.43	93.26	99.898
400	—	8.28	91.11	99.864
500	—	4.44	89.02	99.830
600	—	2.38	86.97	99.796
700	—	1.28	84.97	99.762
800	—	0.69	83.02	99.729
900	—	0.37	81.11	99.695
1,000	—	0.20	79.24	99.661
1,200	—	0.06	75.88	99.593
3,000	—	—	50.15	98.985
17,000	—	—	1.91	94.384
38,000	—	—	0.01	87.880
70,000	—	—	—	78.820
150,000	—	—	—	60.000

*Distribution shifted $\pm 1.5\sigma$.

performance improves from 88.29% to 93.96%. If the sigma level is simultaneously improved to five sigma, performance improves further—to 99.768%.

Tactically speaking, such improvements may occur sequentially rather than simultaneously. A traditional DMAIC project might lead to a need to improve process efficiency, for which Lean principles and tools could be leveraged. Conversely, a Lean project should reveal whether process simplification is a sufficient approach to improvement or whether variation reduction or other types of defect elimination, vis à vis DMAIC or DFSS, are required. Another tactical relationship involves the notion of designing a process to embody both Lean and Six Sigma characteristics, which has been termed by some as Design for Lean Six Sigma. This may be particularly relevant to software organizations that are implementing the CMMI and will be further discussed in Chapters 6 and 7.

3.2 Deployment

3.2.1 Certification of Six Sigma Practitioners

Six Sigma deployment typically begins with a senior management decision to adopt. This is followed by the training and certification of a critical mass of Black Belt practitioners, who are charged with executing improvement projects that yield significant bottom-line benefit to the organization. Organizations may also choose to build a cadre of Master Black Belts, Green Belts, and other levels of expertise. Black Belts, however, are the keystone of a Six Sigma deployment. They shoulder the majority of the project leadership, with Green Belts working on project teams and leading some projects. Master Black Belts teach courses and mentor Black and Green Belts. They also are often assigned to handle the most complex projects.

Six Sigma training curricula are organized by framework and belt color. Black Belt DMAIC certification typically involves four to five weeks of classroom training, taken over the course of six months in parallel with implementing a certification project. Due at least in part to the efforts of the Six Sigma Research Institute, DMAIC-based training enjoys a moderately standardized core curriculum, although every organization does tend to tailor it for its own particular culture and business needs. DFSS and Lean trainings often are two to three weeks in duration and also require a certification project. Many corporations require multiple projects and/or satisfactory demonstration of specific analytical skill prior to granting the certification.

Green Belt training is typically a two- to three-week subset of Black Belt training. Master Black Belts are usually identified based on experience and performance, although some organizations have developed training curricula and certification requirements.

Black Belt training is broad and comprehensive; it presumes that certification candidates have already demonstrated themselves to be effective leaders and change agents and already have experience in both the theory and application of analytical methods. As such, the purpose of the training is to broaden their toolkit, to enrich their ability to know when to use which tools, to place everything in a commonly used Six Sigma framework, and to build a community of practice that will serve as a long-term professional network.

Once certified, a Black Belt practitioner is responsible for leading projects in the organization's improvement project portfolio. In most organizations, Six Sigma Champions and Sponsors hold the responsibility of identifying and advocating for the Six Sigma improvement project portfolio. In many organizations, practitioners remain in this role for a finite number of years. They may be part of a central service organization, or they may be embedded with the organizations they serve. Some organizations have required certification as a condition of promotion into managerial positions.

An overseeing certification body was not established. An inferred reason is that the emphasis on project completion and business success was essentially self-correcting: Organizations that gamed or short-changed the process ultimately did not realize the benefits needed to ensure the institutionalization of the Six Sigma way. There is still no official certifying body, although different organizations have established bodies of knowledge and examinations. Others have pursued standardization of training and certification criteria as an indirect means of ensuring the quality of certified practitioners. While earning Six Sigma credentials via examination is possible, many still believe this is a participation sport and that skills demonstration and successful project completion are the only acceptable ways to verify competency.

3.2.2 Six Sigma Black Belt Projects

Six Sigma projects are selected based on their business importance (strategic alignment) and their potential impact on critical process performance and the bottom line. Requiring a savings of U.S. $100,000 to $150,000 per project is not atypical. Breyfogle cites that certification projects average $550,000+, with an average investment of $200,000 [Breyfogle 02]. All projects are to be endorsed and approved by the appropriate managers and governance boards within the organization. A project duration of three to six months is recommended. Projects that begin with a longer timeframe are descoped or split into multiple projects.

A rigorous project selection process is a critical success factor in Six Sigma deployment. Objectives must be clear and quantitative. Sometimes a project begins with a fuzzy goal, in which case it must quickly be focused on a specific objective. Typical objectives include the following.

- Improve customer satisfaction.
- Optimize the supply chain.
- Reduce defects.
- Reduce the cycle time.
- Improve the first-pass yield.
- Reduce variability.
- Optimize product performance.
- Optimize process performance.
- Reduce costs.
- Reduce the cost of quality.

Once a project is identified, a charter or contract is established to ensure commitment of resources, agreement to a plan and schedule, synchronization of expectations between all stakeholders, and so on.

3.3 Applying Six Sigma to Software

An underlying presumption of this book is that Six Sigma can be applied to software engineering processes and products. There are different ways to examine this: logical reasoning about the initiative and its applicability, analysis of what people are writing and saying, and evaluations of examples and illustrations. In this section, we will focus on logical argument. Other sections will focus on examples and illustrations. Citations of others' publications are incorporated throughout.

Six Sigma is technically a domain-independent initiative. Six Sigma, whose adoption decision is often made at an organizational level higher than the software engineering organization, was originally designed for processes and disciplines that are significantly more mature than software engineering. As a result, it can be difficult to envision how to apply Six Sigma in software engineering. The difficulties relate to both the strategic aspects of implementation (e.g., project portfolio management) and the tactical aspects (e.g., case studies for training curricula). Yet Six Sigma's commitment to the customer and the business bottom line is appealing to those working in software engineering, particularly in the current environment of increasing software pervasiveness, size, complexity, market globalization, and so on.

From a logical standpoint, the creation of software-intensive products and systems is done via a process, albeit one that often involves innovation and creativity (as does any engineering process). This process may be ad hoc, it may be different every time, or it may be highly repeated and repeatable, but it is a process nonetheless. Numerous measures may be collected about the process: the time it takes to complete each process step, the number of outputs, the quality of the outputs, the estimated product performance, and so on. The intent is for all of this to work together to result in a product that meets customer needs and performs well in the field. This, along with an intense interest in improving performance every step of the way, provides the basic foundation for Six Sigma to be applied.

There are differences between applying Six Sigma to software or other engineering disciplines and applying it to manufacturing, but these do not render Six Sigma inapplicable. Rather, they require additional thought, as demonstrated in these examples.

- The overall process cycle time may be much longer for creating a software product than for creating a machine-manufactured item. Six Sigma projects in software may take longer or may need to be conducted with greater risk, due to having smaller amounts of data.
- Software development is human intensive (as is some manufacturing) and involves a creative element throughout its lifecycle. Six Sigma project teams may need to focus on the more routine, repeated subprocesses within the software development lifecycle (e.g., inspections), or they may need to determine how to characterize the human factors. Careful attention must be given to normalizing data to be sure comparisons are appropriate (apples to apples rather than apples to oranges).
- The software development factory focuses on building one of each product. Copies of software can be easily made, without worries that the software itself will vary from copy to copy. The implementation of software into the user environment may involve a lot of variation, but that has more to do with systems, environment, and users than with the core product. In contrast, the hardware factory (i.e., manufacturing) is about making copy after copy of the product, with much concern about variation across the copies [Hallowell 03]. Accordingly, a software development Six Sigma project team would direct its attention to different types

and sources of variation than a manufacturing team would. A software Six Sigma project team may have to address process and product robustness, as well as variation in the user environment. Accomplishing this may require the team to leverage all the frameworks of Six Sigma—DMAIC, DFSS, and Lean—rather than becoming expert in just one of them.

Presentations and publications about the applicability of Six Sigma in software have increased with time. Topics have ranged from general applicability to ways to apply analytical methods at every step of the development lifecycle to Six Sigma training tailored for software developers to project case studies. Additional Resources at the back of this book provides references and reading lists.

3.4 Six Sigma Myths

There are many misconceptions about Six Sigma, especially in software organizations in the early stages of adoption. As such, it is important to examine what Six Sigma is not, along with what it is. Several myths related to the content of this book are briefly addressed here, with subsequent chapters elaborating on them as noted.

- **Myth: Six Sigma is just about statistics.**
  Six Sigma, the title itself, has been a significant contributor to the misunderstandings of what Six Sigma actually is. The term *sigma* is used by statisticians in association with standard deviation. Certainly, the sigma statistic and the underlying concepts of variability are critical aspects of Six Sigma, along with other statistical analyses. However, many nonstatistical methods are used in the Six Sigma toolkit. Many of these, such as process mapping, are perceived as being much more widely used than individual statistical techniques. Furthermore, Six Sigma embodies philosophies, principles, and problem-solving frameworks that transcend the use of statistical and nonstatistical methods and maximize their relevance. (Chapter 9 includes illustrations that depict several different tools.)
- **Myth: Six Sigma is only for manufacturing.**
  Six Sigma was first adopted by manufacturing and was associated with monitoring short-cycle, automated processes and tangible products. Software engineering organizations often hesitate in adopting Six Sigma because software is different than manufactured products. As with many

quality and improvement initiatives, the differences have been allowed to overshadow what Six Sigma can offer software development: a way to drive process improvement, a way to manage the software lifecycle, a way to find control levers to ensure software quality. (Chapters 6 and 7 address the strategies and tactics for applying Six Sigma in software process improvement; Chapter 5 describes two particular cases, and Chapter 8 abstracts an overall process. Chapter 9 provides project illustrations.)

- **Myth: Six Sigma is exclusively about defect density.**
  When an organization adopts Six Sigma, frequently asked questions include these: "How do I calculate sigma?" "What is a defect?" "What is an opportunity?" In manufacturing, these measures are sometimes calculated based on product features and performance, and sometimes organizations choose to use entirely different measures of performance such as savings or cycle time. When faced with these same questions, some early adopters of Six Sigma in software have used defect density for sigma measures. Part of the rationale often is that the data is available. But defect density is an in-process engineering measure. As with manufacturing, final product features and performance, in the context of customer usage and customer satisfaction, should be used when sigma measures (or alternative Six Sigma–based measures of product performance/quality) are pursued in software. Defect density and other critical in-process factors should be related to these customer-oriented metrics, noting that this is not necessarily an easy relationship to make. (Chapter 9 provides examples showing how to align defect density with business objectives as well as how to address other improvement measures.)
- **Myth: All Six Sigma projects must yield direct bottom-line benefits.**
  Six Sigma adopters often hail the significant bottom-line benefit that has resulted from their efforts. Indeed, focus on the bottom line is a strength of the initiative and a feature that contributes to its ability to complement CMMI implementations. Sometimes, however, a Six Sigma project does not directly yield bottom-line benefits. This may occur when an improvement objective is identified, only to discover that the requisite measurement system is not in place, or the underlying process is ad hoc. Before the improvement can be pursued, measurement or process infrastructure must be established—which often requires time and resources well beyond the three- to six-month time period of a typical Six Sigma project. In such cases, an enabling project is often established. One may well imagine that this is a frequent occurrence in the software engineering area—and it points directly to the synergistic relationship between Six Sigma and software best practices. The concept of an enabling project, however,

is anathema to some Six Sigma adopters. This can lead to resource and budget tensions and catch-22 situations that the Six Sigma community and software process improvement community (if different) must strive to resolve. Explicitly allowing enabling projects as part of the improvement project portfolio and requiring that they be aligned (and tracked) with longer-term business objectives are means of managing the situation. (Chapter 6 discusses enabling projects.)

- **Myth: Six Sigma success equates to compliance with domain standards and models and vice versa.**
  Domain models and standards, such as the CMMI, ISO and IEEE standards, and SPICE, frequently demand measurements, monitoring and control, and process optimization. Six Sigma can be used to achieve compliance with aspects of these standards. However, interpreting the usage of Six Sigma as the automatic equivalent of total model compliance is a misconception. A primary reason for this is that while Six Sigma involves enterprise-wide deployment considerations such as training a critical mass of Black Belts, its actual application is not mandated to be enterprise wide. In fact, it may be applied only in niche areas of high need and high payoff, if that is appropriate. In contrast, domain standards and models, particularly those for establishment of process infrastructure, involve organization-wide usage and institutionalization. (Chapter 6 describes strategies, and Chapter 7 describes design connections that shed light on this subject. Chapter 8 describes an affinity matrix that helps distinguish the differing roles of each type of model.)
- **Myth: Implementing Six Sigma and achieving level 4 are synonymous.**
  One of Six Sigma's overlaps with the pursuit of model compliance is that it is increasingly being used as a means to attain CMMI maturity level 4 and level 5. As a specific instantiation of the previous myth, some organizations believe that pursuing Six Sigma in this way equates to achievement of high maturity. However, the CMMI level 4 process areas require attention to organizational views of process performance that is not required (although may be desirable) by Six Sigma. Accordingly, the implementation of Six Sigma supports and enables but does not guarantee achievement of level 4. (In addition to the chapter elaborations mentioned for the previous myth, which also apply here, Chapter 9 contains an illustration set in the context of an organization pursuing high maturity.)
- **Myth: Six Sigma can be used only by high-maturity organizations.**
  In CMMI organizations, many people associate Six Sigma only with the high-maturity process areas. As will be described later, there is an intuitive spirit of commonality between them. However, there is also a direct

connection between Six Sigma and the generic practices, which are used for all process areas, regardless of maturity level. Six Sigma can serve as a tactical engine for implementation of the generic practices and thereby can enable high-maturity thinking (high capability) for any process, including those categorized as low maturity (such as Project Planning). (Chapter 4 further discusses Six Sigma as an enabler of CMMI adoption at low and high maturity and the hypothesis that their joint implementation results in "better, faster, cheaper" process improvement. Chapter 7 further explores particular relationships between Six Sigma and generic practices.)

- **Myth: Six Sigma is the performance goal.**
  In their quest to implement Six Sigma, many organizations believe that achieving a *six*-sigma level of performance is the objective. As organizations strive to address the needs of the business and the needs of the customer, they translate organizational objectives into goals that can be related to performance as well as such things as productivity, overhead, sales, increased profitability, customer satisfaction, and employee satisfaction. By understanding the interrelationships, it is possible to connect customer-driven specifications for the final product to specifications and performance targets for upstream processes. These may be in terms of sigma or other measures, and they may be less or more strict than six sigma. (This chapter has elaborated on sigma measurement; Chapter 8 provides additional explanation about aligning business objectives and process improvement portfolio projects; Chapter 9's illustrations provide examples of process improvement using performance targets other than sigma measurement.)
- **Myth: Six Sigma is a competitor to the CMMI or to other process models and standards.**
  Debunking this myth is a main premise and motivation for this book. Many models, standards, and practices can be leveraged for software (or other) process improvement; each serves a specific purpose and none stands alone as a "silver bullet" answer. In the software and systems engineering domains, the CMMI is a well-recognized model for process improvement. In these domains, Six Sigma is increasingly becoming mandated as part of enterprise-level decision making about and selection of improvement governance, strategies, and tactics. Because the decision making and resource management for these different initiatives are typically handled by different organizations, tensions and perceived competition between their implementation often emerge. To resolve this, an understanding of their synergistic relationships is needed. Also, lessons learned and best practices for their joint implementation—at both

the strategic and tactical levels—need to be shared. This is the main purpose of this book.

3.5 Example Benefits

Driving bottom-line benefits is a key tenet of Six Sigma. When published, results are typically stated at a corporate or enterprise level. For instance, GE has cited savings of U.S. $320 million in 1997, $740 million in 1998, and $1.5 billion in 1999 [Thawani 02].

Most organizations that are succeeding with their software and IT Six Sigma implementations view their efforts as a competitive advantage and seldom discuss them publicly. Here is a sampling of benefits realized in software and IT as a result of Six Sigma implementation.

- "Textron used the DMAIC process and the Voice of the Customer tool, among others, to tackle data-center sprawl. . . . By making customer needs the top priority, Textron has been able to consolidate or shut down 40 of [over 80] data centers, which were supporting legacy or underused applications. [Their] long-term goal is to get down to five data centers" [Mayor 03].
- "One Six Sigma team at Raytheon . . . [developed an approach] to allow applications to share servers logically and securely. The result: a 40 percent consolidation in servers, with the attendant time and labor savings added back to the bottom line" [Mayor 03].
- Chase Financial Services focuses "black belts full-time on a project, and in most cases [sees] between $1 million and $3 million in benefits" [Mayor 03].
- "Raytheon Aircraft's IT department has used Six Sigma to improve claims processing and save the company $13 million" [Prewitt 03].
- "Seagate's IT department booked direct savings from Six Sigma analyses of $3.7 million during the previous fiscal year. Since instituting Six Sigma two years ago, the IT department has saved $4.5 million overall. (The company as a whole reports saving more than $956 million from Six Sigma since adopting the methodology five years ago.)" [Prewitt 03].
- The senior vice president and CIO of computer manufacturer Seagate Technology said, "[Seagate is] being a lot more rigorous with maintenance contracts. We got a team together, analyzed what was needed and defined what maintenance level we wanted. That saved $1.5 million right there" [quoted in Prewitt 03].

- "In the fixed deposits area of [Wipro's] financial services division, [there is] a process in place to eliminate non-value-adding steps and mistake-proof the system. [Wipro is] projecting a 30 percent cycle time reduction in [its] computer business. The estimated short-term gains will be six to eight times the total investment . . . put into Six Sigma" [Erwin 01].

3.6 Summary

Six Sigma is a multifaceted initiative comprising strategic and analytic elements:

- A philosophy
- A collection of performance measures
- Multiple improvement frameworks
- An analytical toolkit

Together these elements provide a structured approach for business improvement.

While software engineering is different than manufacturing, Six Sigma still applies. A Six Sigma project team may face the realities of human-intensive processes, long overall cycle times, and minimal amounts of data. Nevertheless, software engineering is a process. And while the products may vary from project to project, the underlying process itself can be designed to be measurable and repeatable.

Six Sigma offers demonstrated frameworks and analytical methods that can be leveraged to navigate these realities. By using Six Sigma's proven frameworks and methods, a software Six Sigma team can expend its energy on the actual improvements rather than on inventing an approach to use. This is not unlike how the use of engineering process models enables software engineers to focus on creative solutions and elegant product designs and to avoid spending time reinventing processes from scratch.

An organization using Six Sigma can expect to see results such as reduced process variability, reduced time to market, improved product performance and reliability, and improved customer satisfaction. These lead to bottom-line monetary benefits.

Chapter 4

Multimodel Process Improvement: The Value Proposition

Numerous domain-specific models, standards, and technologies are available to software and systems engineering organizations. But implementing multiple initiatives simultaneously, while not uncommon, is not necessarily easy.

Because software engineering is a relatively young discipline, as is the systems engineering of software-intensive systems as we know them today, the role of models and standards is critical. Each model or standard provides collective community experience for the adopting organization to use and allows the organization to focus on its product and business rather than on the need to "invent" engineering. However, community experience is evolving, and the codification of these young engineering disciplines via models and standards is also evolving. So, it can be a daunting task for an organization to select and implement domain-specific initiatives, whether they are oriented toward improvement or toward definition of the basic engineering tasks to be done.

For each initiative being adopted, an organization must go through all of the classic change management steps, including such things as business case development, management sponsorship, deployment planning, training, and monitoring. If each initiative is implemented independently, there are numerous implementation risks: competition for resources, excessive amounts of time spent in training, the perception that each initiative is the "flavor of the month," and so on. Many of the initiatives are interdependent, with some providing guidance on what to do and others providing guidance on how to do it. This points to an additional set of risks: building an independent business case for each domain-specific initiative may be very difficult; the overall cycle time to achieve desired results may be very long, particularly if resource constraints dictate that initiatives are implemented sequentially; and the impact of each initiative may be impossible to separate from the others.

Those who have seriously examined both domain-specific initiatives and the domain-independent Six Sigma approach often see intrinsic value in both but are also often left with the quandary of how to make them work together. One of the first connections usually made is to leverage Six Sigma's focus on business value to justify or show the value of domain-specific initiatives. Some organizations seek a more strategic approach, however, and aim to effectively and synergistically integrate what is domain specific with what is enterprise oriented. The escalation of software in our global market demands such integration. Software process improvement is an investment that

Challenges and Benefits from Multimodel Improvement

Numerous models, standards, and technologies are available to software and systems organizations. Each has been developed to address specific things—establishment of processes or measurement, software architecture guidance, and so forth.

If each selected model/standard/technology is implemented independent of the other, there are risks of resource competition, overwhelmed engineers with too many simultaneous improvement efforts, a feeling of "program of the month," and more. Interdependency and overlap between models point to additional risks that increase the difficulty of building business cases for adoption, such as perceived redundancy of purpose, sequential implementations with unacceptably long overall cycle times to achieve desired results, suboptimal results if they are independently or sequentially implemented, and inability to separate the impact of one initiative from another.

The value proposition of multimodel process improvement is to leverage the best that each model offers and to implement them in an integrated fashion that mitigates risk. Ultimately, this should lead to "better, faster, cheaper" process improvement.

should have a business case and whose results should be measurable. And, following in the footsteps of other portions of the enterprise, software organizations are increasingly being pressured to achieve performance improvements faster and with less investment. Through the effective joining of enterprise and domain-specific initiatives, software engineering organizations can achieve their desired results more effectively, more quickly, and more efficiently.

The research described in this chapter and the case studies described in the next chapter substantiate, through both data and logical reasoning, the premise that joining initiatives yields better results.

4.1 Six Sigma as a Strategic Enabler: An Investigation

Several software and systems engineering organizations have sufficiently codified and reaped benefits from their approach to integrating the CMMI, Six Sigma, and other initiatives that they have begun sharing via presentations and publications. Each such organization has designed and implemented an approach suitable for its organizational culture and business needs. Based on preliminary observations of such successes, the Software Engineering Institute conducted a research project in 2004 regarding synergies between software process improvement initiatives and Six Sigma.

The primary purpose of the project was to examine whether Six Sigma, when used in combination with another process improvement technology or technologies, makes the transition[1] of that technology more effective. The initial project supposition was that Six Sigma might enable or accelerate the adoption of SEI or other technologies and/or facilitate the integration of said technologies within an organization. Preliminary discussions led to a more specific set of hypotheses: that Six Sigma, used in combination with other software, systems, and IT improvement practices, results in:

- Better choices of improvement practices and projects
- Accelerated implementation of selected improvements
- More effective implementation
- More valid measurements of results and success from use of the technology

[1]By *transition* we mean all of these: adaptation and introduction of technology by developers or champions, implementation of technology by organizations and change agents, and adoption of technology by its intended users.

This project primarily focused on organizations that were at least progressing both with one or more variants of Six Sigma and with the CMMI, Information Technology Infrastructure Library (ITIL), and/or Control Objectives for Information and related Technology (COBIT). Secondarily, it focused on architecture best practices and Design for Six Sigma. Information was also gathered on other technologies in use, running the gamut of Capability Maturity Models other than the CMMI, the People CMM, ISO standards, the SEI Team Software Process (TSP), Architecture Tradeoff Analysis Method (ATAM), Goal-Question-Indicator-Metric (GQIM), and Electronic Industries Alliance (EIA) standards.

The research project data included information from 11 case study interviews, 8 partial case study interviews, and survey responses from more than 80 respondents, representing at least 62 organizations and 42 companies. Generally speaking, the organizations from this research that are achieving success in their use of Six Sigma as a transition enabler ranged from low to high maturity, spanned nearly all commercial sectors, ranged from medium to large in size, and included organic and contracted software engineering as well as IT development, deployment, and operations. Note that small organizations' use of Six Sigma as an enabler remains on the project hypothesis list, having been neither refuted nor supported by project evidence.

Because of the proprietary nature of the data and the nondisclosure agreements in place, the results of all public reports are intentionally at a high level.

Examples of Successful Multimodel Improvement

Several software organizations, such as those mentioned here, have begun sharing their successes with multiple models and standards via presentations and publications.

- Lockheed Martin IS&S has integrated the CMMI, EIA 632, ISO 12207, and Six Sigma via its Program Process Standard. This particular approach, detailed in Chapter 5, has resulted in accelerated achievement of process and performance uniformity across a geographically dispersed organization [Penn and Siviy 02].
- Northrop Grumman Mission Systems has integrated the CMMI, ISO 9001, AS9100, and Six Sigma, as well as a formal approach to knowledge management. The results have included visible change toward a

measurement-oriented culture and accelerated achievement of CMMI goals [Hefner and Sturgeon 02; Hefner and Caccavo 04].

- Wipro has an enterprise integrated approach, via its VelociQ system, comprising ISO 9001, CMM, People CMM, TL 9000, British Standard 7799, and Six Sigma. "Six Sigma methodologies brought in quantitative understanding, cost savings, and performance improvement toward product quality" and "brought about a focused customer-centric and data-driven paradigm to product and process quality" [Subramanyam et al. 04].
- Tata Consultancy Services has incorporated the CMMI, ITIL, ISO 9001, and People CMM into a modular framework called the Integrated Quality Management System. This allows the company to effectively address its business goals for productivity, capacity, agility, reliability, and service [Srivastava 06].
- University of Pittsburgh Medical Center (UPMC) is simultaneously engaged in the CMMI, Sarbanes-Oxley (SOX), and ITIL. Though UPMC started implementing these separately, it realized that one collaborative effort would be most effective. Through prioritization of processes to implement, alignment of practices across models, and other factors, this center was the first nonprofit medical system in the country to be certified compliant with the most stringent provisions of Sarbanes-Oxley [Carmody 07].

Each organization has designed and implemented an approach suitable for its organizational culture and business needs. Several have integrated the models and standards of choice into a process infrastructure known internally by its organizational name or label, not by the respective name of each model or standard. In these cases, the software engineers are more likely to assert that they conduct their work using their organization process than they are to say that they use the CMMI or another model. They say this with the confidence that their organizational process infrastructure is compliant with the models and standards that are important to the business.

There is not yet a universally used set of terminology for this approach. *Integrated process architecture* and *interoperable process architecture* capture the intent, as does the term *internal integrated standard process.* Regardless of the label, the idea is that the organization establishes a set of processes that incorporate and align with the features of the process methodologies, initiatives, and standards of choice. It presumes that conscious decisions have been made at the organizational level to adopt these initiatives. It also presumes that the process is adaptable with time (i.e., iterative refinement), it is instrumented (i.e., measurable and measured) and it is robust to the realities of the organization (e.g., types of work done, degree of organizational acquisition, and so on). An underlying assumption is that the organization has chartered a qualified group of people to design and implement the process solution. These people, who are likely part of an engineering process group, are rightly called process engineers or process architects.

4.1.1 Key Findings

The research data showed Six Sigma to be feasible as an enabler of the adoption of software, systems, and IT improvement models and practices.

- Rollouts of process improvement by Six Sigma adopters are mission focused as well as flexible and adaptive to changing organizational and technical situations.
  - Six Sigma is influential in the integration of multiple improvement approaches to create a seamless, single solution.
  - Six Sigma is frequently used as a mechanism to help sustain (and sometimes improve) performance in the midst of reorganizations and organizational acquisitions.
- Six Sigma adopters have a high comfort level with a variety of measurement and analysis methods. They appear to be unfazed by high-maturity or high-performance behaviors, processes, and methods, even when they are at a low level of maturity.
  - When Six Sigma is used in an enabling, accelerating, or integrating capacity for improvement technologies, adopters report quantitative performance benefits, using measures that they know are meaningful for their organizations and their clients (e.g., returns on investment of 3:1 and higher, reduced security risk, and better cost containment).
- Six Sigma can accelerate the transition of models and practices.
  - For instance, Six Sigma helped one organization move from CMMI level 3 to level 5 in nine months and another from SW-CMM[2] level 1 to level 5 in three years, with the typical time being twelve to eighteen

[2]At the time of the research study, the SW-CMM was not yet retired, and data about its implementation with Six Sigma were gathered where available and relevant.

months per level rating. Underlying reasons were both strategic (change in focus) and tactical (how the processes are implemented).

CMMI-specific findings include the following.

- Six Sigma is effectively used at all maturity levels.
- Case study organizations did not explicitly use Six Sigma philosophies or methods to aid in decision making about CMMI representation or process area implementation order; however, project participants consistently agreed that this is possible and practical.
- Project participants asserted that the frameworks and toolkits of Six Sigma exemplify what is needed for CMMI high maturity and high capability. They asserted that pursuit of high maturity or high capability without using Six Sigma results in much reinvention of the wheel.

Additionally, aspects of the CMMI, such as the process asset library, were shown to enable Six Sigma.

Architecture-specific findings include the following.

- Of survey respondents implementing DFSS, the majority were at least progressing with the CMMI (but some were not using the CMMI at all), and few were using ATAM.
- Those pursuing the joint use of Six Sigma, the CMMI, and ATAM noted the strong connections among DFSS, ATAM, and the Engineering process areas of the CMMI.

Appendix E contains a previously unpublished complete list of findings, inferences, and remaining hypotheses. Included are more findings about how the CMMI or domain-specific initiatives enable Six Sigma success.

4.1.2 Deployment Notes and Success Factors

Frequently, Six Sigma was adopted at the enterprise level, and the software, systems, or IT organization was called upon to follow suit. In some cases, the adoption decision was made based on past senior management experience (e.g., often at the direction of a newly hired senior manager). In other cases, a burning business platform (e.g., lost market share) drove the adoption decision. In all cases, senior management sponsorship was definitive.

Regardless of why Six Sigma was selected, successful organizations consistently deployed it fully: senior management sponsorship, a cadre of trained practitioners, project portfolio management, the philosophy, one or more frameworks, appropriate measures, and the analytical toolkit were all present.

Line of sight or alignment of improvement projects to business needs was consistently clear and quantitative. CMMI or ITIL process areas were implemented based on business priorities and were integrated with the organizational process standard (even in organizations at lower maturity). Organizations varied as to whether the CMMI or ITIL started first, Six Sigma started first, or they all started together. The variance was sometimes strategic and sometimes happenstance—a side effect of enterprise and SEI timing. The other aspect of deployment that varied was whether Six Sigma practitioners and engineering process group members were the same or different people and within the same or different organizational divisions. Organizations were successful either way.

4.2 Summary

Simultaneously implementing multiple models, standards, and improvement initiatives has become commonplace in organizations. While many organizations struggle with what is often perceived to be competition for their attention, time, and effort, research has shown that joint implementation of initiatives can lead to accelerated and more measurable, sustainable improvement and performance. Organizations that have effectively blended initiatives, the CMMI and Six Sigma in particular, have realized benefits such as:

- Alignment of domain-specific improvement activities with business needs
- Efficiency of improvement efforts due to initiative synergy—with Six Sigma increasing business focus and the CMMI providing domain knowledge, thereby mitigating the risk that implementers of either initiative will reinvent what already exists
- Accelerated achievement of organizational maturity
- Recognition and use of relevant performance measures, bridging engineering and customer viewpoints
- Culture change, to become a data-driven organization
- Cost savings

A common characteristic of the organizations that realized these benefits was that they recognized that the initiatives were synergistic, not competitive. While a generalized causal model was not developed from the research project results described in this chapter, there were several commonly observed success factors, including the following:

1. Senior management sponsorship
2. A focus on mission
3. A focus on quantifiable results
4. The establishment of internal business and process architectures comprising models and standards of interest, in an integrated and/or interoperable manner

The first three of these factors transcend and are critical to the success of any individual model or initiative. The fourth one is particular to the multimodel environment.

Chapter 5

Two Case Studies

In this chapter, we present two organizations' approaches to the joint implementation of the CMMI and Six Sigma. These cases are complementary and reflect different organizational characteristics as well as different improvement strategies and tactics.

Both organizations benefited from innovative and visionary thinking, with one showcasing innovations in process design strategy and the other showcasing innovations in deployment and training. Both exemplify the imperative of multimodel process improvement, and together, they show that there are multiple paths to success.

5.1 Case Study: Lockheed Martin Integrated Systems & Solutions

Integrated Systems & Solutions (IS&S)[1] is a software development and systems integration organization, whose scope of work includes large-scale software development, system of systems architecture, and system integration.

[1]The organization name was Management & Data Systems for the timeline associated with this case study. It was subsequently renamed Integrated Systems & Solutions and is, at the time of publication, Information Systems and Global Services.

At the beginning of this case study, the organization's name was Management & Data Systems (M&DS), with approximately 4,500 software and systems engineers split across two locations on the eastern seaboard. Over time, it changed its name to IS&S and grew both organically and via acquisitions to 10,000 engineers located in six geographic zones across the country and internationally.

As one of the largest business units of Lockheed Martin Corporation (LMCO), IS&S shares the business heritage of its parent company, including the experiences of Lockheed, Martin Marietta, GE Aerospace, and IBM Federal Systems, among others. The executive vice president of IS&S reports directly to the LMCO CEO. As one organization within the corporation, IS&S is not divided into separate companies and operates as a single enterprise. It's important to know this fact to understand the process standards and the implications of such a complex and diverse organization.

IS&S provides transformational solutions for intelligence, surveillance, and reconnaissance; command and control; communications; and combat support to the U.S. Department of Defense and the intelligence community. Its engineers build the systems that connect the networked battlefield, integrating systems and sensors, people and platforms into a seamless, synchronized war-fighting force. From cutting-edge satellite constellations to real-time battle management systems, IS&S delivers the solutions that give military and intelligence operatives the speed, precision, and confidence they need to accomplish their missions. With a focus on whole-systems thinking, IS&S approaches solutions from the top down, creating open, flexible architectures that can easily support joint and multiagency operations.

We chose IS&S as a case study for this book for multiple reasons. As part of the aerospace industry where maturity models are frequently used, this particular organization was an early adopter of the CMM and the CMMI. And, with General Electric in its heritage, its CMMI-based process improvement journey was heavily influenced by Six Sigma thinking. Along the way, the organization grew significantly, in size as well as in its adoption of additional models and standards. The resultant case study spans its journey from low to high maturity with Six Sigma initially implicit in its CMMI adoption, then later explicit. Throughout, the organization focused on its mission and evolved its process culture to match its growth.

The journey comprises three main phases:

1. Creating a foundation for multimodel improvement
2. Adopting Lean en route to high maturity
3. Moving beyond high maturity

We discuss these phases in the following subsections.

Lockheed Martin IS&S's Journey to High Maturity

Key milestones:

- Organizational acquisitions
- Expansion of the Program Process Standard to include more program types
- Implementation and institutionalization of a measurement infrastructure (implied usage of DMAIC)
- Achievement of SE-CMM Level 4 and SW-CMM Level 3
- Integration of Lean
- Achievement of SE-CMM Level 5 and SW-CMM Level 5

5.1.1 Creating a Foundation for Multimodel Improvement

The journey described in this case study began with the executive vice president of M&DS, who observed issues with a growing organization that needed some consistency. The organization was at SW-CMM Level 2, with a variety of program-level metrics but few enterprise metrics in place. Up to this point, process improvement had been achieved via Software Engineering Process Group (SEPG) and project-level efforts and had resulted in the *Software Engineering and Management Manual* (SEMM), seven 3-inch binders about "how we did business." The binders were filled with standard operating procedures. At face value, there were procedures, and projects were being conducted and products built. One of the underlying issues, though, was that few people actually used the binders, and the procedures were stagnating. The business was growing, but the processes were not growing with it. The M&DS vice president was proud of the binders (he had helped build them), but he determined that maximum value was not being derived.

Two significant external dynamics were occurring in parallel with this growing realization. The Department of Defense (DoD) standards to bid certain contracts had changed to require SW-CMM Level 3. Since M&DS's business was primarily DoD oriented, achieving Level 3 became a significant milestone. Also, Lockheed was merging with Martin Marietta. An organization being integrated into M&DS as a result of the merger had already achieved a degree of process maturity and performance that the vice president desired for the entirety of M&DS. The subsequent information exchange served as a de facto benchmarking exercise, which shaped the vice president's vision for M&DS and resulted in his recognizing the importance of hiring a process improvement champion and strategist.

Organizational Infrastructure

The M&DS vice president established process management as an organizational priority. This decision was based on the combination of several factors:

- A personal passion for process
- The recognition of organizational opportunity
- An external forcing function
- A serendipitously available internal benchmark

He set the ultimate organization goal of SW-CMM Level 5, with interim milestones of one level rating increase every 18–24 months. Perceived as "best in class," the Level 5 goal was associated with better productivity, reduced defects at product delivery, and increased customer satisfaction. Accordingly, quantitative performance targets were set for such things as software productivity improvement, earlier defect detection, and increased customer award fees (as indicators of customer satisfaction). In parallel, other Lockheed Martin organizational units had set goals related to the implementation of the SE-CMM and ISO 9000. And, while there was interest in coordinating efforts across organization units, the implementation of these three models was not yet integrated.

To accomplish the newly set objectives, the vice president began by hiring an M&DS process manager. The primary responsibility of the newly hired process manager was to transform the organization's existing SEPG process improvement efforts to an organizationally managed program (across functions and across business lines). To do this, management commitment and oversight were established and made visible, which assured planning, resource commitment, funding, and scheduling. At the same time, the organization's business case for process change was established, based on (1) industry data available at the time that SW-CMM adoption costs were generally 2% to 3% of an organization's total software sales and (2) the expectation that this investment would enable the organization to meet newly established requirements (level 3) to bid on defense contracts.

Figure 5–1 shows the newly established organizational structure. The technical director reported directly to the president. The technical director was the direct manager of the process manager and the cochair of the integrated Process Control Board (PCB). The organization was a matrix organization. Therefore, the lines of business or product lines got their engineering

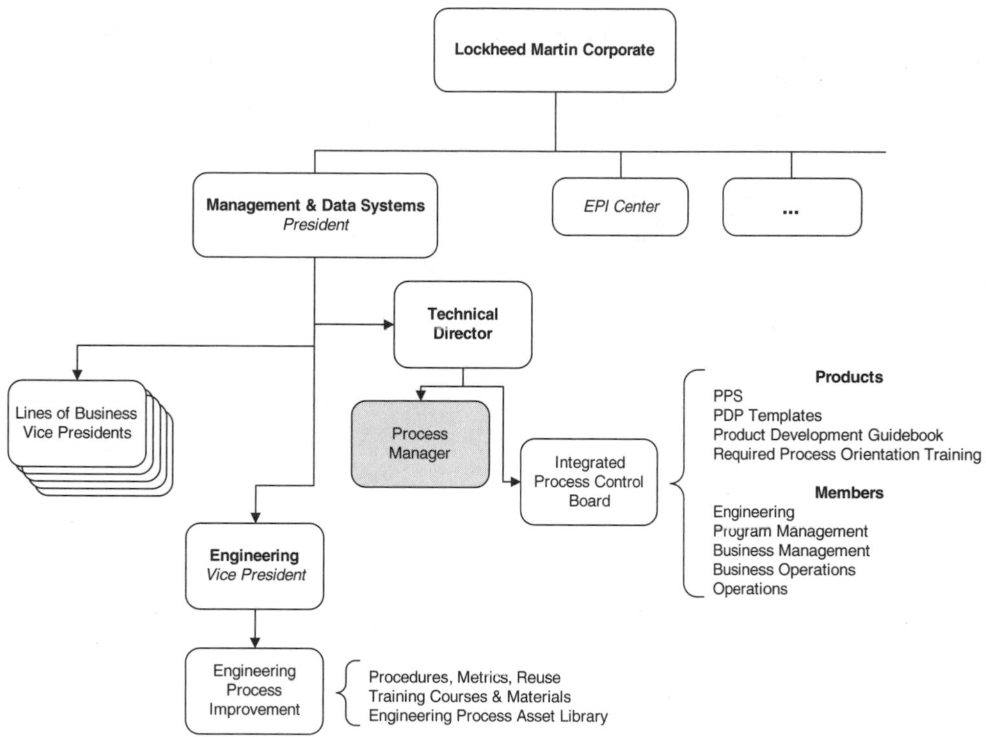

Figure 5–1: *LMCO M&DS organization for process improvement*

resources from the engineering organization, via the vice president of engineering. There was an Engineering Process Improvement group at the corporate level; therefore, the internal engineering organization had represented M&DS at the corporate engineering level. It is clear from the products listed on the right side of Figure 5–1 that the PCB established the organizational focus on process—definition, oversight, measurement, compliance, and improvement.

Figure 5–2 illustrates the newly created process roadmap as it existed at that time. This figure demonstrates a simple structure moving from documentation at the organization level to program documentation (enhanced by a process asset library) to continuous process improvement. This simple process compliance flow introduced the organization to the key elements of its process journey. The structure accommodated multiple program types (applicable through tailoring the organization's standard process), and the standard was simple enough (less than 100 pages) to allow for easy adoption by the programs and program management. The process framework had to also be adaptable to communication, training, and improvement—all built into the infrastructure itself.

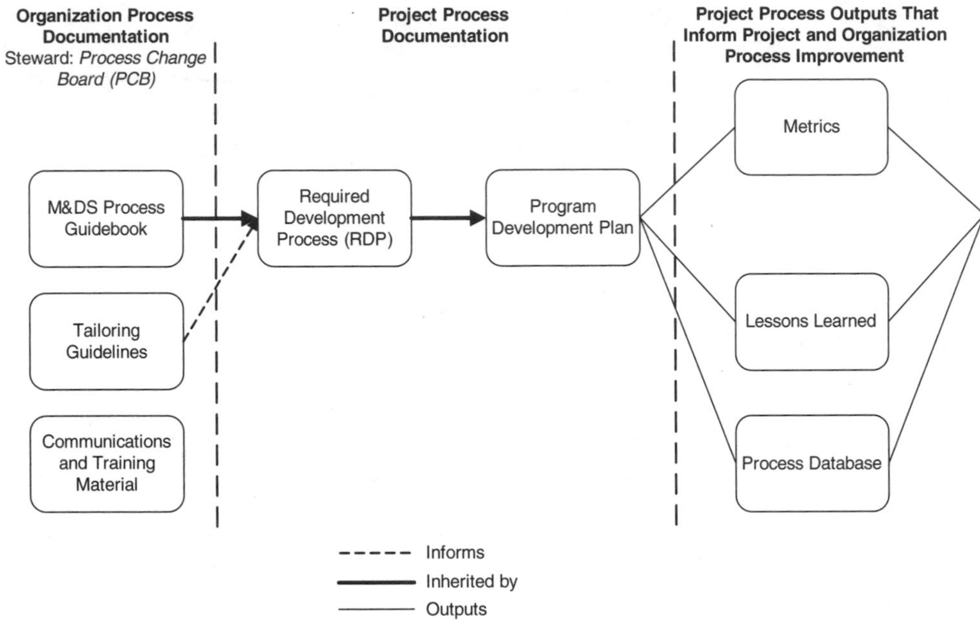

Figure 5–2: *LMCO M&DS process roadmap*

Integrated Process Design

Working closely with the vice president, the process manager launched a transition plan for the newly initiated process improvement program. The plan comprised organizational structure updates, policy, communications, and measures.

The standard operating process, which would eventually become known as the Program Process Standard (PPS), began as the required development process (RDP). The vision associated with the standard operating process was that it would be feasible to introduce only one new process to the organization. That process standard had to reflect the tasks and functions necessary to fulfill organizational project and product commitments. It also had to reflect the features of three standards of interest to the organization: the SW-CMM, the SE-CMM, and ISO 9000. The long-term vision was that new standards, process methodologies, and process initiatives would be integrated with this single operating process, thus allowing the organization to grow and evolve its capability via new releases of its standard process.

Chartered by the process manager, a working group consisting of all the functional process owners extracted the critical processes and created a high-level workflow diagram, across all disciplines. The diagram focused on what work needed to occur, not on how to do it (the latter was the focus of the foundational *Software Engineering and Management Manual*, consisting mostly of procedures). The SEMM was displaced by the newly created RDP. The "how" information associated with the SEMM was kept as collateral documentation to assist rather than direct programs in process adoption. Organizational consensus was obtained for the resulting workflow diagram. This was not a trivial task, and the diagram became known as the "million-dollar diagram," reflecting the cost to produce, review, and approve it.

Portrayed at a high level in Figure 5–3, the diagram consisted of two tiers, with a matrix relationship to the capability lifecycle as indicated by DoD 5000 (now DoDAF[2]). The two tiers were management and control (support

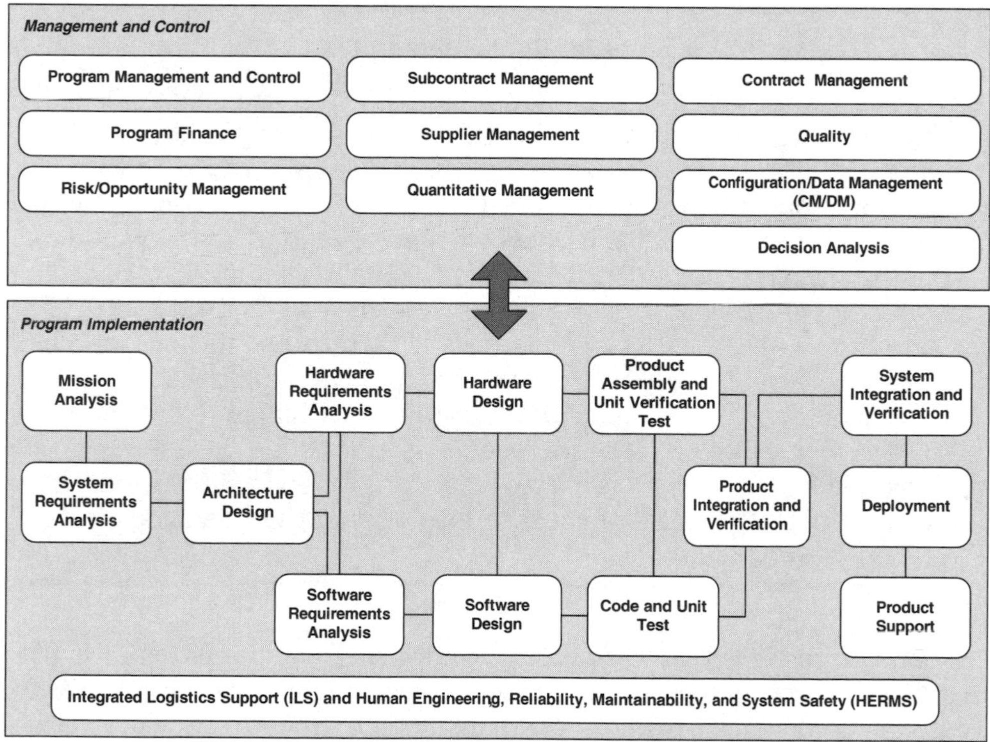

Figure 5–3: *LMCO M&DS Program Process Standard for development programs*

[2]DoD 5000 was a directive and set of instructions from the Defense Acquisition System that defined an acquisition policy environment. DoDAF (DoD Architecture Framework) is a framework for developing a systems architecture or an enterprise architecture. Programs are expected to have DoDAF views developed to pass acquisition milestones. It is applicable to the commercial sector as it applies to systems architecture frameworks.

tasks) and program implementation (repeated development/engineering processes). Development programs were the core of the business, and thus all processes existed in this program type. However, there were other program types, such as operation and maintenance, engineering services, studies, prototypes, and so on. These other types basically adhered to a subset of the processes, and specific activities changed within the processes as well. Tailoring based on program type was a viable implementation of the RDP across this diverse organization. The operating standard was used by all program types, allowing the definition of the program type to define the tailoring of the implementation. Guidance was supplied for all types as well as assistance in determining the appropriate program type.

Did IS&S "Create" the Equivalent of DMAIC?

DMAIC, although not the official label for the IS&S approach to process, was clearly used by IS&S. When initiating the process journey, the first stage was to define the process—the IS&S Program Process Standard. After the organization achieved SW-CMM Level 3, the process journey turned to high maturity. The defined process needed to be measured in order to baseline the performance; this was done with the *Quantitative Management Manual*. Measurements were defined against the PPS. Once the process was baselined, goals for improvement were set and actions were put in place to improve and correct the process. Improvement was done using Lean and Technology Change Management Working Group pilots. The improvements were then measured and monitored to assure that the improvement was indeed as expected. The elements of DMAIC were all present; they were defined as a logical sequence of process maturity.

A specially convened process group, comprising standards experts, then mapped the process standard to the SW-CMM, the SE-CMM, and ISO 9000. The book containing workflow diagrams for the processes in each tier became the minimum mandatory set of processes for all programs. By design, the organization could follow one document, and the reward would be compliance to the SW-CMM, the SE-CMM, and ISO.

Adherence to the newly established process was not achieved simply by distributing the document. Several elements of technology transition were implemented:

- Policy
- Communications
- Training
- Measurement

At this time, the organizational infrastructure (Figure 5–4 in the next section) was updated to support and sustain organizational change. Two process groups were added to the organization to further enhance process management:

1. The Executive Process Steering Committee (EPSC) (as an alternative to a traditional SEPG and the formal name for the integrated Process Control Board introduced previously)
2. The Technology Change Management Working Group (TCMWG)

Routine communications took place via weekly process tips, a monthly newsletter, and posters. Training was accomplished via a mandatory two-hour process orientation, consisting of a video presentation and an in-person moderator to handle questions and ensure interpretation consistency from session to session. Executives completed their training first, so that they could assist the moderators in the training sessions. A one-day common module training session was conducted for those responsible for authoring compliance matrices or program plans.

Deployment was rapid. Within 60 days of training, projects were required to submit a compliance matrix. No grandfathering of the previous process was permitted. Programs unable to comply were required to request a waiver. Waivers were granted for programs midway through a lifecycle phase, with the stipulation that if the program recommenced the lifecycle, it must use the new process. Also, all follow-on work bid for that program was subject to the standard process.

The responsibilities of the Executive Process Steering Committee, comprising all functional process owners and lines of business, included the review and approval of all organizational policies, all cross-functional procedures, and all project compliance (to organizational process standard) matrices as well as program plans. Additionally, the group reviewed quarterly metrics reports and improvement plans. This type of group was chosen rather than a traditional SEPG for two main reasons: to emphasize the need for integrated efforts by the different engineering disciplines (remember, this was well ahead of the CMMI), and to break out of a "model implementation" mindset and into a "process design and execution" mindset. Members of preexisting SEPGs were offered the opportunity to participate in this new approach. The

EPSC, in order to keep the documentation current, documented the requirement to review all process documentation every two years.

The Technology Change Management Working Group was established to manage technology changes associated with process improvement. The TCMWG was chartered by the organization's EPSC to solicit and evaluate improvement project proposals.

By the end of this year-long period, M&DS had achieved SW-CMM Maturity Level 3. Achievement of this objective enabled the organization to continue to compete for contracts. Additional benefits included much less rework and replanning and fewer 60- to 80-hour workweeks, which in turn dramatically reduced engineers' and managers' stress levels. An additional benefit of achieving Level 3 was that the process uniformity across the organization allowed workforce mobility across programs—previously unheard of in an organization where programs lasted for decades. The cost was less than anticipated, at 1.2% of software sales. Critical success factors were a dedicated cross-functional process team and the support and direction of senior management.

5.1.2 Adopting Lean en Route to High Maturity

As the organization began its pursuit of high maturity, it faced the need to streamline and improve its infrastructure. The process standard, boards, and measurement programs were maturing with the organization, and the foundation needed to be rebaselined to serve a more mature organization. Figure 5–4 illustrates the new process infrastructure for the high-maturity process outlook.

To enable this scope expansion and to mark a new beginning for everyone, the Executive Process Steering Committee expanded, evolved, and renamed the RDP to become the Program Process Standard. And, to achieve business goals—including sustainment of existing and achievement of new performance targets and achievement of maturity model level goals—the next priorities of the process improvement program were to establish and use a measurement infrastructure and to identify new ways of doing business, including the integration of Lean.

RDP Expansion: The Standard Process

With the foundational elements of the process improvement program solidly in place, the Executive Process Steering Committee again established a cross-functional working group to reexamine what was renamed as the PPS, which was now on a regular two-year review cycle. The PPS was expanded to

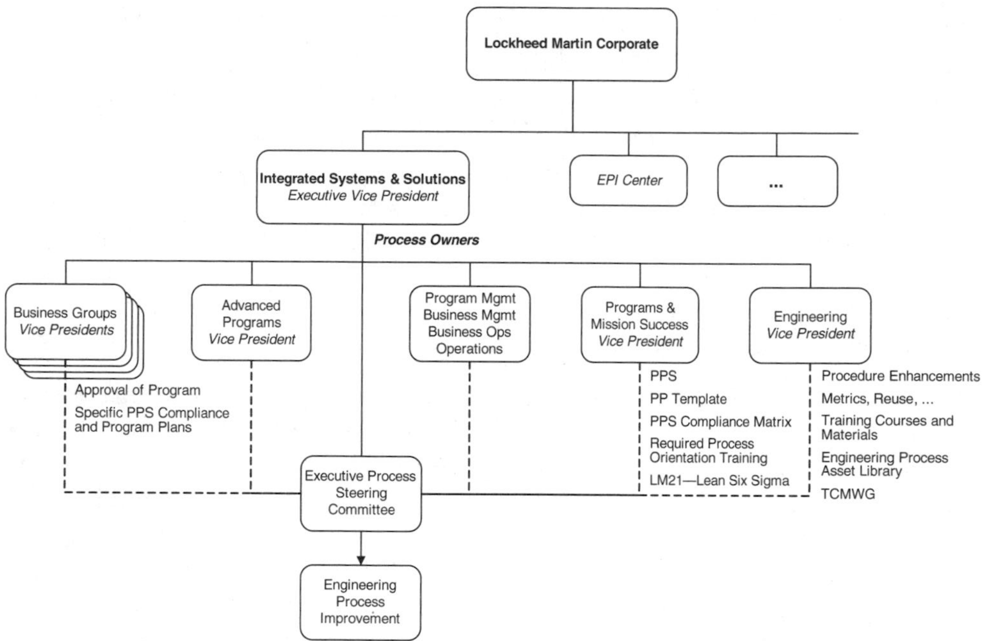

Figure 5–4: *LMCO IS&S organizational infrastructure for enterprise process improvement*

include additional program types. The organization provided specific compliance matrices, program plan templates, and guidance specific for each program type. These artifacts formed the program type tailoring guidelines for specific PPS usage. The following program types were defined for the organization:

- Operations and Maintenance
- Engineering Services
- Facility Outsourcing Services
- Technical Outsourcing Services
- Systems Integration
- Systems Engineering and Technical Assistance (SETA)
- Development
- Independent Research & Development (IR&D)
- Research and Technology Contract

The PPS had grown since the original RDP to include much more detail on the mandatory side. During this period, the programs had become very comfortable with the requirements. Improvement in the document focused on the addition of process activities that had previously been optional or not required of all program types.

With the acquisition of two organizations of lower maturity, the Executive Process Steering Committee established Regional Control Boards in each geographical region in order to align with the organization's EPSC. This assisted in the adoption of the processes and made all acquisitions feel more a part of the whole. The level of detail within the PPS became a key issue. Focus was given to not lose anything the heritage organization had determined was sound business process, but the PPS level of detail had to be adaptable to the acquired organization.

To supplement the PPS, a cross-functional working group was chartered to establish the *Quantitative Measurement Manual* (QMM) as the minimum mandatory set of measurements for all programs. As with the PPS, it included tailoring guidelines. To do this, the working group leveraged historical data (program measures that had been collected for years), including that from heritage companies, as well as Practical Software and Systems Measurement (PSM) as the primary reference. The measurements started with the basic cost and schedule, defect detection, and productivity. The list was expanded to look at the PPS processes and determine what granularity would be necessary to enable program managers to proactively manage their programs. Requirements allocation, traceability, and stabilization measurements were put in place. Inspection data were collected to assist with the defect detection profile. Trends and control limits were based on a few programs' actual data and industry surveys.

As the measurement program matured, more programs used the standard measurements, controls, limits, and trends based on actual data. The QMM required development of an organizational metrics repository, now known as the organization performance database. Similar to the PPS, programs now were required to produce a metrics plan based on the QMM and to produce a metrics compliance matrix.

Although DMAIC was not formally adopted, the organization established a similar technique during the establishment of the process roadmap. The process was defined (PPS) and measured (within programs as directed by the QMM), trends were analyzed as the data were collected (performance database and historical database), and then the process was formerly corrected (TCMWG or Lean techniques).

As with the PPS, the organization implemented elements of transition and organizational change management to support the institutionalization of the QMM. These are further detailed in Chapter 8.

- Establishment of a Metrics Process Steering Committee to support measurement implementation and sustainment
- Measurement training
- Measurement communications and reporting, including a President's Goal Book

At the end of two years, the metrics database had expanded to all the business and functional areas. The organization had achieved SW-CMM Level 4 and SE-CMM Level 3 against all process areas. The President's Goal Book was institutionalized. Equivalent to an enterprise metrics report, it included all the critical measurements associated with the organization. It was constructed using program data rolled up by product line, which was the beginning of a product line scorecard. The organization was also ISO registered.

Lean, the CMM, and the CMMI

This was also the time for new corporate process initiatives. The Lockheed Martin Corporation had decided to implement Lean technologies across the enterprise, as a means of reducing costs. The proper name for the LMCO Lean activity was LM21 (Lockheed Martin—21st Century). LMCO set goals for each of its business units, which in turn were rolled down to the business and functional areas within the units. In order to establish a common understanding of Lean across the corporation, the first training was given to the executive staff. The executives were taken out of the office for three days to be trained in Lean techniques. As a result, there was an understanding coming from the top. Subsequently, the corporation initiated Lean for Leaders training, which is still required of management today. Other formal training associated with Green Belt and Black Belt certifications was also offered.

The Lean toolkit fit perfectly into the high-maturity initiatives within IS&S.

- Lean enabled the institutionalization of the CMM in the newly acquired organizations.
- Lean accelerated the adoption and implementation of new processes associated with the CMMI.
- Lean supplemented the CMMI by addressing critical business processes outside of the CMMI's scope.
- The CMMI enabled Lean by providing defined, documented processes as inputs to Kaizen Events.

For the most recent acquisitions, the initiative served as a way to expedite the adoption of the PPS and therefore CMM compliance. By using Lean methods,

IS&S worked with the acquired organizations to map their existing processes. Using this technique to understand the current situation gave IS&S the capability to set a path toward the future, which ultimately was the adoption of the PPS. The acquired organizations were not truly cognizant of the current state of their processes. Lean techniques gave these organizations the insight. Establishing a data structure (QMM) that was compliant with both PPS and Lean allowed IS&S to monitor the process as it was being adopted by the new organization. This insight into the adopted process performance allowed IS&S to tailor the PPS processes appropriately for the new organization. It served as a real learning experience for both the acquired organization and IS&S. It became increasingly evident that the acquired organizations needed to be monitored and trained to the PPS process in order to realize their true potential.

Lean was significant to the organization for a number of reasons. Although the decision to implement was not directly associated with the organization's decision to achieve high maturity, Lean's introduction afforded the organization other benefits along with its achievement of high maturity.

For example, Lean assisted with institutionalizing processes. The journey to high maturity relies on institutionalization, which is achieved via the CMMI's generic goals. These goals require gathering improvement data for and ultimately optimizing appropriate process areas that will best benefit the business and positively influence the business objectives. With Lean, there was an added drive to collect data not only for management and prediction, which is a focus of the CMMI, but also for Lean-based optimization. In the initial Lean rollout, the organization set cost savings objectives for each process organization. These had to be demonstrated using Lean methods. As a result, there was a natural competition between process owners to demonstrate optimization and cost benefits. This was quite an incentive for the use of Lean, and a side benefit was satisfaction of the CMMI generic practices through which process institutionalization is achieved. This incentive from management gave an added push to overall process improvement activities.

In addition to its overall effect on process institutionalization, Lean was useful within the design of CMMI-based processes involving the TS, DAR, CAR, QPM, OPP, and OID process areas. Lean techniques clearly accelerated the adoption of these new process areas.

For example, the use of Lean, along with the organization's performance database, allowed for the mature, highly capable implementation of CAR. Lean's toolkit of methods (specifically Kaizen Events and value stream mapping) were used in conjunction with the practices of CAR to provide relatively immediate problem identification and resolution results. Specifically, this was accomplished by leveraging the process measurement capability already instituted via Kaizen Events and value stream mapping. With quantitative understanding of process performance and effectiveness as well as causal relationships, the organization more quickly and accurately analyzed problems and identified their root cause. Such mature use of CAR gave the organization the ability to more predictably and effectively deploy improvements.

Another process area introduced with the CMMI, not present in the SW-CMM, was DAR. By the time this process area was formally introduced to the Program Process Standard, Lean's methodologies for process decisions were already in place and became the basis for the organization's formal decision process. As a result of this opportune timing, the organization institutionalized DAR quickly.

Lean's assistance in the adoption of CAR and DAR resulted in the increased capability of these process areas. Although the organization had achieved a higher maturity level, in focusing Lean techniques and methodologies on these two process areas, the capability levels of the individual process areas increased. Both CAR and DAR, through the establishment of performance measurements and statistical techniques, were individually optimized. This use of Lean to enhance capabilities within process areas, theoretically, demonstrates that Lean techniques can be used if the continuous representation is adopted on any set of process areas. These two were specific examples used at LMCO, but it should not be implied that they are the only two that could benefit from such a collaboration with Lean techniques.

Another key advantage of using Lean was the fact that it could focus on organizational processes beyond software and systems engineering, thus showing process benefits to the entire business. The implementation of Lean techniques extended to business processes that the CMM and the CMMI did not address, but for which the process group (and the organization) was a stakeholder and held responsibility for effective execution. An example of such a business process related to software/systems engineering was the standard recruiting and hiring process. A series of small Kaizen Events focusing on each activity throughout the process ultimately yielded a 25% reduction in the time expended to get an individual in the door and placed for productive work. Another example was the process used to identify and obtain approval to bid on new opportunities for the organization. Again, via a series of small events that focused on each decision point, the time was reduced by 30%.

Thus far, we have described IS&S examples that show that Lean can accelerate the adoption of the CMMI. However, the reverse is also true. The deployment of Lean techniques required the organization to look at all established processes and introduced an effort to truly understand that the existing process indeed was the most applicable for the organization. Since this organization was already at high maturity, existing performance databases assisted in defining clearly the as-is states and thus enabled the ability to identify waste and model the to-be states with authority and definition.

Beyond the process improvement approaches just described, at least four significant new ways to do business were identified. These included new inspection methods, a new architecture-based design methodology, a design adequacy assessment (with percentage completion criteria), and in-process quality goals. These methods were difficult to differentiate and were piloted, then rolled out simultaneously for adoption.

By the end of this time period, approximately four years, the organization had achieved high maturity. Figure 5–5 shows the benefits that were

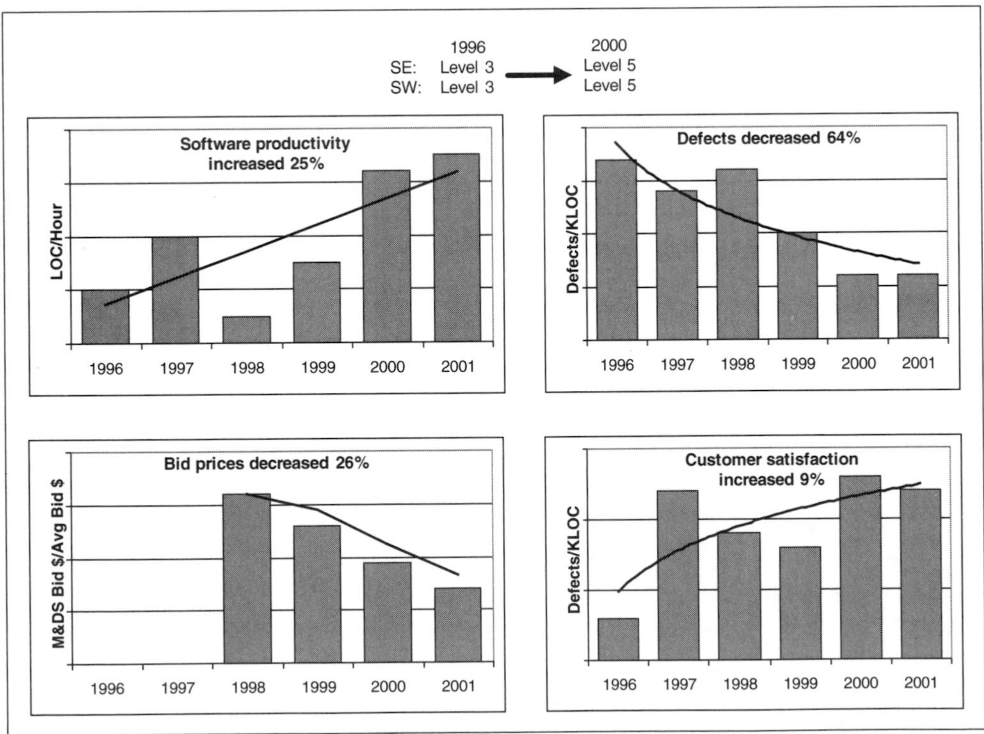

Figure 5–5: *LMCO IS&S benefits realized after achieving SW-CMM Level 5*

realized, including productivity improvements, defect reductions, and customer satisfaction increases. The productivity is based on lines of code (LOC) or thousand lines of code (KLOC). Also, the journey to level 5 had resulted in visible culture change. Lean techniques were fully adopted across the business unit; measurements in all functional and business areas were accepted and managed by the organization. Decisions were made based on data rather than on "trust me" factors, greatly improving the capability and credibility of program managers. Likewise, process improvement and optimization occurred based on data. For instance, when the organization instituted peer reviews, data were used to show that finding defects early in the lifecycle was significantly less costly than finding them later. As the peer reviews were rolled out and programs began finding defects early, their trust in the data used to justify the use of reviews outweighed their concerns about total defect counts (regardless of lifecycle phase) accumulating at a much higher level than previously experienced.

5.1.3 Moving Beyond High Maturity

With the achievement of SW-CMM Level 5, IS&S entered the growth and sustainment phase of its journey. This phase was and continues to be marked by operational excellence and the requisite continuous improvement and optimization of processes. Also, it has included improvement events such as adoption of the CMMI and other models. Some changes result directly from the process improvement effort, such as the removal of the Regional Control Boards. Other changes result from the business environment and drive improvement needs and strategies, such as the acquisition of new organizations.

On the recommendation of the Executive Process Steering Committee, the organization made a strategic decision to adopt the CMMI at the outset of this phase. This was driven by a logical progression from its joint SW-CMM and SE-CMM roots as well as from a growing customer base, primarily the U.S. government, which required CMMI compliance for new work. Based on the organizational focus on software engineering and systems engineering, and customer requirements for maturity levels in acquisition and contract monitoring, the Board selected CMMI SE/SW in a staged representation for adoption. A cross-functional group including model experts, the organization's EPSC and selected individuals took the CMMI introduction training. A subset of this group proceeded to CMMI intermediate and lead appraiser training. The scope of the gap analysis and appraisal was set at the whole organization, now employing 8,000 and spanning four regions. The adoption was planned, based on the traditional mechanisms of gap analysis, gap closure, and appraisal. While some extra effort was invested into the communications plan, the deployment of the CMMI followed the pattern set from the beginning: update and release the PPS, update and execute a training and communications plan, and require compliance matrices with minimal waivers and on a non-negotiable timeline.

The organization perceived the adoption of the CMMI to be the perfect opportunity to advance the PPS drawing. Depicted in Figure 5–6, the renewed diagram was the next evolution of the "million-dollar diagram," previously shown in Figure 5–3. In the center of the revised diagram are three concentric circles, but the circles are at different levels. The inner circle represents the IS&S process architecture, the next circle represents the organizational process assets, and the outer circle represents the programs' implementation of the process assets. The circles define the lifecycle of a system of systems, from procurement through transition and operations. Two groups of processes related to the two tiers of the existing version of the PPS: management and control (support tasks) and program implementation (repeated development/engineering processes). The program management and control processes, listed at the bottom of Figure 5–6, span all processes within the PPS.

The list on the right in Figure 5–6 represents program implementation and contains all processes—from requirements to operations and maintenance—associated with the development, delivery, and maintenance of an actual

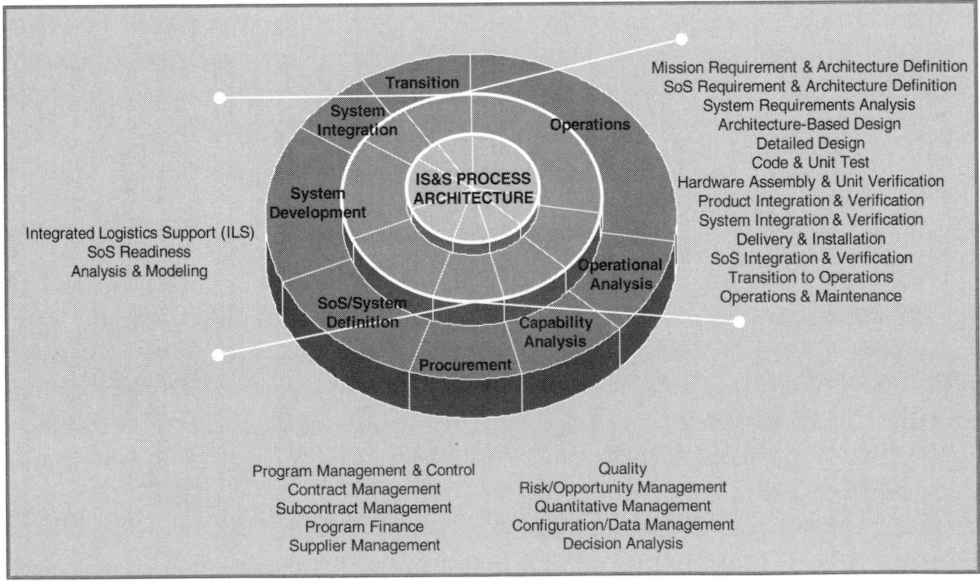

Figure 5–6: *LMCO IS&S PPS architecture*

system. The list on the left was added to address system of systems concerns and the system support activities, which had now become very important in the organization.

Implementation was completed six months ahead of schedule, due in part to the integrated organization process standard (the PPS) and the institutionalized Lean techniques. The overall schedule showed less time in filling the gaps between the CMMI and existing processes.

- The process asset library had been using Lean techniques to make sure that requirements were defined and optimized so gaps were easy to identify and appropriate fills were identified.
- New areas within the CMMI that were not currently identified in the organization's processes used Kaizen Events to define future states.

Thus, adoption of the new standard was clearly less onerous. Lean techniques identified the business cases, and the Lean methods defined the gaps and subsequent process fillers. Lean was used as an enabler for CMMI adoption. Figure 5–7 depicts bottom-line benefits realized as a result of the

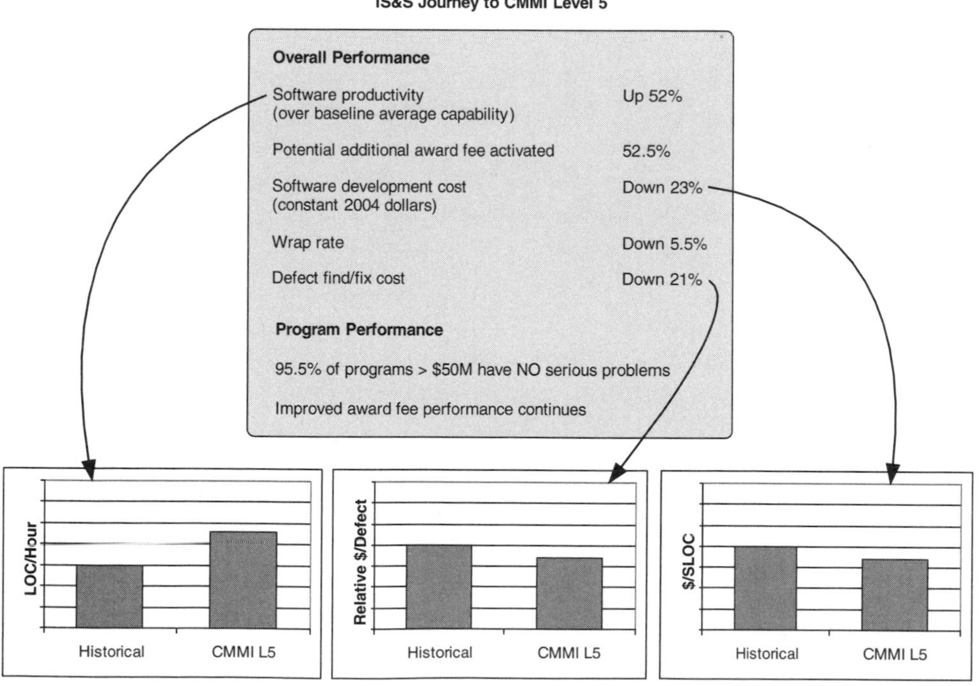

Figure 5–7: *LMCO IS&S benefits realized after achieving CMMI Level 5*

journey to CMMI level 5, including significant productivity increases and cost reductions.

The PPS was mapped to standards including the CMMI, ISO 12207, and ISO 15504. The mapping was published as a new artifact in the organization's process asset library. Also, it was communicated that if any customer mentioned a new standard during acquisition or negotiations, the process group should be notified so that it could conduct a gap analysis to the PPS, then update and release a new mapping.

The PPS and QMM are now in long-term sustainment mode. To support continuous improvement, a Process Improvement Recommendation (PIR) process was established to make it easy for individuals to submit PPS changes. Figure 5–8 shows the new environment and its advancement from the heritage process infrastructure.

Lockheed Martin Corporation has recognized the advances of this business unit in the area of process and has initiated an Integrated Enterprise Process (IEP) document at the organization level. This is the corporation's process standard. Each business unit then documents its processes within an organizational standard process (e.g., the PPS). This method implements a uniform minimum of CMMI maturity level 3 across its diverse business units. This is quite an innovative step for such a large organization but, combined

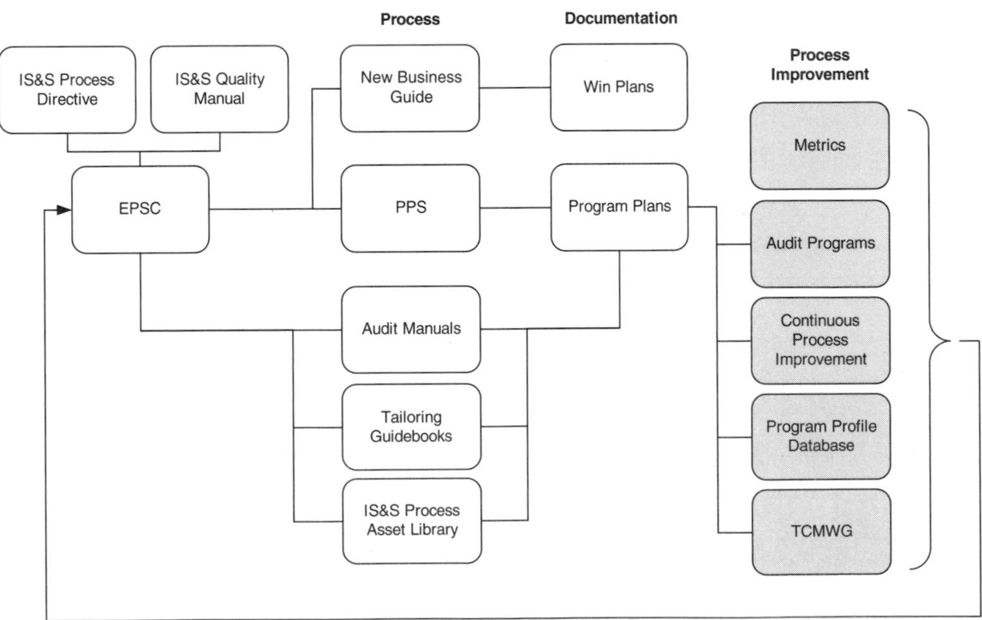

Figure 5–8: *LMCO IS&S current process roadmap*

with its Lean corporate initiatives, will further its production possibilities [Weszka 06].

5.1.4 Lockheed Martin IS&S Summary

The Program Process Standard is the keystone of Lockheed Martin IS&S's process improvement journey. Coupled with an effective transition plan, it has enabled the organization to achieve SW-CMM Level 5 and then to seamlessly adopt the CMMI and other models and standards—ultimately leading to CMMI Maturity Level 5.

Lean and Six Sigma assisted the organization in defining processes as well as adopting and identifying process improvements. Techniques have assisted in setting and predicting trends and variances in the program and business measurements. Although started as separate initiatives, the union of the CMMI and Lean was inevitable. The marriage has proved beneficial on all fronts—program and organization. Today at IS&S, the Lean/Six Sigma program is managed by the same function, Quality Systems and Process Management (QS&PM), that manages the CMMI.

IS&S's process adoption and maturation have resulted in many qualitative as well as quantitative benefits. Processes are managed quantitatively, with performance goals set for those that are critical. The process discipline has yielded productivity improvements and cost reductions. Qualitatively speaking, the expectations of the organizational personnel have changed. Program processes are so disciplined that the organization has started expecting that same discipline in everyday business processes. The organization has begun to expand the scope of CMMI adoption into many disciplines that have not yet experienced process focus and improvement.

5.2 Case Study: Motorola

Originally founded as the Galvin Manufacturing Corporation in 1928, Motorola has come a long way since introducing its first product, the battery eliminator. For more than 75 years, Motorola has proven itself a global leader in wireless, broadband, and automotive communications technologies and embedded electronic products. Inspired by a vision of Seamless Mobility, Motorola is committed to helping consumers get and stay connected simply and seamlessly to other people, information, and entertainment. A *Fortune* 100 company with global presence and impact, Motorola had sales of U.S. $35.3 billion in 2005. Motorola's primary businesses, as of the writing of this book, consist of the following.

- Enterprise Mobility Solutions: This group includes the mission-critical communications offered by the government and public safety sectors and enterprise mobility business. This includes analog and digital two-way radio, as well as voice and data communications products and systems. Product capabilities include mobile computing, advanced data capture, wireless infrastructure, and RFID solutions.
- Home & Networks Mobility: This group provides integrated, end-to-end systems that seamlessly and reliably enable uninterrupted access to digital entertainment, information, and communications services over a variety of wired and wireless solutions.
- Mobile Devices: This group designs, manufactures, sells, and services wireless handsets. The collection spans all cellular and wireless systems and includes integrated software applications, as well as a large complement of Bluetooth-enabled accessories.

At the time of this case study, Motorola employed software engineers worldwide across three major business units. Notable organizational structures that would influence the growth of both the CMMI and/or Six Sigma included the establishment of worldwide software design centers in addition to software staff embedded within each major business unit. The product development lifecycle generally ranged from months to multiple years.

5.2.1 Historical Foundations

Motorola Product Development Lifecycle

The deployment of the Six Sigma methods over the years cannot be fully understood without considering the context of the product development and management processes that also evolved within Motorola. The general framework that served as a corporate standard began with a system of Quality Gates (QGates), which by 2000 was replaced by a more complete product development lifecycle framework called Management Gates (MGates). QGates focused on specific points in which an independent quality organization would conduct quality reviews. MGates served as a more balanced and complete approach to the different types of management reviews that should occur during product development. Although believed to have been initially rooted in early Six Sigma deployments, QGates and MGates evolved on an independent path from both Six Sigma and software process improvement, until the early 2000s.

MGates, at the time of this case study, consisted of 16 gates and provided the framework for making business decisions that radically improved time-to-market and business predictability. By 2003, MGate reviews had become integrated into all normal product development processes, and the MGates had become the common language for all Motorola employees with regard to product development, quality, and process improvement

Six Sigma

Motorola is widely recognized as the birthplace of Six Sigma. In parallel with its internal deployment, Motorola influenced other corporations' adoptions of Six Sigma via the Six Sigma Research Institute (SSRI) and also via both internal and external training offered by Motorola University. It is important to distinguish the internal and external development of Six Sigma. Externally, through the experience and influence of other companies, Six Sigma evolved from its roots to become a holistic business methodology, with several frameworks being applied throughout the enterprise. Internally, however, the initial instantiation of Six Sigma continued successfully for a number of years, without being affected by Six Sigma adoption and evolution elsewhere in industry. Motorola University served an internal corporate role of providing Six Sigma training and deployment, which evolved as external contract instructors became involved. Ultimately, as will be described in this section, the internal and external evolutions of Six Sigma were reconciled.

Motorola's initial internal Six Sigma program contained Six Steps to Six Sigma, as follows.

Step 1: Identify the product you create or the service you provide.
In other words . . . *What do you do?*

Step 2: Identify the customer(s) for your product or service, and determine what they consider important, that is, the customer requirements.
In other words . . . *Who uses your product and services?*

Step 3: Identify what you need in order to provide a product or service so that it satisfies the customer.
In other words . . . *What do you need to do your work?*

Step 4: Define the process for doing your work.
In other words . . . *How do you do your work?*

Step 5: Mistake-proof the process and eliminate wasted efforts.
In other words . . . *How can you do your work better?*

Step 6: Ensure continuous improvement by measuring, analyzing, and controlling the improved process using DMAIC (Define-Measure-Analyze-Improve-Control).
In other words . . . *How perfectly are you doing your customer-focused work?*

The initial deployment philosophy of Six Sigma within Motorola was to train and certify Six Sigma change agents as Green and Black Belts and to have them return to their domains and job roles to lead by example in using the Six Sigma methods and tools. There were no full-time Green or Black Belts within the business entities other than the small core team located within the Motorola University SSRI. A major contributor to the success of this part-time approach to Green and Black Belts was the CEO's continual focus and pull for Six Sigma. A significant factor to the success of the Six Sigma deployment was the focus on developing Black Belts to become effective change agents. A full 25% of the original curriculum of Six Sigma Black Belts at this early stage was focused on managing change in an organization and included five days of training focused on building sponsorship for change, working with influence leaders and early adopters, and personally leading change efforts.

In 2001, the Personal Communications Sector of Motorola (now called the Mobile Devices Business) recruited a new president from the executive ranks of GE who, two years later, moved into the position of chief operating officer (COO) for Motorola. In this corporate role, he recruited another executive from GE to lead a dramatic renewal of the Motorola Six Sigma deployment based on the GE Six Sigma experience. The new Motorola Six Sigma deployment was called Digital Six Sigma (DSS) and was led by a new Corporate Initiatives Group (CIG) consisting of a core team of Six Sigma Master Black Belts, in partnership with a group from within Motorola University. Essentially, the word *Digital* represented not only a changed title to highlight the new flavor of Six Sigma but also a stronger focus on digitizing Six Sigma DMAIC solutions to increase their institutionalization. Finally, the word *Digital* also represented the increased role of e-learning in the successful deployment of Six Sigma, as well as automating the trivial or repetitive work, thereby enabling a stronger focus on the important challenges of quality, productivity, and cycle time.

The initial Digital Six Sigma approach was based on getting away from the legacy program of a "Belt factory," in which a large contingent of Belts would be trained to work on a variety of small, uncoordinated, individual improvement projects. Instead, the Digital Six Sigma approach aimed to develop a lean, well-trained force of full-time Black Belt and Master Black Belt leaders who, in turn, would work on a small, prioritized set of very high value improvement projects ($250,000 to $5 million) that were aligned with the business goals of the company. The new Digital Six Sigma mandated each business entity to have 1% of its headcount as full-time, dedicated Six Sigma Black Belt and Master Black Belt staff within each business entity. In this manner, it was felt that critical mass would be achieved for sustained deployment and application of the new Digital Six Sigma toolset. Accomplishing this degree of dedicated staff was not feasible initially. As a result, the Motorola CIG recruited candidates based on leadership skills and potential and then certified them via training with Motorola University during their first 12 months in the role. Full-time Belts were to be in their dedicated roles for two to three years, followed by promotion into more senior roles within the company.

In 2003, a new Green Belt class was developed and offered within Motorola. Shortly thereafter, a significant investment was made into the development of an 8-hour introductory e-learning module for all Motorola employees, as well as a 40-hour e-learning module for Green Belt training targeted for internal use in Motorola worldwide. This e-learning marked phase 1 of the Digital Six Sigma deployment. During the latter stages of phase 1, Motorola University conducted research and a series of benchmarking activities to ascertain the latest in Six Sigma practices. Through these activities, Motorola University became interested in the process and product reengineering focus of Design for Six Sigma and added a DFSS component to the existing Digital Six Sigma deployment. In addition to expanding the scope to a broader set of Six Sigma frameworks, Motorola University expanded its training team to five full-time, certified Six Sigma Master Black Belts with complementary backgrounds (product engineering and design, manufacturing, transaction and software engineering). The diversity of the team enabled Motorola University to evolve its Six Sigma training program to include core common training for all Belts, followed by domain-oriented training. The training specific to software engineering was strengthened following the realization that Digital Six Sigma and the CMMI could be jointly leveraged, as described in later sections.

Software Process Improvement

Motorola's history with software process improvement actually predates the founding of the Software Engineering Institute in 1984. Initial software process improvement efforts were joined with the Motorola Quality organization and deployed within the context of the other quality initiatives. This accelerated the formation of corporate software process improvement groups and centralized Quality vice presidents who championed software process improvement and the SEI CMM.

Most of these early experts also collaborated in establishing what was then called the Motorola Global Software Group and is now called the Motorola

Software Group. The Motorola Global Software Group arose from Motorola's need in the 1980s and 1990s to attract a sufficiently large software engineering workforce to meet product development demands. During this time period, software engineers were scarce due to the expanding technology bubble and the lead-up to the year 2000 software crisis. Software engineers were so scarce that dramatic measures were undertaken to expand the Motorola software engineering population, including the creation of Global Software Design Centers. The early leaders of the software process improvement initiative decided to pursue the framework of the Global Software Design Centers as the incubator and deployment mechanism of mature software development and quality processes. The Global Software Group quickly gained a reputation as the software maturity leader in the corporation and the embodiment of the very latest in software processes, technologies, and tools. In parallel with the formation of the Global Software Group, the Motorola Software Quality Council was formed to provide corporate leadership and coordination of software process improvement and software maturity assessments. These activities led to significant improvements in both CMM and CMMI maturity results, as well as overall improvements in software quality, productivity, and time-to-market.

5.2.2 Bridging Initiatives

At the enterprise level, Motorola launched activities to bridge the Six Sigma and SEI CMM/CMMI initiatives beginning in 2002. It was perceived that the recent pursuit of Digital Six Sigma would transform the corporation and, ultimately, provide the basis for a new, unified approach to business improvement—including leveraging the SEI CMM and the CMMI.

However, by 2003, Motorola leadership had decided to postpone the transition from the SEI CMM to the CMMI model for an interdependent set of reasons, including the following.

- The realities of severe economic conditions followed by the technology bubble burst and global competitive pressures. This combination highlighted the Six Sigma focus on delivering near-term business results and on software cost and productivity.
- The desire for more business case information—specifically, in the financial language of executives, in order to support the approach of Six Sigma business cases, which called for bottom-line results in a 6- to 12-month period.
- The belief that Digital Six Sigma—which did include a software training track—was the primary path to addressing issues of the current business

climate, coupled with the misconception that the CMMI was a software-only model. Together, these fueled the perception that converting from the CMM to the CMMI was not necessary due to its redundancy with the significant prior investment of maturing many off-shore design centers to SEI SW-CMM maturity level 5. At best, the CMMI was perceived as a subset of, and therefore a distraction from, the DSS deployment.

In reaction to Motorola's leadership desire to stay with the tried and true SEI CMM model, the Motorola Software Quality Council promulgated that all formal, internal software assessments would continue using the SEI SW-CMM. And, in parallel, a significant amount of resources and funding were diverted to the Digital Six Sigma deployment. It was estimated that the financial resources for Digital Six Sigma deployment in several software units exceeded that of the SW-CMM activity by a factor of at least five. Nevertheless, the Global Software Group continued informal activities toward transitioning to the CMMI—including initial CMMI training. The Global Software Group also participated in an SEI-led industry team to develop SCAMPI B and C that included a precedent-setting $100,000 for an SEI project involving three different Motorola organizations.

Impetus to Integrate Digital Six Sigma and the CMMI

During 2003, however, as challenges in the deployment of Digital Six Sigma grew, additional analysis was performed to investigate how the deployment might be accelerated. It was soon recognized that the organization's deployment of and experience with the SW-CMM could be leveraged. This realization arose when the Motorola Corporate Initiatives Group decided to develop an assessment methodology for Digital Six Sigma compliance. At first, this effort proceeded without knowledge of the history and corporate competency already established to conduct SEI CMM assessments; then, during a 2004 workshop when the integration of DFSS and the MGates was first formally discussed, the leverage opportunity finally surfaced.

In spring 2004, a high-maturity CMM Motorola business, one that was not slated to roll out DSS training for another six months, decided to investigate the required investment and benefits of converting to the CMMI. The business participated in one of the last pilots of the SCAMPI C assessment method conducted under the auspices of the Motorola Global Software Group and the SEI-led industry team. Although this high-maturity CMM Motorola business possessed a number of forward-thinking process champions, it needed the results of SCAMPI C, at least, to credibly demonstrate to management what the delta investment/benefit would be to pursue

CMMI-based process improvement. Motorola University participated in this SCAMPI C pilot to identify areas of overlap and synergy between the CMMI and Digital Six Sigma.

The final analysis showed that all of the major challenges in transitioning from the SEI SW-CMM to the CMMI would be addressed by the planned Digital Six Sigma training. The SCAMPI result provided the motivation and stamina for the business process champions to continue their push for CMMI-based improvement within their organization coupled with Digital Six Sigma. Although Digital Six Sigma provided much of the implementation of the CMMI process areas, the CMMI remained the reference improvement model to strategically connect business goals, organizational competencies, and the process improvement tools of Digital Six Sigma.

Tactical Approach to Integrating DSS and the CMMI

As a result of the SCAMPI C experience, Motorola University embarked on a campaign to integrate the training, deployment, and subsequent implementation assessment of both the Digital Six Sigma and CMMI improvement approaches. In addition to the corporate value due to accelerated results, Motorola University, itself, would benefit from integrated training that would simplify and reduce the cost of the separate offerings needed for each business entity.

The key tactics were the following:

- Develop mappings to show how DFSS and DMAIC frameworks and tools would resolve capability gaps revealed during CMMI appraisals
- Develop training that integrated concepts of the CMMI, and other software best practices, into the DSS curricula
- Promote cross-training of the two deployment communities (DSS and the CMM/CMMI), in order to bridge the cultural divide and to build a cadre of personnel with expertise in both initiatives
- Leverage Six Sigma Jumpstart workshops

Mappings

The mapping of Digital Six Sigma tools and methods to the process areas of the CMMI became an effective communications vehicle, providing just the correct amount of detail to convince management of the synergy of the two improvement approaches. The specific mapping shown in Table 5–1 lists the CMMI process areas and a subjective assessment of the contribution of the Design for Six Sigma and DMAIC tools and methods to the CMMI process

Table 5–1: *Motorola Mapping of DFSS and DMAIC to the CMMI*

CMMI Process Area	DFSS Contribution	DMAIC Contribution
Causal Analysis and Resolution (CAR)		++
Organizational Innovation and Deployment (OID)		++
Quantitative Project Management (QPM)	++	++
Organizational Process Performance (OPP)	++	++
Decision Analysis and Resolution (DAR)	++	++
Integrated Project Management (IPM)	++	
Organizational Process Definition (OPD)	+	++
Organizational Process Focus (OPF)	+	++
Organizational Training (OT)		+
Product Integration (PI)	++	
Requirements Development (RD)	++	
Risk Management (RM)	++	+
Technical Solution (TS)	++	
Validation (VAL)	++	
Verification (VER)	++	
Configuration Management (CM)		
Measurement and Analysis (MA)	++	++
Project Monitoring and Control (PMC)	++	+
Project Planning (PP)	++	+
Process and Product Quality Assurance (PPQA)	++	++
Requirements Management (REQM)	++	
Supplier Agreement Management (SAM)	+	

KEY

++ Strong or significant contribution

\+ Moderate contribution

☐ Minimal or no contribution

areas. With this diagram, the audience would see that DMAIC and Design for Six Sigma both contribute, in supplementary fashion, to provide coverage against the CMMI process areas. The diagram served well to convince management of the benefits of using both DMAIC and Design for Six Sigma in implementing the CMMI process areas.

Mappings were expanded to accommodate several different perspectives. One perspective was the CMMI audience seeking to understand how Digital Six Sigma complemented and bolstered the implementation of the CMMI process areas, especially the process areas added from the SW-CMM baseline. The other perspective was the Digital Six Sigma community seeking to understand how the CMMI structure, process framework, assessment methodology, and product/system view could accelerate the adoption of Digital Six Sigma within software-intensive organizations. Consequently, customized views into the mapping proved worthwhile in bridging the two disparate communities, for example, a mapping table with the different columns taking turns in the first column position.

Training

Motorola University saw the need for two curricula—one for DMAIC and one for DFSS. Both would need to be interpreted for software engineering, including identifying the unique software engineering methods and tools that performed the intent of many of the DMAIC and Design for Six Sigma methods and tools. The unique methods ranged from straightforward translations of traditional manufacturing Six Sigma methods into software case studies to additional methods unique to software engineering, such as software architecture evaluation and optimization approaches By late spring 2004, Motorola University and the Corporate Initiatives Group decided on a dual Digital Six Sigma curriculum, consisting of training in both DMAIC and Design for Six Sigma. Table 5–2 depicts the 2004 curriculum for the Six Sigma DMAIC program. The curriculum for the Design for Six Sigma program has continually evolved over the past several years and is not shown here. A discussion of the initial thoughts for the Design for Six Sigma curriculum appears in Chapter 6.

To meet the immediate challenge of rolling out both the DMAIC and Design for Six Sigma training programs simultaneously, Motorola University decided to outsource the DMAIC curriculum development to separate consultants while retaining the responsibility to internally customize the Design for Six Sigma curriculum based on a collection of software best practices internal and external to Motorola. This had advantages and disadvantages. The positive impact was the immediate increase in resources to deploy training,

Table 5–2: *Motorola Training*

Course/Audience	Content	Tools and Techniques
Green Belt	Basic statistics	DMAIC, descriptive statistics, ANOVA, MSA, SPC, process capability
Leading DSS	Leadership skills	DMAIC, DMADDD, DMADV; Big Y-to-x Schematics
Black Belt, Weeks 1–3	Advanced statistics	Green Belt plus VOC, DOE, regression, RSM
Week 4, Software	SW DMAIC and DMADV	SW examples, decision aids, optimization of VOC and VOP
Week 4, Hardware	HW optimization	Pugh's concept selection, Robust Engineering, Parameter Design
Week 4, Transaction	Business process improvement	Discrete Event Simulation, Data Reliability, COPQ
Week 4, Manufacturing	Manufacturing optimization	Lean Manufacturing, Process Mapping, Simulation, MSA, SPC

while the disadvantage was that it became more difficult to integrate and customize the training to include Motorola MGates context as well as synergy with the SEI CMM/CMMI topics.

Deployment Communities

Within Motorola, the community of individuals charged with the deployment of Digital Six Sigma tended to be completely separate from the community of individuals deploying and practicing SEI SW-CMM improvement. Understanding the following dimensions of separation helped to bridge these two initiatives of the CMMI and Digital Six Sigma.

- Discipline: The individuals deploying Digital Six Sigma tended to be from disciplines other than software engineering or from manufacturing, whereas the individuals active with the SW-CMM and early CMMI deployments were almost strictly software engineering professionals.
- Organization: The individuals deploying Digital Six Sigma were organized in a central Corporate Initiatives Group or in central functions

embedded within each business entity (usually the quality function), whereas the individuals within organizations deploying the SW-CMM and early CMMI practices were, for the most part, software process engineers located across a wide variety of distributed process or quality teams (usually in process or quality teams at the business entity or department level).

- Funding: Digital Six Sigma deployment staff were almost exclusively funded by corporate or special business entity funding set-asides that were effectively provided by an eventual organizational "tax," whereas the individuals deploying the SW-CMM and early CMMI practices were funded, for the most part, by organizations and departments that historically had prioritized the effort as a course of doing business.
- Recruiting: The Digital Six Sigma deployment staff were recruited internally and, to a significant degree, from external sources by corporate functions in conjunction with dedicated human resource staff support, whereas the recruitment of deployment staff for the SW-CMM and early CMMI practices was conducted at a project or department level, with some recruitment conducted by the business entity quality function, and usually from internal Motorola staff.

Once these differences were acknowledged, two mechanisms were pursued to resolve the situation:

1. Training to level the playing field of knowledge and skills
2. Organizational alignment to resolve perceived (and real) competition for funding and resources

To help bridge the chasm between these two deployment groups, Motorola University, in conjunction with the CIG, began identifying individuals who had background with both Digital Six Sigma and the SEI SW-CMM/CMMI. Initially, this amounted to only a few individuals, but the number grew after a concerted effort to enlist more seasoned SW-CMM lead appraisers and team members into the Digital Six Sigma training program. It was recognized that to ultimately integrate these two deployments and secure the benefits of such an integration, more individuals throughout the business entities would need to have a working understanding of both worlds.

The primary challenge, during this period of cultivating individuals who could understand both worlds, was that these two deployment groups perceived that they were fighting for the same budget and headcount. It is believed that this initial perception over budgets fueled the misconception that the two deployments were competing and therefore redundant. A secondary issue that further built this misconception was that the Digital Six Sigma methodology included an eventual governance process in which the methodology governed which improvement projects would be funded and staffed. Digital Six Sigma dashboards and cockpits were appearing in staff meetings at various levels of the organization and were used to prioritize significant business needs and projects, as well as to status improvement projects. By the latter part of 2004, engineering process groups within some of the businesses were aligned under the Digital Six Sigma improvement project pipeline process and were no longer working in isolation when deciding which improvement projects to pursue. The net effect was dramatically increased management support, funding, and staffing of improvement projects with heightened visibility of progress and results.

Six Sigma Jumpstart Workshops

Another mechanism to accelerate the deployment of Six Sigma was the use of Six Sigma Jumpstart workshops. These workshops were initiated through successful experiences of such workshops by the External Motorola University Six Sigma business. The workshop basically supported a kickstart on the Big Y to Vital x improvement teams with initial team charters. These workshops were conducted either annually or biannually within businesses and decentralized down to the department level. They became the impetus for project planning most improvement projects and from which SEPGs and engineering process groups would gain direction and guidance. It became the responsibility of the Six Sigma Master Black Belts to facilitate these workshops within their businesses and ensure proper participation and alignment of business goals to improvement projects. As the use of these workshops grew, it became an excellent opportunity to inject topics and priorities from the context of the SW-CMM and CMMI. In several Motorola businesses, these workshops became the best way to begin integrating SW-CMM/CMMI activities with the Digital Six Sigma projects.

5.2.3 Enterprise Deployment Leads to Local Results

A number of success stories have been recorded within Motorola software engineering with respect to Digital Six Sigma DMAIC, DMADV, and DFSS projects. Motorola hosts a number of sharing events throughout the year in which significant projects are showcased for the entire Motorola community. Examples of significant software engineering Six Sigma projects, which built on the improvement journey of SW-CMM topics prior to Six Sigma, have included the following:

- New requirements elicitation and voice of the customer approaches
- New development approaches, including Agile and Extreme Programming
- Architected and designed performance of key product platforms
- New and improved methods for various types of testing
- Technology solutions for new products, including patented approaches for software control of key product operations
- Reduced field failures and improved warranty projections
- Several customer-delighting experiences in which DFSS-designed products propelled Motorola to number one supplier status

Subsequent sharing events since formal adoption of the CMMI have also showcased improvement projects for specific CMMI process areas and have begun to show the joint benefits of the CMMI and Six Sigma.

5.2.4 Motorola Summary

As the Motorola history of SEI CMM/CMMI process improvement and Six Sigma deployment has demonstrated, separate deployments of the two can be successful, but with each exhibiting strengths and shortcomings. Both retrospective and initial Motorola experiences of integrating the SEI CMMI and Six Sigma methods offer the chance to gain an appreciation for pursuing an integrated approach to improvement, reflecting a holistic approach imprinted onto the MGates model for new product development.

5.3 Summary

This chapter presented the journey of two organizations—one defense, one commercial—each with compelling business needs to improve its software and systems engineering processes. Both organizations leveraged multiple models and initiatives in their efforts but used different combinations, strategies, and tactics.

Lockheed Martin IS&S envisioned and engineered an integrated process standard while still at low maturity. This standard focused on the practices and processes needed to conduct its business. Models and standards were mapped to the standard as a means of ensuring completeness and leveraging the best thinking of the larger software and systems community. The SW-CMM and the SE-CMM, then the CMMI, played a significant role in mapping and in guiding how the organization institutionalized its processes and measured its practices. Six Sigma, particularly Lean, was integrated as a tactical engine for implementing specific improvement projects and for bolstering quantitative-oriented organizational practices. It also played a strategic role as one part of a multitiered improvement project selection process. Critical to Lockheed Martin IS&S's success were key personnel gifted with the ability to architect the process and design a robust (and multiphased) implementation and transition strategy, as well as strong senior management sponsorship.

Motorola, at the enterprise level, experienced parallel and independent development of phase gate processes, Six Sigma (including application to software), and software process improvement via domain practices. The initial impetus to join the initiatives, particularly Six Sigma and software domain practices, came when the corporation began reinventing its internal deployment of Six Sigma. The joining of initiatives was not easily realized, though, as there was perceived competition between them—driven partly by lack of mutual understanding of the initiatives by their respective implementers and partly by how budgets and resources were managed. To address this, a detailed mapping of the initiatives as instantiated at Motorola was created to show how DFSS, DMAIC, and the CMMI each filled different organizational needs—and therefore were mutually enabling. This provided the needed bridge between the different communities and helped inform the creation of an integrated training program, the cornerstone of a tactical, joint implementation effort.

Chapter 6

Integrating the CMMI and Six Sigma: Strategies

If one accepts the value proposition that synergistic implementation of multiple standards and initiatives accelerates the improvement journey and renders it more effective, then the next question is how to go about it. There is not a "one size fits all" solution to this question. However, several common approaches and considerations can be leveraged.

In this chapter, we build on Chapter 4's research and Chapter 5's case studies and highlight possible sequencing scenarios, followed by frequently observed strategic approaches to the joint implementation of the CMMI and Six Sigma. Then we proceed with a discussion of integrated deployment tactics. The Motorola case is revisited here, with a field report on Six Sigma deployment, specifically focusing on integrated training.

6.1 Sequencing Scenarios

One way for an organization to begin reasoning about a joint implementation is to consider its starting point in terms of CMMI and Six Sigma deployment and performance. Figure 6–1 shows several possible paths, with different possible starting points.

- Path 1 (solid): Implement the CMMI to high maturity, and then implement Six Sigma. In this approach, the CMMI is likely to be the organizational

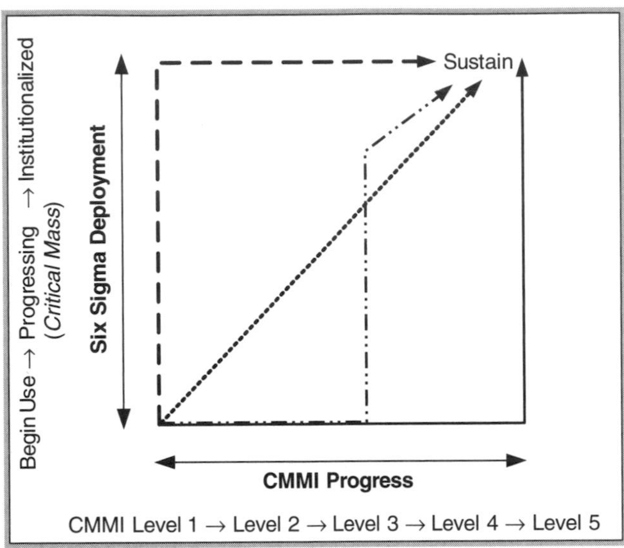

Figure 6–1: *Sequencing scenarios*

governance model, with Six Sigma methods used in an isolated fashion to help with the implementation of specific process areas and practices. After high maturity is achieved, Six Sigma is formally adopted as the means for continuing process improvement.

- Path 2 (dash): Institutionalize Six Sigma fully and then the CMMI. In this approach, Six Sigma is likely to be the governance model, with the CMMI (and other standards) being selected to close problematic gaps in process infrastructure.
- Path 3 (dot): Jointly implement and institutionalize Six Sigma and the CMMI from the beginning. In this approach, the two initiatives may alternate as the governance model or the tactical engine. For instance, Six Sigma may lead the organization to deploy particular CMMI process areas, and it may dictate a lean process infrastructure. The CMMI may lead the organization to quickly identify critical process factors as well as opportunities against which to apply the Six Sigma frameworks.
- Path 4 (dash-dot): Implement the CMMI to level 3, then establish Six Sigma and proceed with a joint implementation. In this scenario, the organization first establishes its defined processes and then uses Six Sigma in its quest for high maturity.

The question that arises by examining joint deployment from this perspective is whether there is strategic advantage in implementing the CMMI first and then Six Sigma, or vice versa, or implementing them in tandem. In truth, the choice about which path to pursue depends on the organization's circumstances when it decides to pursue synergistic, rather than parallel/independent implementation of the initiatives. In some cases, a sequential path is dictated by current reality. For instance, a CMMI adoption may be well under way when the enterprise levies the adoption of Six Sigma on the organization. Or an enterprise may have institutionalized Six Sigma and be well into the process of extending it into engineering when the non-software-oriented Black Belts realize that there is no established software process infrastructure or measurement system (as there is in manufacturing). Presuming they have awareness of domain-specific models and standards, they then face the equivalent of a "build or buy" decision: invent software process infrastructure from scratch or tailor what the community has codified.

Thoughtful, joint implementation throughout the entire improvement journey (path 3) is likely to be the most efficient path, but only if the engineering process group and the organization are ready for that approach. In some contexts, due to politics, previous organizational training, and many other factors, implementing one and then the other may be more ideal. Either way, it comes back to the matters of choice, conscious strategic decision making, and thoughtful designs.

Happenstance and timing issues notwithstanding, an organization can be successful with any of the paths.

6.2 Joint Implementation Strategies

From the published information available and our research, we have abstracted the following strategies for using these initiatives together. This is not an exhaustive list, but rather reflective of patterns we have observed, overlaid with what our experience tells us works well. These strategies, which range from coordinated to fully integrated implementations, are not mutually exclusive. In fact, in some organizations, all of them have been leveraged. These strategies do not presume that the CMMI precedes Six Sigma adoption or vice versa.

Chapter 7 continues the discussion by describing dimensions of design connectivity between the CMMI and Six Sigma that can (and should) be leveraged to execute these strategies. Understanding these relationships enables the successful execution of the chosen strategies.

Strategy 1: Implement CMMI-based processes (or, more simply put, CMMI process areas) as Six Sigma projects.
This strategy establishes the objective(s) of the Six Sigma project team as implementing a process area or a group of process areas. The team is responsible for defining the problem or opportunity that would be addressed by the new process(es) and for using data and analytical methods to inform the design, redesign, and performance improvement and thereby achieve the organizational mission and model compliance. Depending on whether the process area implementation involves updating existing processes or defining new processes, DMAIC, DFSS, or Lean might be appropriate.

Process Implementation via Design for Lean Six Sigma

As described in this chapter, there are different strategies for jointly implementing the CMMI and Six Sigma—including such choices as implementing an internal process standard comprising all models of interest and implementing process areas as Six Sigma projects. Either way, an oft-observed phenomenon in CMMI adoption is that the organizational collection of processes gets larger before it gets smaller. This has been shown pictorially in a presentation about the joint use of the CMMI and

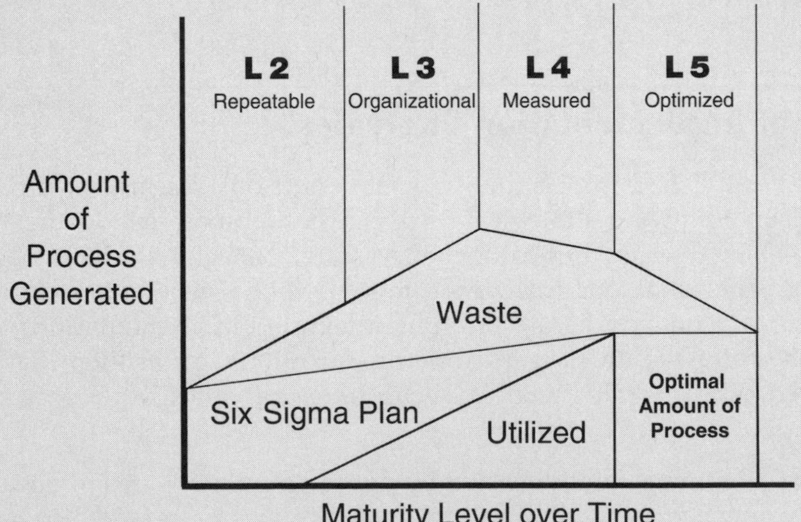

Figure 6–2: *Relative amount of process with maturity level (Reprinted with permission [Beardsley 05]).*

Six Sigma, with specific attention to planning an approach that seeks a direct path to the optimal amount of process [Beardsley 05].

Such a planned approach calls for a systemic architecture and design of the organization's processes. In the Beardsley presentation, Design for Lean Six Sigma is implied as a technique to use in this quest.

The advantages of having an architecture and a process design extend beyond CMMI implementation—to the world of multimodel process improvement. When multiple models and standards are implemented, especially in different timeframes, one might imagine an ongoing version of Figure 6–2—a profile with periodic peaks and valleys as each new model or standard is implemented and then optimized. A robust architecture should minimize (if not prevent) such peaks and valleys and maximize the amount of time an organization spends with just the right amount of process.

Strategy 2: Apply Six Sigma to improve process performance and serve as the tactical engine to achieve high capability and/or high maturity.
There is natural synergy between the high-maturity process areas and the tenets of Six Sigma's DMAIC framework. As such, the tactics of Six Sigma can be used to directly enrich the defined processes that correspond to the high-maturity process areas.

In one aspect of this strategy, Six Sigma steps can enrich the process design, in conjunction with the specific practices of the high-maturity process areas. For instance, the processes to which Quantitative Project Management (QPM) and Causal Analysis and Resolution (CAR) map would obviously reflect the specific practices of both process areas. They could also reflect the steps and tools of DMAIC and/or Lean.

In another aspect of this strategy, the DMAIC steps and toolkit can be used to actually achieve high performance, via Six Sigma projects and high-maturity process execution. Similarly, the steps and tools of DMAIC and Lean support the implementation and execution of the generic practices associated with high capability—those that mature a process to be quantitatively managed and then optimized.

Specific design connections between DMAIC and groupings of process areas will be further discussed in Chapter 7 and in the example on product quality improvement in Section 9.1.

Strategy 3: Apply Six Sigma, specifically DFSS, as a tactical contributor to achieve highly capable engineering processes.

A variation on the previous strategy is to use Six Sigma as a tactical engine underlying the Engineering process areas, alongside architecture and engineering technologies such as ATAM. In this instance, tenets of DFSS would be used to enrich the engineering process. This could be coupled with the usage of DMAIC and the generic practices to institutionalize, optimize, and achieve high capability in those processes.

Strategy 4: Apply Six Sigma to improve or optimize an organization's improvement strategy and processes.

Six Sigma can be used in making decisions about the adoption of improvement initiatives and in the management and overhead associated with adoption. Possible ways to apply Six Sigma in this manner include the following:

1. Appraisal process streamlining and cost reduction
2. Identification of highest-priority organizational problems, which informs decisions about improvement project selection and portfolio management
3. Optimization of the CMMI and overall improvement program execution

DMAIC and Lean seem particularly well suited to these approaches. If a process redesign is warranted, DFSS might be leveraged. Combining with the previous strategies, an organization might use the Define, Measure, and Analyze steps of DMAIC to define an improvement project portfolio that serves the organization's mission. Using the CMMI for guidance and possibly as governance for specific improvements, the organization could then employ DMAIC, Lean, or DFSS for each respective improvement effort and propel itself toward control and optimization one project at a time. A focus on mission and performance ultimately results in compliance to the model.

Strategy 5: Institutionalize Six Sigma project results, and culture, via the CMMI's institutionalization practices.

While the Six Sigma deployment approach (sponsorship, training, belt certification, and so forth) ensures that it is pervasively used in an organization, it does not have formal, codified mechanisms to leverage and disseminate the learnings of individual projects. Many Six Sigma organizations rely on their informal networks of Belts, internal community of practice conferences, and sometimes intranet-based data-sharing systems.

In CMMI organizations, however, the generic practices and such things as the organization's asset library provide ready-made institutionalization mechanisms for Six Sigma project results [Bergey et al. 04; Andelfinger et al. 06; Kirwan et al. 06]. Usage of these mechanisms typically becomes a de facto strategy for those pursuing joint implementation of the CMMI and Six Sigma. It enables an organization to maximize the value of every Six Sigma project.

Strategy 6: Develop an internal process standard that maps to or integrates the CMMI, Six Sigma, and all other improvement initiatives of choice. This standard defines the process by which every project is to be executed, across its entire lifecycle. While the previous approaches are tactical, very oriented toward the use of Six Sigma projects and very oriented toward supporting a CMMI deployment, this strategy is longer term and more visionary. It embodies the idea that an organization should take control of its destiny and manage its initiatives rather than be managed by them. In this strategy, the focus is on embedding Six Sigma alongside other initiatives in the organizational business and engineering processes. It builds Six Sigma thinking into the fabric of the organization, supporting culture change and, in a way, becoming the ultimate enabler of Six Sigma. It also builds every other initiative of choice into the organizational DNA.

Many people describe this idea in different ways. It has been called, among other things, integrated process architecture, interoperable process architecture, and internal integrated standard process. Lockheed Martin IS&S labels its approach the Program Process Standard [Penn and Siviy 03]. Regardless of the label, the idea remains the same: The organization establishes a set of standard processes that incorporate all the features of the initiatives of choice. This idea assumes that the process is adaptable with time (i.e., capable of iterative refinement) and instrumented and robust to the realities of the organization (e.g., the types of work done and the degree of organizational acquisition). This approach can be executed at any maturity level, with any maturity level as the end goal. When possible, it's best to start while at low maturity.

In addition to Lockheed Martin IS&S, whose mapped Program Process Standard has been presented at a high level at conferences, Northrop Grumman Mission Systems (formerly TRW), Wipro, Tata Consultancy Services, JPMorgan Chase, EDS, and others have also presented their enterprise strategies, showing how they jointly leveraged the CMMI, Six Sigma, and other initiatives. (See References and Additional Resources near the end of this book for pointers to some of these presentations.)

6.3 Considerations for Staged and Continuous CMMI Representations

When considering the joint use of the staged representation of the CMMI with Six Sigma, the most frequently asked question relates to whether and how Six Sigma can be applied at lower maturity levels. The answer is that yes, Six Sigma can be applied at lower maturity. Two of the previously described sequencing scenarios call for Six Sigma to be used at lower maturity, and all of the strategies allow for this. The use of Six Sigma at lower maturity is different than at higher maturity and, in fact, contributes to an accelerated attainment of high maturity.

As depicted in Figure 6–3, Six Sigma philosophy, frameworks, and toolkits can all be leveraged at lower maturity. Even its measures can be used, although they may not reflect organizational performance (yet). If Six Sigma project portfolio management and methods are being employed, there is reasonable assurance that local improvements provide added value for the organization and are not just isolated exercises that will not contribute to the greater good. As such, there is a likelihood that these efforts will accelerate the CMMI solution—a key aspect of the value proposition for joint model implementation—because people will gain experience with the effective use of measurement and analysis to gain control of a situation and possibly optimize a process, albeit a local one. CMMI-compliant processes may be piloted

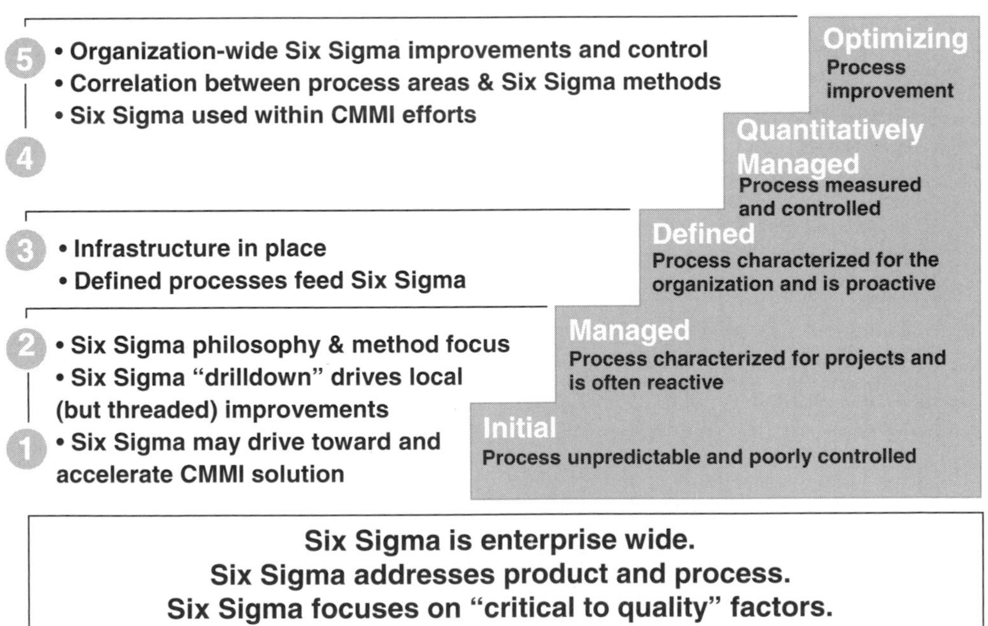

Figure 6–3: *CMMI staged representation and Six Sigma*

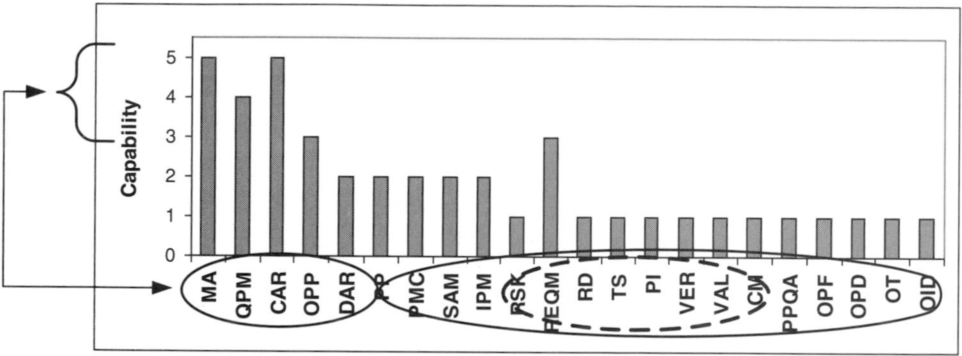

Figure 6–4: *CMMI continuous representation and Six Sigma: a possible scenario*

and refined as part of individual project efforts. As an organization climbs the maturity ladder, the use of Six Sigma can continue, but now applied across organizational processes.

In the continuous representation, Six Sigma may be used to drive the design and/or improvement of any process area that has been selected for implementation, much as it may be used in the staged representation.

An additional usage of Six Sigma for the continuous representation relates to the selection and sequencing of process area implementation. An organization could use Six Sigma thinking to establish its highest-priority issues and the requisite process areas that need to be implemented to solve them [Vickroy 03]. It might also blend in a strategic prioritization of processes. For instance, an organization might choose to develop its capability in process areas that are tightly coupled with Six Sigma skills and methods—those that would enable it to effectively baseline and characterize process performance and issues, such as MA, QPM, and CAR. Figure 6–4 shows a possible scenario that could result when Six Sigma is used to prioritize issues and decide the order of implementation of the CMMI process areas. Alternatively, if new product introduction or market growth were a priority for the organization, it might choose to select the Engineering process areas as first priority. This is also indicated in Figure 6–4, by a dashed line.

6.4 Considerations for Joint Deployment

Fundamentally, CMMI deployment focuses on establishing and improving process infrastructure. In contrast, Six Sigma involves a portfolio of improvement solutions across many domains. Both require management sponsorship and trained change agents. However, the sponsorship and resources are often at different levels of the organization or different parts of the enterprise. When the two initiatives intersect, such as what is currently happening in many organizations, significant gaps emerge. Traditional Six Sigma practitioners often do not have the software, systems, or IT experience that enables them to see how to apply their toolkit in that domain. And they often do not have sufficient awareness or understanding of the CMMI and other domain best practices to build in their adoption as a critical part of the Six Sigma project portfolio. Similarly, CMMI implementers often don't have the depth of analytical or cross-discipline experiences to extrapolate from traditional Six Sigma examples into their own domain and bridge gaps in communications and applications.

To address this, we recommend attention to three fundamental elements of joint deployment:

1. Shared organizational roles, particularly the primary change agents of each initiative
2. Training that is designed to bridge gaps
3. Synchronization of improvement project portfolios

Of the three, the first requires the least amount of explanation. It suggests that engineering process improvement experts should also hold expertise in Six Sigma and vice versa. If expertise in both topics is not held by the same people, the respective experts should work in the same group or otherwise have a seamless partnership. Either way, the objective is for the CMMI people and the Six Sigma people to have a shared sense of organizational mission and goals as well as a shared sense of responsibility to establish an improvement program that achieves its objectives.

One way to bridge gaps between different roles is to conduct cross-training—minimally at the awareness-building level and, for some, at the proficiency-building level.

- Manufacturing Six Sigma Black Belts who are trained in basic software development principles and in the CMMI will more easily recognize the "software factory" and the advantages of leveraging standards and models when establishing process infrastructure.
- CMMI implementers with Six Sigma training will more easily recognize how to achieve quantitatively managed processes and statistically managed subprocesses.

Such cross-training may require adaptations of existing training curricula. Numerous organizations have begun specializing or supplementing their Six Sigma curricula with domain-specific training. This allows the presentation and practice of domain-specific case studies, thereby alleviating the need for trainees to make the leap from the use of analytical tools in manufacturing to their respective disciplines. It also allows the inclusion of awareness sessions about domain-specific topics. This might include special analysis considerations, such as non-normal distributions, and it might include an introduction to improvement technologies, such as the CMMI or software measurement best practices, or to architecture practices (the latter being particularly well suited in a DFSS curriculum). Conversely, CMMI training might include an awareness session about relationships between the CMMI and Six Sigma.

Shared roles and cross-training enable synchronized project portfolios. One risk of not synchronizing is competition for resources, particularly funding. In the worst situation, CMMI-oriented projects get shortchanged, and Six Sigma projects are launched on the false presumption that instrumented software processes stand ready for Six Sigma improvement—a mutually disabling situation. One way to bootstrap synchronization is to create a project identification and definition process that is more efficient due to the presence of both the CMMI and Six Sigma. This approach might include the following features.

- The use of Six Sigma methods to transform fuzzy problem statements into quantitative improvement objectives against which specific improvement projects (including those serving CMMI goals) can be launched. An example of this type of project is included in Section 9.2.
- The recognition of the need for enabling projects that establish processes and measures required for subsequent Six Sigma efforts and the incorporation of the CMMI and other domain model implementation as a critical driver of an enabling project portfolio. The enabling projects might be

executed via the aforementioned strategy to implement CMMI process areas as formal Six Sigma projects.

Specific approaches for project portfolio identification and alignment with mission are discussed in Chapter 8, as part of the general case of multimodel process improvement.

6.4.1 Motorola Retrospective: Integrated Training Curriculum

At Motorola, the fourth week of the traditional Six Sigma DMAIC Black Belt program involved choosing one of four different discipline-specific training options: Software, Hardware, Transaction, or Manufacturing (refer back to Table 5–2). This approach enabled cross-discipline classes during the first three weeks of the DMAIC training and helped to both bridge the communication gap on the methods and enable some degree of cross-training between disciplines.

Within the Design for Six Sigma Black Belt program, a similar type of cross-discipline training took place with the approach of training product development teams in a single class. Table 6–1 shows the initial customized DFSS curriculum, which included a number of SEI technologies and training in the CMMI as well as software-specific topics. During the actual training, at times the class broke out to side rooms to cover discipline-specific topics for that point in the Design for Six Sigma methodology.

6.4.2 Motorola Retrospective: Roles and Responsibilities

Table 6–2 depicts software engineering and management functional roles and job categories mapped to the recommended software DFSS curriculum, as well as recommended supplementary training in software practices. The champion training brought senior management up to speed on the concepts taught to the DFSS Black Belts so that the champions could help create demand for the use of the DFSS toolkit. The gatekeeper training brought senior and middle management up to speed on the DFSS product team scoring process and additional probing questions to ask during the MGates management reviews.

Examples of supplementary software specialty training are shown in Figure 6–5, targeted to specific job categories. This supplementary training spanned the CMMI as well as the SEI's architecture and product line practice technologies, depending on the role.

Table 6–1: *Motorola DFSS Curriculum Tailored for Software*

Week 1 Topics	Week 2 Topics	Week 3 Topics
DFSS Overview	Critical parameter management	Linear and multiple regression
CDOV Process	DFMEA	RSM
DFSS tools and project management	Basic Stats (statistics package)	Monte Carlo
Voice of the customer/KJ analysis	Hypothesis testing	Robust design
QFD	Confidence intervals	Tolerance optimization
First Principle Modeling (Monte Carlo)	ANOVA	CPM
Pugh	MSA	Architecture and design-based software reliability modeling
DFSS Scorecards	SPC	Software reliability growth testing and modeling
Six Sigma and CMMI synergies	Design and Process	Motorola Lab's TRAMS (Test Planning using fuzzy logic)
Parametric SW project forecasting	Statistical capability analysis	Taguchi Noise Testing
Requirements management processes	Design of Experiments (DOE)	Small memory management
Developing SW operational profiles	Full factorial designs	Throughput and timing analysis
SW Quality Attribute Workshops	Fractional factorial designs	Orthogonal Defect Classification
Attribute-Driven SW Architecture	Modeling	Advanced SW inspection
Active Reviews for Intermediate Designs	Advanced DOE	Human error analysis
SW Architecture Tradeoff Analysis Method (ATAM)		Cleanroom Software Engineering
Cost/Benefit Analysis of Architecture Decisions		Agile/Extreme Programming
Software Product Line Planning and Execution		SEI Personal and Team Software Process and relationships to DFSS
		Usability engineering

Table 6–2: *Motorola Role-Specific Training Plan*

Functional Roles	Job Categories	DFSS Training for Software Engineering	Primary Responsibility in DFSS Deployment for Software Engineering
Management and leadership	Senior resource managers Senior software managers Senior test managers Gate review team members Operations managers Software directors Senior software architects	Attend champion training (1 day for each of the DFSS Weeks 1–3 for software engineering) Gatekeeper training	Serve as gatekeepers in DFSS gate reviews for software engineering Use software scorecard measures and explanations Require DFSS training for software engineering within organization Ensure sufficient SW Green, Black, and Master Black Belts exist
Feature team leaders and working-level architects	Test team managers and leaders Feature team leaders First-line software supervisors Senior technical experts, architects	Attend 3 weeks of DFSS training for software engineering Attend software specialty training as required	Ensure the timely use of DFSS tasks, tools, and deliverables for software engineering Present data at DFSS gate reviews for software engineering Identify team members for follow-on in-depth training
Specialists	Designers Programmers Testers	Attend 3 weeks of DFSS training for software engineering when selected Attend follow-on training as requested by management	Perform tasks in a timely fashion

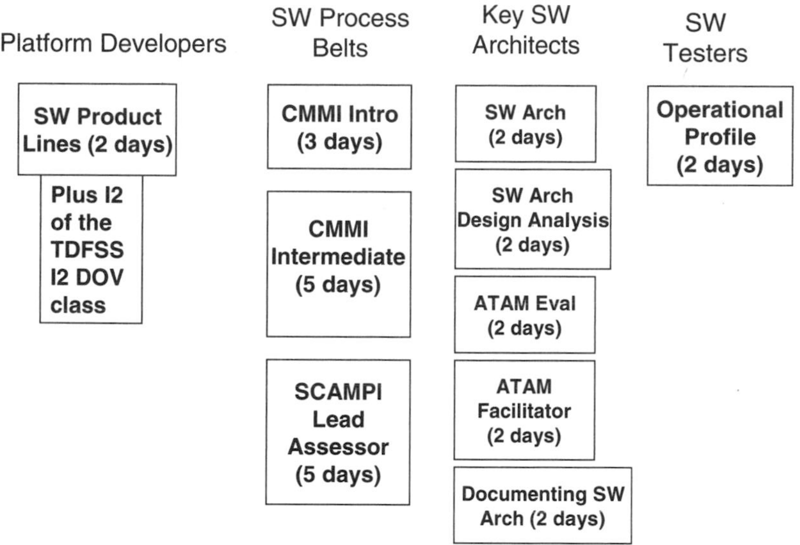

Figure 6–5: *Motorola software specialty training to supplement the DFSS curriculum for software engineering*

6.5 Summary

The joint implementation of the CMMI and Six Sigma should be considered from a strategic viewpoint, with attention to sequence, to their relationship when simultaneous deployment begins, and to several deployment execution factors.

Due to history and legacy, organizations' sequencing of the two initiatives varies. When they reach the point in their timeline to deploy both initiatives simultaneously, several frequently successful strategic approaches may be employed. These approaches, which range in their extent of coordination versus integration, are not mutually exclusive and do not presume that the CMMI precedes Six Sigma or vice versa.

- Implement CMMI process areas as Six Sigma (DMAIC, DFSS, and/or Lean) projects.
- Apply Six Sigma (DMAIC and Lean) as the tactical engine for high capability and high maturity.
- Apply design for Six Sigma as a tactical contributor to achieve highly capable engineering processes.

- Apply Six Sigma to improve or optimize an organization's improvement strategy and processes.
- Institutionalize Six Sigma (including Lean) project results and culture via CMMI's institutionalization practices.
- Integrate the CMMI, Six Sigma, and all other improvement initiatives of choice to provide a standard for the execution of every project throughout its lifecycle.

From the viewpoint of CMMI representation, Six Sigma can be used at all levels of maturity (staged representation) and can be used to guide the priority of process area implementation (continuous representation).

Deployment execution should also be managed in an integrated fashion, which might include the following fundamental shared activities: shared organizational roles, training designed to bridge gaps, and synchronization of improvement project portfolios.

Chapter 7

Integrating the CMMI and Six Sigma: Design Connections

Successful joint implementation of the CMMI and Six Sigma requires an examination of their relationships.

In this chapter, we focus on design connectivity between the CMMI and Six Sigma. Both common and complementary characteristics and relationships must be understood to successfully knit them together in a joint implementation.

The information we provide is not exhaustive and is intentionally not presented in a mapping format as we have found detailed mappings to be useful only within specific organizational instantiations of the initiatives. The connections offered here may provide a framework for mappings and also should provide a design foundation for the execution of whichever joint implementation strategies the organization chooses.

7.1 CMMI Process Areas and Six Sigma Frameworks

There are natural synergies between each of the Six Sigma frameworks and selected groupings of CMMI process areas. Following are brief explanations of connections between CMMI process areas and each of the three Six Sigma approaches discussed in this book—DMAIC, DFSS (DMADV), and Lean (Kaizen Events and value stream mapping). Understanding these connections provides the technical underpinnings for translating Chapter 6's strategies into tactical implementation plans and for defining and implementing processes that are rich with the features of both technologies.

Note: For each explanation, a diagram shows an example of an organizational defined process, overlaid with CMMI process areas and Six Sigma framework steps. These diagrams are based on actual case studies. They are illustrative and are not intended to be comprehensive.

7.1.1 Process Areas and DMAIC

Several CMMI process areas—in particular, Measurement and Analysis (MA), Quantitative Project Management (QPM), Causal Analysis and Resolution (CAR), and Organizational Process Performance (OPP)—align with the DMAIC roadmap steps. The diagram in Figure 7–1 shows a flowchart of one particular organization's defined measurement and analysis process. While this organization's process was designed with model compliance in mind, it represents a holistic approach to the overall use of measurement instead of a replication of the specific practices of each CMMI process area. Similarly, this organizational process leverages ideas of DMAIC but is not a replication of the DMAIC steps.

The figure is overlaid with DMAIC steps and selected process areas. For instance, the process steps for gathering and analyzing data are associated with the Measure step of DMAIC, which includes collecting and baselining the data. And they are overlaid with the MA process area of the CMMI (where gathering and analyzing data are two of the specific practices of this PA). As noted, this diagram does not present an exhaustive mapping of Six Sigma and CMMI PAs to this particular process. For instance, in another organizational setting, Decision Analysis and Resolution (DAR), Technical Solution (TS), and Lean concepts might also be placed on the diagram.

The incorporation of DMAIC into the fabric of an organization's processes, such as what Figure 7–1 shows, would be effected via Organizational Process Focus (OPF) and Organizational Process Definition (OPD). Note that such incorporation of DMAIC into the organization's defined processes does not necessarily mean that every execution of the process equates to a Six Sigma project. It just means that the best practices of a successful initiative are being incorporated into the DNA and day-to-day routine of the organization, to support incremental, evolutionary, and also revolutionary improvement.

Additionally or alternatively, the organization's measurement process could be mapped to the generic practices. This would be advantageous for an orga-

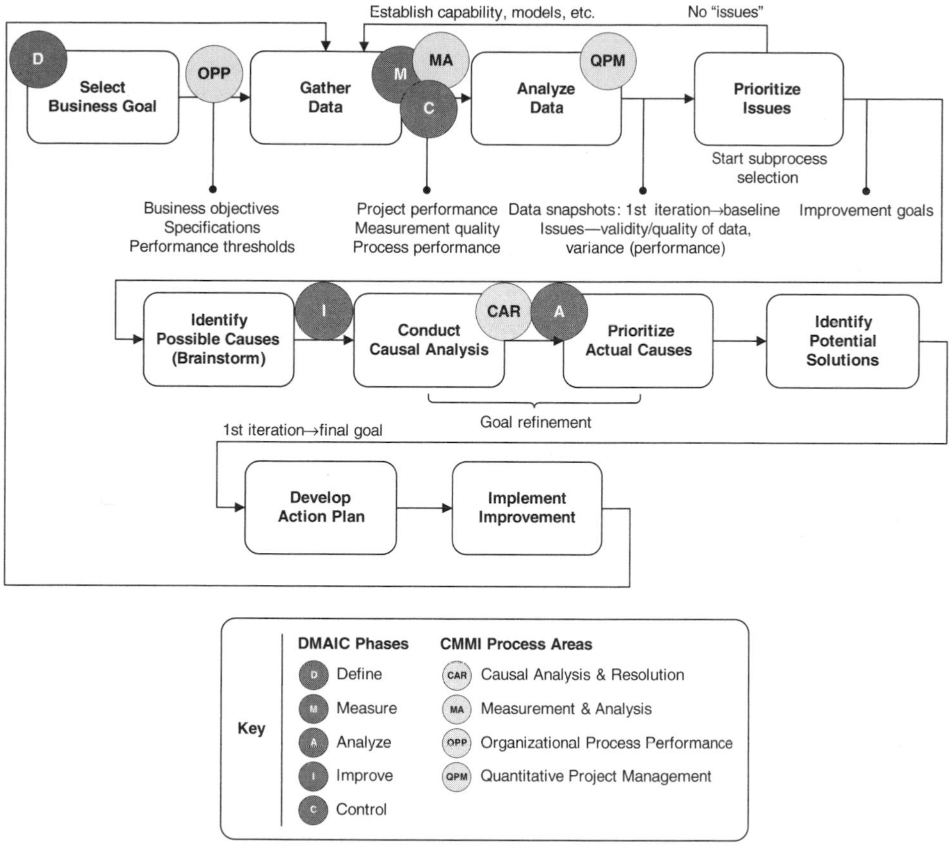

Figure 7–1: *CMMI process areas and DMAIC steps*

nization at lower maturity or one that is pursuing the continuous representation of the CMMI rather than the staged representation. The following generic practices are oriented to this organization's measurement process:

- Generic Practice 2.8, Monitor and Control the Process
- Generic Practice 3.2, Collect Improvement Information
- Generic Practice 4.1, Establish Quality Objectives
- Generic Practice 4.2, Stabilize Subprocess Performance
- Generic Practice 5.1, Ensure Continuous Process Improvement
- Generic Practice 5.2, Correct Common Causes of Problems

Appendix B lists additional connections between the CMMI and process areas' specific goals and generic practices.

7.1.2 Process Areas and DFSS/DMADV

The frameworks of DFSS have an intuitive synergy with the Engineering process itself (software, systems, or otherwise). After all, engineering is about designing and implementing effective products. Accordingly, DFSS—and in this case, we will discuss the DMADV framework—has a design connectivity to the CMMI's Engineering process areas. Figure 7–2 shows an example of a high-level Engineering process map (from our Lockheed Martin IS&S case study in Chapter 5), overlaid with DMADV steps and PAs.

This diagram begs the question about whether the infusion of the DMADV framework with the CMMI into the defined engineering process means that every engineering or product development project is a full-blown Design for

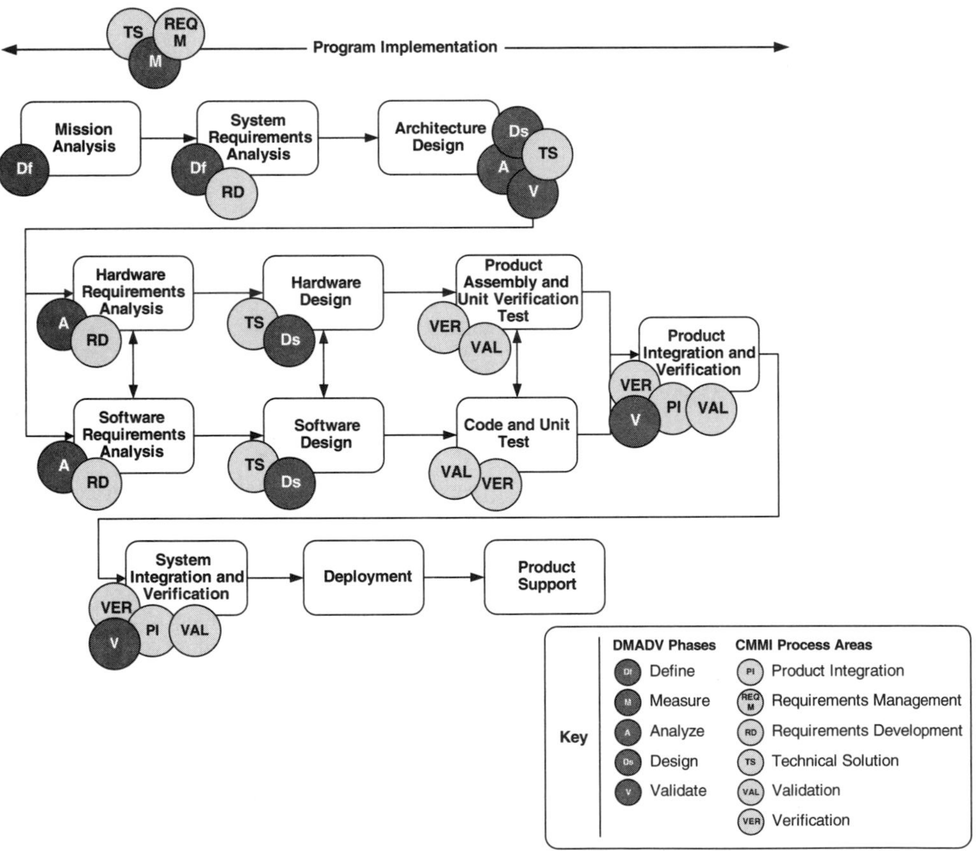

Figure 7–2: *DFSS (DMADV) and CMMI process areas*

Six Sigma project. Most definitely, the infusion and integration of these methodologies can and should incorporate the best thinking of each into the daily engineering routine. However, there still may be a place for sanctioned Design for Six Sigma projects. Particularly visible or critical products may require the full benefit of Six Sigma's resources and tools—drawn from across the enterprise—to maximize the likelihood of success.

7.1.3 Process Areas and Lean

Much as DMAIC shares a kindred spirit with high-maturity process areas, and DFSS with Engineering process areas, Lean's value stream mapping (VSM) and Kaizen Events are related to the Process Management and Project Management process areas. Figure 7–3 shows one organization's instantiation of the process for process definition and institutionalization. In this case, the organization defined this process based on the steps of VSM. CMMI process areas are overlaid.

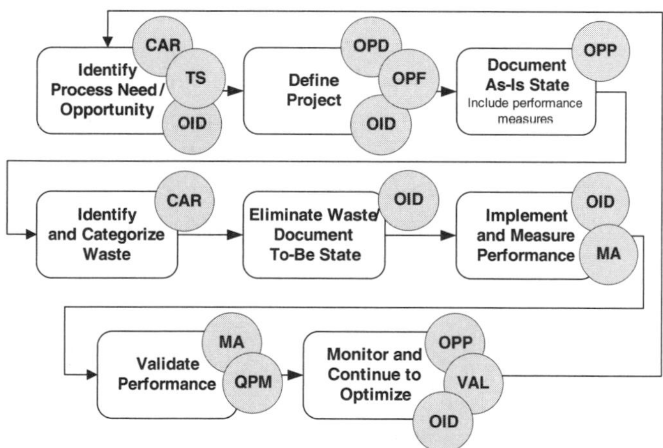

Note: Value stream mapping and Kaizen Events served as a basis for defining process steps and are not shown separately on this diagram.

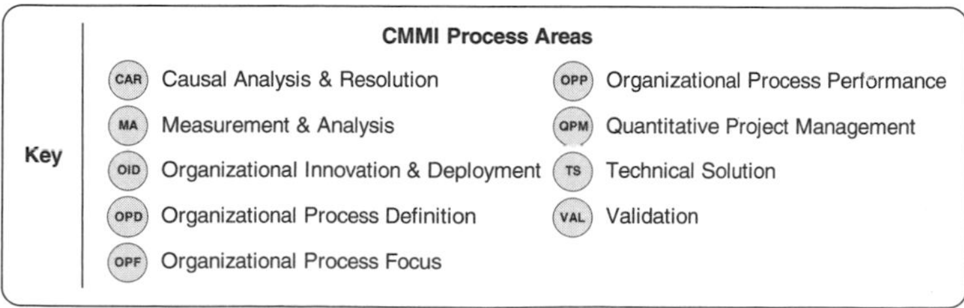

Figure 7–3: *Kaizen, value stream mapping, and CMMI process areas*

7.2 CMMI Process Areas and the Six Sigma Toolkit of Analytical Methods

Quite different from the process design connections just described, another dimension of design connectivity is the use of Six Sigma's toolkit of analytical methods within defined processes. Here are some examples.

- Decision Analysis and Resolution (DAR) can use concept selection methods such as Pugh's concept.
- Risk Management (RSKM) can use failure modes and effects analysis (FMEA).
- Technical Solution (TS) can use design FMEA.

Within an organization, the selection and use of analytical methods is dynamic over time, based on mission and current process and product performance. Analytical methods will change within a project as the lifecycle unfolds. (There is specific evidence of this in DAR.) How methods are used within process areas varies across organizations, based on their business focus, typical issues, culture, available skills, and so forth. For instance, a growth organization focused on bringing many new products to market may wish to exploit the entire DFSS toolkit within its Engineering process areas (and commit to the requisite training for its engineers to use these methods on a routine basis). A small organization with fewer personnel trained in analytical methods and a limited training budget may choose to build into its processes a smaller number of methods (i.e., those it will use most routinely). The list of possible scenarios is endless.

A strategy that uses this dimension of connectivity is the implementation of processes as Six Sigma projects. As each process is implemented, its documented definitions include which analytical methods are relevant, with necessary usage guidance, training plans, and so on.

Appendix C contains a longer list of analytical methods that may be used to support specific process areas.

7.3 CMMI Project Management Process Areas and Six Sigma Project Management

In contrast to the use of Six Sigma tools within CMMI-based processes, another design connection involves leveraging an organization's CMMI-based project management processes to manage Six Sigma projects. Six Sigma projects, which were briefly described in Chapter 3, are launched via a project charter. Through agreement to the charter, the project sponsors, process owners, and team members agree to the project objectives, resources, deliverables, timeline, and measures. Projects typically are completed in less than one year. Six Sigma projects vary widely in scope. Team membership changes from project to project, with composition being determined by project scope. While Black Belts and Green Belts move from project to project, non-Belt team members may serve on only a few projects throughout their careers.

The CMMI process areas involving project management can be leveraged in the management of Six Sigma projects. This enables Six Sigma project teams to rely on the organizational norms for such things as project launches, resource commitments, schedule tracking, and progress tracking. This enables teams, and particularly those team members who do not frequently participate in Six Sigma projects, to quickly focus on their objectives.

The following process areas can be useful in this context:

- Project Planning (PP)
- Project Monitoring and Control (PMC)
- Integrated Project Management (IPM)
- Organizational Process Performance (OPP) (for organization-level execution, management, and oversight of the aggregate set of Six Sigma projects)
- Quantitative Project Management (QPM) (for aspects of Six Sigma project execution that are repeated and which the organization wishes to place under statistical management)

Strategies that benefit from this dimension of connectivity are the implementation of CMMI PAs as Six Sigma projects and the use of Six Sigma as the tactical engine for high maturity and capability.

7.4 CMMI Process Outputs as Inputs to Six Sigma and Vice Versa

When the CMMI and Six Sigma are implemented in a coordinated but not necessarily tightly integrated manner, there can be informational handoffs from one initiative to the other.

Several CMMI process areas can be leveraged to provide inputs to Six Sigma projects. For instance, Requirements Development (RD) may result in inputs to Six Sigma's Define step and to voice of the customer methods. The routinely generated outputs of MA, OPP, and QPM stand as ready baselines for any Six Sigma project. The process definitions of OPD stand as ready process maps for any Six Sigma project.

7.5 Summary

The CMMI is a domain-specific model for creating organizational process infrastructure. Six Sigma is an enterprise, domain-independent initiative for focusing on specific (often narrowly scoped) problems and opportunities that will yield significant business benefits.

There are several dimensions of design connectivity between the CMMI and Six Sigma:

- Commonality of purpose between groupings of CMMI process areas (including generic practices) and Six Sigma frameworks
  - DMAIC and MA, QPM, CAR, OPP, and others
  - DMAIC and generic practices
  - DMADV (DFSS) and Engineering PAs
  - Lean and OPD, OPF
- Use of the Six Sigma analytical methods within CMMI process areas
- Six Sigma projects as the object of the CMMI's project management processes
- CMMI process outputs as inputs to Six Sigma, and Six Sigma process outputs as inputs to the CMMI

Understanding these design connections helps with both strategy selection and implementation.

Our lists of strategies, tactical connections, and deployment considerations—across Chapters 6 and 7—are not exhaustive. We invite you to contact us with other differences, synergies, and thematic connections between the CMMI and Six Sigma that you have leveraged in your work.

Chapter 8

Multimodel Process Improvement: The General Case

Thus far, we have described examples of jointly integrating the CMMI and Six Sigma (and other models) and have offered observations, strategies, and design connections related to how and why this joint integration works.

We offer in this chapter an emerging framework for reasoning about multi-model improvement via the broader set of models and practices in play at any given time within an organization. Because there is no "silver bullet" answer for how to combine models, we perceive the need for a reasoning framework comprising a process definition (with guidance questions), reusable selection and implementation patterns, reference case studies, and relevant best practices.

This chapter reflects our current thinking, as well as elements of the thinking of others, as noted. The Lockheed Martin IS&S case is revisited in this chapter, with retrospectives related to key points. We hope that, in combination with the other chapters of this book, this emergent framework serves both the practitioner and the research community—and that, through their and our subsequent work, we will soon have a more complete, robust framework to use.

8.1 Depiction of the Process of Process Improvement

Figure 8–1 depicts three high-level process steps associated with process improvement. While this process may seem intuitive, even obvious, it is useful to make it explicit, to serve as the structure on which to build our reasoning framework. It shares similarities with diagrams used to describe CMMI transition as well as those used within CMMI deployment to support process areas such as Technical Solution.

8.1.1 Overview of Process Steps

Select Technology

Process improvement groups are typically charged with the task of process improvement by their organizational management. Their charter may come with a mandate to use certain models or standards as part of their efforts. Beyond this, improvement groups often have a reasonable degree of decision authority to select the appropriate technologies to accomplish their objectives. Depending on the level of investment and the organizational norms for approving projects, they may need to submit formal proposals and business cases prior to launching their efforts.

The degree of difficulty in making technology selection decisions varies with the clarity and alignment of the objectives, organizational constraints, and team experience. Decisions may be easier (although not necessarily easy) when the improvement objectives and the relationship to mission are thoughtful and clear. Decisions are much more difficult when the improvement drivers and initial goals have a degree of vagueness and are disconnected from business improvement, such as maturity level goals that are not related to business performance. In such situations, the group must add specificity to the problem statements and align them with the business. Once the motivation for change is established and the performance expectations

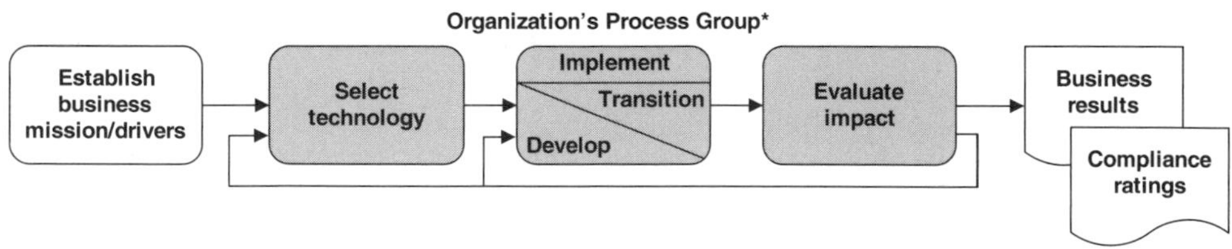

* The shading in Figures 8–1 through 8–5 is used only to distinguish different organizational roles and responsibilities.

Figure 8–1: *Process steps of process improvement*

are understood, the improvement group is then in a better position to select one or more relevant models, standards, practices, technologies, and so on for implementation—those that will solve the problem or enable the opportunity.

Implement Solution

Once a technology is selected, it must be rolled out to the organization. This involves two main phases: development or design of the organization-specific solution and transition of the solution to the organization [Forrester 03].

Via the development or design step, the improvement group determines whether the selected technology can be effectively implemented as is. If it can—which may be the case for very specific, tactical tools—the group's main task becomes determining how to effectively transition the technology. Frequently, though, technologies are tailored, adapted, or supplemented with additional detail, then integrated with the rest of the organization's processes, tools, and so on, in order to be usable. For example, when implementing the CMMI, decisions must be made about the selection of process areas to be implemented and the order of implementation. The processes themselves must be designed (because the CMMI says what to do, not how to do it).

Even as the design process begins, attention must be given to its transition. *Technology transition* is the process of creating or maturing a technology, introducing it to its intended adopters, and facilitating its acceptance and use, where *technology* is

- Any tool, technique, physical equipment, or method of doing or making, by which human capability is extended [Forrester n.d.]
- The means or capacity to perform a particular activity

Process improvement activities referred to as maturation, introduction, adoption, implementation, dissemination, rollout, deployment, or fielding are indicative of transition activities [Forrester n.d.; Schon 67; Gruber and Marquis 65].

The level of perceived risk with each solution, based on clarity of business objectives/problems and strength of design, may cause an organization to pilot its process solutions before a widespread rollout.

As indicated by Figure 8–1, development and transition are both present throughout the implementation process, with the early effort being nearly 100% focused on design and the latter effort being nearly 100% focused on transition [Forrester 04].

Designing and rolling out technologies and associated solutions is the bread and butter of the engineering process group, although they may not think of what they are doing in these terms. It is not traditionally the focus of Six Sigma practitioners because they often work in domains where infrastructure, standards, and best practices have largely been implemented. However, those Six Sigma practitioners working in software engineering may find themselves in the role of the traditional software engineering process group out of necessity.

Evaluate Impact

Since the premise of implementing models, standards, or other technologies is that they will solve a problem or enable a higher level of performance, measurement of impact is the third main step. Impact measures may be in terms of absolute performance ("We achieved abc goal") or relative performance ("We have improved by x%"). The latter requires baseline data, which is not always available in the early stages of software process improvement.

In engineering, impact measurement is a long-term proposition. Depending on the size and quantity of projects, it may take multiple years to determine the effectiveness of an improvement strategy. And the measured results will reflect the impact of all activities that have occurred in the timeframe of interest: the selected improvement initiatives, the evolving skill and experience of engineers, technology changes, and so on. Decomposing the impact into a cause-and-effect model for each individual factor is rarely a practical endeavor. As a result, metameasures of performance become a crucial part of the picture: performance snapshots based on single projects or even subprojects, engineering measures, and measures of model/standard institutionalization (such as maturity levels).

8.1.2 Organizational Context

Figure 8–2 expands on Figure 8–1 by depicting the added relationship of the project teams to the process group's efforts. The main objective of the project team is to deliver its product. This is done by executing a project lifecycle, whether ad hoc or organizationally defined. As they proceed through their project, most project teams are called upon to integrate the process improvements being rolled out by the improvement group. Such projects probably are most effective at integrating new process solutions when they address project performance goals and/or pain points. Clear line of sight between project objectives and business drivers will foster this, as will well-designed process solutions.

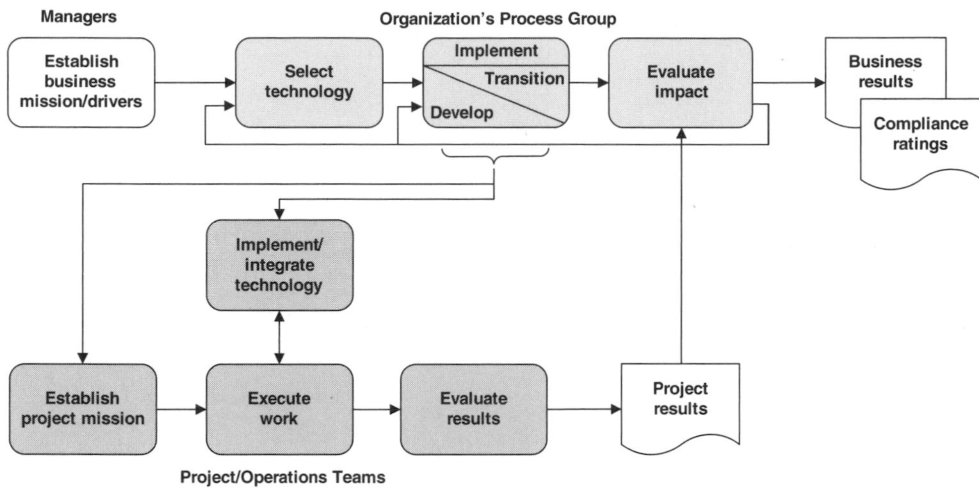

Figure 8–2: *Relationship of project teams to process improvement*

8.1.3 Technology Provider Context

Process improvement technologies chosen during the "select technology" step shown in Figure 8–1 may come from research institutions such as the SEI, the Fraunhofer Institute for Experimental Software Engineering, the USC Center for Software Engineering, and others. They may be derived from public bodies of knowledge, such as the Project Management Body of Knowledge (PMBOK), or they may come from another branch of the enterprise, such as the organization's central Six Sigma deployment group. Other types of technologies, such as tactical tools to directly support code development, may come from tool vendors.

Each of these technology providers also follows a "develop, then transition" process, as shown in Figure 8–3. An improvement group may select a technology anywhere along its development/transition cycle. A consequence of this is that the improvement group will likely need to cycle back through the selection process as the technology evolves and determine whether and when to implement new versions.

As an example, Figure 8–4 shows a blend of selections: the CMMI, which is mature; IT best practices and technologies, which are just beginning to be codified into standards and best practices; and Six Sigma, which is mature, notwithstanding new variants that are emerging across industry. This figure also shows a glimpse of the added complexities that a process group faces—different bodies of research interrelate with each other, such as Six Sigma's presence in the development of IT practices.

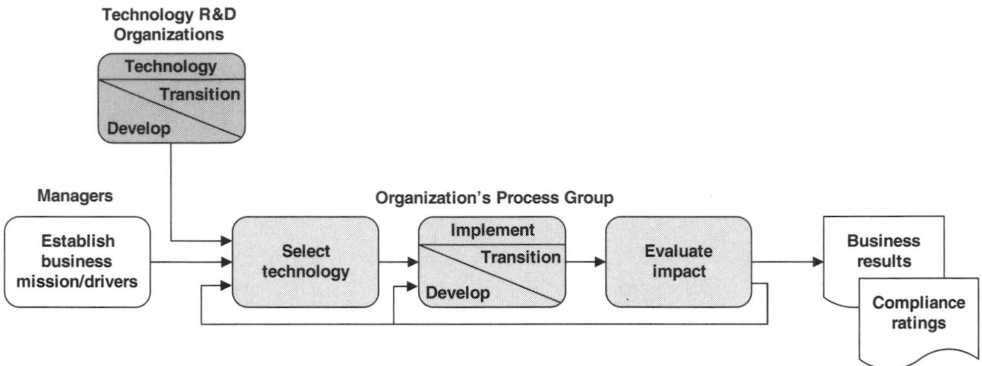

Figure 8–3: *Process improvement steps, showing inputs from R&D organizations*

8.1.4 Usage Guidance

This process is suitable for both infrastructure implementation projects and for specific process, project, or product improvement projects. Most of this chapter (actually, most of this book) focuses on the former. The latter, which may be done in conjunction with infrastructure implementation projects, is addressed in Chapter 9.

To accompany the process and enrich its execution, we have developed a base set of guidance questions and a short list of relevant best practices. By using this process and the guidance questions, the engineering process group is essentially filling the role of process/practice engineer for engineering execution, rather than simply being the group that rolls out each new model.

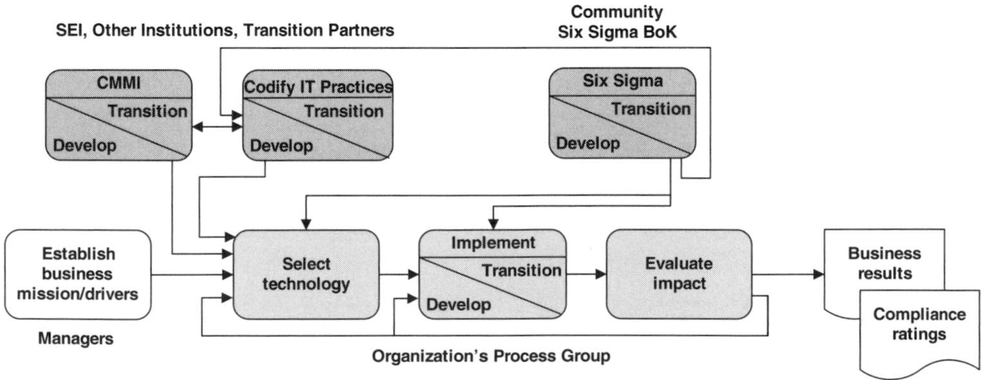

Figure 8–4: *Selecting technologies at different stages of development and transition*

1. What is our mission? What are our goals?
2. Are we achieving our goals? What stands in our way?
3. What process features or performance do we need to support our goals? What standards and models provide or enable these features?
4. How do we join them into a cohesive internal standard process (new or existing) that we can rapidly and effectively deploy? How do we design an internal standard process that we can easily update as new regulatory or process requirements occur?
   a. How do we deploy our newly designed or updated standard process?
   b. How do we determine the effectiveness of our designed standard process?
5. Once enabling (i.e., infrastructure implementation) projects are under way, how do we manage a portfolio of projects aimed at improving process, project, and product performance?

To those with many years of experience, some of these questions, and their answers, may seem obvious; however, many organizations are embarking on this journey without the benefit of past experience. And in the rush to improve, even those with experience may not allow themselves the luxury of stepping back and approaching their efforts in an engineering-like way and fully leveraging best practices and current research.

Figure 8–5 shows relevant practices and emerging research to leverage for each process step. This is neither an exhaustive nor a prescriptive list. Rather, this serves as a reminder to reuse, rather than reinvent, whenever possible.

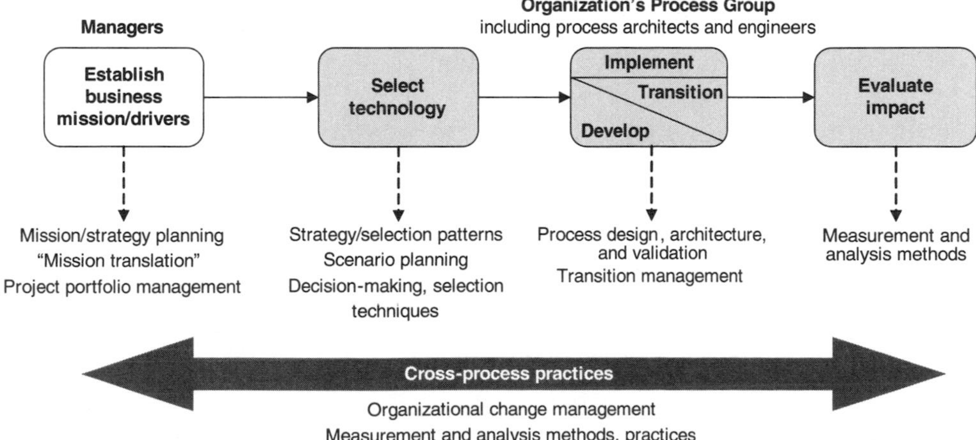

Figure 8–5: *Practices to support multimodel improvement*

Specific methods that are already institutionalized in the organization would be appropriately leveraged, in order to speed the design process and enable optimum communications across the organization.

In the remainder of this chapter, we have selected a subset of these practices for further discussion, as we perceive them to be highly relevant in the pursuit of multimodel process improvement. As will be described in the subsequent sections, each of these informs the next.

- Mission translation and project portfolio management (maturing practices)
- Model selection and strategy patterns (new research)
- Process architecture (new research)

In addition to their relevance, we also see these practices as needing to be specifically tailored to the multimodel situation.

Measurement and analysis, transition, and organizational change management are briefly addressed in the Appendices G, H and I. With the exception of the aspects of transition and change management that were discussed in Chapter 6, these disciplines are not particularly unique to the multimodel situation. We do, however, believe that each of these is critical to multimodel success. Because of this, we did not want to exclude them from our book and have chosen to share with our readers some of our favorite and most useful references in the appendices.

8.1.5 Case Retrospective: LMCO IS&S's Technology Selection Process

IS&S's adoption of standards is planned, monitored, measured, and improved just like any other program within the organization. For each standard that is proposed, a formal business case is performed. The following activities must be completed prior to a proposal to the Executive Process Steering Committee for adoption across the organization.

- Determine the business need to adopt this standard (e.g., customer requirement, corporate requirement, and/or country requirement).
- Perform a gap analysis against the existing Program Process Standard (PPS) and other process documentation to determine the gaps or overlap (i.e., aligning requirements).
- Map the gaps to actions, and assemble an appropriate plan. The plan must include resources (staff, documentation changes, training, communication, process products).

- Perform an analysis against the current measurements to predict what the adoption may give the organization in terms of cost savings.
- Weigh the benefits against the cost of implementation. At this time, the organization also looks at the scope of the standard adoption. The scope of the adoption will include whether the entire organization needs the standard and will adequately benefit. If the organization is the recipient, changes to the PPS will be red-lined to show direct impact. If the organization as a whole is not the recipient, determine who is, and how they will benefit.
- Develop a plan to show adoption (piloting, if necessary), measurement indicators, success criteria and ROI.
- Present the plan and business case to the Executive Process Steering Committee for adoption.

8.2 Mission Translation and Project Portfolio Management

In their article "How the Learning Organization Manages Change," Ronald Recardo, Kathleen Molloy, and James Pellegrino state, "Translating organizational goals and metrics to individuals and teams continues to be one of the most difficult management activities and is often a stumbling block to implementation" [Recardo et al. 07]. Managing change is one of an Engineering process group's roles. In order to maintain a line of sight between its activities and the organizational mission, an Engineering process group needs to translate the mission into actionable goal statements and drivers. This translation serves multiple purposes, such as guiding the initial selection of best practices and models, clarifying how seemingly overlapping models can effectively work together, prioritizing specific process performance improvements, and providing the backbone for organizational success measures.

Approaching this translation methodically is important for ensuring objectivity. As with any type of measurement or analytical technique, the consequences of being methodical may be unexpected and highly valuable conclusions. Several existing practices may be brought to bear for this translation, such as:

- Function Analysis Systems Technique (FAST) goal structures
- Six Sigma's Y-to-x decomposition

- Critical success factors, as developed by Daniel and refined by Rockart [Daniel 61; Rockart 86]
- Systems thinking's current and future reality trees
- Traditional strategic planning methods
- Balanced scorecard strategy maps

As stated earlier, the intent of listing practices such as these is not to recommend that organizations immediately investigate and adopt every one of them. Rather, those that are already known within an organization are ready candidates for usage in mission translation and project portfolio management. Others are candidates for addition to an organization's toolkit, on an as-needed basis.

Of these, FAST goal structures are particularly suited to the Engineering process group's task to connect enterprise objectives and strategies to engineering improvement efforts and to identify accompanying measurements. Adapted from the Functional Analysis Systems Technique, a FAST goal structure is essentially a goal and function decomposition. A topmost goal is decomposed repeatedly by asking the question "How?" Each goal and subgoal is ideally expressed as a verb-noun pair. The structure is validated by answering "Why?" from bottom to top. Figure 8–6 shows a simple goal structure, using the universal goal of customer satisfaction, ultimately linked to tactical goals and functions—for instance, product inspection and project cost and schedule management.

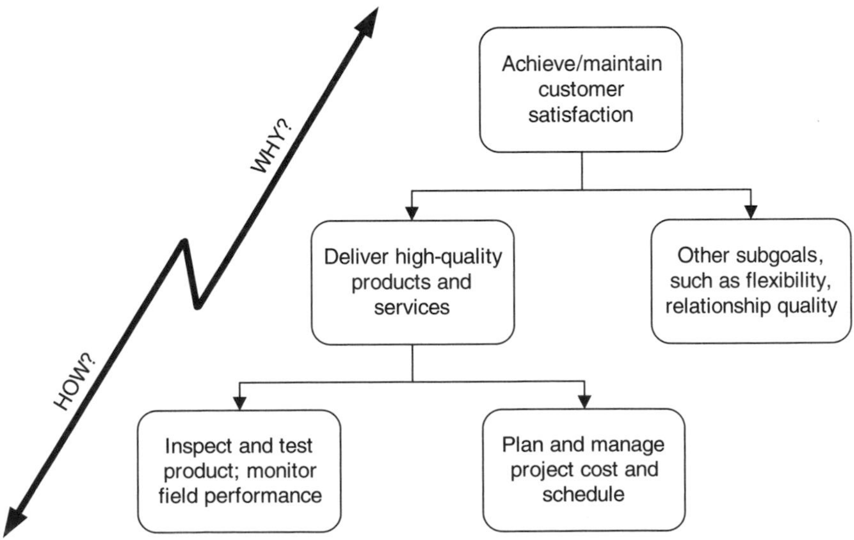

Figure 8–6: *Example of a FAST goal structure*

In the case study from which Figure 8–6 was extracted, baselines for inspection, cost, and schedule data were established; improvements in cost and schedule variability emerged as a notable improvement opportunity. (This case is described in Chapter 9.) However, the organization faced an interesting juxtaposition: It perceived a real need for cost and schedule performance improvement, yet the customer survey data indicated high levels of customer satisfaction. Pursuing a cost/schedule improvement project aligned to customer satisfaction risked becoming process improvement for the sake of process improvement. Herein lies the value of mission translation through goal structures. Figure 8–7 depicts a redrawn goal structure that further delineates subgoals and shows alignment of cost and schedule performance both to customer satisfaction and to the organization's competitive position in the marketplace. This provided a more credible position to motivate process change.

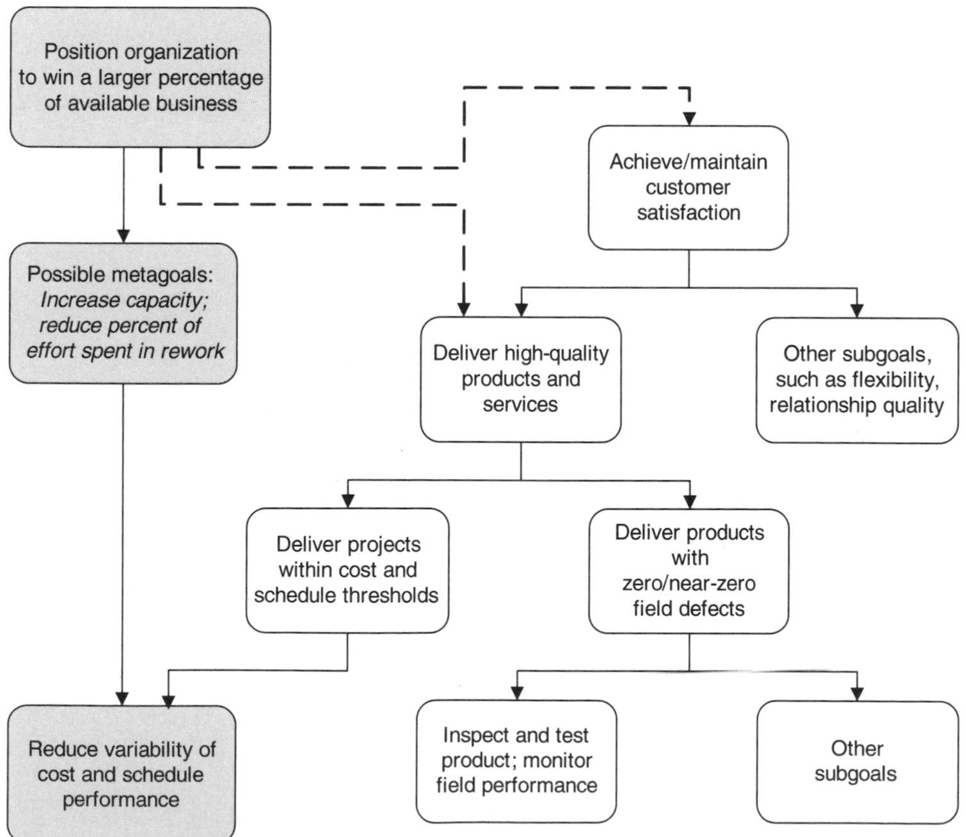

Figure 8–7: *Improvement project realignment, using a FAST goal structure*

A similar scenario about misalignment may occur with inspection data. In the pursuit of CMMI implementation and the development of process models, many organizations seek to develop a defect or quality model; however, they often neglect to properly align the model to business goals. Making it clear whether the defect model development is serving primarily customer satisfaction (i.e., field failures) or business productivity (e.g., internal efficiency, cost of quality, and so on) may not change the specific process changes being made, but it may significantly affect the organizational change management effort and also the success measures used to monitor results.

The examples in Figures 8–6 and 8–7 use some of the most universal objectives related to customer satisfaction—cost, schedule, and defects. These simple examples illustrate alignment. To go to the next step of identifying a multimodel strategy based on mission translation, Figure 8–8 shows the goal

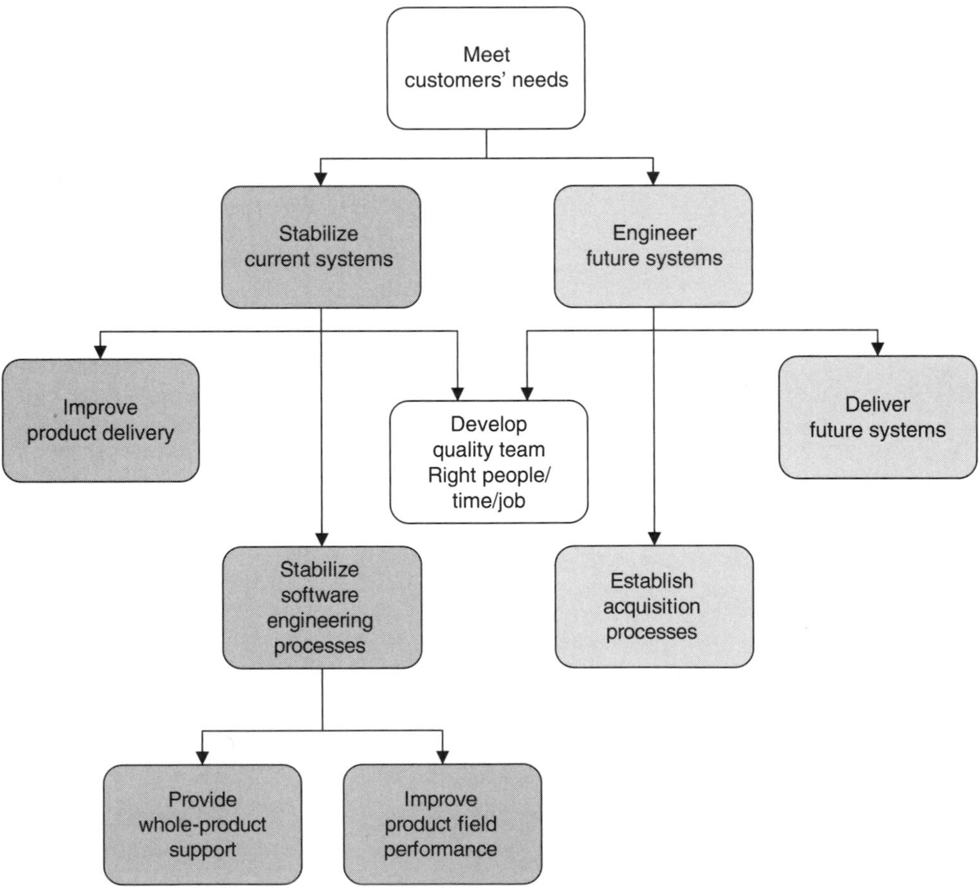

Figure 8–8: *Example of a goal structure for an IT development organization*

structure for an IT organization charged with maintaining and then replacing an HR database system. It shows that meeting customer needs is achieved via product-oriented objectives: stabilizing the current systems and creating future replacement systems. In the third tier of the decomposition, product-oriented objectives are further detailed, and process infrastructure objectives are made explicit.

One of the subgoals shown in Figure 8–8 is to establish acquisition processes. Figure 8–9 shows a slice of the strategy and task plans that support this goal. In this particular case, the process of making the goals, strategy, and model selection explicit allowed the organization to develop a blended model implementation plan for the establishment of acquisition processes and the stabilization of engineering processes. In this particular case, CMMI implementation was already under way to support the subgoal of stabilizing the engineering processes. This implementation, with its already-developed processes, was leveraged by the acquisition-oriented portion of the organization. It was supplemented with the acquisition-specific processes of the Software Acquisition CMM (SA-CMM).

Linking this to the "evaluate impact" step of the overall process improvement process, Figure 8–9 is annotated for three different types of indicators that an organization needs [Goethert and Siviy 04].

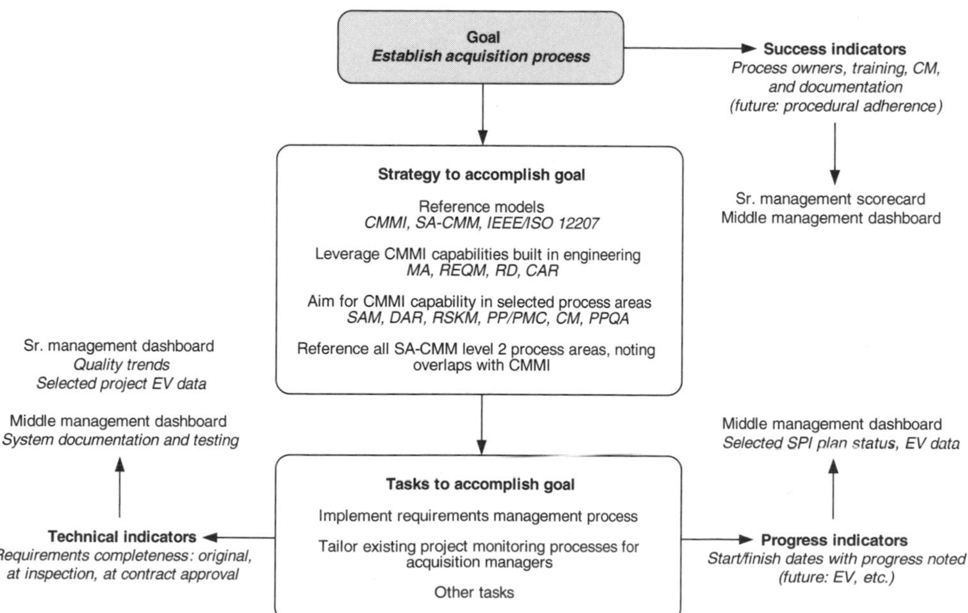

Figure 8–9: *Goal-strategy-tactic alignment for an IT organization subgoal*

1. *Success indicators*: These indicators are constructed from the defined success criteria and are used to determine whether the goals have been met.
2. *Progress indicators*: These indicators are used to track the progress or execution of the defined tasks. A Gantt chart is a good example of this type of indicator. The successful execution of all the defined tasks does not necessarily guarantee that the goal has been successfully met.
3. *Analysis or technical indicators*: These indicators are used to assist in analyzing the output of each task. The analyses help test assumptions about the data used to judge progress and success.

8.2.1 FAST Goal Structures and Six Sigma Y-to-x Decomposition

Six Sigma's Y-to-x decomposition is similar to goal structures, but rather than focusing on the "how and why" relationship, it focuses on connecting business performance (Y) with process performance/output (y) with process factors (x), as shown in Figure 8–10. Its purpose is to identify the vital few process factors—those that are critical to quality—from the trivial many. A Y-to-x flowdown tree enables an organization to depict hypothesized (and later verified) causal relationships between customer-critical performance

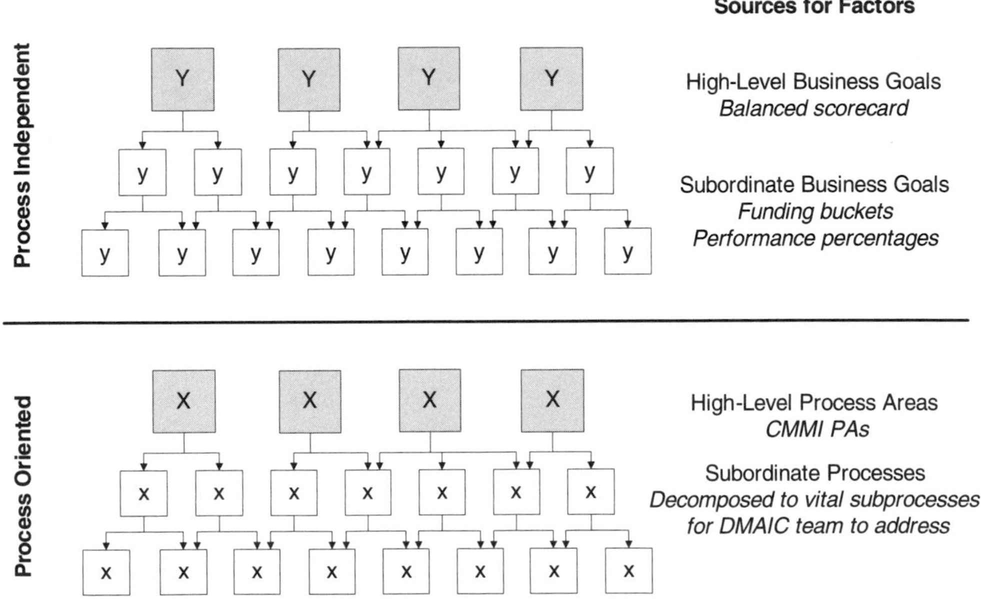

Figure 8–10: *Y- to-x decomposition. (Adapted with permission from the SEI course "Improving Process Performance Using Six Sigma" [SEI 07].)*

measures and process factors. However, in absence of extensive process understanding, it may be difficult to construct the decomposition.

FAST goal structures are easier in that they presume less a priori process understanding and are relatively intuitive for a broader cross-section of people to develop. One might quip that they are the 5 Hows—to complement the 5 Whys and the 4 Whats that are often used in problem solving. (These methods are explained in Appendix F.) When blended with Six Sigma's Y-to-x decomposition, as shown in Figure 8–11, goal structures enable alignment of improvement strategies and tasks (as shown in Figure 8–9) and also enable identification of Y's, y's and x's.

Going to the next step and categorizing process factors (x's) as uncontrollable versus controllable helps prioritize data collection and analysis—baseline at first, and then exploratory and in-depth analysis. This in turn reveals the most critical process factors and the most significant improvement opportunities, which enables development and prioritization of the organization's improvement project portfolio. Blending the FAST goal structure with Y-to-x decomposition, along with related analysis, provides a tight coupling between business objectives and process performance management (whether high capability or high maturity).

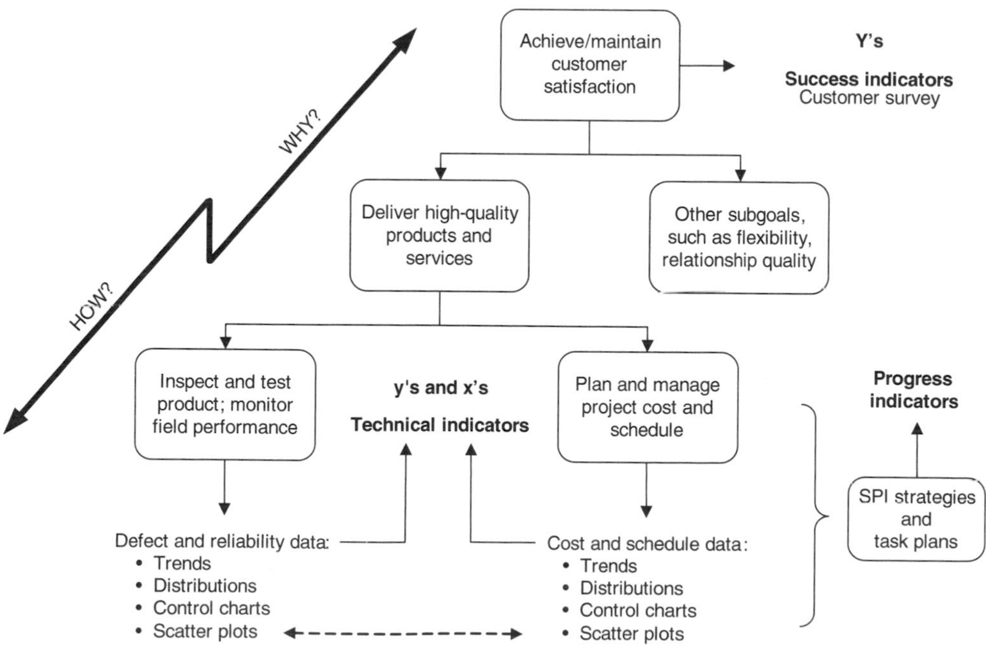

Figure 8–11: *FAST goal structure, annotated with Y-to-y and x relationships*

8.2.2 Case Retrospective: LMCO IS&S and Organizational Aspects of Project Portfolio Management

FAST goal structures and Y-to-x decomposition may be done at any level within an organization. Ideally, the most significant problems and priorities are evaluated at an organizational or enterprise level, to guide the prioritization of resource investment. But practically speaking, the methods may be broadly applied in the spirit of continuous improvement, small and large. In a large organization, there must be multiple routes into the process improvement arena in order to ensure that relevant process suggestions have a path. Once within the system, FAST goal structures and Y-to-x decomposition may be completed. This subsection describes the approach used by Lockheed Martin Integrated Systems & Solutions to manage and collect improvement projects and process innovations.

IS&S uses three methods to implement a process innovation:

- Process Improvement Recommendations (PIRs)
- Technology Change Management Working Group (TCMWG)
- Lean/Six Sigma Projects

The PIR and TCMWG projects and suggestions are monitored by the Executive Process Steering Committee (EPSC), which is the sponsor of the annual IS&S Process Improvement Plan. This plan covers the process aspects of the annual IS&S Strategic Plan. There is also an IS&S Technology Plan. When process improvement initiatives are reviewed, whether PIR or TCMWG, the EPSC reviews them in context with the Process Improvement Plan. Therefore, there is an alignment with the overall IS&S business objectives set forth in the IS&S Strategic Plan. The Lean/Six Sigma Projects are much more diverse. Although there is continuity with the Strategic Plan in those projects planned as objectives (annual Functional and Program Excellence Plans) at the beginning of the year when the Strategic Plan is published, there are also many ad hoc projects that may or may not apply to the Strategic Plan.

Process Improvement Recommendation

This is a simple electronic "employee voice" that automatically generates a request for a process change. The suggestion is routed to the process owner for a determination of whether or not to proceed. The employee suggesting the change is kept informed as the suggestion goes through the process. If it is determined to implement, a decision must be made as to either piloting, performing, or postponing the change for a later implementation (resource constraints). After the change is implemented, a validation must occur to determine whether rollout including communication and training is complete before closing the PIR.

Technology Change Management Working Group

Years before there was a CMMI, while still at SW-CMM level 3, M&DS established a Technology Change Management Working Group (TCMWG). The working group at the time was a combination of the old SW-CMM key process areas (KPAs) of Technology Change Management (TCM) and Process Change Management (PCM).[1] Similar to an R&D organization that pilots and implements technologies for future products, the TCMWG was chartered to evaluate technologies that could influence process.

Once a year, the TCMWG hosts a call for projects. The defined project proposal process includes evaluating the expected effect of the improvement on the process performance as well as relevance to the organization's strategic plan. After a project is chosen, a formal plan, schedule, and budget must be developed. This plan must be consistent with the organization's standard process, which means that the plan for the project must have those elements that any project would have within the organization. Program management, engineering, and support processes (including identification of measurements) must be planned. The project is reviewed on a monthly basis against its formal plan.

The project is also assigned a sponsor, who will take ownership of the process within the organization. Projects are expected to be completed within one year. Pilots are generally completed within one year—sometimes they take longer. The completion means the pilot is complete with measurements, organizational process documentation is red-lined and ready to be released, training material is established, and a formal communication plan is established. The process owner identified early in the process then takes responsibility for the process rollout.

Multiyear projects must have agreed-upon deliverables for the proposal year, and their justification is revisited prior to continuing work in subsequent years. A set of measurements are identified for each specific project, and these measurements are monitored throughout the pilot implementation.

TCMWG projects are those changes that need piloting—process changes that are generally based on a specific technology project plan. If a project can be implemented without a pilot, it does not get identified with the TCMWG.

---

[1]The CMMI incorporated these two KPAs into one process area—Organizational Innovation and Deployment (OID).

The technologies identified for immediate implementation, if found in the selection process, are sent to the EPSC as a Process Improvement Recommendation or to the Lean/Six Sigma group for a value stream mapping, a Kaizen Event, or immediate implementation.

Once the pilot is completed and the measurements analyzed, the board determines where the process change should be implemented. This determination is made based on the data and its relevance to the organizational performance, as well as ROI. The final plan must include current process performance data, projected performance data, and actual pilot performance data. The final plan also includes the investment (which can be tools, training, and so on) that the organization should make to implement the process change.

The sponsor then analyzes the data and determines whether the improved process should be

- Made mandatory for all projects (thus part of the organization's standard process)
- Used as tailoring guidance for specific project types
- Incorporated into a best practice library for artifacts

In order to determine the true effectiveness of this process, the organization continues to monitor the process change in order to determine real ROI. It is also important to do this in order to determine whether the overall process improvement project selections are effective for the organization. The TCMWG is further explained in Figure 8–12.

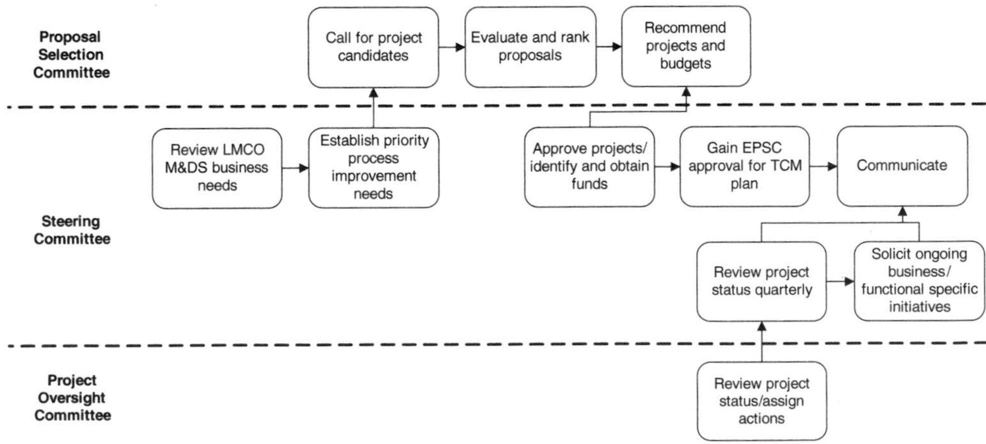

Figure 8–12: *LMCO IS&S organization and operations of TCMWG*

Lean/Six Sigma Projects

In contrast to TCMWG projects, Lean/Six Sigma projects are usually presented as a result of a causal analysis activity or a specific suggestion, related to either an improvement or an observation; they can be proposed throughout the year. Unlike PIRs, these do not need to be organizationally focused. Any employee within the organization or customer who works with the organization can identify a potential project, for any process within the organization: management, overall business, or engineering. Individual programs within the organization are encouraged to write Program Excellence Plans (PEPs) to identify processes that will be monitored for possible improvement and cost savings as the program proceeds. The plan documents by years possible projects and cost savings to be realized over the life of the program. The improvements can be a collection of formal projects and improvements implemented without pilots.

The project must be formally presented, with a sponsor identified. Sponsorship comes from various functions (as opposed to TCMWG, which is funded by the organization). Lean/Six Sigma projects are generally program or functionally sponsored and funded by the sponsor.

An organization within Lockheed Martin Corporation supplies the infrastructure to identify and execute overall Lean process improvement initiatives. Although the members of this organization support LMCO IS&S with enterprise events, they are also deployed to the specific lines of business, projects, or functions as needed. This organization formally trains a core of Green Belts, Black Belts, and Master Black Belts (who are dedicated resources to support this infrastructure).

Approved projects are planned by an assigned Black Belt and Green Belt. A team of subject matter experts are asked to participate on the project. Then, based on the project suggestion, the team determines whether a Kaizen Event or value stream mapping (VSM) is more appropriate. Kaizen Events generally look at one process and are very focused. VSMs can look at a process or business practice that spans different processes. The results of a VSM are a Get to Excellence Plan, which documents a systematic rollout of the changes. It may or may not include elements of a pilot activity. Particular implementation of the VSM and Kaizen are very similar.

When a formal Kaizen method is used, the team must be trained in the method prior to the start. Kaizen Events generally are limited to no longer than three days. It is not uncommon to change scope on day 1, once the project is understood. Both projects start with mapping the as-is process. Variances and waste within the current process (Kaizen) or business practice

(VSM) are identified. Those variances and waste that are not value added and not required by some regulation or customer constraint are removed, and a to-be process is designed. After each event, an implementation team is assigned, including a financial representative who verifies the investment and future savings. Variances are adjusted to the new process performance, and a rollout plan is put in place, including communication and training for the organization.

8.3 Model Selection and Strategy

In a multimodel implementation strategy, each selected model and practice ideally addresses a particular need or opportunity. However, this is easier said than done. There may be multiple models that address the same need. Among those that address different needs, there may be significant overlap. And, unto themselves, models may be used in different ways. So, the decision to simultaneously adopt multiple models can be complex and can depend as much on how they will be implemented as on their specific features and benefits. For instance, in the earlier example depicted in Figures 8–8 and 8–9, the CMMI was used for the acquisition process implementation to leverage an existing CMMI investment within the engineering portion of the organization.

To help with the complexities of multimodel decision making, an improvement group might consider a few approaches to inform their decision making:

- Affinity groupings or taxonomies of models and technologies
- Selection and implementation patterns of models, standards, and other technologies
- Rigorous decision methods

All of this—the affinity groups, the patterns, and the decision models (as applied to multimodel improvement)—is an area of emerging research and the subject of increasing numbers of papers about model combinations. The following list notes several papers that consider a variety of dimensions associated with model relationships and selection. They touch on process design considerations—which both may inform and is informed by selection decisions and is the subject of Section 8.4.

- In 2004, *CIO* magazine published a process model selection framework that depicted several models and methods by the dimensions of IT relevance and level of abstraction [Mayor 03].

- Presented at the Software Engineering Process Group Conference in 2006, a framework called Unified Process Improvement Approach (UPIA[2]) examines models by their component elements, which are categorized as institutionalization, good practice, and improvement methodology [Andelfinger et al. 06].
- Armstrong's paper "A Systems Approach to Process Infrastructure" shows the components of process infrastructure to be best practices and supporting tools, a process improvement infrastructure, and measurement [Armstrong 05].
- After observing that the choice of a software process improvement (SPI) framework is mostly subjective and seldom based on objective evidence, Halvorsen and Conradi tackled the challenge of comparing frequently used comprehensive frameworks via a 25-factor taxonomy, in "A Taxonomy to Compare SPI Frameworks" [Halvorsen 01].
- Bendell, in his paper "Structuring Business Process Improvement Methodologies," presents a problem-solution decision model, with such things as Lean being selected to address chronic waste, Six Sigma for variation, and ISO 9001 for market pressures [Bendell 05].

8.3.1 Strategic Classification of Models

Our contribution to this body of work is a multimodel affinity matrix that groups models by their strategic value and application focus, indicates typical decision authority, and serves as a backdrop for pattern analysis. Figure 8–13 shows this matrix, populated with a selection of models (not exhaustive, by any means). Coupled with observed case-based patterns and descriptions of model relationships, this can be useful when developing a multimodel strategy. It can enable making the link from an organization's mission translation to its strategy, such as what was shown earlier in Figures 8–8 and 8–9. And, while this generalized matrix is informed by the design features and characteristics of the models, its usage informs an organization's process architecture and process designs. Essentially, an organization's instantiation of this matrix can serve as a framework for its process architecture.

With additional research, this matrix might be enhanced using the aforementioned UPIA dimensions or product-oriented versus process-oriented categorizations.

---

[2]The model element classifications of UPIA are now housed under the SEI project named PrIME, Process Improvement in Multimodel Environments.

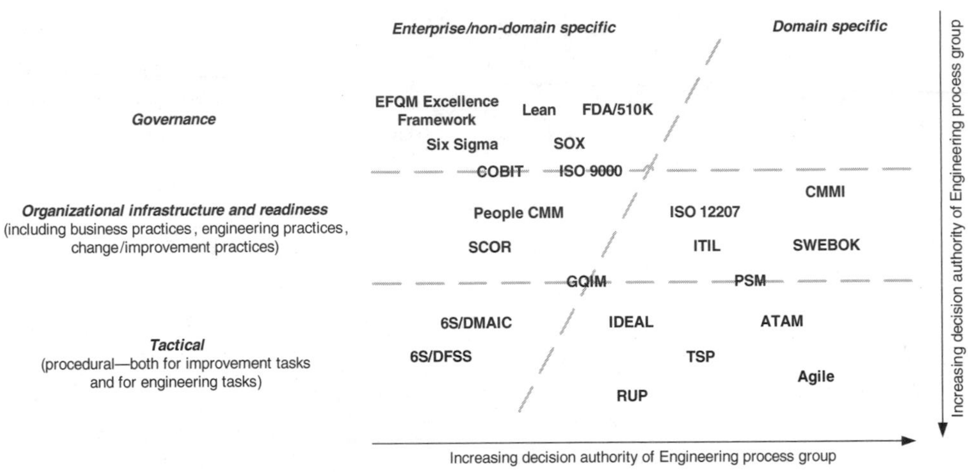

Figure 8–13: *Multimodel affinity matrix (not exhaustive)*

Following are guidance questions to support the use of this matrix as a decision aid.

- What decision-making authority do you have?
- For governance models (whose selection is typically outside the engineering process group) or for non-domain-specific models (which also may be outside your authority):
    - What selections have been made—by both customer dictates and senior managers or other decision authorities?
    - Do you need to leverage models to solve a particular problem? Do you have a business case? A champion to help sell the decision makers?
- For types of models within your authority:
    - Have you translated your mission into actionable goals and baselined performance? What particular problems need to be solved? What new capabilities are needed?
    - What efforts are already under way?
    - Minimally, have you identified a reference model or practice for measurement, for lifecycle practices, and for improvement methods? At the infrastructure and at the procedural levels?
    - Which models enable others?

Despite their usefulness, the matrix and guidance questions alone may be insufficient to develop the minimum list of reference models and practices that enable an organization to address customer requirements, solve their product and process problems, and optimize operations without reinventing any wheels.

Pattern analysis—the evaluation of frequently used combinations of models or the examination of combinations from just a few successful similar organizations—may serve as a supplementary, and needed, decision aid.

The next stage of decision aids would be the creation of detailed decision models to compare business and process needs with the features of individual or integrated models, possibly akin to what is often pursued within the Technical Solution PA of the CMMI. Such decision models might be sophisticated variants of quality function deployment, or they might involve simpler, comparative evaluations using techniques such as Pugh's concept.

Comparison taxonomies and affinity groups, libraries of model integration patterns, and decision models are all emerging areas of research that promise to grow significantly in the coming years.

8.3.2 Case Retrospective: LMCO IS&S's Model Selection Patterns

Together, Figures 8–14 and 8–15 show the categories and timeline associated with Lockheed Martin IS&S's journey, as described in Chapter 5.

The selection of the standards shown in Figure 8–14 was often dictated by customers; therefore, there was no hesitation in adoption. It became adoption by direction. Some standards, such as Systems Engineering Capability Maturity Model (SE-CMM), Rational Unified Process (RUP), and People CMM, filled gaps in IS&S's overall organizational process infrastructure. Their adoption expanded the process discipline into new areas and therefore

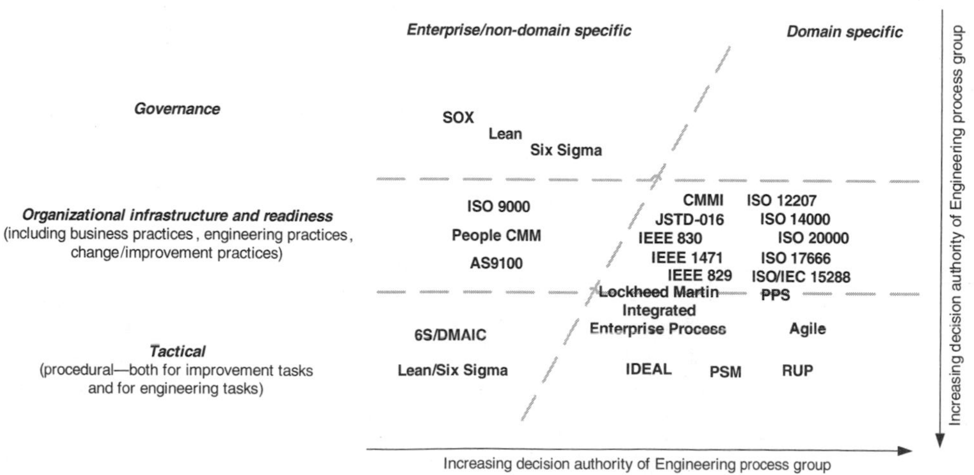

Figure 8–14: *LMCO IS&S technology selection pattern*

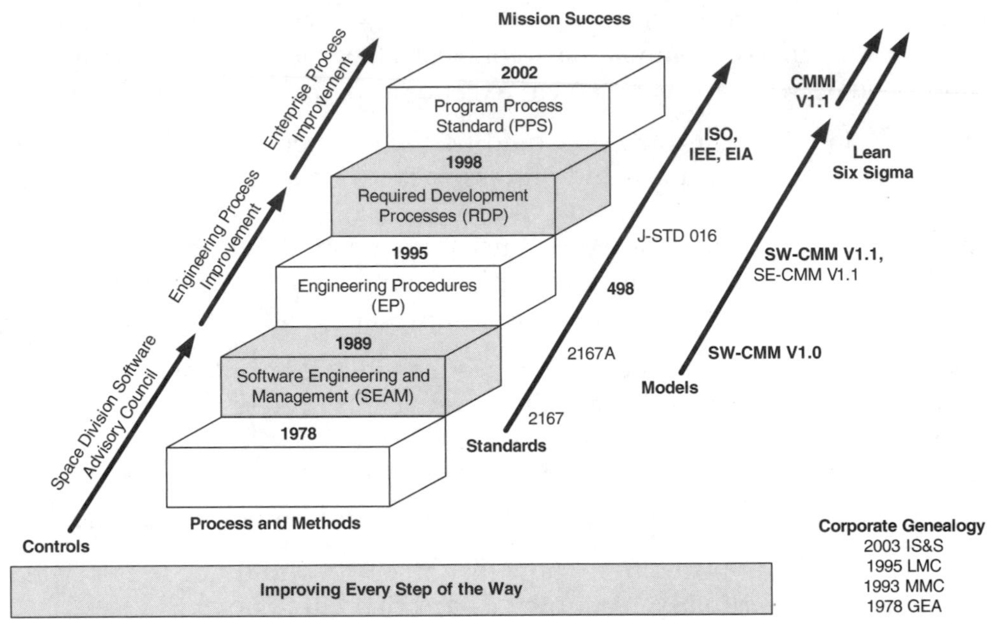

Figure 8–15: *LMCO IS&S process improvement timeline*

put process in an all-inclusive light. During the process benchmarks, it became evident that the organization was starting to adopt some Agile concepts without the formality of organizational direction. A value stream mapping was held to define the meaning of Agile within the IS&S organization. An Agile Requirements Manual (ARM) was generated, which basically was tailoring guidance on how to implement Agile using the IS&S PPS. Once adopted, a CMMI benchmark was conducted to see if use of the ARM was CMMI compliant.

Note that the PPS, the organization's internally developed process technology, is included in the figure. Also included is LMCO's Integrated Enterprise Process (IEP), which was a PPS-like approach at the overall enterprise level. These two are included not only as tactical standards but also as the formative documents for the actual process infrastructure.

Figure 8–15 distills the infrastructure-oriented standards to show those of significant impact to the organization at each major phase of process improvement. Note that this diagram begins significantly earlier than what was described in Chapter 5. The maturity models are shown because with their best practices they became a common means to institutionalize process at IS&S. Their advancement, from the SW-CMM to the CMMI, became IS&S's process advancement. Lean/Six Sigma is included on this chart because of permeation across the entire organization. Those infrastructure standards shown in Figure 8–14 but not in Figure 8–15 were auxiliary or supplemental standards that were mapped and tracked but not foundational to the organization's overall process assets.

Lockheed Martin IS&S continues to identify standards and address their applicability to the organization and the potential rollout, scope, schedule, and ROI. M&DS started with the SW-CMM, which quickly advanced to the SE-CMM and ISO. The reasons for adopting these standards were to continue to advance the benefits seen by adopting the SW-CMM.

8.4 Solution Implementation: Process Architecture and Design

Before we begin a discussion about process architecture in the context of multimodel process improvement, consider the following definitions.

- The CMMI defines process architecture as the ordering, interfaces, interdependencies, and other relationships among the process elements in a standard process. The process elements are the fundamental units of a process, each of which covers a closely related set of activities.
- With a slightly more granular, more program-level focus, Kasser states that "the major organisational function of process architecting is to design, set up and continuously optimise the process for the development of the specific system being produced by the specific organisation over the specific time period of the SDLC to optimise productivity" [Kasser 05].
- From the archives of the Business Analysis Body of Knowledge, process architecture is defined as the processes an organization needs to conduct its business, how those processes interact, and how they are managed and modified over time. A process architecture should remain fairly intact even as the details of process execution evolve and change [BA Insight 06].

Noting these views, the formal design and architecting of software (or any) engineering processes are, at the time of this writing, emergent (maybe pre-emergent) research topics. An underlying motivation for the research is to enable organizations both to reach a mature process state with a minimum of waste and to create a process system that is robust and efficiently updated as new models are adopted (or other changes are made). While there does not yet seem to be a universally agreed-upon set of architecture characteristics for engineering processes, the following list should be considered:

- Functional properties, including classes, flow, and attributes
- Outputs, including flow and relationships
- Roles and responsibilities, including users and actors
- Information flow
- Overall interrelationships, dependencies, and constraints

The architecture characteristics should consider relevant, multiple views; attributes and properties; documentation rules such as showing things once and only once; and so on. More specifically, views might include functional, behavioral, organizational, and data. Properties might include modularity, cohesion, and minimized coupling [Mutafelija and Stromberg 06].

The aggregate collection of architectural components and features informs the functional description of the processes, including classes, flow, tasks, and so forth—the types of things typically documented via process structuring and definition tools such as ETVX diagramming (IBM's model, where E represents entry criteria, T is tasks, V is verification and validation, and X is exit criteria) or process mapping.

A critical success factor of creating a process architecture is the ability of the process engineers and architects. Likening their task to that of systems engineers who are charged with creating a software-intensive system comprising many interoperable and integrated components, it stands to reason that the engineers and architects responsible for creating process infrastructure should have skills similar to those of systems engineers [Kasser 05]. Their skills and talents should include the ability to see the big picture and to communicate complex ideas. They need to be objective, creative, and experienced in business as well as in the software domain.

8.4.1 Existing Methods for Process Architecture

As research on this topic progresses, the requisite tradeoffs between effort, complexity, and practicality (fit for use) will need to be made. While invention of new approaches may be necessary, numerous existing methods such as the following might be applied or extended to support engineering process architecture and design.

- Design connectivity between specific initiatives, such as:
  - The connections described in Chapter 7 of this book
  - Element classifications of UPIA [Andelfinger et al. 06; Kirwan et al. 06]
  - Descriptions by numerous presenters, as listed in the References and Additional Resources at the end of this book

- Design for Six Sigma, Design for Lean Six Sigma, and other robust design techniques
- Software and related engineering technologies, such as:
  - Interoperability, including business process interoperability and service-oriented architectures
  - The validated architecture process of the Evolutionary Process for Integrating COTS-Based Systems (EPIC) [Albert and Brownsword 02]
  - The Unified Modeling Language, including structure, behavior, and interaction diagrams
- Architectures and models for business process management, such as:
  - Architecture of Integrated Information Systems (ARIS) applied to business process modeling [Scheer 00; Davis 01]
  - Riva's process definition technique (using role-activity diagrams) and process architecture technique [BA Insight 06; Ould 05]
  - Goal-Oriented Business Process Modeling [Bider 05]
- Beer's Viable Systems Model, which organizes systems in a way that meets the demands of surviving in the changing environment; subsystems include primary activities, information channels, controls, environmental monitoring, and policy [Beer 85; Beer 94; Espejo and Harnden 89]

A relevant related long-term research interest is to develop preimplementation modeling and simulation to accompany the work-in-process architecture. Much like software product architecture, engineering process architecture approaches include sound analytic mechanisms to analyze the behavior of a system with respect to quality attributes. The analysis would enable the following:

- Prediction of behavior before process systems are deployed
- Understanding of process behavior after process systems are deployed
- Design decisions during design and during evolution

Organizations that have already institutionalized one or more of these technologies may be in a position to apply them to their engineering process architectures. Other organizations may choose to wait for research to be conducted or to sponsor research by others.

8.4.2 Case Retrospective: LMCO IS&S's Program Process Standard

As with many topics of emerging research, case studies are a frequent starting point for eliciting good practices and success factors. This subsection provides a description of Lockheed Martin IS&S's approach to its PPS architecture, design, and implementation. (Some text is repeated in part from

Chapter 5. This is intentional, to improve the readability of this retrospective.)

As described in Chapter 5, the standard operating process, which would eventually become known as the Program Process Standard, began as the required development process (RDP). (The name change resulted from the ultimate desire to eliminate the word *development* and expand the defined process into different types of programs.) The vision associated with the standard operating process was that it makes it feasible to introduce one overall process to the organization. It also had to reflect the tasks and functions necessary to fulfill organizational project and product commitments. And it had to reflect the features of three standards of interest to the organization: the SW-CMM, the SE-CMM, and ISO 9000. The long-term vision was that new standards, process methodologies, and process initiatives would be integrated with this single operating process, thus allowing the organization to grow and evolve its capability via new releases of its standard process.

The RDP and PPS both started with an overall workflow diagram of what processes were necessary for the organization. Each process defined was then given a functional owner, a group that had primary responsibility for the process itself. Other functions that also had responsibilities for tasks within that process were defined as support functions. A table was generated to illustrate functional responsibilities, primary or support, for each process. The process was then dissected and tasks within the process enumerated. Once tasks were enumerated, entry and exit criteria as well as inputs and outputs were defined. Once the entry and exit criteria and inputs and outputs were represented by the functional process owners, they were modeled to define relationships and interfaces between processes. Every entry or exit criterion needed a task in another process. Every input had to be an output from some process. This modeling not only represented a simulation of the workflow but also enabled the organization to illustrate and streamline the overall process implementation.

The PPS architecture started with describing the processes that the projects within the IS&S organization needed to operate. This was coupled with a mapping of the process to the organization's business objectives and goals. The document was designed to be flexible enough to adapt to the requirements of multiple industry standards and models. The organization needed a project-focused document that would be simple enough to be accepted but comprehensive enough to meet all needs. The document met these needs.

Lockheed Martin IS&S used process-mapping techniques to evolve the initial PPS and develop an architecture for the standard process. Figure 8–16 represents a high-level view of the overall process map, showing specific processes linked to various organizational functions. In the center three concentric circles, but the circles are at different levels. The inner circle represents the IS&S process architecture, the next circle represents the organizational process assets, and the outer circle represents the programs' implementation of the process assets. The outer circle defines the lifecycle of a system of systems, from procurement through transition and operations. Two groups of processes related to the two tiers of the existing version of the PPS: management and control (support tasks) and program implementation (repeated development/engineering processes). The program management and control processes, listed at the bottom of Figure 8–16, span all processes within the PPS. The list on the right in Figure 8–16 represents program implementation and contains all processes—from requirements to operations and maintenance—associated with the development, delivery, and maintenance of an actual system. The list on the left was added to address system of systems concerns and the system support activities, which had now become very important in the organization.

After the high-level diagram was developed, the underlying processes were defined by functional process owners and subject matter experts. Program responsibilities for each process were identified. One of the challenges the process designers faced was what level of detail to define. Using

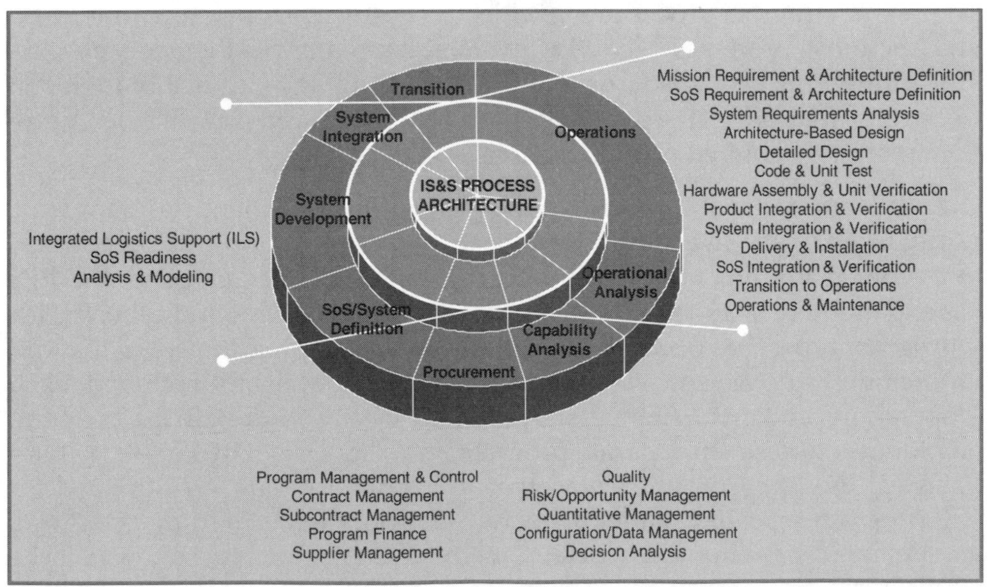

Figure 8–16: *LMCO IS&S process architecture*

the philosophies of "keep it simple" and "the process should reflect how we do business," they created a process template and limited each process description to one page. The template was designed to focus on what the program needed to know: purpose, intent, entry and exit criteria, inputs and outputs, activities and tasks, with the latter written in terms of what to do. Where a SW-CMM KPA matched the process, the KPA goal was used as the primary reference for the process purpose. The KPA practices helped identify the needed process activities.

A small process group, comprising standards experts, then mapped the process standard to the SW-CMM, the SE-CMM, and ISO 9000. The book containing the workflow diagrams became the minimum mandatory set of processes for all programs. Each process was identified as part of management, engineering, or support/sustainment. Each activity within the process could be mapped to a recommended procedure within the process asset library. The organization did not require the use of these procedures, but if they were used, full compliance to the PPS would be assured. However, the procedures could be tailored and still meet the intent of the process purpose (the required portion of the process). By design, the organization could follow one document, and the reward would be compliance to the SW-CMM, the SE-CMM, and ISO.

The product suite also included a compliance matrix, which each program was required to complete, demonstrating how the program was compliant (pointers to program procedures), which processes were being tailored, and which of those processes needed waivers. A template was then created for a typical program plan based on the standard process, with elaborations on procedures that programs could adopt in order to assure compliance. A program plan was required on all programs.

After the foundational elements of the process improvement program were solidly in place and in a routine two-year review cycle, and as the organization evolved via organic growth and organizational acquisitions, the PPS was expanded to include tailoring guidelines based on program type; the list of program types was updated as well. For instance, program types that did not include full-scale software development were explicitly included, such as operations and maintenance, support, and special studies. In all, the organization recognized ten separate program types, as shown in Table 8–1. Templates for the PPS Compliance Matrix and Program Plan were defined for each program type. In Chapter 5, the two Development program types were not separated based on their design methodology. This table shows all the definitions.

Table 8–1: *LMCO IS&S Program Types*

Program Type	Description
Operations and Maintenance	Supports a customer in maintaining existing operational software/hardware
Engineering Services	Supports a customer in a time and materials manner (level of effort), performing those tasks directly identified by the customer
Facility Outsourcing Services	Provides one or more of the following for a customer's workplace: security, cleaning and maintenance, reconfiguration/renovation, telecommunications, general administrative services, general facility planning
Technical Outsourcing Services	Provides one or more of the following aspects of a customer's operational IT needs: data center operations, network design and installation, computer equipment repair and maintenance, software installation and configuration
Systems Integration	Performs systems engineering and integration work of a system of systems
Systems Engineering and Technical Assistance (SETA)	Is responsible for or provides the principal support for one or more of the following functions for a customer: program management, requirements analysis, technology and product evaluation/assessment, systems specification and design, systems acquisition planning and support, independent system testing and evaluation, training, operational support
Development—Architecture-Based Design (for all development programs initiated after 2004)	Develops (using the Architecture-Based Design Process) new software/hardware or integrates reused and/or nondeveloped software or hardware (COTS/GOTS/FOSS/third party) in order to meet a customer's requirements
Development—Non-Architecture-Based Design (for heritage programs prior to 2005)	Develops new software/hardware or integrates reused and/or nondeveloped software or hardware (COTS/GOTS/FOSS/third party) by using heritage structured design techniques in order to meet a customer's requirements

(continued)

Table 8–1: *LMCO IS&S Program Types (Continued)*

Program Type	Description
Independent Research and Development	Produces research reports, proof-of-concept demonstrations, or operational products using advanced technologies
Research and Technology Contract	Performs research, analysis, and studies; produces research reports; includes proof-of-concept demonstrations, data collections, and analysis

8.5 Summary

Process improvement is itself a process with several key steps, including these:

- Selection of technologies to support or enable the improvement journey
- Development and transition of improvement solutions, ranging from large-scale process infrastructure implementation to smaller-scale, narrowly focused performance improvements to specific processes
- Measurement and analysis of results

Numerous demonstrated practices and technologies, as well as emerging research, can be leveraged by an engineering process group in the improvement journey. Measurement practices and transition science are among the fields that are well established, albeit not necessarily well adopted. Engineering process groups should develop expertise in these areas to ensure that their time is spent solving problems, not inventing existing methods. An area that is maturing is what we call mission translation. These techniques enable an engineering process group to effectively translate the business mission into actionable engineering-level goals and to identify critical-to-quality process factors. This enables a process group to develop a prioritized and strategically aligned improvement project portfolio—essential in an era of limited and competing resources. Goal structures and Y-to-x flowdown diagrams are useful tools for this. In the emerging research category are model selection and design patterns and process architecture. While mission translation helps clarify the problem space, these emerging research areas will help clarify and efficiently converge on the solution space. While there is still much to be developed and codified in these topics, an engineering process group would benefit from familiarity with what knowledge is available.

Chapter 9

Sustainment: Your Improvement Project Portfolio

Improvement projects take many shapes and forms. The main focus of this book has been to describe the joint use of the CMMI and Six Sigma, along with other models, primarily for the establishment of process infrastructure. A robust improvement project portfolio, however, contains far more than infrastructure projects.

The purpose of this chapter is to describe different types of projects that an improvement group may realistically expect to implement over time, in the context of a joint CMMI and Six Sigma deployment. Some of these examples reflect strategies mentioned earlier for the joint implementation of the CMMI and Six Sigma, such as the use of DMAIC as the tactical engine for high maturity or the use of Lean to establish a new process. Others more simply focus on the resolution of particular product, project, or process problems—in the context of a CMMI and Six Sigma organization. By design, this chapter's examples touch on software development, systems engineering, and IT, as well as on DMAIC, Lean, and DFSS.

Six Sigma Case Studies in Software and Systems Engineering

In addition to reinforcing points made in previous chapters about process infrastructure and performance improvement, the examples in this chapter enable CMMI practitioners to gain awareness of the full analytical toolkit at their disposal and thereby more effectively implement analysis-oriented practices. They also will help Six Sigma Belt candidates from these domains to more easily connect the dots between their manufacturing-oriented training and their day-to-day reality. For organizations in which the CMMI and Six Sigma communities are separate, these case studies can serve as a common ground for discussion—a means of bridging communication gaps.

Accordingly, we intentionally selected examples to address a variety of project contexts.

- Product quality improvement in software development via defect resolution, inspection practices, and defect prevention (Section 9.1)
- Cost and schedule process improvement in a software and systems engineering environment, via baselining to identify the project portfolio, application of basic tools, and integration with existing project management practices (Section 9.2)
- Implementation of an organizational decision-making process, to be compliant with the CMMI, via Lean techniques (Section 9.3)
- Application of Lean techniques to improve the relationship with and operational support from an IT organization to its systems engineering (internal) customer (Section 9.4)
- Instantiation of DFSS in a systems engineering organization and development of performance models and simulations (Section 9.5)

Other examples are becoming increasingly available, although many organizations still limit the amount of information shared because they view their successes with these initiatives and methods as competitive advantages. The Additional Resources section near the end of this book contains ideas for further reading, including sources that present more examples such as those found in this chapter. For example, the following papers by Holmes are available via an SEI-led special series on Six Sigma applications in *Software Quality Professional* during 2003–2004.

- "Software Measurement Using SCM" describes a way to use configuration management historical data to identify problematic areas of the code, which are then addressed using DMAIC

- "Optimizing the Software Life Cycle" illustrates productivity improvements achieved via the design of experiments and regression modeling, applied within the DMAIC framework.
- "Identifying Code-Inspection Improvements Using Statistical Black Belt Techniques" explains how a team used Six Sigma methods to identify the statistically significant factors driving its inspection process.

The intent is to provide enough detail for readers to be able to envision similar projects in their own context. While we do offer examples of final analysis and Appendix F contains overviews of selected methods, step-by-step instructions and data analysis guidance (which would more appropriately appear in a handbook for analysts) are not included here.

Please note that the sources of these case studies vary. As such, they are written in different voices and with different styles.

9.1 Product Quality Improvement

This section presents a case study in:

- Aligning defect reduction and inspection best practices to business objectives
- Applying defect prevention practices and prediction models

Software engineers and software process groups sometimes measure quality in terms of bad lines of code, at the exclusion of customer- or business-driven definitions of quality. For instance, they may pursue implementation of formal inspections and creation of a defect detection model without first understanding whether the root problem is one of field quality (customer dissatisfaction) or rework reduction (business efficiency). While the inspection and analysis tasks may be the same either way, the approach to project justification and transition varies significantly based on these problems.

This case study demonstrates the use of the Six Sigma philosophy and the use of the Six Sigma toolkit to supplement and provide business context for an effort to reduce defects through the implementation of the Team Software Process (TSP) and inspections. It then proceeds to describe basic, progressing, and advanced defect models. It is a *composite example*, in that all of the information is real but comes from multiple sources to enable a complete story to be told. It relies heavily on *individual* TSP data to show how improvements at an individual level can be readily aligned with and made more meaningful by business objectives. In the human-centric business of engineering, it may require an accumulation of numerous and varied individual changes to reach performance objectives. The lessons and methods may be applied to organizational data as well. The models are presented at an organizational level.

9.1.1 Organizational Context

The organization discussed in this case study develops software that is provided to others for system integration. It has established a strategic objective to reduce costs by 10% in order to complete in a fiercely cost-conscious market.

It recently began the adoption of the TSP as part of a CMMI implementation strategy. It also is in the process of adopting Six Sigma, as dictated by senior management. One innovation-oriented team has embraced both initiatives. The team members have used TSP long enough to have reliable baselines of their own data. One of its members, Joe, is enrolled in Six Sigma Black Belt training, and the team's project manager is considering enrolling. They are personally interested in process improvement and have periodically served as liaisons to the organization's Engineering process group. The Engineering process group leader recently completed her Six Sigma Black Belt certification.

9.1.2 Initial Project Definition

The Engineering process group leader and the team's project manager perceived in this team a ready-made pilot opportunity for organizational cost reduction ideas. They conducted a preliminary evaluation to verify that reduced development labor costs per product will translate directly to organizational cost reductions (i.e., there is more work readily available) and that improvements to defect reduction and prevention are low-hanging fruit (relative to reengineering or "leaning out" other aspects of the process). As a result, they have asked each team member to determine how he or she can contribute to the organizational cost reduction objective by improving defect reduction and prevention. After working with each team member to improve his or her performance, their plan is to compile guidance for all individuals to use in their personal improvement efforts and also to identify frequently occurring problems/solutions for widespread implementation.

Figures 9–1 and 9–2 show simple process maps for the development and inspection processes, respectively.

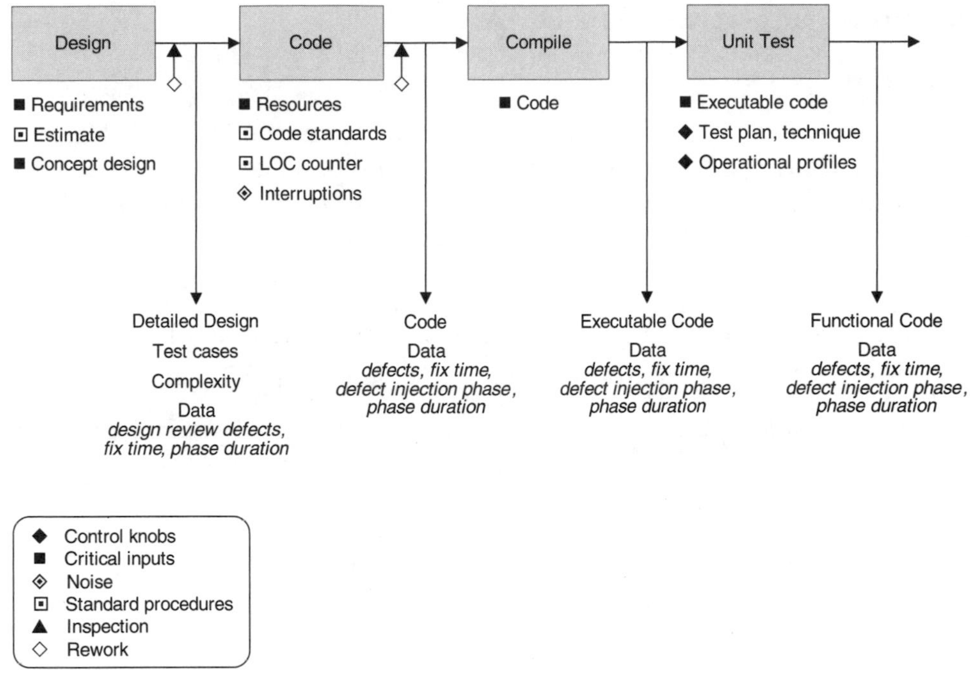

Figure 9–1: *Development process map*

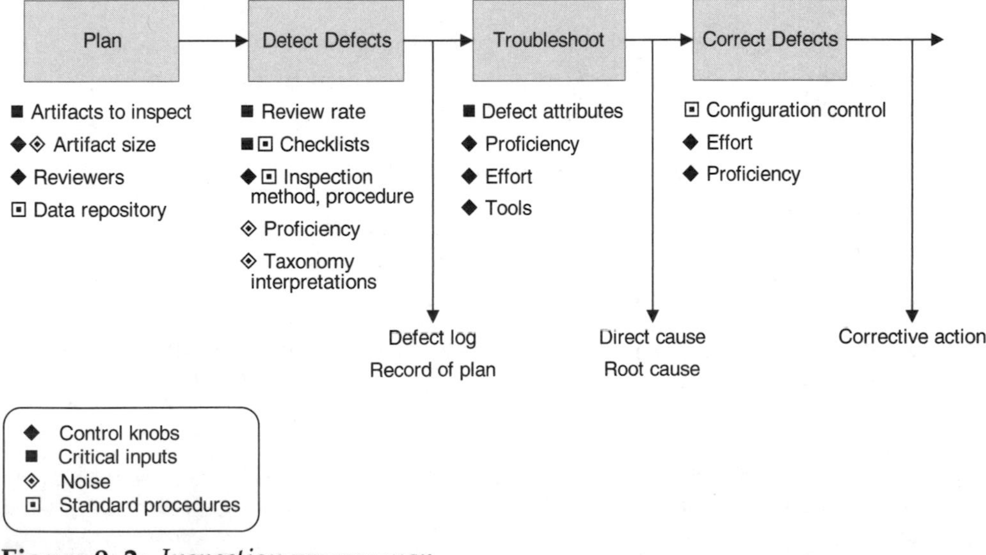

Figure 9–2: *Inspection process map*

9.1.3 Project Implementation: DMAIC

Measure

Joe set out to identify how he can address the cost reduction goal. He had previously validated his personal measurement practices, and his team's data quality manager routinely uses a data validation checklist to ensure that everyone's data quality remains high. He has the following baseline data:[1]

- Average productivity: 19 LOC/hour
- Average time spent fixing defects: 33% of development time
- Average defect density: approximately 250 defects/KLOC

After due consideration and a bit of math, he identified several possible ways to state a quantitative improvement objective:

- Reduce cycle time by 22 minutes/module.
- Reduce fix time by 1.3 minutes/defect.
- Reduce defects by 6/program.
- Reduce defect density to 190 defects/KLOC.
- Use any combination of these reductions to yield a new productivity of 21 LOC/hour.

Joe perceived these targets to be measurable and not confounded with the normal variability of his baseline data.

Analyze

Joe then analyzed his data with the improvement objectives in mind. He discovered several opportunities to reduce the amount of time spent repairing defects (also depicted in Figure 9–3):

- Defects removed in test: 78% of repair time
- Defects injected in design: 25% of repair time
- Defects injected in code: 56% of repair time
- Syntax defects in general: 63% of defects

Further analysis revealed that syntax defects were high in number but, on average, required less than 10 minutes each to repair. And defects injected in

[1] In practice, individual TSP data is not shared in an organization unless a person expressly permits it. Rather, individual data is rolled to the team or organizational level for analysis and reporting.

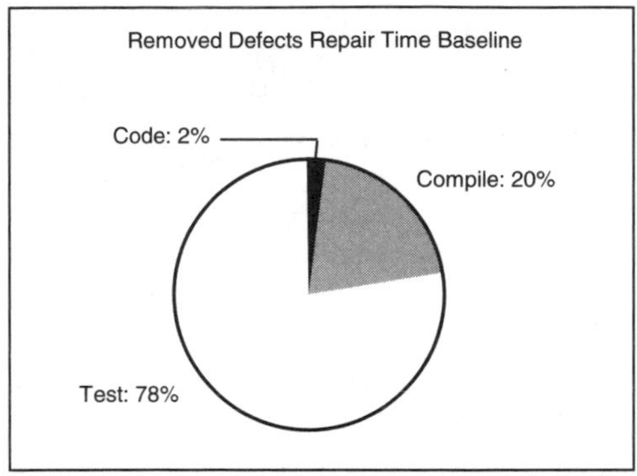

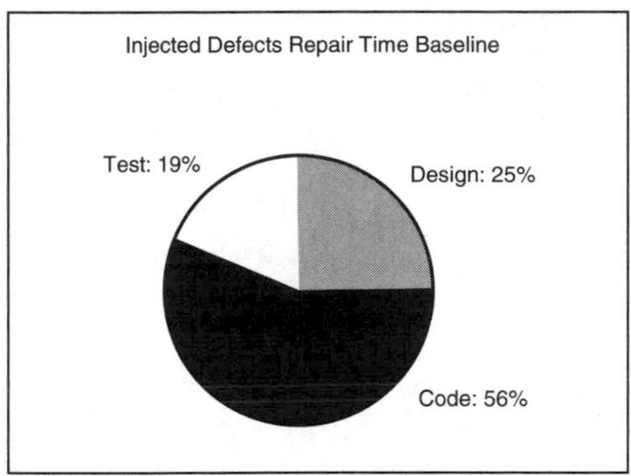

Figure 9–3: *Analysis of defects*

design but removed in test were fewer in number but, on average, took significantly longer than 10 minutes to repair.

Joe used the management by fact (MBF) summary template, shown in Figure 9–4, that he learned in Six Sigma training to summarize his improvement project. The completed MBF is shown in Figure 9–5.

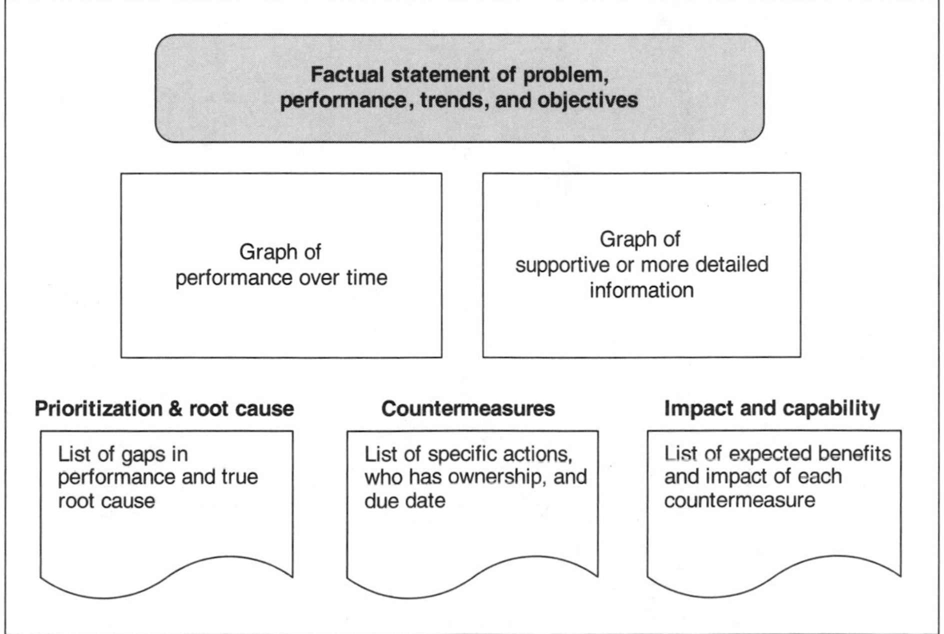

Figure 9–4: *Management by fact template*

Improve

Recognizing that immediate and complete eradication of all defects was unlikely to happen, Joe developed an improvement strategy to:

- Reduce the quantity of easily repaired syntax defects
- Reduce the quantity of defects injected in design
- Use more effective and efficient troubleshooting when defects occur

Some specific improvement ideas that he instituted were the creation of a syntax checklist and a phase completion checklist, the enhancement of his defect taxonomy to include subcategories of defect types, and the creation of cause-and-effect diagrams to aid his troubleshooting efforts.

Joe monitored the effect of his improvements by tracking total defect density, changes in defect density by phase injected and phase removed, and productivity, as shown in his MBF in Figure 9–5. He also conducted mean comparison tests, as shown in Figure 9–6.

An increase in productivity, the removal of defects in earlier lifecycle phases, and the reduced injection of defects all support the effectiveness of the

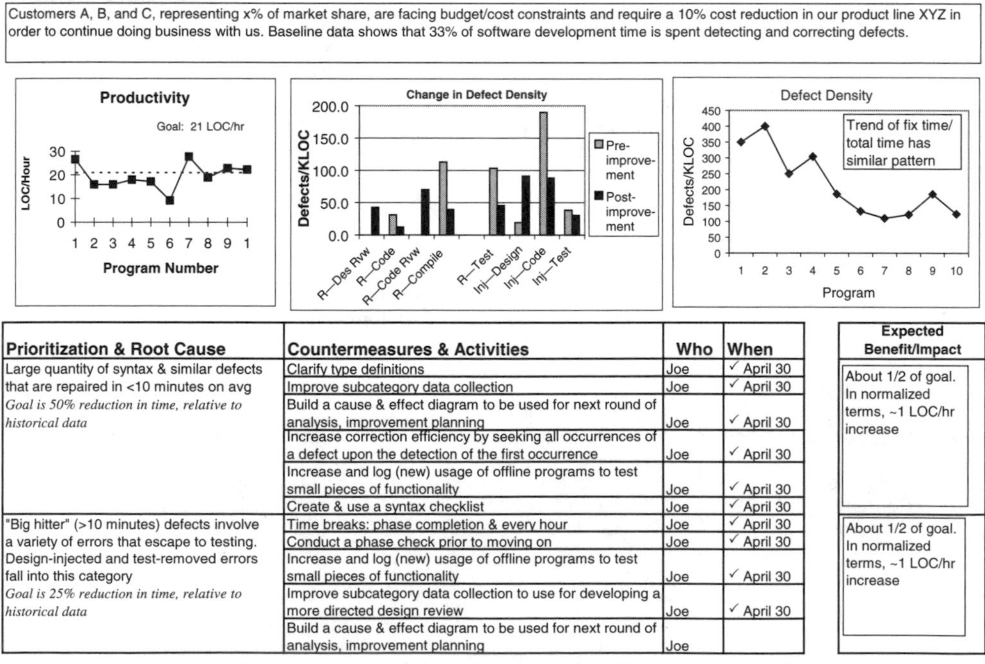

Figure 9–5: *Management by fact for defect reduction*

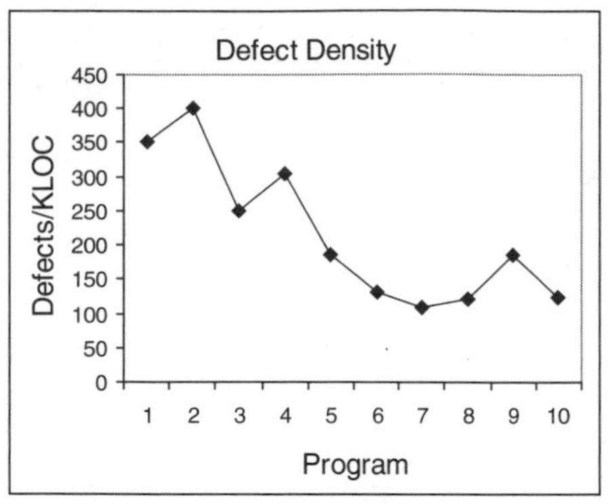

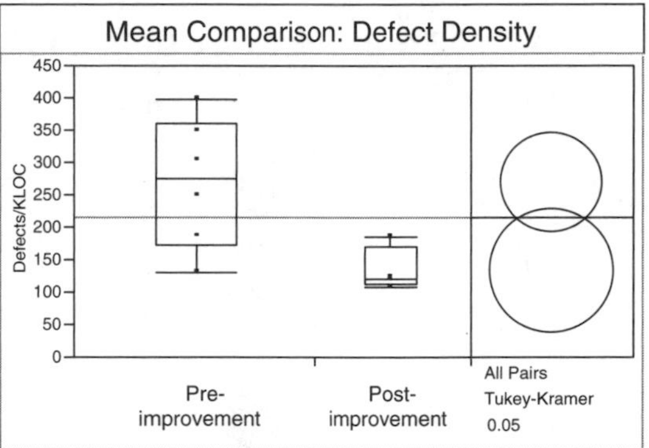

Figure 9–6: *Defect density analysis*

improvements. The examination of the total defect data, however, presented a less clear picture. In a perfect world, the effect of improvements would be seen as a step change from one steady level to a new steady level. While the pre- versus postimprovement mean comparison of the total defect density points to an improved situation, the total defect density trend chart shows a downward trend rather than a step change. Joe concluded that his improvements had an effect, but that there was also something else (something not controlled) contributing to improvements. He hypothesized that it was the effect of the learning curve while he increased his experience with a new software language.

Control

Once Joe's performance stabilized, he developed a control chart for his productivity and defect density. However, he also wanted a more real-time control mechanism. After searching the literature, he discovered that some organizations use their historical performance data to estimate defect detection levels for each lifecycle phase, based on the size and complexity of the product being developed, as shown in Figure 9–7. By comparing actual detection to estimated, they can make informed decisions about proceeding to the next phase. As a step toward this, Joe decided to build a control chart for his defects detected in each phase. After he gathered sufficient data, he would attempt to build a prediction model.

9.1.4 Closing Comments: From Individual Results to Organizational Results and Models

As a pilot for organizational improvement, Joe's project was quite useful. It provided a template approach, as well as some reusable chart types and

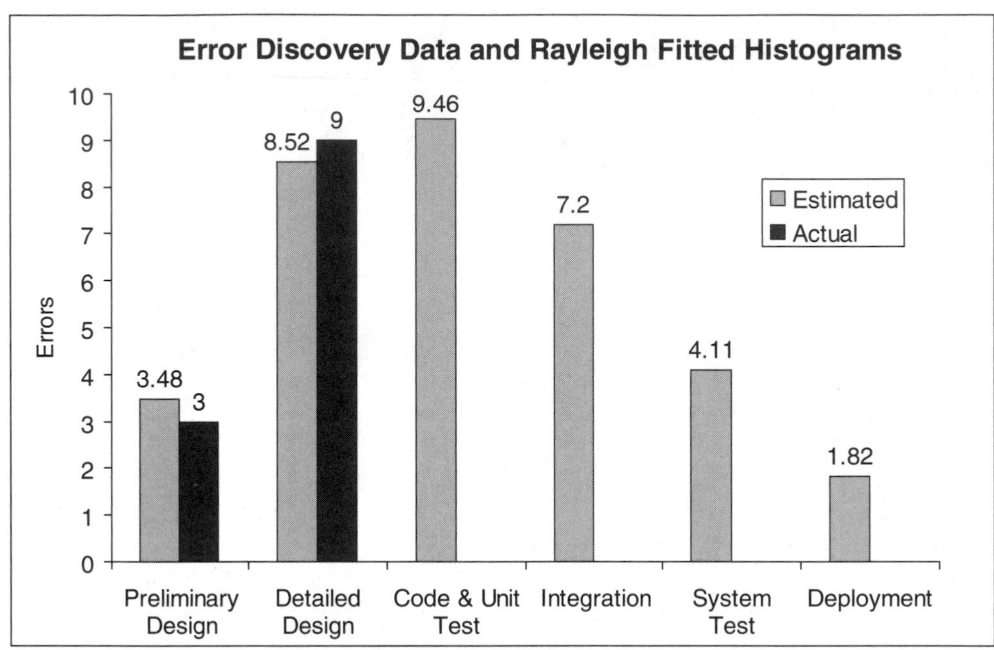

Figure 9–7: *Rayleigh curve-based pattern analysis*

analyses, for others' individual improvements. The approach was also reusable at the organizational level, using rolled-up data—with the possible exception of the productivity measure, which, if misused at an organizational level, could result in undesirable behaviors.

Joe's learning curve factor, which confounded his data, was acknowledged as an organization-wide factor because technologies and skills needs constantly change. Explicit recognition of it as a factor influencing quality and efficiency was viewed as an aid for the organization and individuals to make judicious decisions about technology and tool change.

The Rayleigh fitted histograms were selected as the organizational defect model. While Joe planned to build personal control charts for each phase, the organizational approach was to conduct a pattern analysis and build a Rayleigh profile with a range of expected values, rather than a single point, for each lifecycle phase. Initially, the range would be based on historical data.

Long term, the Six Sigma Black Belts would put their modeling expertise to work and build a prediction model. The predictions might be used to create more exact ranges on the Rayleigh model. Or the organization might adopt models similar to what the Engineering process group leader learned about at a recent SEPG conference presentation about applications of Six Sigma to

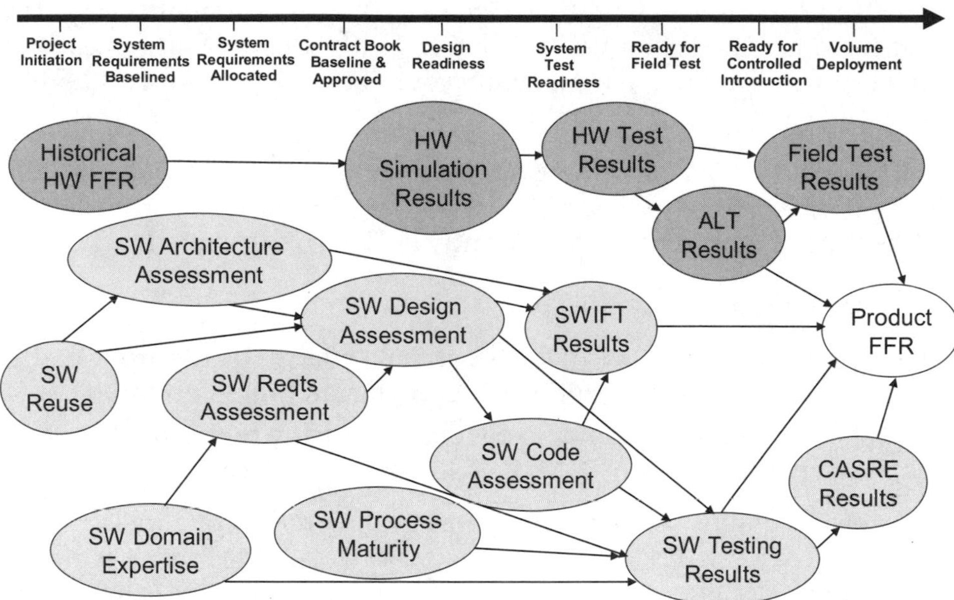

Figure 9–8: *Cause-and-effect model*

software engineering, as shown in Figures 9–8 and 9–9. Figure 9–8 shows a causal system that affects field reliability, and Figure 9–9 shows a prediction model for actual field defects based on knowledge of the underlying causal

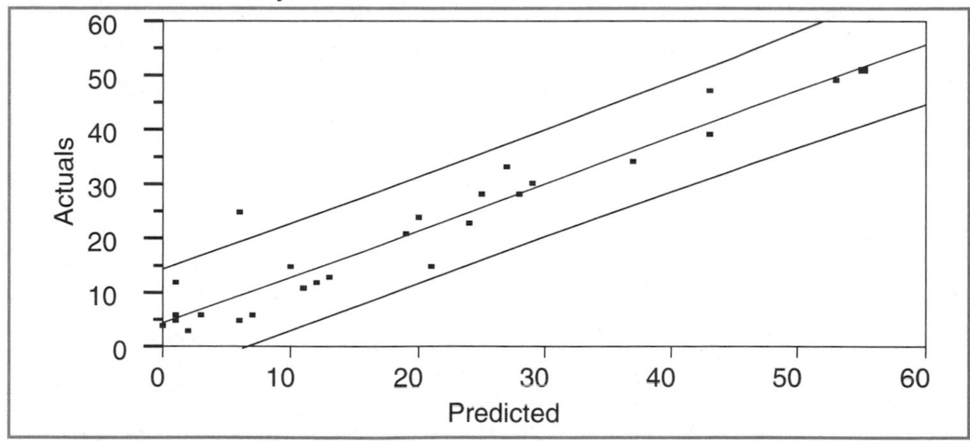

Actual field defects = f(CASRE predicted defects)
CASRE predicted defects = f(weekly arrival rate of SW failures, weekly test intensity measures)
$3M/year savings from premature SW releases

Figure 9–9: *CASRE predictions*

system. While these were long-term visions for the organization, their potential business benefit warranted their being in the idea pipeline as early as possible so that foundational capability could be built and so that the idea development and transition would be well timed.

9.2 Cost and Schedule Performance Improvement

This section presents a case study in:

- Using goal structures and DMAIC to navigate the fuzzy front end of problem definition and identify an improvement project portfolio
- Using a blended CMMI and Six Sigma approach where DMAIC served as the tactical engine for CMMI high maturity or high capability

A critical factor influencing customer satisfaction, product quality is a rather universal basis for setting organizational objectives. However, it is not always the most significant issue facing an organization. In this example, the Define, Measure, and Analyze steps of DMAIC, coupled with goal structures, are used to discover the highest-priority improvement opportunities and to establish SMART[2] objectives for a portfolio of improvement projects. In the ensuing effort, the analysis, improvement, and control mechanisms served as the necessary evidence to demonstrate compliance with several CMMI process areas' practices.

While case studies are often designed for simplicity and singular representation of problems and solutions, this particular one focuses on the fuzzy front end of problem definition and involves the balancing of several methods, models, and tools on the journey to improvement. Relative to the CMMI and Six Sigma joint deployment strategies, it shows the use of Six Sigma as a tactical engine to achieve high maturity. More specifically, in the pursuit of CMMI high maturity, organizations must select subprocesses for statistical management, with the aim of optimizing them and achieving the desired level of process capability. Often organizations face this challenge with limited experience in applying quantitative methods to processes. As a result, they look to the literature and try to emulate the success stories they read about. This example describes how this organization navigated this situation. Lastly, this example also portrays the reality that software improvement personnel sometimes must manage the risk of moving forward with limited data.

---

[2] Specific, measurable, attainable or agreed-upon, relevant or realistic, timely or timebound.

Note that while much of this case study focuses on organization-level metrics and improvement, it does contain useful information for those who may be pursuing improvement efforts in a more localized fashion, whether at low or high maturity. In particular, the project management model developed as part of the analysis effort could be easily implemented using project data, in the absence of organizational baselines. In fact, were such a model built while at lower maturity, it could have created the foundation on which the achievement of high maturity could have been accelerated—thereby exemplifying the synergistic relationship of the CMMI and Six Sigma.

9.2.1 Organizational Context

This large organization develops and maintains software-intensive systems of varying size and complexity. Project durations range from less than 1 month to more than 18 months. The organization was assessed at SW-CMM level 3 five years prior to the effort described here. At the time of this project, it was working toward CMMI high maturity, striving to implement process areas to add value, not just achieve compliance.

Figure 9–10 depicts the organizational structure established to support the process improvement journey.

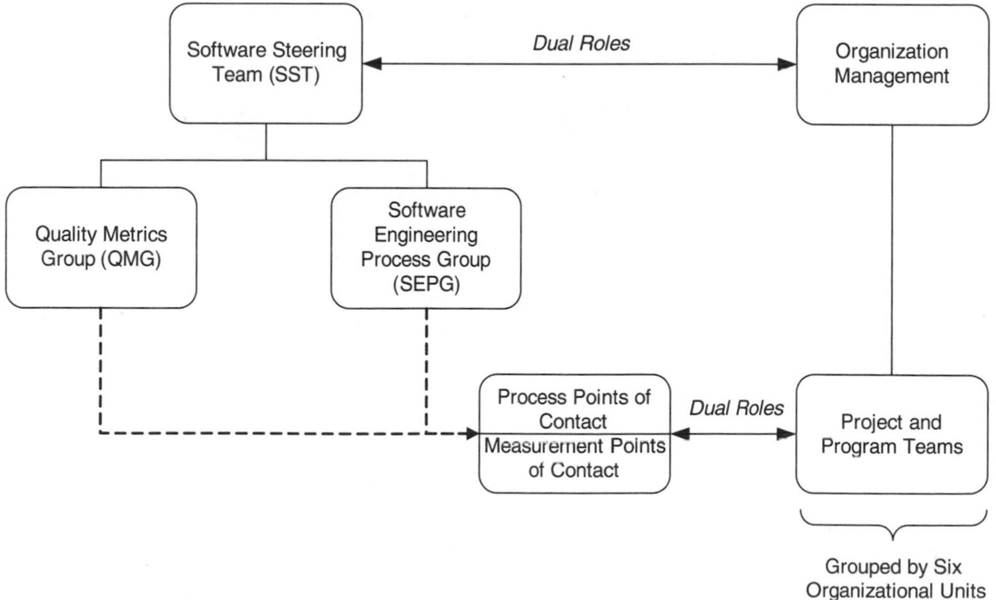

Figure 9–10: *Organizational structure*

9.2.2 Initial Project Definition

The organization had established several strategic business objectives.

- Improve customer satisfaction.
- Establish a common organizational process.
- Improve employee satisfaction.
- Improve business opportunities.
- Improve communications.
- Establish a skills database.

Improving customer satisfaction was selected as the objective to focus on to satisfy CMMI high-maturity process area requirements. Because this organization was relatively new to the use of analytical methods, it engaged with an external resource to determine how to proceed.

Together, they began by creating a simple goal structure to further narrow attention to cost and schedule performance and product quality, as shown in Figure 9–11. As described in Chapter 8, establishing an explicit line of sight to

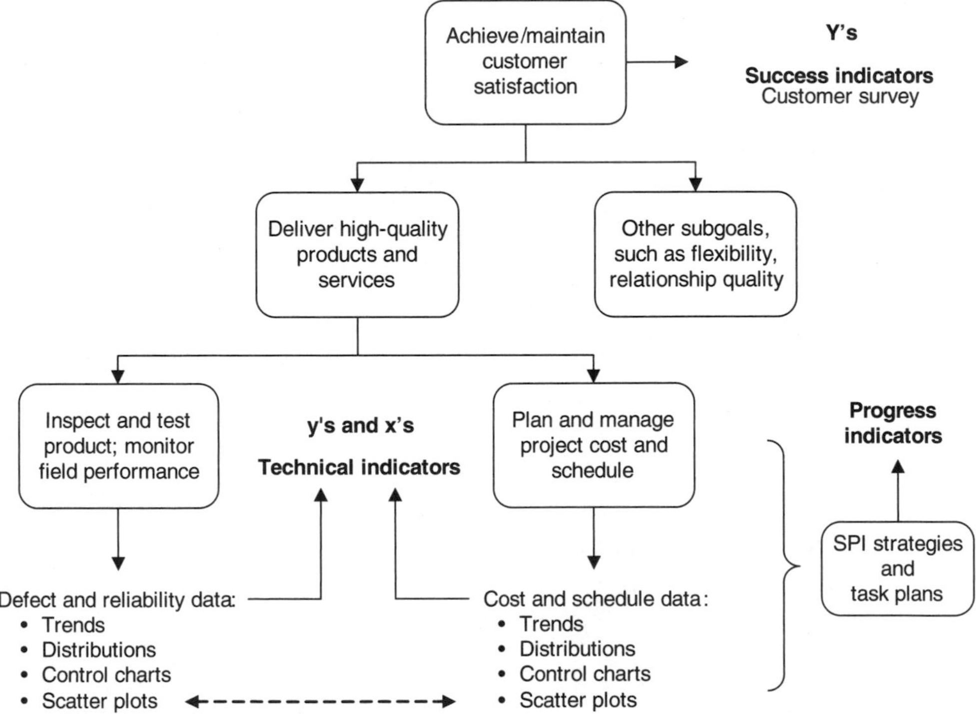

Figure 9–11: *Goal structure*

the strategic objective was useful for engaging the organization in the development, transition, and success measurement of the resulting improvement efforts.

Figure 9–11 is annotated with analyses and indicator types. This diagram was used early in the effort to explain the proposed analysis approach to both managers and newly appointed measurement points of contact. The proposal included several areas of effort.

- Define a measurement process and update the existing organizational measurement plan based on the practices and tools of the CMMI, DMAIC, and GQIM. This process is shown in Figure 9–12. The measurement plan document, which listed required organizational and project measures, was updated to include indicator templates for all graphically displayed data.
    - Note that the defined process includes an iterative loop to gather and analyze data and prioritize issues prior to commencing causal analysis of specific opportunities that would drive business value. In Six Sigma parlance, this roughly equated to conducting a DMA-DMAIC project.
- Conduct data analysis for the high-level objective of customer satisfaction as well as for the key process results of cost and schedule performance as well as product quality. Baselines for and relationships between these measures would be constructed. Additionally, relationships to other factors would be explored. The intent was that the analysis would inform and enable the creation of a detailed process performance improvement plan.
    - Note that all exploratory analyses would be conducted offline but in partnership with innovator and early adopter measurement points of contact. A series of working meetings was scheduled with all measurement points of contact. In turn, these points of contact held key responsibilities to champion and aid the transition of the analysis method to the rest of the workforce.
- Build process performance models, to serve business needs as well as comply with the CMMI due to resource and time constraints. Pending the results of initial data analysis, it was decided to develop organizational models that would be initially inherited by all programs and projects. These models would be tested or piloted with projects associated with the innovator and early adopter measurement points of contact. People working on projects or programs who wished to tailor the models or develop their own would be permitted to do so, within the constraints of the defined process and the CMMI implementation requirements.

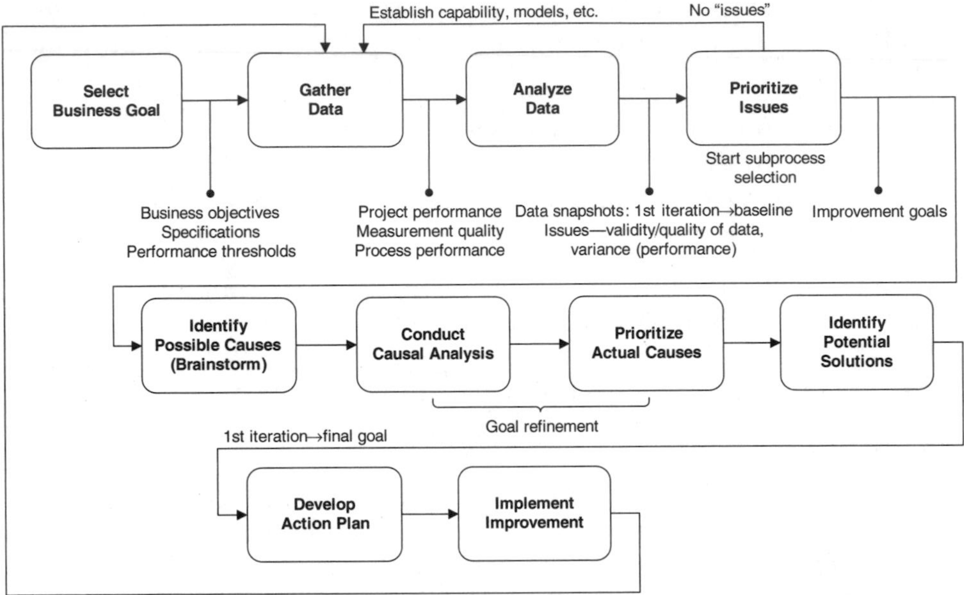

Figure 9–12: *Measurement process*

9.2.3 Project Implementation: DMAIC

Measure

The initial data collection included the measures listed in Table 9–1. At the beginning of this project, survey data, inspection data, and monthly cost and schedule variance data were available in manually maintained databases. All other data sets were constructed manually, using source data from project managers' files.

Data were quickly examined for quality and charted for the purpose of narrowing the scope of the project. Two primary outcomes resulted.

1. Numerous measurement infrastructure improvements were identified, such as:
   - Updating the customer satisfaction survey to use scoring aligned with organizational objectives and goal structure
   - Establishing real-time data validation guidelines
   - Improving data collection automation
   - Incorporating closed project data into a central repository

Table 9–1: *Initial Data Collection and Evaluation*

Y or y	Data	Performance Goal	Initial Data Quality	Initial Evaluation
Customer satisfaction	Postproject survey Client e-mails	Not yet established	Few data points Qualitative responses	Satisfied customers
Product quality	Inspection data, including defect types, inspection effort, rework Field defect data	0 field defects	Data skewed toward low-priority defects because significant defects are preinspected out during desk checks Significant variance in operational definitions of in-process defects	Effective inspection process Few field defects (4 per year for previous 2 years)
Cost and schedule performance	Monthly cost and schedule variance relative to most recent estimate Final project cost and schedule variance, including categorization by causes and lifecycle phase*	+/– 20% monthly variance (for some portions of organization, +/– 10% variance, based on customer requirements)	Effect of replanning on performance not well understood In the monthly data set, a mix of projects at all stages of completion, even though performance is expected to be different Sparse data, with some parts of organization barely represented Extreme outliers present	Overall averages nearly centered at 0% variance But, significant variability, with approximately 20% of monthly data outside of spec and 40% of closed project data outside of spec

*Closed project variance was calculated using the initial plan and the final actual values. This formula did not mask customer-driven changes or project replans.

- Grouping project data according to lifecycle phase or percentage complete
- Clarifying operational definitions of all data

2. Cost and schedule data performance was identified as the primary improvement opportunity and the higher priority for process modeling for the CMMI implementation.

Noting that the surveyed customers indicated satisfaction with products and services provided by this organization despite the variability in cost and schedule performance, cost and schedule performance (and proposed improvement) was realigned to a new strategic objective, as shown in Figure 9–13.

The second iteration of the data collection, data quality evaluation and baselining, focused on the cost and schedule data. Extreme values and suspected outliers were evaluated and dispositioned. The evaluation of data quality issues was completed at a more detailed level.

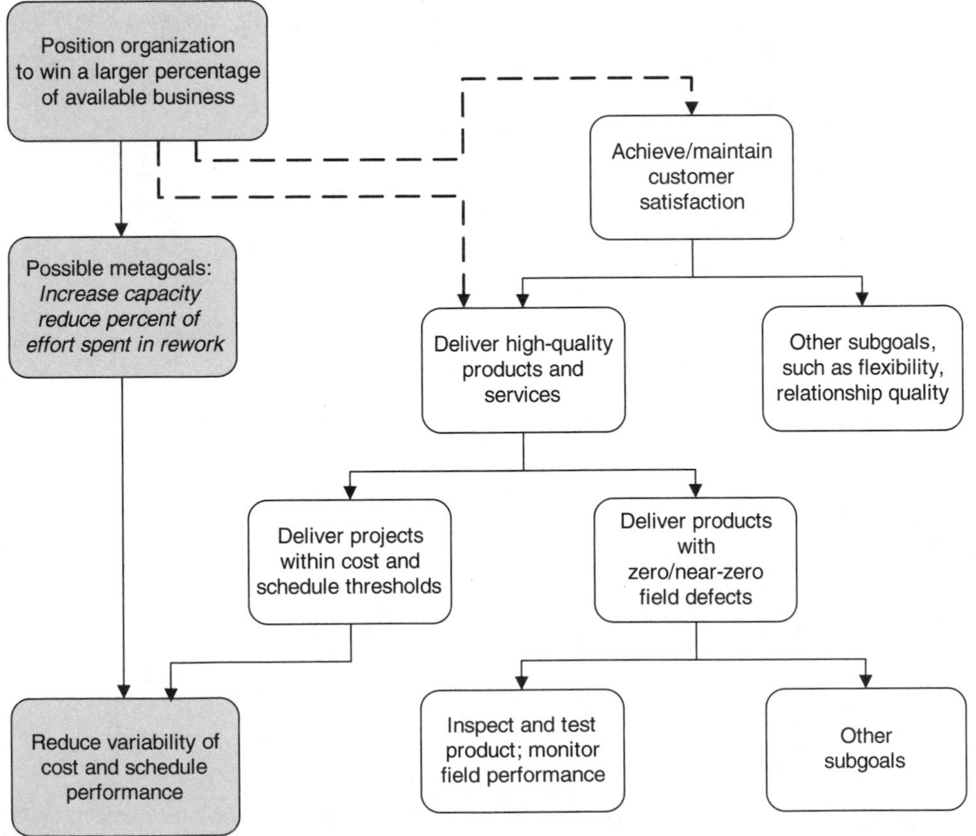

Figure 9–13: *Goal realignment*

- Accuracy
  - Biased data due to rebaselining, promoting the perception that performance is better than it actually is
- Repeatability
  - Different estimating methods across the lifecycle, across projects
  - Unclear definition of *project*
  - Incomplete records about project replans
- Completeness
  - Some needed project types excluded from the data set
  - Sparse data—some parts of the organization better represented than others
  - Completed project data missing from organization data
- Sampling
  - All monthly data rolled together, regardless of the part of lifecycle represented

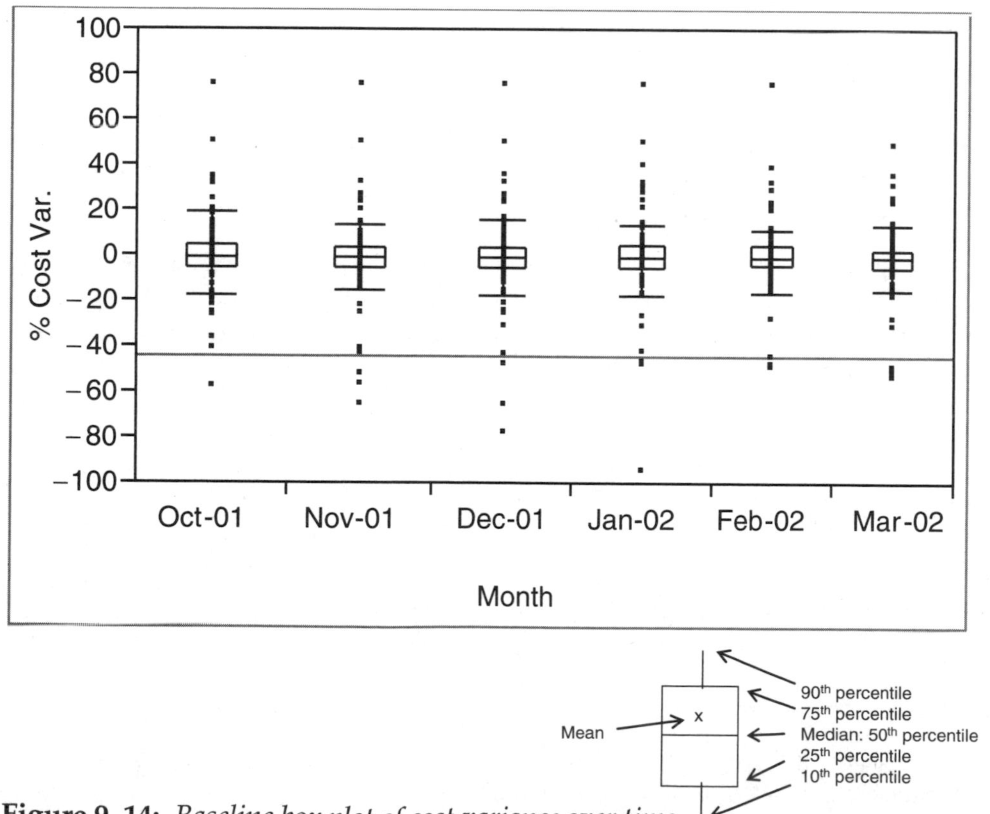

Figure 9–14: *Baseline box plot of cost variance over time*

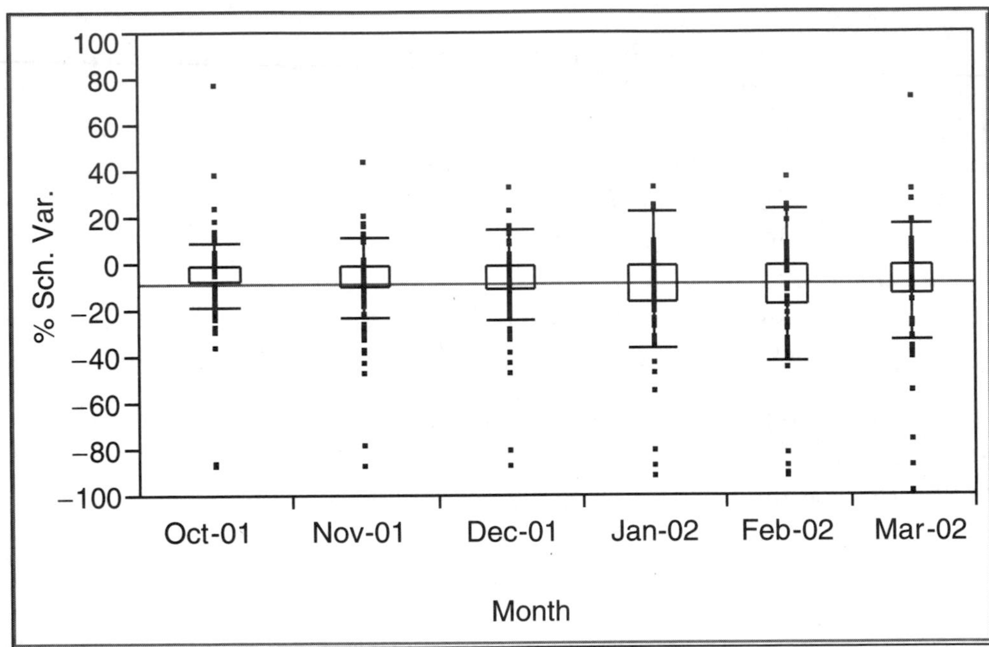

Figure 9–15: *Baseline box plot of schedule variance over time*

Baselines were represented as simple descriptive statistics, as well as histograms, box plots, and trend charts. Figures 9–14 and 9–15 and Table 9–2 show a sampling of these charts.

A management dashboard was assembled to monitor customer, defect, cost and schedule, and measurement infrastructure improvement data. This helped mitigate the risk that the organizational focus on cost and schedule might divert attention from and allow undesirable trends in other areas to occur.

Table 9–2: *Baseline Descriptive Statistics*

Statistic	Cost Variance	Schedule Variance
Average	–2%	13%
Standard deviation	33%	36%
Median	2%	7%
Minimum to maximum	–95% to +50%	–128% to +71%
Capability notes (specification = +/– 20%)	43.8% outside specification	39% outside specification

Analyze

The cost and schedule data were explored for possible drivers of variation. The initial exploration was limited to sources of variation included in the initial data set. For instance, completed project data were segmented by lifecycle phases where variances were perceived to have originated and also by causal categories of internal (i.e., project, organization) versus external (i.e., customer requirements). Monthly data were segmented by organizational unit and by percentage completed.

The initial exploration helped to characterize the cost and schedule variability but did not reveal definitive drivers of variation. A causal analysis workshop was held with the measurement points of contact to establish a cause code taxonomy for cost and schedule variance:

- Missed requirements
- Underestimated task
- Overcommitment of personnel
- Skills mismatch
- Unavailable tools
- Earned value problem
- Planned work not performed
- External
- Other

In addition to building these cause codes into the data collection system, they were retrospectively assigned to over a year's worth of data. Pareto analysis was conducted for both schedule and cost (effort) for the overall organization and for two organizational subsets. Recognizing the issues with data archaeology, this analysis, summarized in Table 9–3, revealed that underestimated tasks, unavailable tools, earned value problems, and missed requirements were the high-priority issues. Each cause code was further evaluated for possible root causes of variation—both common cause and special cause. And for each of these causes, the measurement points of contact identified relevant processes and subprocesses to characterize, to statistically manage (in CMMI parlance), and possibly to improve.

For instance, the underestimated tasks cause code was associated with the process of project management and the subprocesses of requirements establishment, project process definition, detailed planning, and requirements management. Root causes of the common cause variation were hypothesized to include two main factors. The first was the organization's inexperience with executing its overall defined estimation process. The second was the inexperience of the estimators in performing estimation tasks, particularly assigning accurate estimate levels to work. Root causes of the special cause variation included budget issues. The prioritization of these root causes involved a balance of logical analysis (e.g., What is in our sphere of influence? What is resolved in-process?), statistical evaluation (e.g., How frequently does the cause occur? How large is the variance that it contributes?), and methodical evaluation (e.g., What are the failure modes and their effects?).

At the completion of this exploratory analysis and problem characterization, the organization was able to update the project scope with SMART goal statements, such as:

Reduce the total schedule variance by decreasing the variance of the top three causes by 50% in one year.

Problem statements, associated performance history, and prioritized root causes were documented in MBF summaries. This tool was integrated into the organizational processes for causal analysis and organizational innovation.

Thus far, all the effort had an organizational focus, which was consistent with the maturity model structure and would certainly benefit the organization's collection of product development projects. However, it did not yet address the day-to-day management of individual projects. Therefore, the organization pursued the establishment of a project-level model that would both incorporate the organizational analysis and integrate with the established project management norms. Because of resource constraints and because the measurement point of contact was still a fairly new role (i.e., early in the learning curve), the improvement group decided to develop a set of common project-level models whose structure and capability limits would be inherited by each project until it could establish project-specific limits and/or models.

Such a model would need to inform the decision-making process of the project manager and help distinguish the need for project-level process corrections versus project-level process improvement versus organizational-level process improvement. Because project managers in this organization routinely used earned value, the organizational cost and schedule historical data were transformed for use on the estimate at completion chart. A different set of ranges was used when projects were between 20% and 80% complete and when they were greater than 80% complete.

Table 9–3: *Pareto Analysis Multimap*

Impact Rank	Schedule	Effort	Organization Slice 1 Schedule	Organization Slice 1 Effort	Organization Slice 2 Schedule	Organization Slice 2 Effort
1	Underestimated task	Unavailable tools	Underestimated task	Underestimated task	Unavailable tools	Unavailable tools
2	Unavailable tools	Assets not available*	EV problems	Underplanned rework*	Skills mismatch	Underestimated task
3	EV problems	Underplanned rework*	Missed requirements	Missed requirements	Underestimated task	Missed requirements
4	Missed requirements	Planned work not performed	Underplanned rework*	EV problems	Missed requirements	Unexpected departure of personnel*
5	Skills mismatch	Underestimated task	Asset availability*	Planned work not performed	Unexpected departure of personnel*	EV problems

*These are other sources of variance, beyond the cause code taxonomy, that were ascertained during this initial analysis.

Figure 9–16 shows the specification and capability ranges for a project as it neared 50% completion. It shows that the capability range, based on the historical variability of the organization's projects, is larger than the specification ranges. This was enlightening for the project managers because most differences between the baseline and the calculated estimate at completion were now recognized as being within the normal variability.

Planned enhancements included the tailoring of limits based on project history, the organizational development of a robust prediction model, and the use of Monte Carlo simulation.

Improve and Control

Numerous improvement ideas were generated, including the following candidates for improving schedule variance.

- Develop tips for implementing Microsoft Project.
- Enhance the interface between project and EV data systems to automate data transfer.

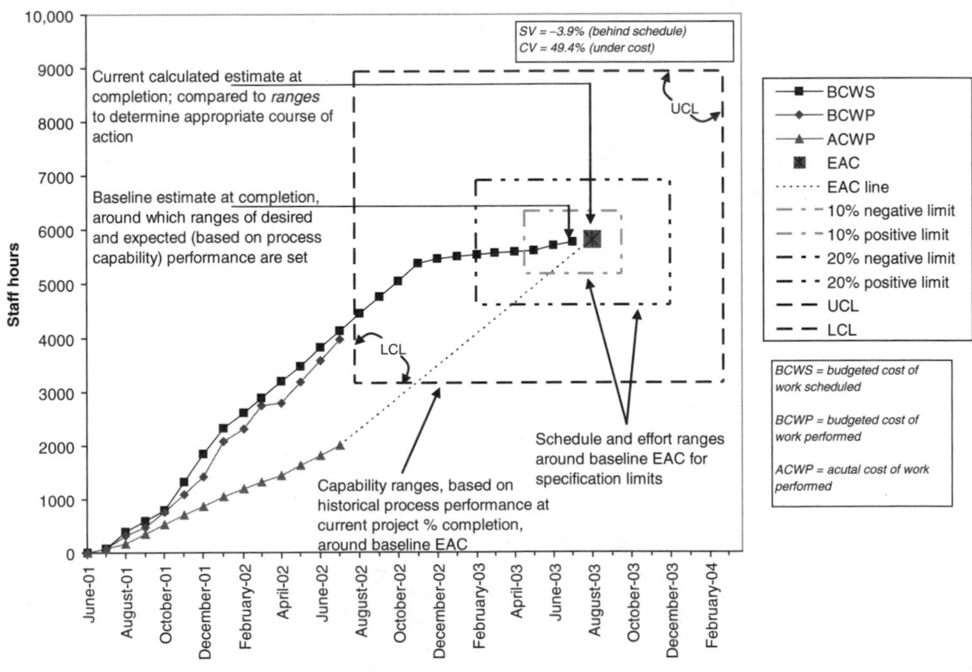

Figure 9–16: *Estimate at completion (EAC) model*

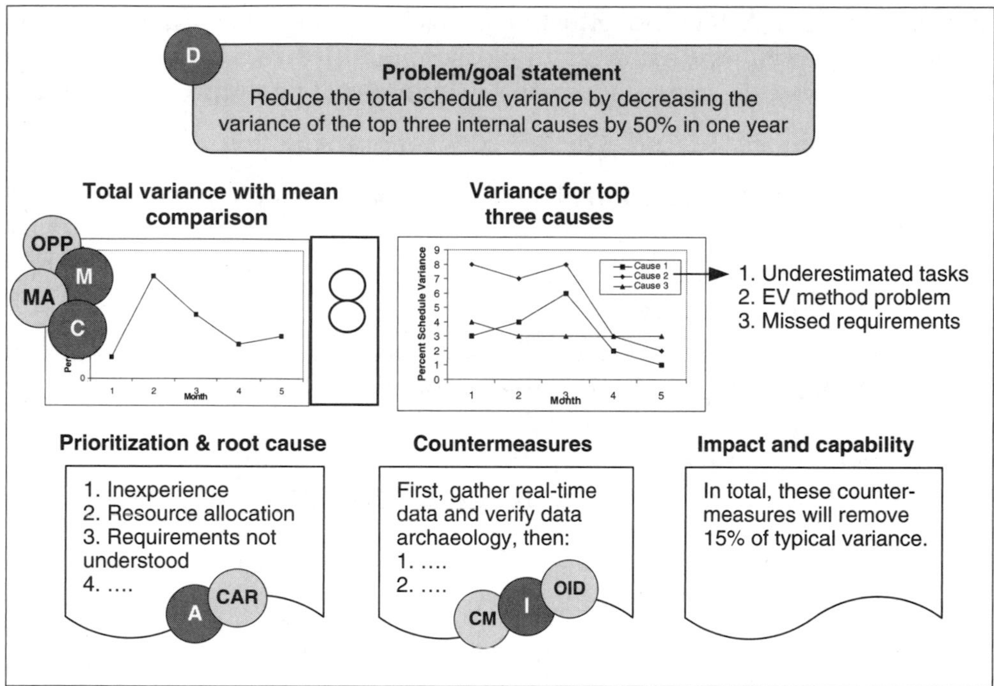

Figure 9–17: *MBF, reflecting improvement ideas*

- Teach an on-site class about successful techniques in project management.
- Identify a course in model-based estimating.
- Require a peer review of the project schedule before baselining.

These were reflected in the MBF (Figure 9–17). In compliance with the organizational innovation process, each selected improvement was chartered as a formal project, with resources, budget, schedule, and reporting requirements.

9.2.4 Closing Comments: Strategic Alignment, Level of Effort, and Results

With a strategic objective of customer satisfaction, this organization may have pursued development of a defect model to satisfy high-maturity practices of the CMMI. By incorporating the tactical engine of Six Sigma's DMAIC framework into the organizational approach, team members realized that a more significant business opportunity was to reduce cost and schedule variability both to address customer satisfaction and to enable business growth. Achieving reduction in cost and schedule variability necessitated numerous improvements to measurement infrastructure. Reduction in cost and schedule variance is a continuing effort at the time of this writing.

The elapsed time for the effort described was approximately two years:

- Seven months from the initial data collection to completion of the analysis
- Five months on hiatus while other CMMI activities consumed the limited organizational resources
- Twelve months to implement initial organizational improvements and institutionalize the use of the project model

9.3 Definition and Design of the Decision Analysis Process

This section presents a case study in:

- Using Lean/Six Sigma techniques to kick off a CMMI-based process implementation

This example demonstrates how Lean/Six Sigma techniques can be used to define CMMI processes within an organization. Establishing process within an organization is the first step toward standards compliance. It establishes the project (level 2) or organization's (level 3) process focus. The definition of the project's or organization's standard process is necessary for consistency within the project and among projects in the organization.

Lean/Six Sigma techniques frequently are used to optimize or monitor a defined process but less often thought to be a tool for process definition. Yet the toolset identified with Lean/Six Sigma gives the user the basis for establishing a process that best fits the needs of the project or organization.

9.3.1 Organizational Context

This example is set in the context of LMCO M&DS's transition from the CMM to the CMMI, as described in Chapter 5. One maturity level 3 process area, new to M&DS due to the switch to the CMMI, was Decision Analysis and Resolution (DAR). In this case study, DAR was integrated into the organizational process, with attention to the following considerations and questions.

- Did the identified decision processes fully represent the needs of the business?

- Did the decision processes comply with DAR?
- Were decisions being analyzed and resolved consistently across the organization?
- Did the decision process contain any waste?
- Were decision resolutions tracked, measured, and improved?
- Did the decision process listen to the voice of the customer?

9.3.2 Initial Project Definition

At the outset of this project, decisions were being made, but formal analysis and methods for decision resolution were not clearly established. People at many engineering organizations think, as did M&DS at this point, that the only decisions that require analysis are associated with trade studies. Trade studies are well established within the development organization, but they are just a small example and one type of functional decisions. The risk process was also very well defined with risk analysis and resolution/mitigation techniques. Again, this did not include all of the decisions made by management. There are also varying levels of responsibilities within a project or organization. These tiers all have their responsibilities; thus, decisions need to be delegated throughout the organization, allowing the appropriate delegation of authority and not allowing a single-point failure.

DAR was clearly an area that needed to be further defined and at the same time refined to assure it was the best process it could be. The organization also needed visibility into the effectiveness of its decision-making capability. This meant not just measuring the consistency and lapsed time but also determining how many decisions were overturned, how many resulted in negative results (a very subjective measure), and whether they were answering the demands internally and externally.

The program needed a single, robust decision process that could be used by many different roles, in many different contexts, and could satisfy both the internal and external customers.

9.3.3 Project Implementation: Kaizen

It was decided that the best approach would be to conduct a Kaizen Event. M&DS started at the program level, to develop an as-is framework. This resulted in the documentation of many required activities. The decision processes documented were frequently rooted in organizational processes for decisions. These were proposal submittal decisions, formal contract change requests, and other business-specific decisions. However, some decisions very specific to particular programs and customers also needed oversight and leaning. M&DS mapped a few typical programs, trying to capture different customers in the mix also. Program mappings included decisions that could be made within the program as well as those decisions that needed M&DS organizational resolution or customer resolution.

M&DS then started peeling the onion. Decisions were evaluated one by one (grouped where possible and appropriate), waste was identified, and a to-be state was determined. The to-be state was then compared to the requirements of the CMMI to determine compliance. The programs that participated then piloted the to-be process and reconvened to discuss results. For decisions that were indicative of this program, the program's operating procedures were modified. For organizational decisions that were optimized during this event, appropriate changes were made to the organizational documentation. Most of the organizational changes were directly to the Program Process Standard (PPS), with very little collateral documentation (with the exception of recommended analysis techniques) needing to be added.

Beyond establishing a decision process at the program level, a goal was set to integrate the decision analysis process into the organizational business rhythm. The process was dissected to identify the following:

- Affected documentation (actions for change and approval)
- Required communications (program communications and organizational communications)
- Required training (determination of existing training courses to be offered and any additional courses to be initiated, as well as who the audience should be)

Another Kaizen Event was then scheduled and conducted at the M&DS level for those program decisions that went upward and for business decisions (typically related to procurement and purchases). The enterprise activities spilled into a number of other process areas, which resulted in improvements that would not have been as easily diagnosed without this event. These process areas included but were not limited to:

- Technical Solution (TS), in the specific use of case studies
- Organizational Innovation and Deployment (OID), in selecting processes for improvement and subsequent deployment decisions
- Causal Analysis and Resolution (CAR), in the sampling decisions and deployment of process improvement

The results of the individual Kaizen Events as well as the other identified process improvements were analyzed. The process definitions and improvements were put into a Get to Excellence Plan. Some specific actions addressed included the following:

- Defining appropriate decision criteria
- Determining how to delegate authority and defining criteria for who could make which decisions
- Choosing and involving other individuals to cross-check and approve decisions
- Defining the communication methods for decisions
- Defining the records to be kept from the decision analysis process

This plan was broken down into actions assigned to the appropriate individuals or functional organizations. The actions were then mapped to an overall rollout, training, and communication plan across M&DS. Some actions required a pilot activity before introduction into the organization. An analysis of each action to determine its point of introduction was also done—a change to the organizational standard process, tailoring guidance depending on the size or type of project, or a best practice recommendation. The actions were also integrated into the organization's existing Process Improvement Plan in order to minimize the impact to the organization and optimize timely rollout.

The Kaizen team also defined measurements of success. Once the rollout commenced, a Kaizen member was responsible for working with the measurement group to track and ensure that the event was a success. These measurements enabled the organization to address questions about why the model and its new processes were being adopted.

Creating the Kaizen final report also included working with a finance person assigned to the particular team to set up the business case figures. Adoption costs were calculated. These included publication changes and generation, process training, and communication and tracking costs. The finance guru then projected the cost of implementing the to-be process in order to determine the business cost of the process definition. Each step of the as-is baseline was required to have a cost. As the to-be steps were established, costs from the as-is baseline were moved over, eliminated, or minimized, or if an additional step were put in, an estimation of effort was required. This financial analysis gave the organization a true cost of doing business.

After the Kaizen Event, there was a facilitated lessons learned session. The biggest lesson learned was that the organization shouldn't limit process definitions to a few participants, but rather should broaden the base. This not only gives buy-in but also allows insights that can often be lost or, worse, never solicited. This is in keeping with good change management practices and the reality that a process group is valued if it embraces the organization and listens to the users.

9.3.4 Closing Comments: Success Factors and Results

Allowing a structured approach to defining the process, involving relevant stakeholders, and being able to baseline the current situation in order to map the new destination were critical to the successful definition and adoption of the process. The team composition and follow-up activities were also critical to the success of the rollout at both the program and enterprise levels. Customer involvement at the program-level Kaizen Events was another benefit since it set expectations against an interface that has the customer's expectations built in. Common communications and understandings by all parties were another critical success factor.

The importance of the Kaizen Event or any other Lean/Six Sigma strategy is to focus on an issue, get the right parties involved, and then talk, analyze, and ultimately roll out a solution. In this case, the issues were related to process integration and DAR adoption as a step toward maintaining the M&DS maturity level 5 within the CMMI. This approach was instrumental in coming up with a lean process definition for a new process area in the CMMI.

When this project began, the process existed but was not fully integrated or documented within the organization. The process was clearly ad hoc and lacked the discipline of a formal process. The new process reduced the time and number of individuals involved when analyzing, resolving, and communicating decisions. Streamlining of the records kept and artifacts produced during the decision analysis phase also occurred. The customer satisfaction level definitely improved. Decision analysis and resolution activities were now auditable to the new process—no subsequent audit findings were initiated after the adoption of the modified process. The process was integrated into the program's business rhythm. There was also a significant reduction in decision reversal, which resulted in less rework.

9.4 IT Operations: Value Stream Mapping with IT Tools

This section presents a case study in:

- Establishing a collaborative customer and IT project management process

Often within an organization various support and services functions exist. These functions support the organization, similar to how subcontractors or suppliers service customers. However, these functions, because they are part of the same organization or enterprise as their customer, often do not have disciplined processes to assist them in providing the services. A subcontractor or supplier outside the enterprise has processes in place to collect requirements, review progress, and formally interface with the customer. With internal support and services functions, since the customer is also "them," this part of the management and delivery of services is often ignored. This is especially bad in setting expectations both ways.

Value stream mapping is an excellent tool used to illustrate the current state, identify problem areas, and design a new process. Having both the customer and the service providers in the same room plotting the course forward saves time and sets the proper expectations for both.

9.4.1 Organizational Context

The activities described in this case study were performed after the adoption of the CMMI and the achievement of CMMI maturity level 5. This example demonstrates the joint use of the CMMI and Lean/Six Sigma to establish an IT process that would meet the needs of a mature organization. This mature organization was accustomed to and expected mature, disciplined processes and data-driven decision making.

Serving only IS&S, the IT organization in this example provides tool support, maintains the overall IS&S portal, assists in tool trade studies, interfaces with the corporate office for IS&S/LMCO alignment issues, and mainly offers tool support to various functional and business areas within IS&S. This project was initiated jointly by the IT group and its internal customers. The IT group had found that many systemic issues among their customers required a scrutiny that a Lean event could accommodate.

IS&S and the IT group have many interactions. These include but are not limited to:

- Maintenance of current applications
- Major upgrades of current applications
- Evaluation of potential new applications

IS&S and the IT group needed to establish a working relationship, with the following considerations.

- A smooth operating interface saves time, money, and rework.
- Both organizations need to understand each other and work well together.

- Both organizations work with specific constraints and guidance.
- This is a long-term relationship that needs to work well!

9.4.2 Initial Project Definition

IS&S application owners had been dissatisfied with the partnership between IS&S and the IT group. Unfamiliarity with the IT group's processes and unclear roles and responsibilities had resulted in the perception of unnecessary rework and unmet expectations.

Lack of communication between the IT group and the application owners had resulted in misunderstanding, rework, and unmet expectations on both sides. The following were major points of concern:

1. Continuity of IT resources
2. Establishment of standard status meetings
3. Clarity of roles and responsibilities

These concerns were manifested basically because of the following:

1. Minimal insight into the processes that the IT group used for project management, application development, and maintenance support
2. Lack of planning and oversight related to:
   - Basis of estimates
   - Schedules without interim milestones
   - Validation of requirements
   - Planning for levels of verification
3. Uneven responsiveness to ad hoc requests

There was a definite cooperation problem between the IT organization and its customer. No clear understanding existed of how they needed to operate throughout the production phase. The idea of buying something off the shelf was not correct. However, the customer was not expected to redesign the product on a daily basis. The actual relationship, including ways to collaborate on product development, needed to be defined. This project was expected to result in better planning, mutually understood requirements, appropriate end user visibility, and less rework.

Expectations were set for the IT and IS&S relationship during the event kick-off.

- Create the basis for understanding, clear roles and responsibilities, and a strong relationship going forward.
- Establish a team attitude.

- No "us versus them" mentality
- Positive and open communications
- One vision to work toward

9.4.3 Project Implementation: Value Stream Mapping

For this particular process activity, a value stream mapping (VSM) was used. A team was identified including IT representatives and various IS&S customers and stakeholders. The as-is process was mapped prior to the start of the event. It was determined that the IT group treated all projects as operation and maintenance, which lacked formal processes. Another difficulty stemmed from the IT group's workload. Different work projects with different required expertise at unplanned times caused resources to be moved from project to project, which disrupted the work being done and was disconcerting to the customers. Also, the IT group had always had limited customer involvement due to the fact that many IS&S customers viewed IT services and projects as a shrink-wrap capability and therefore did not want an interface. Because of the nature of their work, IT staff did not solicit customer involvement and therefore had frequent rework situations because they had not embraced any verification or validation exercises.

Deliverables for the project included clearly defined customer engagement points in the IT process, such as:

- Involvement in creating a comprehensive schedule
- Customer validation milestones
- Entry and exit criteria for customer validation points
  - Clearly defined customer and project team roles and responsibilities throughout the product lifecycle
  - Clearly defined criteria regarding when an operation and maintenance process versus a development process should be followed for mission-critical applications
- A process for management of ad hoc requests, estimation, and work authorization, including a standard status and reporting mechanism with objective evidence

The processes used to assist the customer and the IT group were the processes that had been established when adopting the CMMI on development programs within IS&S. IS&S has a history of bringing the CMMI into areas where it otherwise is not identified. The IS&S IR&D programs—quick one-year production cycles—have used the PPS for years, and the productivity of these projects has increased by 30%.

The as-is evaluation resulted in three specific changes.

1. The IT group and the IS&S customer would define a project as either large or small. This definition would be established as part of the excellence plan.
2. Large IT projects would use tailored processes based on those used for IS&S development projects.
3. There would be much more customer involvement in the planning, tracking, and requirements phases of the IT projects.

The expected outcomes included better planning, less rework, and better requirement maturity, which would enable the IT group to stabilize resources for a customer's IT project. For each specific engagement, the expectations would be set up front between the IT group and its customer.

The following measurements were established in order to determine the effects of the changes identified:

- Planned versus actual cost and schedule
- Defect removal counts at various steps
- No-go decision statistics
- Number of feature requests
- Percentage of hitting milestone dates
- Number of status meeting participants
    - Steady number
    - More or fewer participants
- Customer survey results

A Get to Excellence Plan was generated with 47 specific actions identified—including process documentation, training, communication, deployment, and feedback. Sixteen specific risks were identified and ranked, and mitigation plans were put in place for each. As a result, a budget was established that included projected cost of development and deployment and estimated savings as a result of deployment. This plan was then reviewed with the event sponsor and functional process owners for the go-ahead. Once this occurred, the plan was deployed. The plan included schedule, budget, and resource sections and was monitored on a monthly basis with the owners.

9.4.4 Closing Comments: Results

The results were very successful.

- Rework decreased by 50%.

- Discrepancies at production and acceptance decreased by 20%.
- Customer satisfaction as a result of customer involvement improved 100%.
- Milestone completion on cost and schedule increased to 90%.

Other benefits from the event included the following:

- Improved customer communications
- Better understanding of the process
- Improved product quality, with fewer defects after deployment
- Clear knowledge (rather than assumptions) of what the customer actually values

9.5 Performance Modeling and Simulation

This section presents a high-level case study in:

- Instantiating DFSS in a systems engineering organization
- Exploring how critical-to-customer requirements, quality function deployment (QFD), failure modes and effects analysis (FMEA), and other methods are used to inform the development of performance models and simulations

Many issues are associated with implementing DFSS within systems engineering tasks. However, DFSS cannot be implemented without forethought—formal planning and identification of participants, including roles and responsibilities, and lifecycles. The CMMI plays a role in this execution, specifically associated with the CMMI version 1.2 requirement for modeling and simulation. Discussions here are focused on the benefits of DFSS as it pertains to the modeling and simulation activities.

9.5.1 Organizational Context

DFSS and the CMMI

Design for Six Sigma is a systematic methodology applied to product development. Product development efforts often suffer from the expense of overdesigning systems. There are many reasons for this, including the concern about designing to accommodate worst-case specification limits for requirements. This can also occur when the product performance variation is of so much concern that the product team focuses on the performance variation at the elements level. This low-level-variation concern can overwhelm the design with unnecessary precautions.

The CMMI has been implemented to ensure that the development process is mature, and generally CMMI maturity level 3 or higher has been a prerequisite to implementing DFSS in an organization. Without this level of process maturity, the measurement and analysis processes are inadequate for DFSS.

In contrast to improving the maturity of a product organization to improve the *process* capability of the development organization with the CMMI, DFSS is used to focus the organization's processes toward the *product's* performance. By evaluating the performance variation or probability of nonconformance along the related key characteristics (KCs) to a particular characteristic that is critical to the customer (CTC), the organization can allocate targets to design elements based on achievable parameters in turn based on past performance or modeled future performance.

DFSS and the Product Development Lifecycle

For Design for Six Sigma to be effective in an organization, it is imperative to communicate the key characteristics, specification targets and limits, and responsibilities throughout the organization's functions. The key steps in the DFSS methodology can be summarized into the following three areas:

1. Identifying and tracking, in a detailed way, the characteristics critical to the customer and the underlying features, KCs, driving the performance of these CTC characteristics
2. Predicting the probabilities of meeting the customer requirements by analyzing the capabilities of the underlying features and entering those capabilities into models of the dependence of the critical characteristics on the underlying feature
3. Altering the product design or the processes that support it to attain acceptable probabilities of meeting the requirements

The preceding tasks are accomplished in the design phase, *before* manufacturing begins. As the design is implemented, the predictive performance is validated and verified through testing and evaluation. Figure 9–18 illustrates the general DFSS process for a product development effort.

Unlike other initiatives such as Lean and Six Sigma, Design for Six Sigma is not an add-on function that can be delegated to a quality, mission success, LM21, or other support organization. In successful deployments at Lockheed Martin, DFSS has been built into the company's engineering practices and

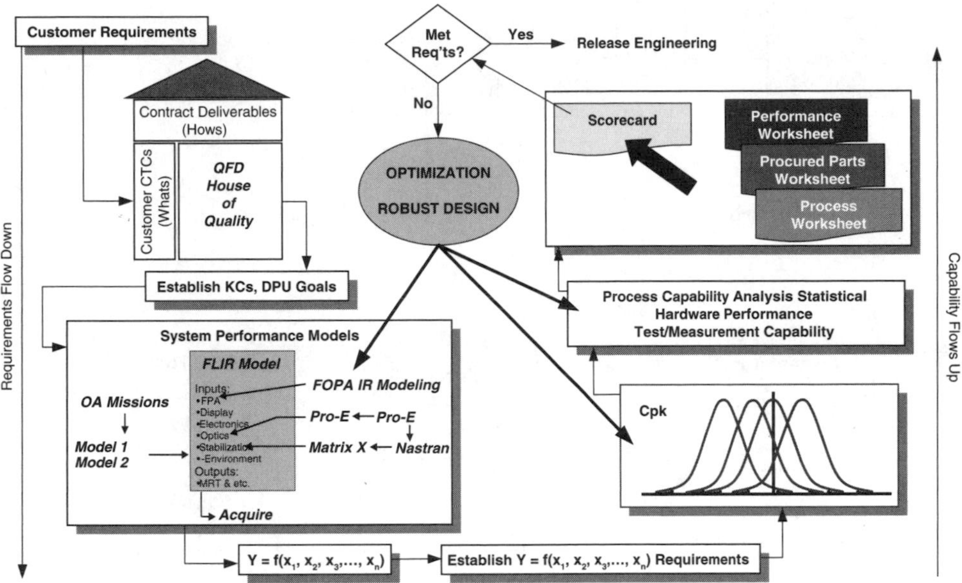

Figure 9–18: *DFSS methodology in product development*

procedures. It has been championed and driven by engineering senior leadership in organizations. Business objectives and personnel evaluations are tied into DFSS objectives.

DFSS can be deployed at the program level, where it is built into the development plan and championed and driven by program management.

DFSS Roles and Responsibilities

A successful DFSS deployment requires a team that comprises all of the key functions that contribute to defining the product (and its constraints), designing the product, testing the product, manufacturing the product, and servicing the product. Some of the representatives see the project from beginning to end; others contribute only during specific phases. Figure 9–19 illustrates the use of subject matter experts (SMEs) in the organization of the DFSS deployment.

Proper representation by function is important; if the selected representative does not have the requisite functional expertise and knowledge, his or her contribution will be negligible (and sometimes negative). Each team member has specific duties and responsibilities that must be effectively carried out to make the project successful.

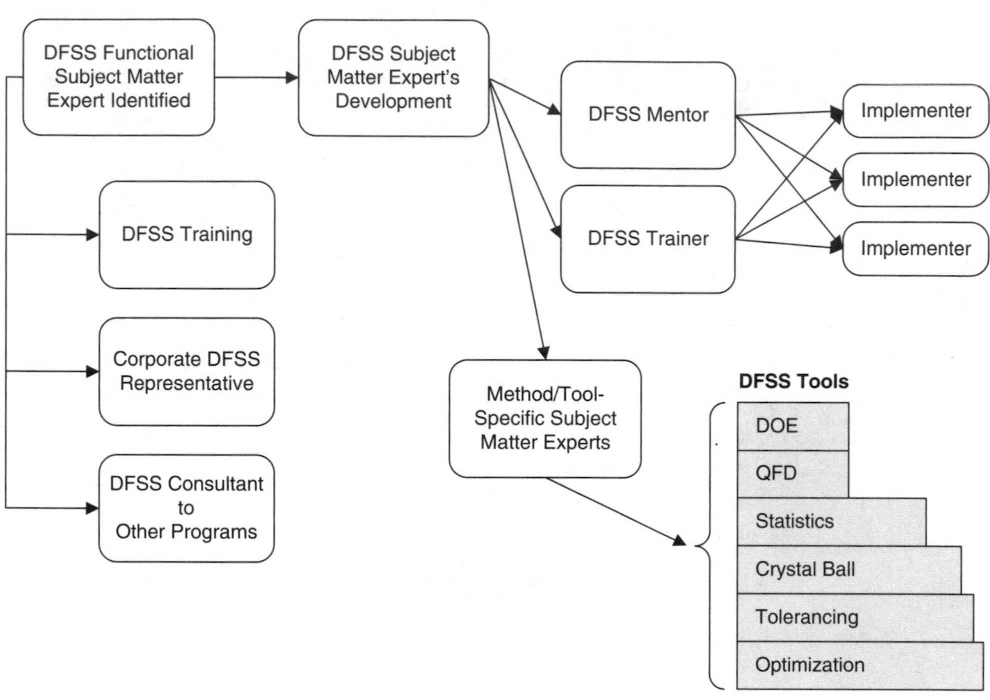

Figure 9–19: *DFSS deployment strategy*

Supporting a DFSS project requires many levels of involvement.

1. *Sponsors*: Sponsors may be at the company or program level and are responsible for allocating resources, interfacing with the company's governing body, and ensuring that the project is kept on track. The sponsor is generally the executive responsible for the new product (e.g., a program manager), but with regard to DFSS his or her primary role is to support the process.
2. *DFSS subject matter experts*: The SMEs are responsible for helping the teams and leaders with the more difficult aspects of a DFSS project. They act more as consultants than as managers. They must be experts in the tools and methods of DFSS and have good consulting skills.

   The SMEs are the primary source for technical knowledge of the DFSS tools and methods. As such, these people must be not only highly respected technically but also able to effectively consult with teams and senior management.
3. *Project leaders*: A project leader is responsible for coordinating the various tasks and activities that contribute to a successful project. Many of these tasks and activities are defined and deployed as part of a company's cur-

rent new product introduction process. The key DFSS challenge for a project leader is effectively integrating the DFSS tools and methods into the current development process.

The project leader might, at times, need help integrating the DFSS tools and methods into the project. This is where the SMEs come in: They provide the guidance and technical support to help keep the project leader on track.

4. *DFSS implementers*: DFSS implementers include everyone else involved in the product development cycle. They bring specific skills and knowledge to the team and include the obvious (design engineers) and the not so obvious (people working on contracts, manufacturing, testing, finance, and so on).

   Implementers participate in implementing the tools and generating the metrics needed to track development, so they must at least be aware of the tools and overall scheme of DFSS.

5. *Suppliers*: A well-deployed DFSS program is driven down to the supplier level. If a key characteristic in the product design is allocated to a subsystem or component assigned to a supplier, the supplier must be involved in controlling variation and meeting the performance target assigned.

Organizational Context: DFSS Methods in Use

The methods used for DFSS usually include the following:

- Requirements traceability along key characteristics
- Structured system design approach
- Quantitative concurrent engineering
- Design accountability (engineering, manufacturing, sourcing, testing)
- Producibility
- Robust design and optimization
- Best customer value, design, and production
- Business case decisions
- Predictive production quality
- Production risk assessment and mitigation

9.5.2 Initial Project Definition

DFSS has been deployed successfully once clear customer target specifications are defined and tied to the elements controlled by design, manufacturing, and subcontractor organizations. The underlying theme of DFSS is to model the performance success of a design, match performance parameters to design and fabrication process capabilities, predict successful design before building the system, validate the performance models, and verify the resulting design.

DFSS has been applied with the most success in precision guidance systems, navigation systems, and complex multidisciplinary systems. Mechanical and electrical systems have traditionally been the focus of DFSS efforts, with software measures playing an increasing role in the key characteristics.

The CMMI and Six Sigma play similar supporting roles in the successful deployment of DFSS. Both initiatives are used to ensure that capable, characterized processes are instituted for design, manufacturing, and sourcing. The CMMI ensures that the organizations involved have mature processes in design and integrated product development by assessing the process areas supporting design. Six Sigma techniques are used to characterize and optimize existing manufacturing processes to reduce variation.

9.5.3 Project Implementation: DFSS

In defining the DFSS project, the customer's critical requirements are identified. They are generally collected in the form of a survey or a storyboard to determine the customer's concept of the system and the critical parameters to maximize success. The critical-to-customer requirements, CTC characteristics, from this effort are used in the DFSS process to determine the key characteristics of the design solution.

The QFD is a powerful tool that gathers, sorts, and synthesizes groups of information, resulting in a weighted representation of critical-to-customer design goals and objectives versus the key characteristics of the organization's design solution. The very nature of the QFD process can often improve communication between cross-functional teams, reveal differences in terminology and perceptions, provide a medium for open technical discussion, and cultivate a spirit of teamwork on all levels. By linking customer CTC characteristics with engineering tasks and objectives, a successfully completed QFD can provide the framework for design initiatives. In cases where a QFD is performed in the middle of a design effort, the resulting information can sharpen the focus of the design team and provide a heightened awareness of tasks and objectives that are of critical importance to customer satisfaction. In comparison to Six Sigma, this effort is focused on design parameters and is a forward-looking effort as opposed to hindsight.

The key characteristics are examined for risk mitigation using failure modes and effects analysis, to identify potential risks in the system architecture, product manufacturing, and/or source selection. At this point, design trades are made to minimize risk to the product design and development.

The key characteristic performance characteristics are used in various models to build a probability model for CTC parameters using historical data, prototype testing, or simulation models. By building the performance model, the effects of variation and the specification limits are modeled to determine variation at the top parameter at the customer level. Figure 9–20 shows an example performance model.

Upon completion of the performance model and analysis, the product solutions are transitioned to design, manufacturing, and sourcing. The performance models are used to guide the specification targets for each contributing group. In design, the modeled performance is evaluated and reviewed at design reviews, and any discrepancies against targets are highlighted. In manufacturing, the statistical process control effort is guided by the target specification, and Six Sigma events are used where necessary to reduce variation that can affect the performance targets. For sourcing, specifications are written to the targets identified by the performance model and used in site surveys and in source inspection to ensure vendor compliance.

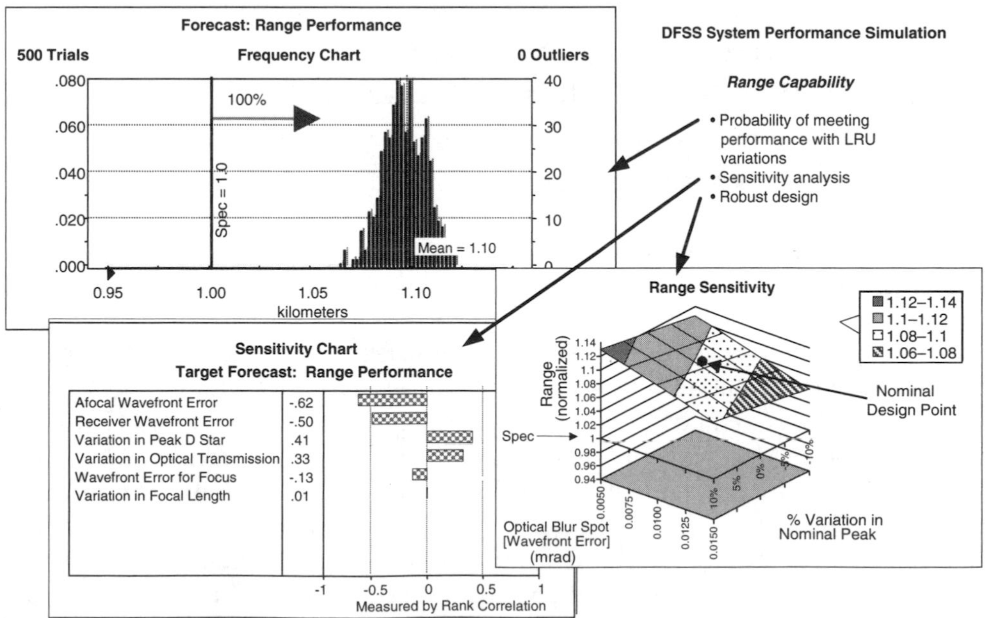

Figure 9–20: *Example DFSS system simulation*

9.5.4 Closing Comments: Results

DFSS efforts have resulted in successful projects with a successful prediction of performance prior to fabrication. By designing to the CTC characteristics and modeling performance prior to transition to manufacturing and sourcing, design rework and incorrect sourcing selection have been avoided.

With precision guidance and navigation systems, small variation errors in components and subelements result in mission failure. DFSS has provided increased confidence in mission success and increased success in actual deployment.

DFSS deployment can provide benefits such as these:

- Proof of principle in design
- Managed risk
- Fewer defects
- Lower unit cost
- Optimal customer satisfaction
- Improved customer perception from proposal to end of life
- Cost avoidance and savings
- Accurate prediction of resources
- Lean design
- Less rework/redesign due to predictive performance modeling
- Waste avoidance through a focus on KCs
- Supply chain integration of KCs into the design
- Reduction of rework by 50%
- Decrease of discrepancies at production and acceptance by 20%

9.6 Summary

In this chapter, we discussed several examples that illustrate the different types of projects that an improvement group may realistically expect to implement in the context of a joint CMMI and Six Sigma deployment. These included projects focused on establishing process infrastructure, which has been the main focus of much of our discussion about the joint implementation of CMMI and Six Sigma. In this context, we presented strategies that use DMAIC as the tactical engine for high maturity or use Lean to establish a new process. Also, we described projects that occur in conjunction with, and long after, the establishment of process infrastructure. These projects focused on the resolution of particular problems—whether product, project, or process—in the context of a CMMI and Six Sigma organization.

Chapter 10

Summary and Final Remarks

Our purpose in writing this book was to provide evidence—logical thinking, data, and examples—not just that the CMMI and Six Sigma should not be viewed as competitors but that their joint implementation leads to more effective process improvement. Research has substantiated the hypothesis that Six Sigma is an enabler of the CMMI (and other domain-specific initiatives) and also has shown that, in turn, the CMMI enables Six Sigma. Six Sigma has been found to be an enabler and an accelerator, to be synergistic and complementary, and to be effective at all CMMI maturity levels.

- The CMMI is a process model for establishing process infrastructure in software and systems engineering and related disciplines. It describes what processes are needed for project management, process management, engineering, and organizational support (including measurement), and it provides mechanisms to institutionalize the needed processes. In software and systems engineering and IT, relatively young compared to other technical disciplines, models and practices such as the CMMI are critical to establishing the processes presumed to exist by Six Sigma.
- Six Sigma is a holistic, business improvement initiative encompassing philosophy, improvement frameworks, measurements, and analytical methods. It is often adopted as an enterprise initiative, focusing an organization on its most critical issues and opportunities. In addition to serving as a tactical engine to improve processes within the CMMI, Six Sigma

can guide the organization through process definition, decision making about which domain initiative to adopt, and development of an improvement project portfolio to which CMMI implementation is aligned.

An organization that pursues one initiative without the other not only misses the synergistic value but actually risks an increased cost of adoption because it must essentially "invent" the initiative it has not selected. Joint implementation is therefore more cost effective than separate, disconnected implementations. Other benefits of joint implementation include accelerated achievement of maturity objectives and mission; robustness to organizational dynamics; high comfort level with measurement and analysis, with a corresponding culture change and ability to report relevant measures; and an aligned improvement project portfolio.

Success factors include the following:

- Senior management sponsorship
- Mission focus
- Quantitative management focus
- Seamless model integration
- Engineering process architecture and design (not just rollout of process descriptions or CMMI areas)

There are no silver-bullet answers for how to blend the initiatives—hence, no easy checklists to follow. But there are some oft-used strategies, including these:

- Implementing CMMI process areas as Lean/Six Sigma projects
- Applying Lean/Six Sigma to improve all processes and thereby achieve high maturity or high capability
- Applying Design for Six Sigma to enrich engineering processes and thereby achieve high capability in them
- Applying Six Sigma to improve or optimize an organization's improvement strategy and processes, including such things as appraisals and improvement project portfolio management
- Institutionalizing Six Sigma culture and project results via CMMI's institutionalization practices
- Developing an internal process standard that reflects the work processes necessary to support the business and product development and that maps to all desired models and practices

These strategies are not mutually exclusive, and all may be leveraged by an organization. The first three embody a spirit that is akin to traditional Six Sigma projects and are arguably the most straightforward (and frequently used) entry points to the joint implementation of the CMMI and Six Sigma. The internal process standard strategy is perceived as more challenging to implement and therefore is not pursued as frequently. However, we recommend that all organizations consider it, if the sponsorship and resources are present. It likely will encompass the other strategies. Furthermore, its inherent design is one that embodies a process architecture paradigm and a multimodel approach—it is the ultimate enabler strategy that builds Six Sigma into the DNA of a CMMI (or other model) organization. As such, it leverages all relevant (for that organization) initiative connections, minimizes deployment conflicts, and provides a degree of robustness that may not otherwise be achieved.

To support the execution of these strategies, there are tactical considerations as well—regarding both the ways in which the initiatives connect and the means by which they are deployed. While mappings between the initiatives may be effectively accomplished within a specific organization's specific situation, the general case is better served by identifying several dimensions of connectivity.

- Commonality of purpose between the Six Sigma frameworks and CMMI process areas, such as:
  - DMAIC versus MA, CAR, and QPM practices (and others)
  - DMADV versus RD, TS, DAR, VER, and VAL (and others)
  - Lean's Kaizen and value stream mapping versus OPF, OPD, and OPP
- Commonality of purpose between the Six Sigma frameworks and CMMI generic practices
- Usage of the Six Sigma analytical methods within CMMI process areas, for instance, FMEA for risk management process or value stream mapping for OPD (with the benefit that via these relationships, Six Sigma frameworks and tools can serve as the tactical engine for achieving high maturity or high capability)
- Six Sigma projects as the object of the CMMI's project management processes
- CMMI process outputs as inputs to Six Sigma, for instance, requirements as inputs to VOC
- Six Sigma process outputs as inputs to the CMMI, for instance, VOP as inputs to planning and estimation

Even when an organization identifies and selects strategies and initiative connections, deployment challenges often remain. In many organizations, the CMMI group and the Six Sigma Belts are not the same people, and their budgets and objectives are separately managed—with the CMMI budgets often subsumed by the Six Sigma budgets. To reconcile this, shared organizational roles, integrated training or cross-training, and project portfolio synchronization are recommended.

As with the two-way blend of the CMMI and Six Sigma, there are no silver-bullet multimodel solutions or easy-to-use checklists for implementation via an internal process standard. There is a process, however, that describes a basic approach that should be followed.

- Identify business drivers, mission, and objectives.
- Select technologies that enable the organization to address its mission, and select a strategy for the overall solution to process improvement. Note that this applies equally well for establishing a project portfolio primarily focused on implementing process infrastructure and for establishing a portfolio after infrastructure has been established.
- Design the improvement solution. For implementing process infrastructure, this includes creating the process architecture.
- Transition the solution.
- Evaluate the results.

Several best practices may be brought to bear to support this approach, for example, mission translation, portfolio selection and management, measurement, transition, and so forth. And there is emerging research (e.g., related to technology selection patterns and architecting engineering processes) that, when matured, will enable this approach to become state of the practice rather than state of the art. The strategies, connections, and deployment challenges of the two-way blend of the CMMI and Six Sigma serve as a foundation for the more general multimodel case—which is everyone's reality.

Appendix A

DMAIC Roadmap Guidance Questions

A.1 Questions for the Define Step

- Define the project scope.
  - What is the current problem to be solved?
  - What are the goals, improvement targets, and success criteria?
  - What is the business case, potential savings, or benefit that will be realized when the problem is solved?
  - Who are the stakeholders? The customers?
  - What are the relevant processes, and who owns them?
- Establish the formal project.
  - Have stakeholders agreed to the project charter or contract?
  - What is the project plan, including the resource plan and progress tracking?
  - How will the project progress be communicated?

A.2 Questions for the Measure Step

- Identify needed data.
  - What are the process outputs and performance measures?
  - What are the process inputs?

    - What information is needed to understand relationships between inputs and outputs? Among inputs?
    - What information is needed to monitor the progress of this improvement project?
- Obtain the data set.
    - Is the needed measurement infrastructure in place?
    - Are the data being collected and stored?
- Evaluate data quality.
    - Does the measurement system yield accurate, precise, and reproducible data?
    - Are any urgently needed improvements revealed?
    - Has the risk of proceeding in the absence of 100% valid data been articulated?
- Summarize and baseline the data.
    - What do the data look like on initial assessment? Are the data what we expected?
    - What is the overall performance of the process?
    - Do we have measures for all significant factors, as best we know them?
    - Are there data to be added to the process map?
    - Are any urgently needed improvements revealed?
    - What assumptions have been made about the process and data?

A.3 Questions for the Analyze Step

- Explore the data.
    - What do the data look like?
    - What is driving the variation?
    - What is the new baseline?
    - What risks and assumptions are associated with the revised data set and baseline?
- Characterize the process and the problem.
    - Do any hypotheses need to be tested?
    - What causal factors are driving or limiting the capability of this process?
    - What process map updates are needed?
    - Are there any immediate issues to address? Any urgent and obvious needs for problem containment?
- Update the improvement project scope and scale.
    - Should the improvement goal be updated?

- Do we need additional data exploration, data decomposition, and/or process decomposition? Additional data?
- Can we take action? Are there evident improvements and corrections to make?
- Have we updated the project-tracking and communication mechanisms?

A.4 Questions for the Improve Step

- Identify possible solutions.
  - What type of improvement is needed?
  - What solution alternatives could address urgent issues and root causes of identified problems?
  - What process factors need to be adjusted?
  - What is the viability of each potential solution?
  - What is the projected impact or effect of each viable solution?
- Select a solution.
  - What are the relative impacts and benefits?
  - What are the relevant technical and logistical factors?
  - What are potential risks, issues, and unintended consequences?
- Implement the solution (pilot as needed).
  - What is the action plan, with roles, responsibilities, timeline, and estimated benefit?
  - Is piloting needed prior to widespread implementation?
- Evaluate.
  - Did the solution yield the desired impact?
  - Has the goal been achieved?
  - If piloted, are adjustments needed to the solution prior to widespread rollout? Is additional piloting needed?
  - How will baselines, dashboards, and other analyses change?

A.5 Questions for the Control Step

- Define the control method.
  - Should data be compared to a range? If so, which range?
  - Does procedural adherence need to be monitored?
- Implement.
  - What updates are needed in the measurement infrastructure?
  - What process documentation needs to be updated?

  - What new processes or procedures need to be established?
  - Who is the process or measurement owner who will be taking responsibility for maintaining the control scheme?
- Document.
  - Have we documented improvement projects for verification, sustainment, and organizational learning?
  - What are the realized benefits?
  - Is the project documented or archived in the organization asset library?
  - Have the documentation and responsibility for it been transferred to the process or measurement owner?

Appendix B

DMAIC and CMMI Specific Goals and Generic Practices

This appendix lists the CMMI specific goals (by number, not name) that reflect intents similar to those of the DMAIC roadmap steps. This list is provided as a simple cross-reference that an organization may choose to use as a guide while defining its processes. It is not exhaustive.

- The Define roadmap steps
  - Define the project scope; align process improvements with business objectives.
    - Organizational Process Focus (SG 1)s Focus (SG 1)
    - Organizational Process Performance (SG 1)
    - Organizational Innovation and Deployment (SG 1)
    - GP 2.2, GP 3.1, GP 4.1, GP 5.1, GP 5.2
  - Establish the formal project; establish improvement projects.
    - Organizational Process Focus (SG 1)
    - Organizational Innovation and Deployment (SG 1)
    - Implied by GP 4.1, GP 5.1
- The Measure and Analyze roadmap steps
  - Identify (define) the needed data; establish repositories.
    - Measurement and Analysis (SG 1)
    - Organizational Process Definition (SG 1)
    - Organizational Process Performance (SG 1)
    - Causal Analysis and Resolution (SG 2)

    - Quantitative Project Management (SG 2)
    - GP 2.8, GP 3.2, GP 4.2, GP 5.1, GP 5.2
  - Summarize and baseline the data.
    - Organizational Process Definition (SG 1)
    - Organizational Process Performance (SG 1)
    - GP 2.8, GP 3.2
  - Explore the data; characterize the process and the problem.
    - Measurement and Analysis (SG 2)
    - Organizational Process Performance (SG 1)
    - Causal Analysis and Resolution (SG 1)
    - Organizational Innovation and Deployment (SG 2)
    - GP 2.8, GP 3.2, GP 5.2
- The Improve and Control roadmap steps
  - Identify improvement alternatives.
    - Decision Analysis and Resolution (SG 1)
    - Organizational Innovation and Deployment (SG 1)
    - Organizational Process Performance (SG 1)
    - GP 5.1
  - Define the control method and implement.
    - Measurement and Analysis (SG 2)
    - Organizational Process Performance (SG 1)
    - Organizational Innovation and Deployment (SG 2)
    - Causal Analysis and Resolution (SG 2)
    - Quantitative Project Management (SG 2)
    - GP 2.8, GP 4.2, GP 5.1, GP 5.2

Appendix C

CMMI Process Areas and the Six Sigma Toolkit

This appendix offers a listing of Six Sigma techniques (statistical and nonstatistical) that are particularly relevant in the execution of several software and systems engineering processes, as categorized by CMMI process areas. This listing is certainly not exhaustive and is intended merely to supplement the main text.

- Integrated Project Management
  - Quantitative baselines with confidence intervals
  - Scorecards
  - Critical dependencies and critical path measured with risk distributions
  - Team charters and project reviews
  - Analysis and reconciliation of different voices (VOP, VOC, VOT, VOM, VOB)
- Risk Management
  - Confidence in meeting the critical path based on modeled schedule uncertainties
  - Process and design failure modes and effects analysis (FMEA)
  - Parametric project forecasting
  - Critical parameter management (CPM)
  - Robust design
  - Capability analysis

- Analytic hierarchy process (AHP)
- Fault tree modeling
- Scorecard metrics
- Project reviews

- Supplier Agreement Management
  - Pugh's concept selection
  - Benchmarking
  - Product line practices
  - Critical to quality (CTQ) flowdown
  - Critical parameter management
  - Statistical process control
- Requirements Development
  - KJ analysis
  - Quality function deployment
  - Voice of the customer and structured interviews
  - Kano analysis
  - Critical to quality (CTQ) flowdown
  - Critical parameter management
  - Quality Attribute Workshops (QAWs)
  - Operational profile development and testing
  - Prototyping
- Technical Solution
  - Pugh's concept selection matrix
  - Brainstorming and concept generation techniques
  - Architecture Tradeoff Analysis Method (ATAM)
  - Attribute driven design
  - Product line management, including platform architecture and reusable components
  - Operational profile development
  - Robust design
- Product Integration
  - Use of variation points built into the software architecture and design
  - Prediction of variation and performance and then tracking of actuals
  - Escaped defect analysis
  - Orthogonal defect classification (ODC)
  - Modeling and simulation (of product)
  - Measurement, prediction, and control of the usage of memory, throughput, and performance, including timing
  - Statistical testing and software reliability analysis and predictions

- Verification
  - Software inspections
  - Modeling and simulation (of product)
  - FMEA
  - Source of error analysis
  - Monte Carlo simulation
  - Rate monotonic analysis (RMA)
  - Architecture Tradeoff Analysis Method
  - SW architecture and design patterns and anti-patterns
- Validation
  - Operational profile testing
  - Structured and sampled end user testing
  - Design of experiments (DOE)
  - Modeling and simulation (of product)
  - Statistical user trials, sampling methods
  - Robust design
- Decision Analysis and Resolution
  - Pugh's concept selection
  - Analytic hierarchy process
  - Probabilistic modeling
  - Scorecards and gate reviews
  - Design of experiments
  - Real Options Analysis
  - Decision trees
- Measurement and Analysis, generic practices, Quantitative Project Management
  - Entire Six Sigma toolkit
- Organizational Process Definition
  - Process mapping
  - Value stream mapping
- Organizational Process Focus
  - Y-to-x decomposition
  - Goal structures
- Project Planning, Project Monitoring and Control
  - Scorecards
  - Management by fact
  - Critical path analysis

Appendix D

"Six Sigma as an Enabler" Research Project: Full Report

This text is excerpted, with permission, from SEI Technical Report CMU/SEI-2004-TR-018 [Bergey et al. 04, ch. 5].

D.1 Purpose

The primary purpose of this project was to examine whether Six Sigma, when used in combination with another process improvement technology or technologies, makes the transition[1] of that technology more effective. While we were interested first in the transition of SEI technologies, what we learned also applies to non-SEI technologies, non-process technologies, and to Six Sigma users in general.

A secondary or implicit purpose of this project was to overcome a frequent misunderstanding about Six Sigma. We realized that many practitioners do not get the transition advantage they could from Six Sigma because they see

[1]By "transition" we mean all of the following: adaptation and introduction of technology by developers or champions, implementation of technology by organizations and change agents, and adoption of technology by its intended users. Most of our research results from this project center on implementation and adoption, but those results have profound implications for developers and champions of technology.

it as a competitor with other improvement practices and models, rather than as an enabler, and therefore do not recognize its potential.

D.2 Background

Six Sigma is an approach to business improvement that includes a philosophy, a set of metrics, an improvement framework, and a toolkit of analytical methods. Its philosophy is to improve customer satisfaction by eliminating and preventing defects, resulting in increased profitability. Sigma (σ) is the Greek symbol used to represent standard deviation, or the amount of variation in a process. The measure *six sigma* (6σ), from which the overall approach derives its name, refers to a measure of process variation (six standard deviations) that translates into an error or defect rate of 3.4 parts per million, or 99.9997 percent defect free. In the Six Sigma approach, *defects* are defined as anything in a product or service or any process variation that prevents the needs of the customer from being met.

During the 1990s, large manufacturing companies such as Motorola, General Electric, and Allied Signal used Six Sigma processes to collect data, improve quality, lower costs, and virtually eliminate defects in fielded products. Using both statistical and non-statistical methods, the approach soon spread to several major service industries, and today software practitioners are exploring ways to apply Six Sigma techniques to improve software and systems development.

D.3 Approach

This project was conducted by two members of the SEI: Jeannine Siviy of the Software Engineering Measurement and Analysis initiative, and Eileen Forrester of the Technology Transition Practices and Capability Maturity Model Integration (CMMI) teams. Siviy is a "Black Belt Practitioner"[2] in Six Sigma,

[2]From isixsigma.com: "Black Belts are the Six Sigma team leaders responsible for implementing process improvement projects within the business—to increase customer satisfaction levels and business productivity. Black Belts are knowledgeable and skilled in the use of the Six Sigma methodology and tools. They have typically completed four weeks of Six Sigma training, and have demonstrated mastery of the subject matter through the completion of project(s) and an exam. They coach Green Belts and receive coaching and support from Master Black Belts."

and Forrester is an applied researcher and consultant in technology transition. In learning about each other's domains we concluded that Six Sigma and technology transition are probably mutually reinforcing. In addition, we hypothesized that the successful transition of Six Sigma itself meant that a persistent community of practitioners, possibly more adept at adopting technology, exists and even pervades the software and systems community we serve. We wanted to discover if the community of Six Sigma practitioners might be more receptive to and capable of adopting SEI technologies and other technologies, thereby serving as a *de facto* community of innovators and early adopters.

Our approach was to use a combination of case interviews and site visits, surveys, field experience, discussions with technology and domain experts, and literature review to examine the use of Six Sigma as a transition enabler and to understand how organizations are using Six Sigma with other technologies. Both the surveys and the literature review were used to elicit hypotheses and candidate case studies. We also elicited hypotheses through interviews and discussions with other researchers and practitioners (see the Collaborators section for participants).

We used an inductive technique to generate our hypotheses, to be tested with qualitative field experience, akin to the "grounded theory" method. Put simply, *grounded theory* calls for the investigators to pose an explicit theory, observe field conditions to test the theory, revise the theory based on that experience, observe again with the revised theory, and so forth. It is a qualitative technique driven by data. We maintained a set of position statements throughout the project that reflected our current theories, and, as the project advanced, added inferences and findings. We periodically reviewed these with other researchers and practitioners for feedback, suggestions, and critique.

D.4 Collaborators

We included about a dozen members of SEI programs (including Software Engineering Process Management, Dynamic Systems, Product Line Systems, and Survivable Systems) as we performed the research, both to get the benefit of their expertise and to foster natural information flows for the project results in other programs. We held interviews and discussions with some to elicit and review our position statements as we progressed. With others, we collaborated to consider how Six Sigma is applied to their domains, or how it could be applied.

Four SEI affiliates participated in scoping this project, setting the research direction and refining survey questions and the interview process: Lynn Penn, Lockheed Martin IS&S; Bob Stoddard, Motorola; and Dave Hallowell and Gary Gack, Six Sigma Advantage. We appreciate their contribution of time and multiple trips to Pittsburgh.

We engaged a small set of practitioners who are thinking about Six Sigma and architecture to improve our potential direction in that domain. These included John Vu of Boeing, Lynn Carter of Carnegie Mellon West, Dave Hallowell of Six Sigma Advantage, and Bob Stoddard of Motorola.

Two members of the Information Technology Process Institute, Gene Kim and Kevin Behr, reviewed our ideas for studying the IT operations and security domain.

The International Society of Six Sigma Professionals and isixsigma.com collaborated with us to formulate and distribute the surveys, and their memberships are interested to hear the results of the project.

Additionally, we would like to acknowledge the time investment of the interviewees and survey respondents whose thoughtful responses provided a rich data set. We estimate their time investment to exceed 150 hours.

D.5 Evaluation Criteria

This project was conceived as a feasibility study. SEI feasibility studies are undertaken to examine the technical and transition issues associated with a promising technology or significant engineering problem. These studies allow the SEI to consider a long-range direction for new work and an assessment of what issues should be addressed if the new work is to be pursued.

The criteria for evaluating feasibility studies are as follows:

- What is the problem in the practice of software or systems engineering or barrier that impedes adoption of new practices?
- Is this unique or critical to software or systems engineering?
- What is the technical or business case for recommending further work by the SEI?

We posited that Six Sigma is a unique *opportunity* or *enabler* (rather than a barrier) that could have the potential to improve transition generally for many software- and systems-related technologies. If we were to express this as a barrier, then the barrier we saw was that too few organizations were aware of—let alone taking advantage of—the possible enabler. Only a few innovative top performers are using Six Sigma as an enabler and it is occasionally in use serendipitously instead of strategically. The enabler is not unique to software and systems engineering but is critical and significant to that domain and to related domains on which software and systems engineering are dependent (administrative science and IT operations, for example).

D.6 Evaluation of Project Data

The project data consisted primarily of language data: text from case study interviews, survey responses, publications, and presentations. Surveys also yielded a limited amount of numerical and countable attribute data, most of which served to characterize the context of and demographics associated with the responses.

The language data was processed qualitatively; each portion of text was evaluated against a list of hypotheses created at the start of the project. This list was revised, as appropriate, using field and case study data.

Minimally, a hypothesis required one credible example of its application to be deemed "feasible." The example had to come from an organization that was at least progressing with one or more variants of Six Sigma and one or more of the improvement models and practices under study.

D.7 Results

Our findings in examining the efficacy of combining Six Sigma with other technologies to get more effective transition are so clear that the technical and business case for further work is simple. Given the field results when SEI technologies and other technologies are applied in concert with Six Sigma, and the wide applicability to a range of SEI technologies that we are uncovering, we see tremendous potential for Six Sigma to serve as a strategic amplifier for SEI technology transition success. The same success should be available for other technologies and other organizations. If the success enjoyed by project participants using CMMI and Six Sigma is emulated, the SEI and its community could have a repeatable transition accelerator for all of its technologies.

Although we faced an unfortunate challenge in gathering information and publishing our results, we see this as a testament to the value and power of Six Sigma: many companies regard Six Sigma use as a competitive advantage and tightly control any information associated with it. Several potential case or interview participants began discussions with us only to suspend our discussions at the direction of their senior management or legal departments. Most of our participants have placed stringent requirements on what we may publish or even share with other SEI staff and collaborators about their use of Six Sigma. In several cases, these same organizations share other data about themselves freely with us and with the community; their treatment of Six Sigma is a departure. We theorize that this is an indirect confirmation of the value of Six Sigma.

The following subsections describe the refined scope and scale of this project, a partial listing of findings that have been abstracted from collected data, an overview of demographic and contextual information, and recommendations for further work. Results are based on the project data set, including information from 11 case study interviews, 8 partial case study interviews, and survey responses from more than 80 respondents, representing at least 62 organizations and 42 companies (some respondents maintained an anonymous identity). Because of the proprietary nature of our data and the non-disclosure agreements in place, the results in this public report are intentionally at a high level. Numerous other findings will be documented separately. Additional publications, with additional detail, are planned, pending review by project collaborators.

D.7.1 Refinement of Scope and Scale

Our initial project supposition was that Six Sigma might enable, accelerate, or integrate SEI and other technologies. Through discussions and an initial project survey, we further theorized that Six Sigma, used in combination with other software, systems, and IT improvement practices, results in

- better selections of improvement practices and projects
- accelerated implementation of selected improvements
- more effective implementation
- more valid measurements of results and success from use of the technology

Based on a combination of SEI interest and community interest and technology readiness, as evidenced through discussions and an initial project survey, we selected the following project priorities:

- primary focus: CMMI adoption and IT operations and security best practices
- secondary focus: architecture best practices and Design for Six Sigma

D.7.2 Primary Findings

Six Sigma is feasible as an enabler of the adoption of software, systems, and IT improvement models and practices (also known as "improvement technologies").

- Six Sigma is influential in the integration of multiple improvement approaches to create a seamless, single solution.
- Six Sigma can accelerate the transition of CMMI (e.g., moving from CMMI Level 3 to Level 5 in nine months, or from CMMI Level 1 to Level 5 in three years, with the typical time being 12–18 months per level rating). Underlying reasons are both strategic (change in focus) and tactical (how the processes are implemented).
- Rollouts of process improvement by Six Sigma adopters are mission-focused as well as flexible and adaptive to changing organizational and technical situations.
- When Six Sigma is used in an enabling, accelerating, or integrating capacity for improvement technologies, adopters report quantitative performance benefits, using measures that they know are meaningful for their organizations and their clients (e.g., returns on investment of 3:1 and higher, reduced security risk, and better cost containment).
- Six Sigma is frequently used as a mechanism to help sustain (and sometimes improve) performance in the midst of reorganizations and organizational acquisitions.
- Six Sigma adopters have a high comfort level with a variety of measurement and analysis methods. They appear to be unfazed by "high maturity" or "high performance" behaviors, processes, and methods, even when they are at a "low maturity."
- Some business sectors are realizing greater success than others regarding the use of Six Sigma as a transition enabler.

Additional, CMMI-specific findings include the following:

- Six Sigma is effectively used at all maturity levels.
- Case study organizations do not explicitly use Six Sigma to drive decisions about CMMI representation, domain, variant, and process-area implementation order; however, project participants consistently agree that this is possible and practical.

- Project participants assert that the frameworks and toolkits of Six Sigma exemplify what is needed for CMMI high maturity. They assert that pursuit of high maturity without Six Sigma will result in much "reinvention of the wheel."

Architecture-specific findings include the following:

- Many survey respondents are in organizations currently implementing both CMMI and Six Sigma DMAIC[3] and many are in organizations progressing or using Design for Six Sigma (DFSS). Of the latter, the majority are at least progressing with CMMI (but some are not using CMMI at all) and none are using the SEI Architecture Tradeoff Analysis Method (ATAM). Note, however, that multiple organizations we studied are pursuing the joint use of Six Sigma, CMMI, and ATAM, focusing on the strong connections among DFSS, ATAM, and the engineering process areas of CMMI.

We found no supporting or refuting evidence for several hypotheses and we have several inferences (conclusions derived inductively from evidence, but not supported directly by evidence) that were not pursued because of time constraints. These will be described in future documents.

D.7.3 Context of Findings

The following questions and answers provide context for our findings and should be helpful for organizations considering the use of Six Sigma as a transition enabler.

What did the case study and survey organizations look like? (Or, more specifically, "Did they look like my organization?")

Generally speaking, the organizations that are achieving success in their use of Six Sigma as a transition enabler ranged from low to high maturity, spanned nearly all commercial sectors, ranged from medium to large in size, and included organic and contracted software engineering as well as IT development, deployment, and operations. (Note that "small" organizations' use of Six Sigma remains on the project hypothesis list, having been neither refuted nor supported by project evidence.)

We did not set out with a research question about which domains were enjoying success—we simply wanted to find evidence of successful use of Six

[3]DMAIC = Define-Measure-Analyze-Improve-Control, one of the improvement frameworks of Six Sigma.

Sigma to improve transition effectiveness. That said, we have evidence from a wide range of organization types and domains, with one exception: We do not have direct evidence from DoD organizations for use of Six Sigma as a transition enabler, except from the field experience of the two researchers. (We do have evidence from industry organizations that serve the DoD.) This does not mean DoD organizations are not employing Six Sigma and enjoying the same benefits, only that we do not yet have evidence. In fact, this may point to an area of needed follow-on work.

What technologies did organizations deploy in conjunction with Six Sigma?

This project focused on organizations that were at least "progressing" both with one or more variants of Six Sigma and with CMMI, Information Technology Infrastructure Library (ITIL), and/or Control Objectives for Information and related Technology (COBIT). However, we gathered data on other technologies in use and they ran the gamut of Capability Maturity Models other than CMMI, the People CMM, ISO standards, the SEI Team Software Process (TSP), ATAM, Goal-Question-Indicator-Metric (GQIM), and Electronic Industries Association (EIA) standards. Demographic statistics will be presented separately.

Why and how did organizations use Six Sigma?

Frequently, Six Sigma was adopted at the enterprise level and the software, systems, or IT organization was called upon to follow suit. In some cases, the adoption decision was made based on past senior management experience (e.g., at the direction of a new senior manager who was just hired from General Electric). In other cases, a "burning business platform" (e.g., lost market share) drove the adoption decision. In all cases, senior management sponsorship was definitive.

Regardless of why Six Sigma was selected, successful organizations consistently deployed it fully (i.e., the following were all present: senior management sponsorship, a cadre of trained practitioners, project portfolio management, the philosophy, one or more frameworks, appropriate measures, and the analytical toolkit). Organizations tailored the focus of Six Sigma and its improvement projects to target key performance measures and the bottom line. "Line of sight" or alignment to business needs was consistently clear and quantitative. CMMI or ITIL process areas were implemented based on business priorities and were integrated with the organizational process standard (even at lower maturity). Organizations varied as to whether CMMI or ITIL started first, Six Sigma started first, or they all started together; the variance was sometimes strategic and sometimes an effect of enterprise and SEI timing. The other aspect of deployment that varied was whether Six Sigma practitioners and process improvement group members were the same or different people and within the same or different organizational divisions. Organizations were successful either way.

Why does Six Sigma work as a transition enabler?

Based on our research and knowledge of both Six Sigma and technology transition, we find that Six Sigma supports more effective transition because it requires alignment with business drivers, garners effective sponsorship, supports excellent and rational decision making, aids robust implementation or change management, and offers credible measures of results for investment. The latter is particularly crucial for convincing majority adopters to transition, and is often the sticking point in failed transitions (popularly labeled after Moore as failing to "cross the chasm"[4]).

D.7.4 Path Forward

Below is a brief listing of several possible follow-on projects that have been identified as a result of project findings and analysis. Pursuit of these areas will depend on available funding and confirmation of value and interest. Additional details will be documented separately.

- The robustness of Six Sigma as a transition enabler, including examination of requisite characteristics for organizational and technology fit, as well as appropriate measures of transition progress (with specific attention to small, acquisition, and DoD organizations and specific attention to both technology developers and technology adopters)
- The codification of DFSS and component-based development techniques to enable organizations to more effectively integrate and deploy multiple models and standards in a way directly focused on mission success
- Use of Technology Design for Six Sigma to contribute to the development of a holistic architecture technology
- Use of Technology Design for Six Sigma to harmonize IT models (or to provide "harmonization guidance" to organizations)
- The application of Six Sigma's analytical toolkit to advance the state of measurement and analysis practice in software, systems, and IT—for instance, the integration of Critical Success Factors, GQIM, and elements of Six Sigma for enterprise measurement and the demonstration of methodologies for language and text data processing

[4] Geoffrey A. Moore. *Crossing the Chasm.* Harper Collins, 1991.

- The ability of Six Sigma's focus on "critical to quality" factors and on bottom-line performance to provide resolution among peers with a similar rating and to provide visibility into (or characterization of) the specific performance strengths of each. As an example, with Six Sigma, an organization might be enabled to reliably make a statement such as, "We can deliver this project in +/– 2% cost and we have capacity for five more projects in this technology domain. If we switch technologies, our risk factor is 'xyz' and we may not be able to meet cost or may not be able to accommodate the same number of additional projects."

Appendix E

"Six Sigma as an Enabler" Research Project: Findings, Inferences, Hypotheses

This appendix contains the master list of findings, inferences, and hypotheses from the SEI-sponsored Independent Research & Development (IR&D) project to explore Six Sigma's role as an enabler of domain-specific practices. While this list was reviewed with each IR&D case study participant as one means of verifying our interpretations, this is the first time it has been publicly documented. It is included for its potential value in seeding other research as well as helping to confirm—via shared viewpoints—the thinking of CMMI and Six Sigma practitioners. For instance, when we shared this list with IR&D project participants, both the preliminary findings and the remaining hypotheses often confirmed locally held beliefs that the organizational resources had insufficient time to investigate or substantiate.

Hypotheses were confirmed as findings based on substantial evidence collected during the IR&D project—either pervasive observations across many case studies, interviewees, and survey respondents or perhaps fewer observations from very significant situations, such as a highly mature and reliable data source, or a scenario where results were conclusive and indisputable. Findings are grouped into several lists: general, CMMI-related, IT-related, and architecture-related.

In many cases, inferences were drawn from findings or from limited evidence. These remain listed with hypotheses. Hypotheses are also grouped into several lists: general, CMMI-related, IT-related, and architecture-related.

Each subsection contains a brief introduction followed by a numbered list, where:

1, 2, 3, . . . = a finding or a hypothesis (inferences, based on findings, are listed with hypotheses)

a, b, c, . . . = clarifications, amplifications, explanations, and examples

E.1 General Findings

Six Sigma makes transition of a range of SEI (and non-SEI) technologies measurably more effective. The following findings elaborate on the general ways in which "effective" has been made evident in case study and surveyed organizations. Findings specific to CMMI implementation, the IT domain, and architecture technologies follow.

1. Six Sigma ensures that model-driven improvement projects are focused on business needs: customer satisfaction and business profitability (or business health).
   a. While this may be a statement of the obvious to people who are approaching improvement this way, it is often observed that model-based improvement can tend to degenerate toward the "check the box" or "get the level rating" mentality. Six Sigma can serve as a valuable check and balance on this tendency.
2. Model-based improvement implementation undertaken in conjunction with Six Sigma consistently shows quantitative results in terms that are meaningful for their business, their internal organizations, and their clients.
   a. Ultimately, organizations implementing both initiatives will measure these results in terms of bottom-line business results. Note that bottom-line results are what is important to the organization. (If level 3 is required to stay in business, then ROI is irrelevant.)
   b. The relationship between customer, business, and internal measures is typically understood.
3. Process improvement efforts led by Six Sigma practitioners tend to be very focused on business results that are mission critical and on how (i.e., what combination of practices) to get there.

   a. Six Sigma practitioners tend to cut to the chase, do what's right, and match the model to the process, rather than getting pulled into the trap of matching process to model and creating a multitude of documents and working to appraisals.
4. Design for Six Sigma (DFSS) and DMAIC-based Six Sigma (or a variant) can be used to roll out model-based practices to an organization. DMAIC Six Sigma is then used to optimize them.
5. Six Sigma can be both part of internal integrated process solutions (or standards) and influential in their design.
   a. Such process solutions are seamless and transparent to the engineer in the field and are viewed as a significant contributor, possibly a "control knob," to the success of the organizations that use them.
6. Those organizations that are realizing significant success in their use of Six Sigma in conjunction with other initiatives are fully utilizing Six Sigma: its infrastructure, philosophy, toolkit, methodologies, and so on.
7. Six Sigma typically spans organizational boundaries as well as enterprise boundaries.
   a. Organizations often teach Six Sigma to their suppliers and outsourcing and co-sourcing organizations.
8. There is a correlation between the presence of Six Sigma and good decision making within an organization.
   a. A Six Sigma deployment involves enhancing and transforming the roles and skills of the existing workforce. As such, a Six Sigma organization has practitioners and a supporting management infrastructure of champions and sponsors who are proficient in using decision analysis methodologies (e.g., Pugh's concept).
   b. This decision-making capability is used for tradeoffs during the adoption process.
9. Six Sigma provides a unifying language across the enterprise and better enables "non-software" managers and engineers and allows technology implementers (e.g., SEPGs) to more effectively implement maturity models and software engineering standards and promotes, as a result, better understanding of their true intent.
   a. Six Sigma provides a unifying language that better enables technology implementers (e.g., SEPGs) to present their models and standards in terms that are more readily understood by intended users, including senior managers (especially "non-software" managers), line of business managers and engineers, technical reps from adjacent domains, and so on.

E.2 Findings Related to the Implementation of CMMI

1. Six Sigma enables the adoption of CMMI, including the transition from SW-CMM to CMMI.
   a. It accelerates in the attainment of a level, with the attendant business results.
   b. It helps in the transition from SW-CMM to CMMI.
   c. It raises effectiveness through characteristics such as flexibility, well-understood interpretation, predictability/assurance of results, and ability to count on certain capabilities in the presence of a certification.
2. Six Sigma accelerates the adoption of CMMI.
   a. CMMI process areas that are implemented as Six Sigma improvement projects are institutionalized faster and more effectively because the potential benefit is clear and measurable, and possibly predictable.
   b. Six Sigma aligns voices of the business, customer, and process (VOB, VOC, VOP), whereas CMMI (in practice) tends to be mostly focused on VOP. Six Sigma strengthens the attention to VOB/VOC that is written in CMMI, but often overlooked or shortchanged in the quest for a level rating.
   c. Within these projects, use of process mapping enables the organization to treat CMMI adoption as a process, with controllable and noise inputs, with normal variation, and with "waste" that can be "leaned" out.
   d. CMMI processes that are designed using voice of the (internal) customer and DFSS principles are more robust to the realities of the organization and therefore less prone to "failure" (disrupted or delayed adoption because they are sent "back to the drawing board.")
3. Six Sigma enables an organization to employ/implement CMMI as it was truly intended, because it requires the organization to link everything to the business and the customer.
   a. Process areas may be implemented as Six Sigma projects. As such, they are implemented as a means to the mission (business goal), and the level rating is no longer "the main goal."
4. Six Sigma may be used at any maturity level.
5. Six Sigma can provide motivation and methods to drive decisions about CMMI representation, domain, variance, and PA implementation order, as confirmed by multiple interviewees. However, in practice, organizations are not explicitly using Six Sigma this way. They are making these decisions based on knowledge of their business and organizational

scope, with Six Sigma influencing their analytical decision-making skills (as previously discussed).

a. The business and customer focus of Six Sigma provides the inputs for prioritizing PA implementation order, when the continuous representation of CMMI is chosen, or within the PAs of each maturity level when the staged representation of CMMI is chosen.
b. The business-driven PA implementation priorities may drive the decision to select the continuous representation.

6. Participants in this project assert that the frameworks and toolkits of Six Sigma exemplify what is needed for CMMI high maturity. They assert that pursuit of high maturity without Six Sigma will result in much "reinvention of the wheel."
   a. If Six Sigma is not explicitly employed in the implementation of the high-maturity process areas, the actions that an organization must take to be successful will eventually embody the tenets of Six Sigma. From this perspective, implementation of Six Sigma makes this process active and, in effect, "leans it out" and improves the cycle time to achieve high maturity.
   b. The experiences of high-maturity organizations that have used Six Sigma to accelerate or enrich their processes are able to reach practical interpretations of the "sometimes-mystifying" language of the measurement and analysis-related CMMI process areas.
7. Six Sigma can be applied to appraisals to reduce cycle time.
8. CMMI-based organizational assets enable Six Sigma project-based learnings to be shared across the software and systems organizations and thereby enable more effective institutionalization of Six Sigma.
9. Appraisers or appraisal team members with Six Sigma experience are better positioned to interpret the many possible ways that an organization may meet the requirements of levels 4 and 5, thus leading to greater clarity of the expectations of a high-maturity appraisal, faster cycle time in the interpretation process, and greater acuity in the findings.
   a. Many organizations use appraisal gap assessment as a key input to their implementation plans. Therefore, accurate appraisal findings are critical to success. They will focus the improvement effort and avoid rework from "chasing red herrings" or conforming to narrow views of acceptable evidence for the measurement and analysis process areas of CMMI.

E.3 Findings Related to IT Development and Operations Organizations

There is much public domain interest and dialogue about Six Sigma in IT, conceivably in response to the plethora of regulations and security issues. But the practice of Six Sigma both on its own and in conjunction with other improvement models generally lags what has been observed in software and systems development. Nevertheless, there are some IT organizations that have leapt far ahead of their peers and are achieving success in this area.

1. High IT (development, deployment, and operations) performers are realizing the same benefits of integrated process solutions, measurable results, and so on, as articulated in the aforementioned general findings. However, they are doing this using the technologies and practices specific to their domain (ITIL, COBIT, sometimes CMMI).
2. CMMI-specific findings apply to IT organizations that have chosen to use CMMI.
3. Six Sigma enables an organization to more effectively identify and manage key risks, including verification that one source of security risk is variance in the operational or production environment.

E.4 Findings Related to Architecture Practices, Design for Six Sigma

DFSS is emerging (in the literature) as a popular variant of Six Sigma. At the outset of this project, it was observed that there is a natural fit between DFSS, ATAM, and the Engineering process areas of CMMI. Based on the findings below, a portion of the project effort was redirected toward exploring possible ways to integrate these technologies.

1. Of survey respondents, many are in organizations currently implementing both CMMI and Six Sigma DMAIC and many are in organizations progressing or using Design for Six Sigma (DFSS). Of the latter, the majority are at least progressing with CMMI (but some are not using CMMI at all) and none are using ATAM.
2. Multiple case study organizations are actively working toward the integration of ATAM as part of their DFSS solution.

E.5 General Hypotheses

We believe it may be true that:

1. Six Sigma has value not only for commercial organizations and government contractors but also for DoD organizations (where its use it limited).
2. Lessons learned from Six Sigma, CMMI, ITIL, and COBIT in large commercial organizations are directly applicable to DoD IT organizations and federal agencies. Also, these learnings can be scaled for smaller IT organizations.
3. Six Sigma can be a key driver in the decision to use integrated solutions of maturity models and proven best practices rather than single, sequential, or isolated implementations, and it can be a key driver in the design of the integrated solution.
   a. One comprehensive view of this goes as follows: Six Sigma and DMAIC and IDEAL and DMADV share common characteristics at the strategic, driving level. People CMM can strengthen organizational fit and readiness for CMMI and other quality management or improvement models. GQIM and PSM can provide tactical approaches to support the measurement-based PAs of CMMI. Similarly, PSP provides an instrumented process.
   b. Unknown: whether this hypothesis is universally applicable or requires special organizational capability.
4. The integration of Six Sigma with domain-specific best practices and improvement models is more critical for success in software and systems engineering organizations and IT than in manufacturing because the industry is relatively new and bodies of knowledge, first practices, and so on are still being defined.
5. Six Sigma's measurement focus can easily be extended to include measures of transition, infusion, and diffusion and make them a standard aspect of the rollout of a technology.
6. Design for Six Sigma, particularly Technology Design for Six Sigma, provides guidance for an organization to effectively design its particular blend of quality management models.
7. Six Sigma training that includes awareness training of proven best practices, in this case CMMI, enables Black Belts to select existing solutions and achieve the desired improvement faster than if they invented (reinvented) the needed processes.

Six Sigma provides a unifying language that better enables technology developers (e.g., SEI technology teams) to present their models and standards in terms that are more readily understood by intended users, including senior managers (especially "non-software" managers), line of business managers and engineers, technical reps from adjacent domains, and so on.

E.6 Hypotheses Related to the Implementation of CMMI

1. Six Sigma allows/enables small organizations to have access to resources, tools, and infrastructure to more easily adopt CMMI.
2. SW-CMM was about software, Six Sigma historically has been about hardware. Some organizations moving from SW-CMM to CMMI struggle with how to extend their model-based processes. Six Sigma bridges that gap.
3. Six Sigma provides the business focus that better positions maintenance organizations to adopt CMMI.
4. Six Sigma enables a tactical approach to several of the generic practices and, thereby, the implementation of the intent of these high-maturity process areas at low maturity or within the continuous representation. This drastically accelerates the cycle time in the final steps toward achieving high maturity because all the building blocks for the high-maturity PAs are already in place.
5. Six Sigma practitioners may help fill a current gap in the ability to lead and populate teams for high-maturity appraisals.
6. Six Sigma can provide resolution among peers with a similar rating and visibility (characterization) into the specific performance strengths of each.
   a. As an example, with Six Sigma, an organization might be enabled to reliably say something like, "We can deliver this project within 2% of the original budgeted cost, and we have capacity for five more projects in this tech domain. If we switch technologies, this is our risk factor, and we may not be able to meet cost or may not be able to accommodate the same number of additional projects."

E.7 Hypotheses and Inferences Related to IT Development and Operations Organizations

The need for process excellence is very acute in the IT operations arena because of the number of regulations that organizations are subject to. The findings stated above should be realizable in this domain. Were IT organizations to embrace these findings, they would in effect build on the lessons of an adjacent community and expedite their progress toward their goals.

We believe that it may be true that:

1. The IT (development and operations) domain can replicate the success that has been observed in software and systems engineering's use of CMMI and Six Sigma.
   a. This is applicable for the CMMI and Six Sigma as well as other combinations of practices and models (i.e., CMMI findings are extensible to other models and practices).
2. Six Sigma provides the business focus that better positions IT service organizations to adopt any maturity-based model (COBIT, ITIL, or CMMI).
3. Six Sigma is the preferred decision-making, implementation, and improvement technique or framework for process improvement in IT operations and security. It is a more apt framework for improvement in IT operations than other models, including IDEAL.
   a. Because IT operations and security are operationally, maintenance-, and service-oriented, Six Sigma may be an easier fit here than in software development. It has features more in common with manufacturing and is a fit for the market discipline of operational excellence.
   b. IT organizations, particularly IT operations, are considerably more focused on bottom-line performance than many software development organizations. Six Sigma is more synchronous with this outlook than the majority of other models available to them.
4. Six Sigma can be used to confirm problem prioritization across the IT lifecycle and to confirm critical-to-quality factors (controllable inputs or driving influences).
   a. The availability of this information at either the organizational or cross-organizational level provides needed input to the codification and selection of improvement methods and practices.
   b. Better-informed selection reduces cycle time and rework.
   c. Understanding the relationship between performance and process within IT operations and IT development, respectively, enables the understanding of performance and process across the supply chain and drives attention to "supplier measures" and a feedback loop that drives improvements "further to the left."
5. Six Sigma enables organizations to identify the context-specific relationships between processes and performance, to quantify the current capability (or lack thereof) of individual and the aggregate set of processes

(regardless of process maturity), and to create a corresponding prioritized list of process needs and improvements.

6. Six Sigma enables an organization to affirm the relevance and priority of each proposed measure (such as privacy, service levels, transaction success rate, repeat business) in its own context and to determine other organization-specific performance measures.
   a. Typical measures might include the business value of:
      i. IT cost avoidance, including avoidance of rework and unplanned work
      ii. IT controls
      iii. Regulatory compliance
      iv. Repairing the root cause(s) of poor service levels
      v. Dimensions of service improvement, sustainability, reliability, availability, integrity as seen by the customer (in IT speak, lower MTTR, greater MTBF, lower MTTD)
7. Six Sigma enables an organization to have excellent operational processes containing well-defined security controls, resulting in the ability to achieve and more importantly sustain a desired security state in a dynamic risk and technology environment.
8. At the technology development level, Design for Six Sigma, particularly Technology Design for Six Sigma (TDFSS), provides frameworks and methods to codify a robust best practice framework for IT operations and security to meet business objectives.
   a. (T)DFSS is used in preference to "regular design methods" to address "new, unique and different" problems. IT, with its proliferation of options and complexities of supply chain relationships, qualifies.
   b. If not a best practice framework, (T)DFSS can lead to standardized guidance for navigating the many choices of standards and frameworks that an IT organization faces.
9. Six Sigma–based process mapping promotes examination of the entire IT lifecycle, including IT infrastructure design, product purchase and installation, and maintenance. This will ensure balanced attention to short-term needs for "survival" and long-term needs for "prevention" in the codification of best practices.

E.8 Hypotheses Related to Architecture Practices and Design for Six Sigma

Following are numerous hypotheses about specific ways in which Six Sigma, DFSS in particular, enables architecture practices. This is a still-evolving list.

Note that it may also be said that the SEI's product line technologies promote or enable both Six Sigma and CMMI. (Which view is the "center" influences the view on which initiative is accelerating which.)

1. Six Sigma for Product Development training provides a foundation for and accelerates the training for SEI Architecture and Product Line Management training.
   a. How? By including ATAM as part of the standard toolkit (along with CMMI TS PA).
2. ATAM deployment is enabled, accelerated, or made more effective via DFSS tasks, tools and deliverables.
3. Cost/benefit analysis method (CBAM) is enabled by DFSS measurement tools already in place to gauge change, impact, and significant factors.
4. DFSS and/or CMMI increases focus on the involvement of stakeholders, which helps ATAM with its needs to involve stakeholders.
5. DFSS uses a robust VOC toolkit and critical parameter management (CPM), which accelerates and creates demand for the SEI Quality Attribute Workshop (QAW).
6. DFSS scorecards on tools, tasks, and deliverables create demand and utilize the aspects of the SEI architecture documentation guidance.
7. The DFSS integration with the product development phases and gates enables a more timely use of ATAM and CBAM.
8. DFSS training motivates architects to take further training in architecture, ATAM, and product line management.
9. DFSS measurement tools readily and immediately provide acceleration to product line management adoption, impact measurement, impact sharing, and structured experimentation for enhanced benefit.
10. The inherent management support and champion development that comes with SSPD provides an essential environment for successful introduction and adoption of both the architecture and product line management practices.
11. The SSPD infrastructure and people skill development motivates and enables organizations to pilot aspects of SEI technologies where otherwise the pilots would not occur.
12. The SEI's product line technologies are leading what "Software TDFSS" should be, excluding measurement infrastructure, which is in place with TDFSS.
13. An effective training strategy would be for the first wave of software DFSS Black Belts to be software architects and ATAM evaluators (not QA).

Appendix F

Overview of Frequently Used Six Sigma Analytical Methods

Evolved from years of process improvement in manufacturing and engineering, the Six Sigma toolkit is expansive. It is also adaptable and dynamic. The decision to adapt, add, or focus on specific methods should be based on the improved ability to deliver on customer needs and business benefit.

This appendix provides short descriptions of several frequently used methods that are readily applicable in software development improvement projects and that have often been included in our conference presentations. They are offered here for ease of reference while reading this book. For more complete descriptions of analytical methods, we recommend using Six Sigma or any of the quality handbooks, as well as specific in-depth texts that are available for many of these methods.

F.1 Descriptive Statistics

Following are formulas for frequently used descriptive statistics.

Measures of central tendency

Mean = (sum of n measured values)/n

Median = midpoint by count

Mode = most frequently observed point

Measures of dispersion or spread

Range = maximum – minimum

$$\text{Variance} = \frac{\sum_{i=1}^{n}(x_i - \mu)^2}{n}$$

Standard deviation = square root of the variance

F.2 Process Mapping

Process mapping is a representation of major activities and tasks, subprocesses, process boundaries, key process inputs, and outputs. Figure F–1 is a simplified, high-level depiction of a process step with its inputs and outputs. Figure F–2 shows the sequencing of steps that make up—and bound—an inspection process. Inputs and outputs are shown and categorized as described below.

The basic steps of process mapping are as follows.

1. For the overall process, list inputs and outputs.
2. Identify all steps in the process: value-added and non-value-added.
3. Show key outputs at each step (process and product).
4. List key inputs and classify process inputs. Figure F–2 shows a process map with a partial listing.

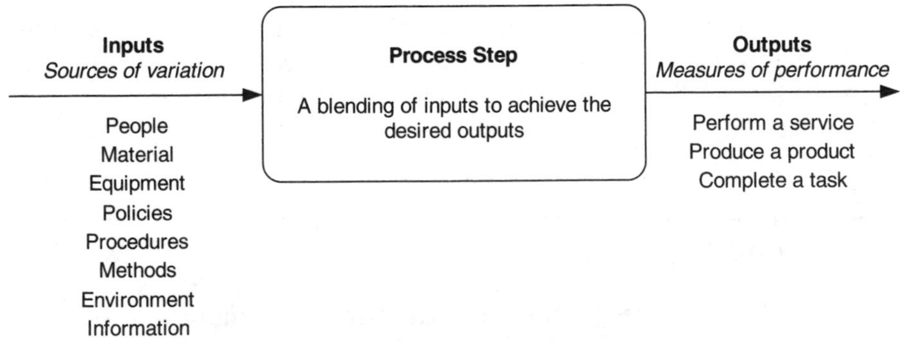

Figure F–1: *Black box process with types of inputs and outputs*

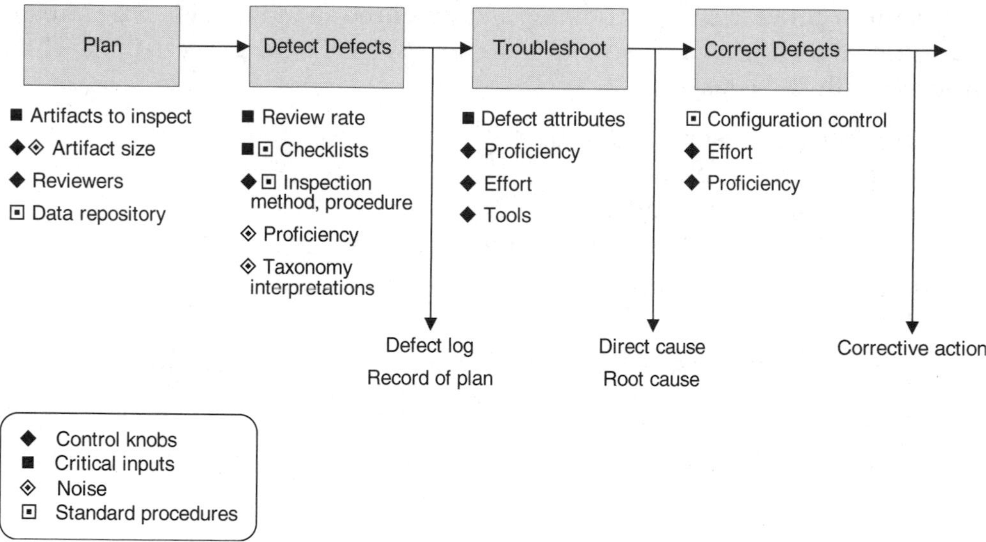

Figure F–2: *Inspection process map*

- Controllable inputs: Key inputs that can be changed to see the effect on key outputs. Sometimes called control knobs.
- Critical inputs: Key inputs that have been *statistically* shown to have a major impact on the variability of the key outputs.
- Noise inputs: Input variables that impact the key outputs but are difficult or impossible to control.
- Standard operating procedures: A standard procedure for running the process.

5. Add the operating specifications and process targets for the controllable and critical inputs.

When developing process maps, it is important to go to the *actual place* where the process is performed, talk to the *actual people* involved in the process, and chart the *actual process*. Few processes work the way we think they do!

In addition to its use as a detailed process descriptor, a process map is often used in the refinement of a Six Sigma project's scope and scale. A process map may be an input to cause-and-effect matrices, failure modes and effects analysis (FMEA), design of experiments planning, and the control plan assembled to sustain performance. A process map may evolve to a value map, in which process steps are evaluated for their value-added contribution to the overall outcome. Unnecessary steps are eliminated to improve cycle time and reduce the risk of error.

A variant of process mapping that is a key technique in Lean is value stream mapping. To create a value stream map, first develop the process map. Then proceed with these tasks.

- Color-code each step to identify value.
    - Green = value-added
    - Red = non-value-added
    - Yellow = non-value-added but necessary
- Identify handoff points, queues, storage, and rework loops in the process.
- Quantitatively measure the map (throughput, cycle time, and cost).
- Validate the map with the process owners.

An example is shown in Figure F–3, where white, dark gray, and light gray are used for green, red, and yellow, respectively.

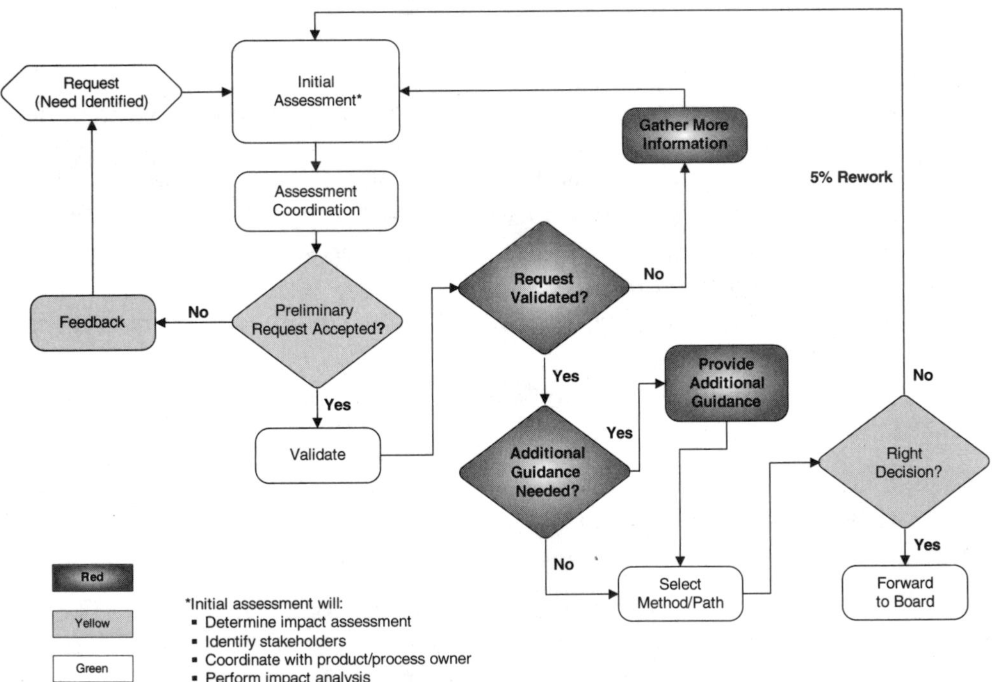

Figure F–3: *Example of a value stream map*

F.3 Failure Modes and Effects Analysis

FMEA is a systematic method for:

- Identifying, analyzing, prioritizing, and documenting potential failure modes
- Determining their effects on system, product, and process performance
- Determining possible causes of failure
- Establishing actions to reduce risk

Unlike statistical process control charts, which flag existing problems and call for response, FMEA is a risk mitigation and reliability improvement method intended to prevent problems from occurring. Ultimately, this will decrease rework, reduce cycle time, reduce cost, and so on. It is most effectively conducted with a cross-functional team. It may be applied during product or process design (design FMEA) to identify weak points during concept development.

Its basic steps are as follows.

1. For each process function, list what could go wrong, that is, the potential failures.
2. Describe the effects of each failure, and rate its severity on a 1–5 scale.
3. Identify the root causes of each failure, and rate their probability of occurrence on a 1–5 scale.
4. Identify means of detecting the failures, and rate for their ability to detect on a 1–5 scale.
5. Calculate risk by multiplying the ratings: severity × occurrence × detection.
6. Prioritize by using the risk factor.
7. Identify (and implement!) ways to reduce risk by decreasing occurrence, reducing severity, or increasing detection.

More information about FMEA may be found at www.fmeainfocentre.com, in addition to the Six Sigma handbooks and other references included in References and Additional Resources at the end of this book.

F.4 The Basic Tools

The basic tools are fundamental data plotting and diagramming tools, such as:

- Cause-and-effect diagrams
- Scatter plots
- Histograms
- Pareto charts
- Run charts
- Flowcharts
- Brainstorming

The list varies with source. Alternatives include the following:

- Statistical process control charts
- Descriptive statistics (mean, median, and so on)
- Check sheets

Figures F–4 through F–13 present some examples of several of these basic tools as well as popular variations, such as box plots.

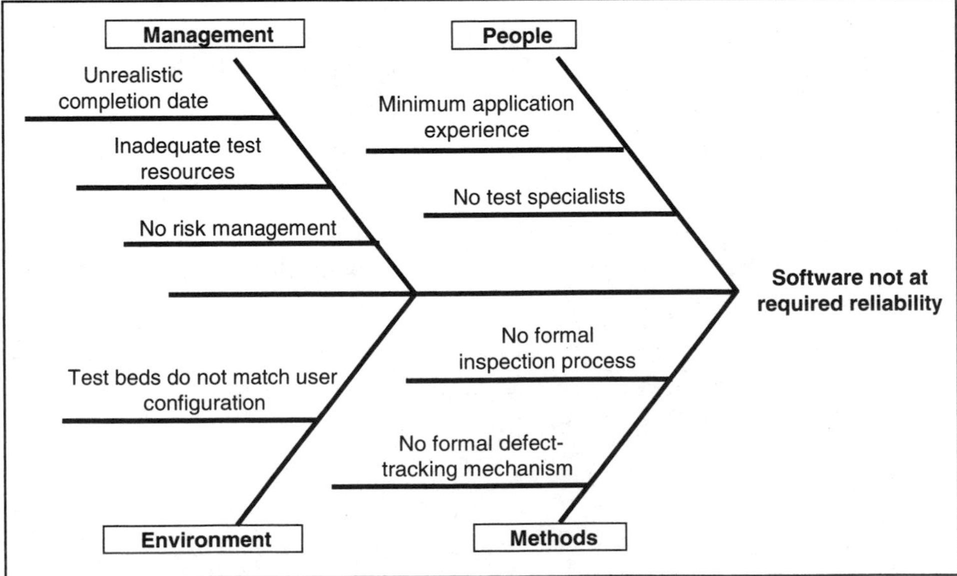

Figure F–4: *Example of a cause-and-effect diagram*

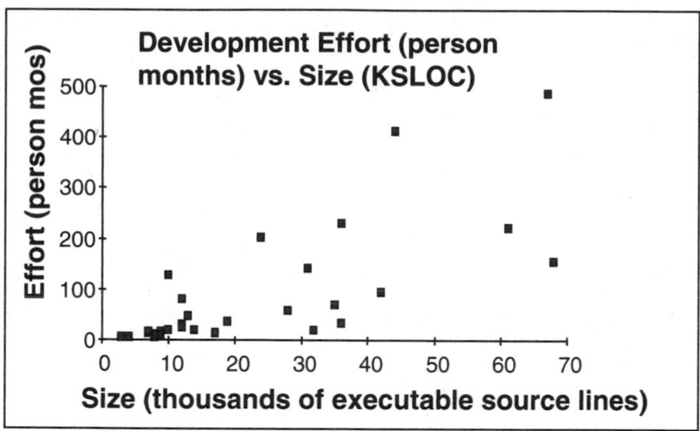

Figure F–5: *Example of a scatter plot*

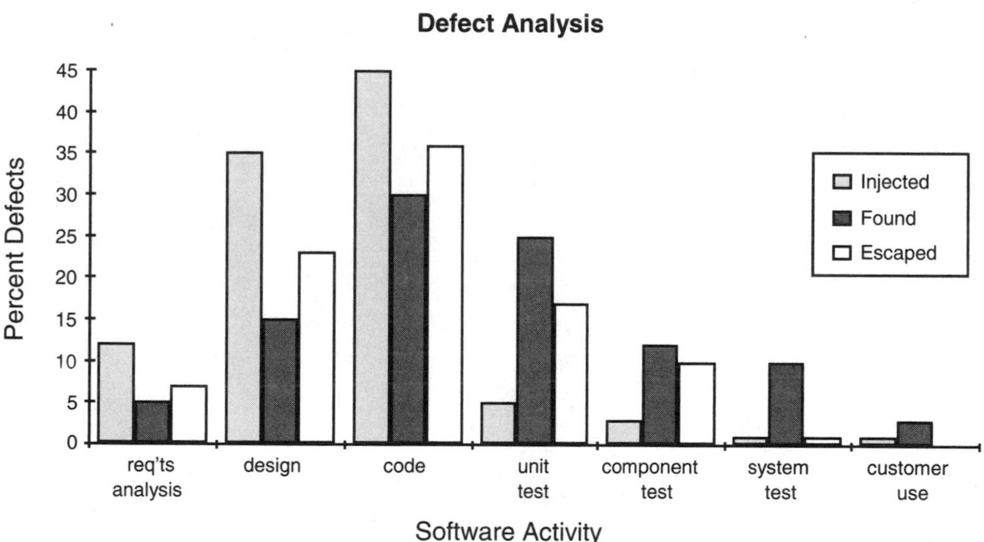

Figure F–6: *Example of a bar chart*

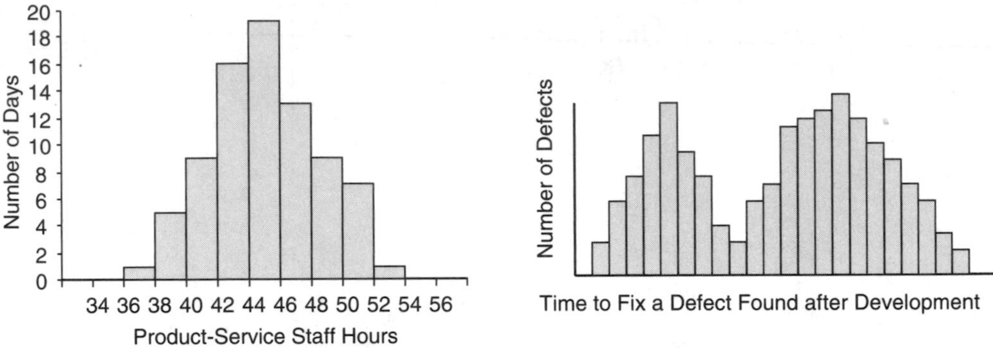

Figure F–7: *Examples of histograms, a special type of bar chart*

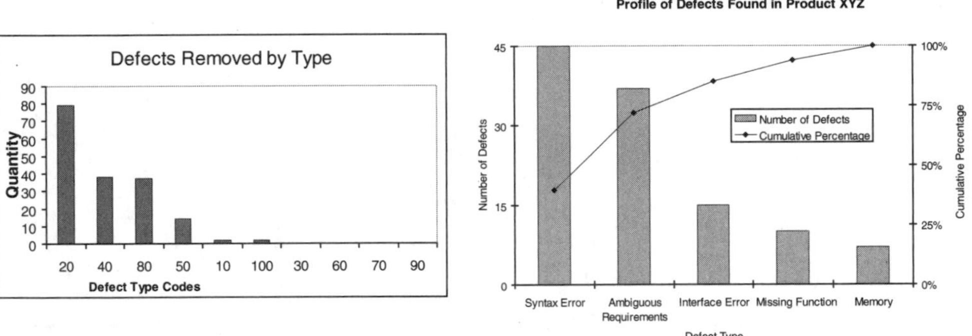

Figure F–8: *Examples of Pareto charts*

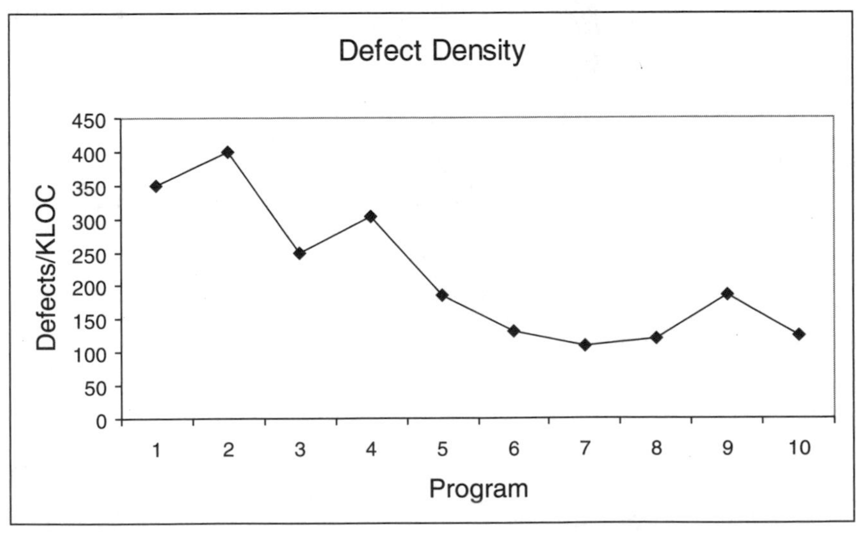

Figure F–9: *Example of a run chart*

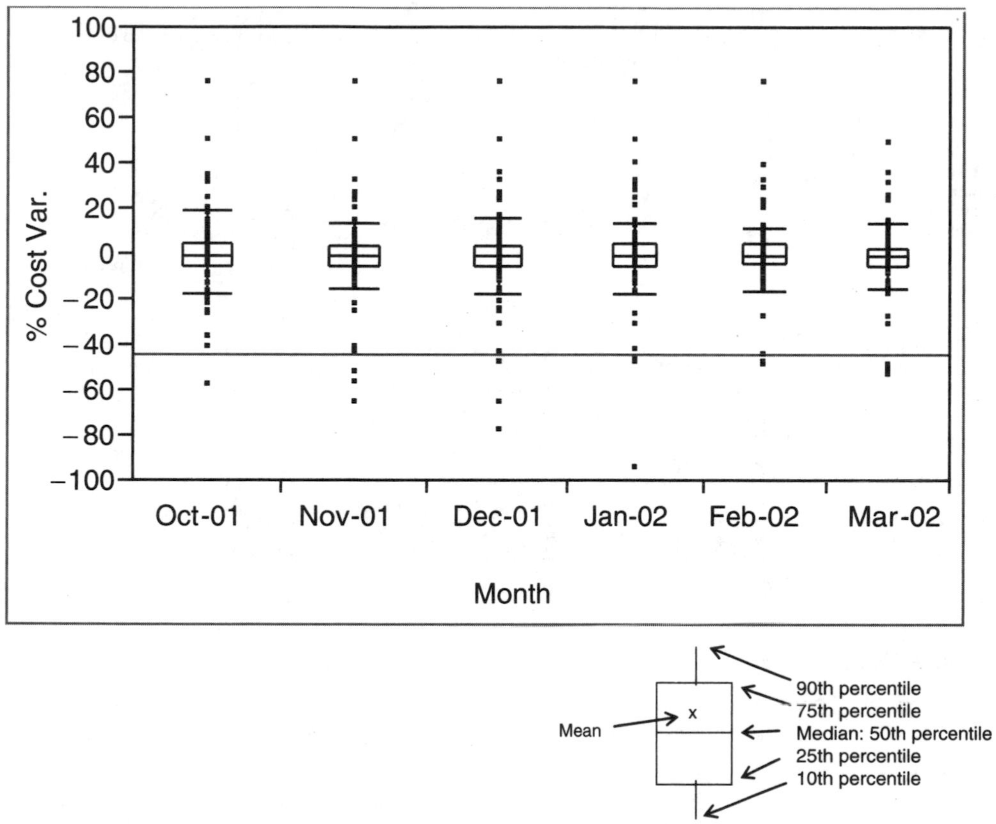

Figure F–10: *Example of a box plot, process data*

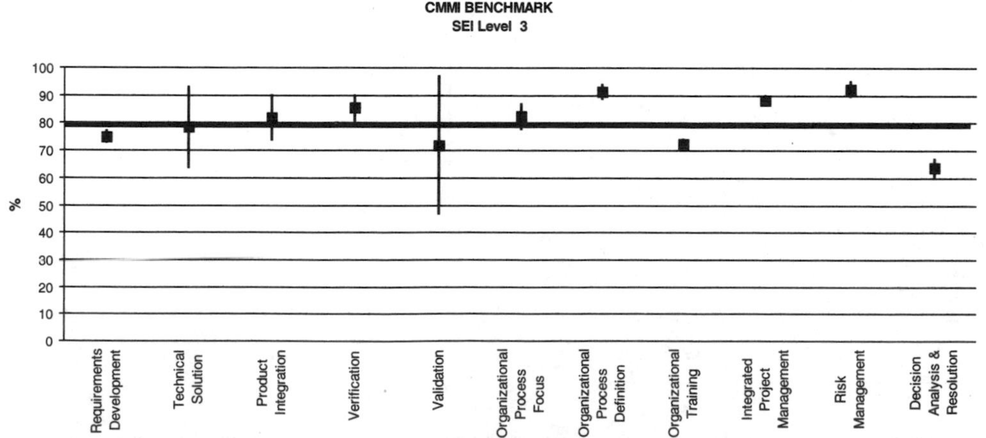

Figure F–11: *Example of a box plot, appraisal data*

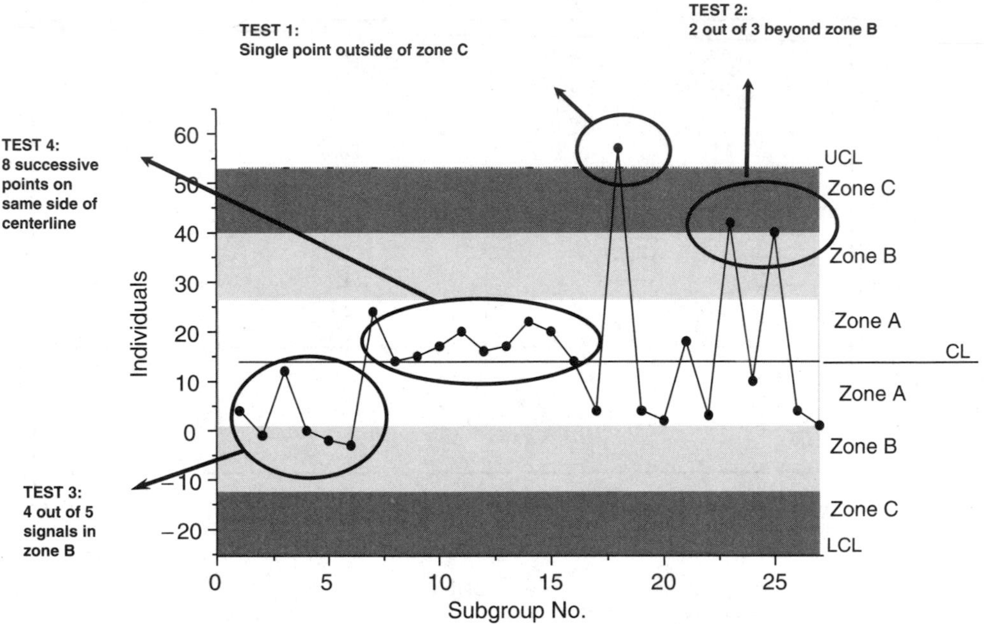

Figure F–12: *Example of a control chart format, with control rules*

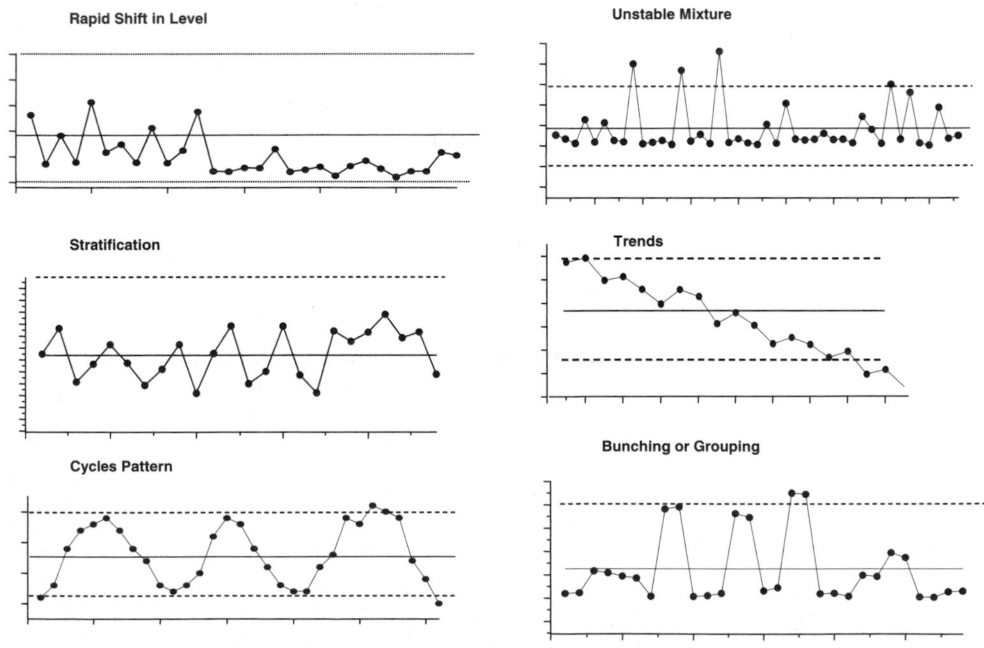

Figure F–13: *Examples of anomalous data patterns (may be viewed via run or control charts)*

F.5 Measurement System Evaluation

Measurement system evaluation addresses whether a measurement system yields accurate, precise, and reproducible data. It involves understanding the data source and the reliability of the process that created it.

Examples of data problems that it reveals include the following:

- Wrong data
- Missing data
- Skewed or biased data

Following is guidance for simple checks of data and an explanation of formal methods. Simple checks may be sufficient, particularly in the early stages of establishing measurement infrastructure.

F.5.1 Simple Checks

Use common sense, basic tools, and good powers of observation.

Look at the frequency of each value:

- Are any values out of bounds?
- Does the frequency of each value make sense?
- Are some used more or less frequently than expected?

Map the data collection process. Know the assumptions associated with the data.

Look at indicators as well as raw measures. Ratios of bad data still equal bad data.

Data systems to focus on include the following:

- Manually collected or transferred data
- Categorical data
- Start-up of automated systems

Supporting tools and methods include these:

- Process mapping
- Indicator templates
- Operational definitions
- Descriptive statistics
- Checklists

F.5.2 Formal MSE

Formal MSE answers the following questions.

- How *big* is the measurement error? (What part of the total error is due to measurement?)
- What are the *sources* of measurement error?
- Is the measurement system *stable* over time?
- Is the measurement system *capable*?
- How can the measurement system be *improved*?

Or, in more statistical terms, formal MSE determines:

- Accuracy (bias)
- Precision (reproducibility and repeatability—R&R)
- Stability over time

Figure F–14 depicts *accuracy*, or the closeness of the measurement (or average of measurements) to the correct value.

Precision is the standard deviation, or spread, of the measurement system distribution. It comprises two sources of variation: repeatability and reproducibility. This is depicted in Figure F–15.

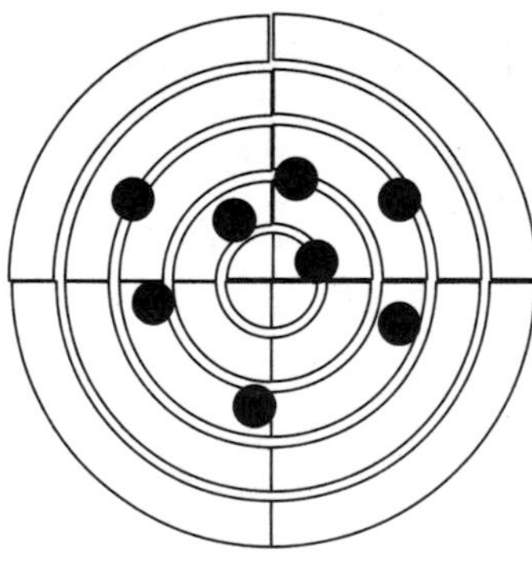

Accurate

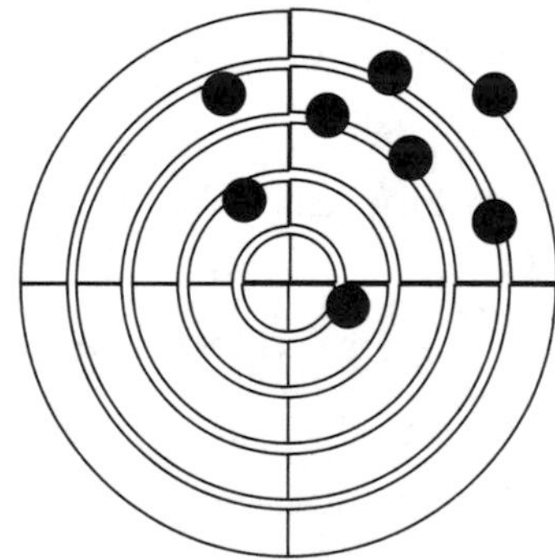

Not accurate

Figure F–14: *Accuracy*

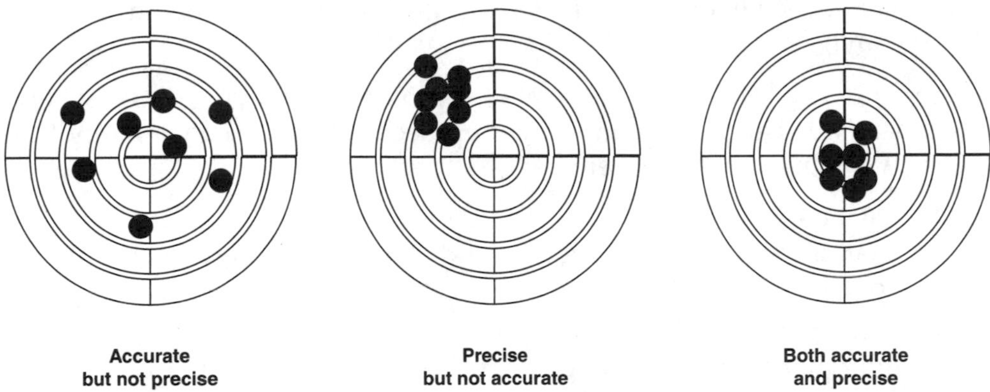

Figure F–15: *Accuracy and precision*

Repeatability is the inherent variability of the measurement system—in other words, it is the standard deviation of the distribution of repeated measurements, when those measurements are made under identical conditions:

- Same inspector, analyst
- Same setup and measurement procedure
- Same software, document, or data set
- Same environmental conditions
- Same short interval of time

Reproducibility is the variation that results when different conditions are used to make the measurement:

- Different inspectors or analysts
- Different setup procedures, or checklists at different sites
- Different software modules or documents
- Different environmental conditions

F.6 Outliers

Through the process of measurement system evaluation, one may identify poor-quality data to exclude from further data analysis. Often, however, there are still data points that don't fit and that one would like to exclude from analysis—potential outliers.

The decision to keep or remove a data point that appears as an outlier must be coupled with knowledge of the data and the process. (Sometimes this knowledge is newly discovered, as a result of troubleshooting an outlier—that is okay!)

There is no widely accepted automated approach to removing outliers; however, there are visual and quantitative approaches that can serve as inputs to decision making about their removal.

- Visual methods
  - Examination of distributions, trend charts, SPC charts, scatter plots, box plots
- Quantitative methods
  - Interquartile range (IQR; procedure described in section F.6.2)
  - The Grubbs test (please consult statistical handbooks for more information on this test)

If an outlier can be attributed to poor-quality, nonrepairable data, the point should be deleted from the data set (and the appropriate measurement system improvements put in place). If an outlier can be attributed to a special circumstance that is unlikely to occur in the future, a judgment call must be made about deleting it from the data set versus keeping it in the data set but excluding it from analysis (easily done in most statistical packages). In both cases, the decision should be properly documented in an analysis log. If it makes sense to keep the data point, observations about its effect on the analysis should be recorded. And, on a practical matter, chart axes may need to be rescaled to maintain visibility into most of the data, if the outlier is significantly different.

Don't remove outliers under the following conditions.

- You don't understand the process.
- You just don't like the data points, or they make your analysis more complicated.
- You think you should remove them just because IQR or the Grubbs test "says so."
- The outliers indicate a second population. In this case, identify the distinguishing factor and separate the data.
- You have very few data points.

F.6.1 Visual Methods

Charts that are particularly effective to flag possible outliers include these:

- Box plots
- Distributions

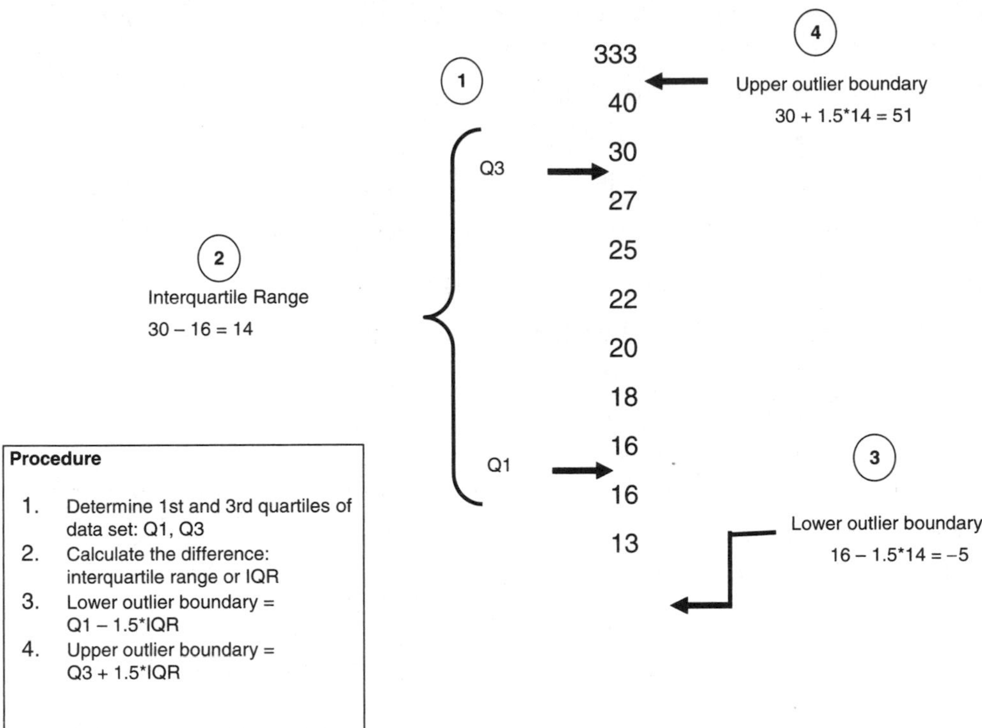

Figure F–16: *Interquartile range method for identifying outliers*

- Scatter plots
- Control charts (if you meet the assumptions)

F.6.2 Interquartile Range

Here is the procedure for the IQR method. Figure F–16 shows an example.

1. Determine the first and third quartiles of the data set, Q1 and Q3, respectively.
2. Calculate the difference, the interquartile range: IQR = Q3 – Q1.
3. Calculate the lower outlier boundary: Q1 – 1.5 × IQR.
4. Calculate the upper outlier boundary: Q3 + 1.5 × IQR.

F.7 Voice of the Customer

Voice of the customer (VOC) is a method for describing the stated and unstated needs or requirements of the customer. These needs and requirements may be captured in a variety of ways: direct discussion or interviews, surveys, focus groups, customer specifications, observation, warranty data, field reports, complaint logs, and so on.

There are inherent risks with VOC techniques.

- They are anecdotal, not quantitative.
- It is difficult to get the "right" answer.
- Humans are perfect filters! And it is very easy to induce bias in VOC.

To mitigate such risks, follow these suggestions.

- Use existing information with care—it may be biased or too narrowly focused.
- Always use more than one source.
- Visit the customers to allow direct discussion and observation. Customer visits also allow immediate follow-up questions and unexpected lines of inquiry.

Here is the VOC procedure.

1. Define the customer.
2. Select customers to interview. Always interview more than one.
3. Plan the interview.
   - Develop a checklist/guideline.
   - Plan to use teams of three: a moderator, a scribe, and an observer.
4. Conduct interviews.
   - Customer statements and observations need to be recorded *verbatim*.
   - Keep asking "Why?"
5. Create a VOC table. Table F–1 shows a possible format for such a table.
   - Interpret verbatim statements into new meanings.

Table F–1: *VOC Table Format*

			Classification						
Customer Comment	**Interpretation**	**I/E**	**Perception, Experience, Context**	**Barrier**	**Root Issue**	**Results, Success**	**Need**	**Solution**	**Keyword for Sorting**
We are already at maturity level x, so why do more?		E	x	x					

Table F–2: *VOC Analysis Guidance*

Prioritization Method	Customer Time	Preparation Complexity	Analysis Complexity	Quality of Resulting Prioritization	Number of Customers Needed	Number of Needs to Prioritize	Recommended?
Frequency of responses	Short	Low	Low	Low	Large	Large	No
Constant sum	Medium	Medium	Medium	Medium	Medium	Small	Yes
Rating	Short	Low	Low	Medium	Medium	Medium to large	Yes
Simple ranking	Medium	Low	Low	Medium	Medium	Small to medium	Yes
Q sort	Short	Low	Low	Medium	Medium	Large	Yes
Paired comparison	Long	Medium	High	High	Large	Small	Yes
Regression	Short	Medium	High	High	Large	Small to medium	Yes

   - Document the source of VOC or reworked VOC.
     - "I" if internally changed or generated (by team)
     - "E" if externally generated (by customer) or not changed by team
   - Classify each statement as:
     - A real need that feeds QFD
     - A technical solution
     - A feature requirement that feeds QFD
     - Not a true need (e.g., cost issue, complaint, technology, hopes, dreams, and so on)
6. Quantify, analyze, and prioritize.
   - Tallying the frequency of certain responses is among the easiest of analysis approaches, however, it is not recommended because it does not adequately account for the significance of responses relative to the problems being addressed, sampling biases, and so forth.
   - Table F–2 provides guidance for other, more effective analysis methods.

F.8 Management by Fact, Including the 4 Whats and the 5 Whys

Management by fact (MBF) is a method of unknown origination that has propagated through several large Six Sigma–adopting corporations as a means of communicating and monitoring Six Sigma projects. It is a concise summary of quantified problem statement, performance history, prioritized root causes, and corresponding countermeasures for the purpose of data-driven project and process management. It is typically documented in a single page, formatted similarly to what is shown in Figure F–17. By its design, MBF uses the facts, minimizes or eliminates bias, and tightly couples resources and effort to problem solving.

Here is the MBF procedure.

1. Identify and select a problem.
   - Use the 4 Whats (see Section F.8.2) to help quantify the problem statement.
   - Quantify the gap between actual and desired performance.
   - State SMART[1] objectives.
2. Determine the root cause.
   - Separate beliefs from facts.
   - Use the basic tools.
   - Use the 5 Whys (see Section F.8.2).

[1]SMART objectives are specific, measurable, attainable or agreed-upon, relevant or realistic, timely or timebound.

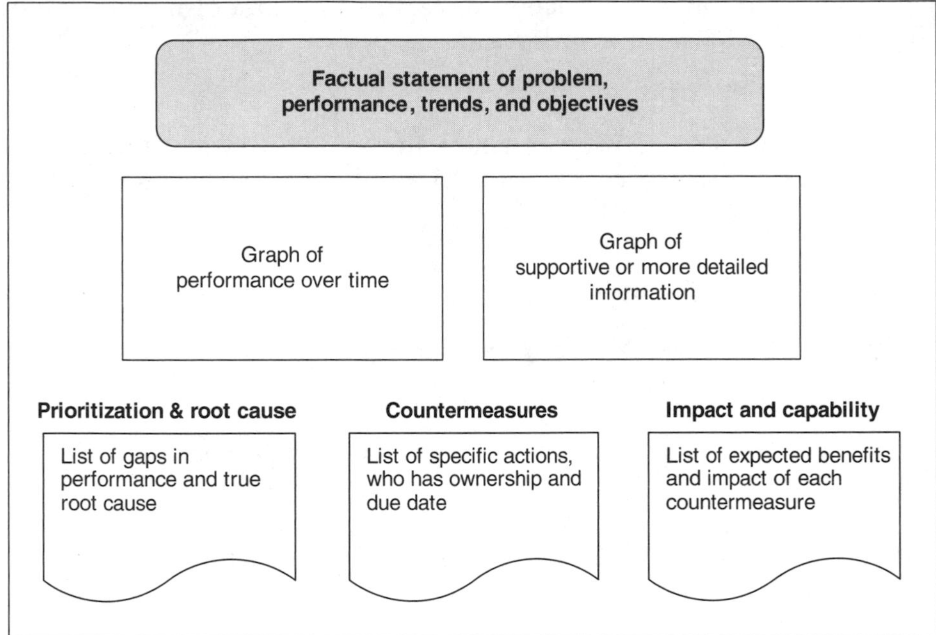

Figure F–17: *MBF format*

3. Generate potential solutions, and select an action plan, which must
   - Be measurable and sustainable
   - Have specific and assignable ownership
   - Clarify the expected results from each action
4. Implement solutions and evaluate.
   - Compare data before and after solution.
   - Document actuals and side effects.
   - Compare with desired benchmarks.

F.8.1 Example of the 4 Whats

Customer satisfaction scores are too low.

What is too low?

Compared to the best-in-class benchmark of 81%, we are at 63%.

What is the impact of this gap?

It represents lost revenue and earnings potential.

What is the correlation between customer satisfaction and revenue?

Each percent of customer satisfaction translates to 0.25% of market share, which equals U.S. $100 million in revenue.

What is the lost potential?

Final problem statement: Customer satisfaction is 18% lower than the best-in-class benchmark, which corresponds to a potential lost revenue of U.S. $1.8 billion.

F.8.2 Example of the 5 Whys

The marble in the Jefferson Memorial was deteriorating.

Why?

The deterioration was due to frequent cleanings with detergent.

Why?

The detergent was used to clean droppings from local sparrows.

Why?

The sparrows were attracted by spiders.

Why?

The spiders were attracted by midges.

Why?

The midges were attracted by the lights.

Solution: Delay turning on the lights until later at dusk.

F.9 Systems Thinking

Systems thinking is a discipline for seeing interrelationships, patterns, and wholes.

- Event-driven thinking: Put out the fire.
- Statistical thinking: Based on the history and likelihood of fires, where should fire prevention equipment be concentrated?
- Systems thinking: How can the fires be avoided?

It leverages both theory of constraints (TOC) and systems dynamics and their diagramming techniques, such as:

- Prerequisite trees (TOC)
- Current and future reality trees (TOC)
- Transition trees (TOC)
- Conflict resolution diagrams (TOC)
- Causal loop diagrams (systems dynamics)

Peter Senge, author of *The Fifth Discipline: The Art and Practice of the Learning Organization* [Senge 90, ch. 4], has put forward these laws, which are fundamental for systems thinkers.

- "Today's problems come from yesterday's 'solutions.'"
- "The harder you push, the harder the system pushes back."
- "Behavior grows better before it grows worse."
- "The easy way out usually leads back in."
- "The cure can be worse than the disease."
- "Faster is slower."
- "Cause and effect are not closely related in time and space."
- "Small changes can produce big results—but the areas of highest leverage are often the least obvious."
- "You can have your cake and eat it too—but not at once."
- "Dividing the elephant in half does not produce two small elephants."
- "There is no blame."

H. William Dettmer, author of Goldratt's *Theory of Constraints: A Systems Approach to Continuous Improvement* [Dettmer 97, ch. 1], offers these TOC principles (partial listing).

- "Systems are analogous to chains"—having a weakest link or constraint.
- "Strengthening any link in a chain other than the weakest one does NOTHING to improve the strength of the whole chain."
- "The system optimum is not the sum of the local optima."
- "All systems operate in an environment of cause and effect. . . . This cause and effect phenomenon can be very complex, especially in complex systems."
- "Most of the undesirable effects in a system are caused by a few core problems."
- "Core problems are almost never superficially apparent."
- "System constraints can be either physical or policy."

- "An optimal system solution deteriorates over time as the system's environment changes."
- "Ideas are NOT solutions."

Goldratt offers a five-step focusing process for dealing with system constraints, with a prerequisite step to articulate the goals that are sought [Goldratt 99; Dettmer 97, ch. 1].

0. Articulate the goals.
1. "Identify the system constraint."
2. "Decide how to exploit the constraint."
3. "Subordinate everything else" to the decision in step 2.
4. "Elevate the constraint."
5. "Go back to step 1" if the constraint has moved.

This section offers just a sampling of systems thinking and TOC principles and methods. If you are interested in this topic, we recommend that you read the Senge, Goldratt, and Dettmer references.

F.10 Pugh's Concept Selection

Several methods may be employed to evaluate the superiority of one solution over another—including benchmarking, decision and risk analysis, and Pugh's concept selection. The latter is highlighted here.

Pugh's concept is a selection technique, set up in a matrix format, that assists in evaluating and synthesizing concept alternatives. Best conducted with a multidisciplined team and defined problem scope and constraints, Pugh's concept selection involves a pair-wise comparison of identified alternatives against each identified acceptance criterion. One alternative is selected as the reference, and in each comparison, the other alternatives are rated for their relative strength of solution—better than the reference, the same, or worse. This is often done using a three-point scale (superior, same, or inferior; +, 0, –; 1, 0, –1) but may also be done with greater resolution. The alternatives are then rank prioritized according to their cumulative strength of solution against the whole set of acceptance criteria. For instance, they would be prioritized according to the most +'s and the fewest –'s. Or, if numbers are used (1, 0, –1), the ratings may be summed. If appropriate, the cumulative strength may be weighted according to the relative importance of the criteria.

Table F–3 shows a generic Pugh's concept selection matrix, as generated in an Excel add-in tool called QI Macros. In this case, concept 4 would be the first selection. This method is intended to be straightforward and relatively quick. Ratings should be made based on data, where available. The objective is to select the best among the choices, not necessarily the perfect choice.

Table F–3: *Example of a Pugh's Concept Selection Matrix*

Pugh's Concept Selection Matrix Comparison Criteria	Current Process (Baseline) or Reference	Design Concept/Alternative 1	Design Concept/Alternative 2	Design Concept/Alternative 3	Design Concept/Alternative 4
Criteria 1		+	0	0	+
Criteria 2		0	–	0	+
Criteria 3		–	+	0	+
Criteria 4		+	–	0	0
Total +'s		2	1	0	3
Total –'s		1	2	0	0

(See www.isixsigma.com/dictionary/Pugh_Matrix-384.htm for more information.)

Appendix G

Measurement Practices

Measurement is essential to both Six Sigma and the CMMI, and it enables their successful deployment in support of performance-driven improvement. This appendix presents brief descriptions of best practices that we recommend considering in the implementation of measurement infrastructure. A retrospective of the Lockheed Martin IS&S case study follows.

G.1 Goal-Driven Measurement Overview[1]

The goal-driven software measurement approach, described in the SEI's "Goal-Driven Software Measurement—A Guidebook" [Park et al. 96], is implemented via the Goal-Question-Indicator-Metric (GQIM) methodology. The GQIM methodology identifies and defines software measures that directly support an organization's business, process improvement, and project goals, ensuring relevance and traceability from the goals to the data collected. Many organizations use the GQIM methodology when deciding what to measure to achieve their business goals. The *I* distinguishes the GQIM methodology from the closely related GQM methodology introduced and described by Basili and Rombach [Basili and Rombach 88; Basili and Weiss

[1] Section G.1 is reprinted (with minor edits) with permission from the Software Engineering Institute Technical Note CMU/SEI-2004-TN-024 [Goethert and Siviy 04].

84; Basili 89; Rombach and Ulery 89]. The steps of the GQIM approach, as implemented by the SEI, are organized into three general sets of activities [Zubrow 98]:

1. Goal identification
2. Indicator identification and data specification
3. Infrastructure assessment and action planning to guide the implementation

The indicator template, shown in Figure G–1, is a key artifact of GQIM. It is used to guide an organization through the three sets of activities and to

Indicator Template

Date ____
Indicator Name/Title ____
Objective ____
Questions ____
Visual Display
100
80
60
40
20
0
Perspective
Input(s)
Data Elements ____
Definitions ____

Data Collection
How ____
When/How Often ____
By Whom ____
Form(s) ____
Data Reporting
Responsibility for Reporting ____
By/to Whom ____
How Often ____
Assumptions ____
Algorithm ____
Interpretation ____
Probing Questions ____
Analysis ____
Evolution ____
Feedback Guidelines ____
X-reference ____

Figure G–1: *Indicator template*

precisely describe and document the who, what, where, when, why, and how of an indicator and its alignment with the goals of an organization. As such, it ensures precise operational definitions, including these:

- Communication: Will others know precisely what was measured, how it was measured, and what was included or excluded?
- Repeatability: Could others, armed with the definition, repeat the measurements and get essentially the same results?
- Traceability: Are the origins of the data identified in terms of time, source, sequence, activity, product, status, environment, tools used, and collector?

Addressing these characteristics ensures consistency in indicator interpretation. The template may be modified as needed. For instance, some organizations add fields for corrective action guidance, to ensure consistency in response to trends or out-of-control points.

G.2 Practical Software and Systems Measurement Overview

PSM[2] provides detailed guidance to establish, use, and sustain an effective measurement process that addresses an organization's technical and business goals. The guidance in PSM represents the best practices used by measurement professionals within the software and systems acquisition and engineering communities. It provides project managers with objective information needed to successfully make decisions related to cost, schedule, and technical objectives; provides a basis for enterprise measurement; and is compatible with the ISO/IEC 15939 standard, Systems and Software Engineering: Measurement Process.[3]

PSM uses its Measurement Information Model to formally relate information needs to specific measures. The information model is based on the identified information need, or in other words, what the measurement user needs to know. An *information need* is identified and described by one or more *measurable concepts*. These measurable concepts identify process or product characteristics that will be measured to satisfy the information need. Each

[2]More information may be found at PSM's Web site, www.psmsc.com, and also in the book *Practical Software Measurement: Objective Information for Decision Makers* [McGarry et al. 02].

[3]CMMI's Measurement and Analysis process area incorporates the basic activities detailed in PSM and required by ISO/IEC 15939.

measurable concept is subsequently formalized as a *measurement construct*, which specifies exactly what and how the measurement will occur; this in turn leads to the *measurement procedure* that defines the mechanics. The collection of measurement constructs is combined to form the *measurement plan*. Through a defined measurement construct, as shown in Figure G–2, the Measurement Information Model provides a foundation for consistent usage

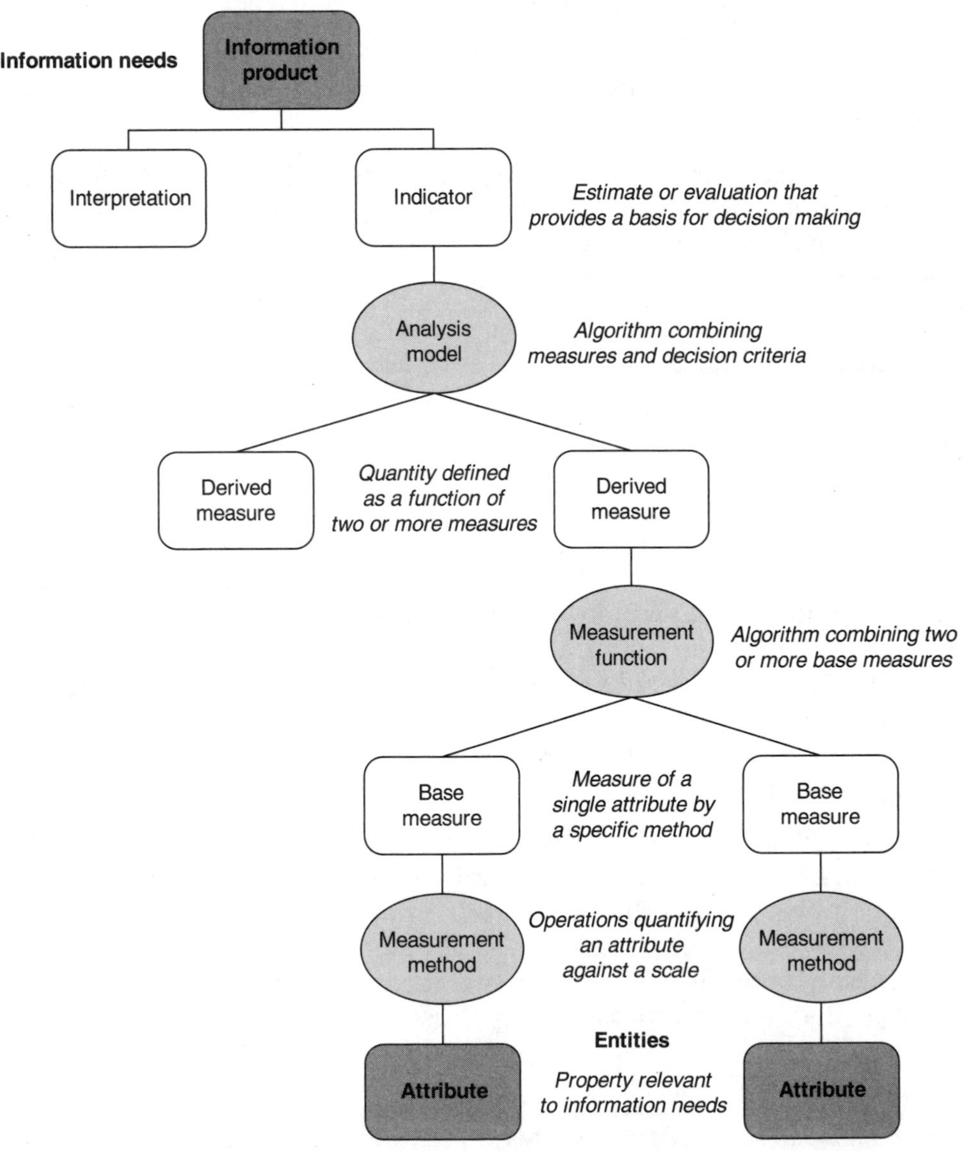

Figure G–2: *PSM detailed measurement construct. (Adapted from ISO/IEC 15939. Reprinted with permission [McGarry et al. 02].)*

of measurement terms and definitions. PSM provides an indicator template to match its detailed measurement construct. In this figure, the base measures, derived measures, and indicators—which are the three levels of measures between the information product and the attributes of the process/product being observed—are shown with the methods, algorithms, relationships, and so on needed for successful measurement definition and fulfillment of the information need [McGarry et al. 02].

PSM includes seven information categories that are common to most organizations.

1. Schedule and progress
2. Product size and stability
3. Process performance
4. Customer satisfaction
5. Resources and cost
6. Product quality
7. Technology effectiveness

Each of these has a corresponding set of measurable concepts. For instance, the measurable concepts of process performance are compliance, efficiency, and effectiveness. For product quality, the measurable concepts are functional correctness, supportability/maintainability, efficiency, portability, usability, and dependability/reliability. In turn, each measurable concept has a candidate set of proven measures. These PSM information categories, measurable concepts, and measures provide a starting point for the selection of appropriate project-specific measures. Additional measures may also be defined.

PSM's Measurement Process Model works in conjunction with its Measurement Information Model and describes the activities essential to implementing a measurement system. Figure G–3 shows this model.

PSM also offers its Integrated Analysis Model, which describes a basic causal system for the engineering process [McGarry et al. 02]. Through its portrayal of leading and trailing indicators, as shown in Figure G–4, the Integrated Analysis Model is used to evaluate multiple indicators for a project, rather than evaluating them singly. For instance, an examination of individual indicators may lead one to address questions about plans versus actual trends, variance growth, and outliers. Examining multiple indicators leads one to address questions about whether growing problems in one indicator are early indicators of other problems (e.g., requirements creep and its effect on

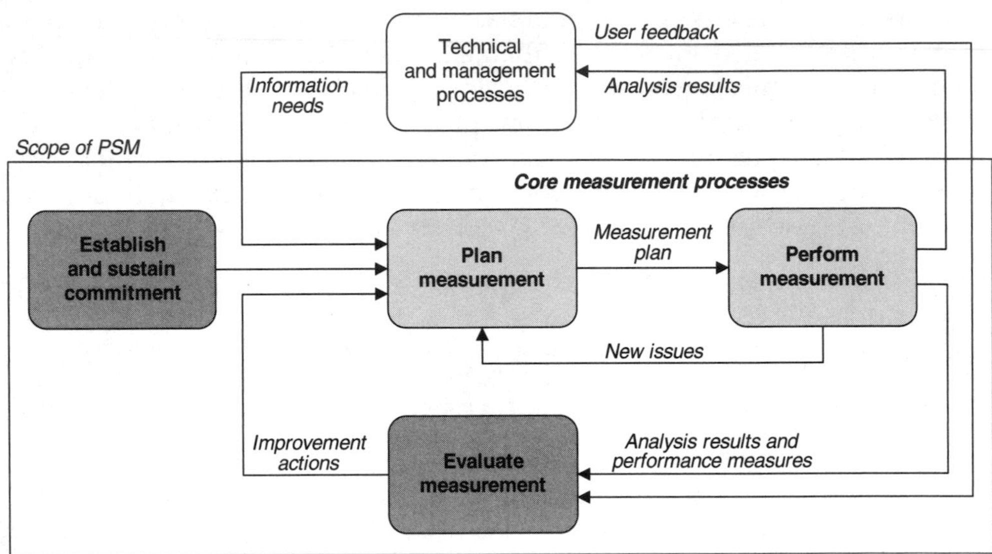

Figure G–3: *PSM Measurement Process Model. (Reprinted with permission [McGarry et al. 02].)*

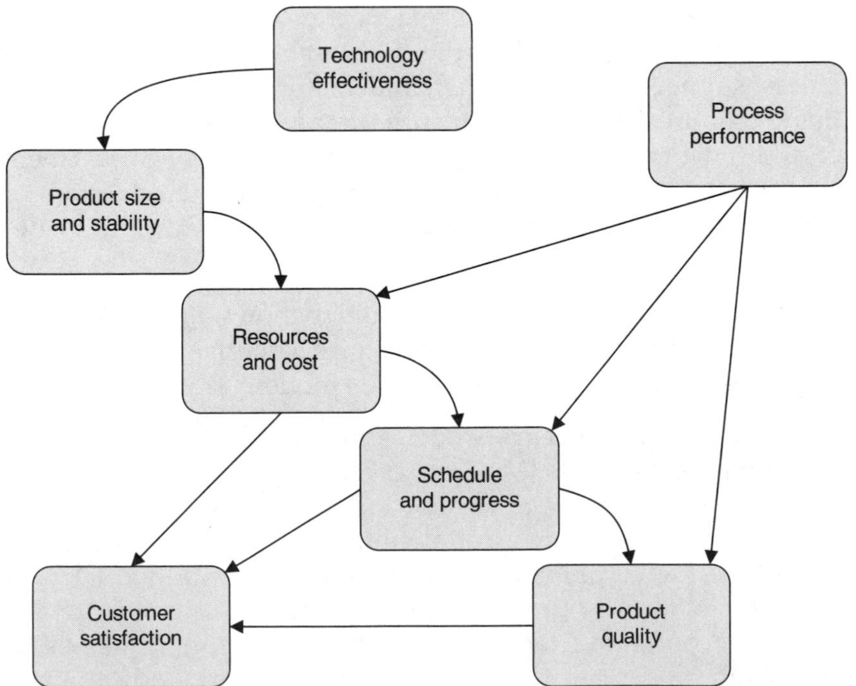

Figure G–4: *PSM Integrated Analysis Model. (Reprinted with permission [McGarry et al. 02].)*

schedule), whether multiple indicators lead to consistent conclusions about direct and root cause, and whether project information contradicts performance (e.g., milestones being met while open defect counts are increasing).

G.3 Case Retrospective: LMCO IS&S's Measurement Program

Following is a summary of how Lockheed Martin IS&S implemented its measurement program, in the context of the case study presented in Chapter 5. Some text from Chapter 5 is repeated here to improve readability.

To supplement the PPS, a cross-functional working group was chartered to establish the *Quantitative Measurement Manual* (QMM) as the minimum mandatory set of measurements for all programs. The members of the working group leveraged historical data (program measures that had been collected for years), including that from heritage companies, as well as PSM as the primary reference in their efforts. The measurements started with the basic cost and schedule, defect detection, and productivity. The list was expanded to look at the PPS processes and determine what granularity would be necessary to enable program managers to proactively manage their programs. Requirements allocation, traceability, and stabilization measurements were put in place. Inspection data were collected to assist with the defect detection profile. Trends and control limits were based on a few programs' actual data and industry surveys.

As the measurement program matured, more programs used the standard measurements, controls, limits, and trends based on actual data. The QMM required development of an organizational metrics repository, now known as the organization performance database. Similar to the PPS, programs now were required to produce a metrics plan based on the QMM and to produce a metrics compliance matrix.

The process improvement program team, now formally named the Quality Systems and Process Management (QS&PM) team, knew from past experience that the adoption of measurement is a difficult step in the rollout of processes. Simply setting a policy to collect measurements and rolling out the prescribed implementation with a new version of the PPS would not likely be sufficient. Accordingly, the organization implemented elements of transition and organizational change management to support the institutionalization of the QMM.

- Establishment of a Metrics Process Steering Committee to support measurement implementation and sustainment
- Measurement training
- Measurement communications and reporting, including a President's Goal Book

The actual collection and usage of the measures involved culture change among managers as much as among the engineers. For example, managers needed to accept answers to their questions only if numbers were produced for backup and clarification. Likewise, all others were expected to base their critical organizational and programmatic decisions on numbers. The president had a set of business objectives that were cascaded down to the executive staff. All were expected to use data in their respective efforts. The goals were tracked monthly, with an associated color being given for goal status. Management could project whether the goal was going to be met that year or whether actions (return to green plans) had to be taken to assure success.

At the end of two years, the metrics database had expanded to all business and functional areas. The organization had achieved SW-CMM Level 4 and SE-CMM Level 3 against all process areas. Additionally, the organization was ISO registered. The President's Goal Book, as shown in Figure G–5, was institutionalized. Equivalent to an enterprise metrics report, it included all the critical measurements associated with the organization. It was con-

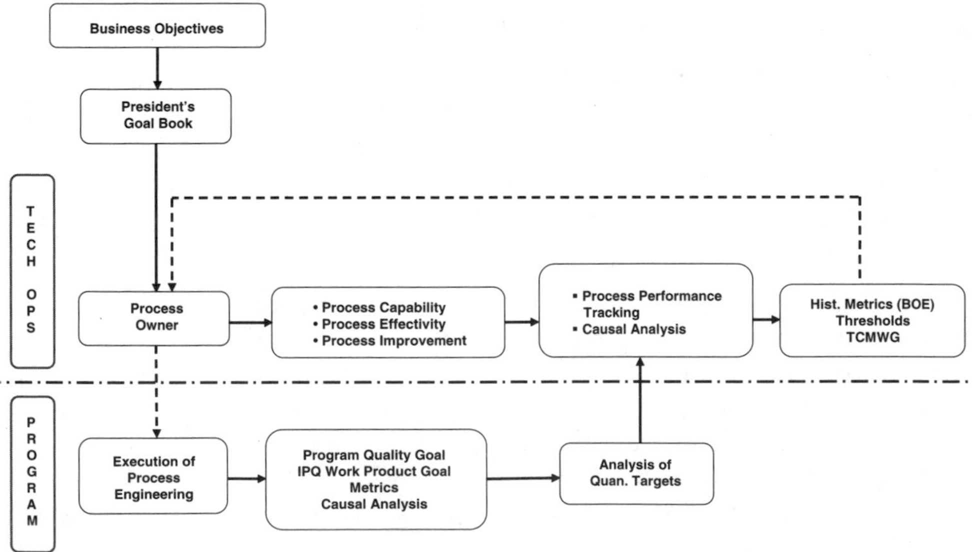

Figure G–5: *LMCO IS&S goals and tracking*

structured using program data rolled up by product line, which was the beginning of a product line scorecard.

To support this culture change, numerous required training mechanisms were established, such as:

- A quantitative management course for all leaders and program managers
- A metrics workshop, to establish the program's specific measurement program, for all team members upon program start-up
- "Measurement to manage" training for all new program managers

In the program metrics workshop, targets, limits, and expected trends were explained and identified, based on the program type and the organizational experience with this program type. Program types included development, engineering support services, research and development, operations, and maintenance. The program profile database was established to store basic characteristics of every program in the organization. In conjunction with the measurement repository, this enabled historical data to be leveraged for effective estimation and to determine past performance, enable effective program start-up (thresholds), and provide another mechanism for process optimization. Figure G–6 shows the data flow and databases that were established.

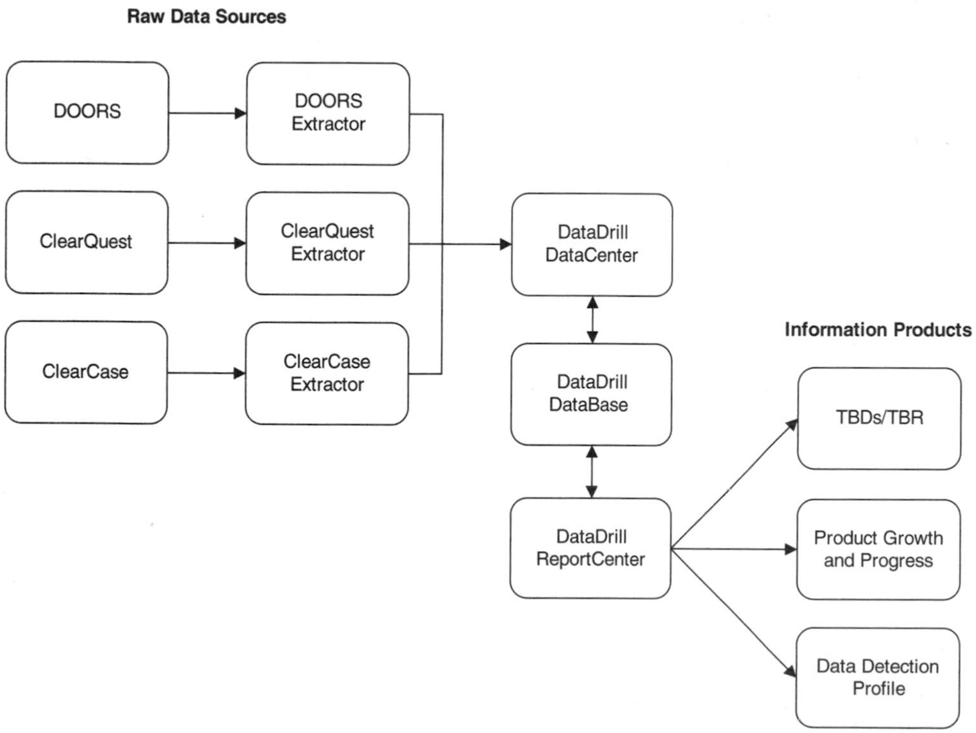

Figure G–6: *LMCO IS&S data flow*

Most metrics program communications were integrated into the overall process communication plan. This included such things as weekly process tips in an online news bulletin, monthly articles in the organization's newspaper, periodic lunchtime briefings, and a section in the two-hour process orientation training course.

Additionally, a quarterly metrics report was established to communicate current performance measurements and program-type-specific data. This is placed in a repository for use in estimation and planning on programs. The individual programs have their own repository with actual program performance data stored in a standard format compatible with the organization's repository.

To ensure ongoing relevance, an organizational survey was established to determine whether the organizational identified metrics still pertain and are being used by the individual programs. The survey goes out annually to about 60% of participating programs (randomly selected but also based on lifecycle, period of performance, and total contract value). Response is high—usually 75% of programs that receive the survey respond. The survey is recognized as a way for program managers to give feedback to the organization on the measurements being collected. The survey results are published in the IS&S newsletter. Each program that participates in the survey is given a training session on the survey, its results, and a chance to comment on the improvement initiatives the organization has defined based on the survey. This communication session is run similar to a value stream mapping.

Appendix H

Transition Practices

As described in Chapter 8, the *transition* of a solution should be considered in parallel with its design. There has been much research on the subject of transition, which includes the activities indicated by such terms as *rollout*, *adoption*, and *implementation*. By leveraging this research, those seeking to improve processes can not only design their technical solution but also design the most effective approach to its implementation in their particular organizational context.

This appendix does not seek to summarize the entire body of knowledge about transition and related topics (such as innovation and organizational readiness). Rather, it highlights a few fundamental concepts that we typically share with process implementers. A retrospective of the Lockheed Martin IS&S case study also appears.

H.1 Highlights of Transition Fundamentals

Included in the transition body of knowledge are several concepts that have been woven into CMMI transition processes and serve as fundamental knowledge for the transition of multimodel solutions as well:

- Diffusion of innovations and the technology adoption lifecycle [Rogers 03; Moore 91]

- "Whole product" [Moore 91]
- Commitment curve [Patterson and Conner 82]

In his book *Diffusion of Innovations*, Everett Rogers presented five categories of adopters of any new technology or innovation, distributed according to a bell curve. Geoffrey Moore, in his book *Crossing the Chasm*, relabeled and further characterized the categories and discussed the gap (the chasm) between the early adopters and early majority that can impede the adoption of a technology. This gap results, at least in part, due to differing expectations about completeness of solution between the early and mainstream adopters.

- Early adopters
  - Innovators or technology enthusiasts (2.5%)
  - Early adopters or visionaries (13.5%)
- Mainstream adopters
  - Early majority or pragmatists (34%)
  - Late majority or conservatives (34%)
  - Laggards or skeptics (16%)

According to Moore, "whole product"—or the "100% solution to the problem"—is the key to engaging the pragmatists. The definition of whole product is "the minimum set of products and services necessary to ensure that the target customer will achieve his or her compelling reason to buy" [Moore 95, 21]. Figure H–1 depicts a whole product wheel that shows examples of whole product components such as training, software, and standards.

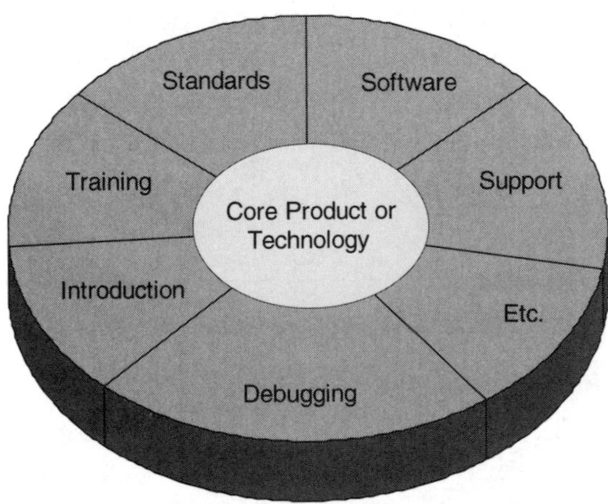

Figure H–1: *Whole product wheel*

The elements of the whole product wheel are examples of *transition mechanisms*. The actual usage of each transition mechanism can be set in the context of Patterson and Conner's curve depicting organizational commitment to change—from contact to awareness to understanding to trial use to adoption to institutionalization. In this context, a variant on the definition of transition mechanisms is that they are the products, activities, and methods that enable and accelerate progress from one commitment stage to the next [Patterson and Conner 82]. Following are examples of activities often used at each stage of commitment [Garcia 02a; Garcia 02b].

- Contact
  - Presentations
  - Examples of implementation
- Awareness
  - Tutorials for different organizational roles
  - Quick appraisals to gauge status (for CMMI implementation)
- Understanding
  - Process implementation approach
  - Detailed training for change agents
- Trial use
  - Measurement system
  - Piloting plan
  - Customized training
- Adoption
  - Leading and reinforcing of change
  - Periodic reappraisal
- Institutionalization
  - Policies and support structures
  - New employee orientation
  - Tailored model

Partnerships with external change agents, technology complexity, degree of change, technology maturity, technology readiness (for adoption by different categories), and organizational readiness (to adopt different types of technologies) are yet more dimensions to consider when assembling a transition strategy. For those who would like to read more, we recommend the following SEI documents, which provide both experience reports and succinct summaries of fundamental research by others such as Moore, Tornatzky and Fleischer, Adler and Shenhar, and many others.

- "Road to CMMI: Results of the First Technology Transition Workshop," CMU/SEI-2002-TR-007 [Carter et al. 02]. (This report addresses adopter populations, whole products, transition mechanisms, and the commitment curve.)
- "Technology Transition Push: A Case Study of Rate Monotonic Analysis," Parts 1 and 2, CMU/SEI-93-TR-029 and CMU/SEI-93-TR-030 [Fowler and Levine 93a; Fowler and Levine 93b]. (These reports include a succinct but broad literature review on transition research.)
- "A Conceptual Framework for Software Technology Transition," CMU/SEI-93-TR-031 [Levine 93].
- "Transition Packages for Expediting Technology Adoption," CMU/SEI-98-TR-004 [Fowler and Patrick 98].

H.2 Case Retrospective: LMCO IS&S's Transition Program

One of the critical factors of Lockheed Martin IS&S's success with its PPS is that the organization had an effective transition plan, consisting of policy, organizational infrastructure, compliance verification, training, and communications.

New standards, process methodologies, and process initiatives are relatively easy to adopt. After the members of the process group map the PPS to the new standard and make any subsequent improvements, they plan the release of a new version of the PPS, including an update of all training and communications mechanisms. In general, processes change on a two- to three-year cycle—if formal change doesn't occur via special events or continuous improvement, it is an indication that the process is not being used. The organization's process asset library automatically notifies process owners when a process reaches two years without having been updated.

The following key training and communication elements were employed when the PPS was initially rolled out.

- Two-hour process orientation training:
    - Made training mandatory for everybody, with executives being trained as a group early in the process so that they could answer questions
    - Used auditoriums and video with live moderator (to ensure consistent message)
    - Arranged training to span a couple of months

  - Took attendance, which was reported to managers
  - Tracked the percentage of personnel trained, which was reported to president routinely
- Common Module training (one day) for some individuals:
  - Compliance matrix authors
  - Program plan authors
- Communications plan:
  - Weekly process tips
  - Monthly newsletter column
  - Posters in lobbies
  - Additional communications as needed

In sustain mode, the key elements are the following.

- Mandatory process orientation training, now one hour and required every two to three years:
  - Is Web based
  - Covers the basics of the PPS, especially focusing on any recent changes
  - Must be completed by personnel before they can be assigned to a program
- Communications plan:
  - Newsletters
  - Brown bag lunches
  - Metric working group networking (facilitated):
    - Information sharing to show how the second layer of data can help answer management questions
    - Guidance on how much data to examine and how it interrelates, to mitigate the risk of attempting to measure everything at once

Appendix I

Organizational Change Management

While this book is not focused on the fundamentals of organizational change management, this is an underlying premise of both the CMMI and Six Sigma. Numerous materials are available to assist an organization with change management. In fact, many CMMI practitioners take supplementary courses in it, and many Six Sigma curricula include it as a core subject.

Senior management sponsorship, including commitment of sufficient resources, is critical to the success of efforts such as the CMMI and Six Sigma. While bottom-up approaches may yield some localized benefits, both of these initiatives are intended as organization-level efforts, and local efforts must soon gain traction and management sponsorship if they are to have the desired long-term, lasting results.

Most change agents, whether members of process improvement groups or Six Sigma Black Belts, have favorite change management references—ones they have found useful time and time again, in many different circumstances. Following are highlights of two of our favorite references: Beckhard and Harris's formulaic approach to change and Senge's *The Dance of Change*.

I.1 Beckhard and Harris's Formulaic Approach to Change

The formulaic approach to change is as follows [Beckhard and Harris 87].

$D \times V \times F > R$, where:

D = dissatisfaction with the present situation

V = vision for the future; a vision of what is possible if today's problems are solved

F = first (or next) steps toward the vision—steps that are achievable

R = resistance to change

As developed by Beckhard and Harris, and based on practitioner experience, all components on the left side of the formula must be present in order to overcome resistance. This formula may be (and is probably most often) used intuitively. It is possible to use survey-style questions and ratings to add some objectivity to the interpretation of its elements.

Following are some key points about the components of this formula. The text here leverages some material from a Web site that is no longer available, www.tbs-sct.gc.ca/fin/sigs/FIS-SIF/communications/framework/2Over_e.asp (accessed March 2006).

Dissatisfaction can be an important lever and motivator when making changes. Organizational initiatives often lack dissatisfaction or motivation for change except at the senior or initiating level. Leaders and change agents may mistakenly assume that because they feel dissatisfied, other people should as well. Yet often these true reasons for change are not well communicated and are not transformed into issues at the working level. (Such a situation was described in Section 9.2, where the driver for change was realigned; this parallels the need to translate goals to the working level, as described in Chapter 8.) If people don't see a problem that needs to be addressed, they are unlikely to invest significant time and attention to change-related issues, although they may do the requested change-related tasks to be politically correct. Identifying sources and a rallying theme of dissatisfaction can be a key strategy when implementing organizational changes.

In this formula, vision refers not to such things as vision statements but to the ability of the people affected by the proposed changes to "see what you mean" with enough detail. Without a clear vision, people keep asking such questions as these: "How does that differ from our current process?" "How will these changes affect me?" "What will things be like once these changes are made?"

First steps are simply a plausible set of initial actions toward achieving the vision. They need to be realistic activities, with clear short- and long-term benefits for those affected by the change. They need to build confidence that the plan is real, that the senior leadership is committed to the change, and so forth.

Resistance may be present as a result of the absence of dissatisfaction, vision, or first steps. Or it may be present due to other factors that may or may not be easily addressed. (For instance, organizational acquisitions and resultant organizational churn may be outside the realm of control.) This formulaic approach offers the option of elevating and strengthening the components on the left side of the equation with the intent of compensating for and overcoming these other sources of resistance.

I.2 Peter Senge's *Dance of Change*

Peter Senge, author of *The Dance of Change* [Senge et al. 99, 26–29], has put forward these challenges of organizational change.

Senge does an excellent job of reminding the change agent that resistance is natural. In identifying the challenges associated with such actions, the agent can assess the organization against the challenges provided and at the same time identify and mitigate the obvious risks. The obvious question associated with these changes is whether the change is adequate and sufficient for this organization. Therefore, the change agent has the opportunity to face these challenges with a more proactive approach, thus preparing for opposition.

Challenges of initiating
These challenges are often sufficient to prevent growth from occurring, almost before it starts. They are consistently encountered at the early stages of significant organizational change. The capabilities to deal with them must be developed under high pressure; but in managing these challenges effectively, organizations develop capabilities much sooner than otherwise for dealing with challenges down the road.

- Not enough time: "We don't have time for this stuff!"
- No help: "We have no help!"
- Not relevant: "This stuff isn't relevant!"
- No corresponding leadership behavior: "They're not walking the talk!"

Challenges of sustaining momentum
These challenges occur sometime during the first year or two, when the group has clear goals and has discovered that new methods save more

than enough time to put them into practice. Now the pilot group's real troubles begin. Sustained activity confronts boundaries—between the work of the pilot group and internal attitudes and beliefs, and between the pilot group's needs and the larger-scale company's values and ways of measuring success.

- Fear and anxiety: "This stuff is ——."
- Assessment and measurement: "This stuff isn't working."
- Believers and nonbelievers: "We have the right way!" say pilot group members. "They don't understand us!" say their other colleagues and peers.

Challenges of system-wide redesign and rethinking

These challenges appear as a pilot group's work gains broader credibility and confronts the established internal infrastructure and practices of the organization.

- Governance: "Who's in charge of this stuff?"
- Diffusion: "We keep reinventing the wheel!"
- Strategy and purpose: "Where are we going?" and "What are we here for?"

References

This section lists sources cited earlier in the book as well as materials we consulted while writing it.

Notes:

- URLs are subject to change without notice.
- Resources and references specific to IT, software, and systems engineering are annotated with this symbol: ♦.

♦ [Abdel-Malek and Hutchings 99] Abdel-Malek, Nabil, and Anthony Hutchings. "Applying Six Sigma Methodology to CMM for Performance Improvement." European Software Engineering Process Group (SEPG) Conference, 1999.

♦ [Albert and Brownsword 02] Albert, Cecilia, and Lisa Brownsword. "Evolutionary Process for Integrating COTS-Based Systems (EPIC): An Overview." SEI Technical Report CMU/SEI-2002-TR-009. Pittsburgh, PA: Carnegie Mellon University, 2002.

♦ [Andelfinger et al. 06] Andelfinger, Urs, Andre Heijstek, Patrick Kirwan, and Hans Sassenburg. "Towards a Unified Process Improvement Approach (UPIA)." SEPG Conference, 2006.

◆ [Anthes 04] Anthes, Gary H. "Quality Model Mania." *CIO Magazine*, March 8, 2004. www.computerworld.com/developmenttopics/development/story/0,10801,90797,00.html (accessed September 2007).

[Antony 06] Antony, Jiju. "Six Sigma for Service Processes." *Business Process Management Journal* 12, no. 2 (2006): 234–248.

◆ [Armstrong 05] Armstrong, James. "A Systems Approach to Process Infrastructure." INCOSE Symposium, 2005.

[Arnold 99] Arnold, Paul V. "Pursuing the Holy Grail." *MRO Today*, June/July 1999. www.progressivedistributor.com/mro/archives/editorials/editJJ1999.html (accessed May 2007).

[ASA 01] American Statistical Association, Quality and Productivity Section. "Enabling Broad Application of Statistical Thinking." 2001. http://web.utk.edu/~asaqp/thinking.html (accessed May 2007).

[ASQ 00] ASQ Statistics Division. *Improving Performance Through Statistical Thinking*. Milwaukee, WI: ASQ Quality Press, 2000.

[BA Insight 06] "Riva's Process Architecture." *Business Analysis Insight*, December 5, 2006. www.bainsight.com/archives/147 (accessed May 2007).

◆ [Basili 89] Basili, Victor R. "Using Measurement for Quality Control and Process Improvement." SEPG Conference, 1989.

◆ [Basili and Rombach 88] Basili, Victor R., and H. Dieter Rombach. "The TAME Project: Towards Improvement-Oriented Software Environments." *IEEE Transactions on Software Engineering* 14, no. 6 (June 1988): 758–773.

◆ [Basili and Weiss 84] Basili, V., and D. Weiss. "A Methodology for Collecting Valid Software Engineering Data." *IEEE Transactions on Software Engineering* 10, no. 6 (November 1984): 728–738.

◆ [Beardsley 05] Beardsley, Gregg. "Pitfalls to Avoid While Accelerating Your CMMI Implementation with Six Sigma." CMMI and Six Sigma Panel, SEPG Conference, 2005.

[Beckhard and Harris 87] Beckhard, R., and R. Harris. *Organizational Transitions*. Reading, MA: Addison-Wesley, 1987.

[Beer 85] Beer, Stafford. *Diagnosing the System*. New York: Wiley, 1985.

[Beer 94] Beer, Stafford. *Brain of the Firm*, 2nd ed. New York: Wiley, 1994.

[Bendell 05] Bendell, Tony. "Structuring Business Process Improvement Methodologies." *Total Quality Management* 16, no. 8–9 (October–November 2005).

[Bennis 69] Bennis, W. *Organization Development: Its Nature, Origin and Prospects*. Reading, MA: Addison-Wesley, 1969, p. 12.

♦ [Bergey et al. 04] Bergey, J., S. Dietrich, D. Firesmith, E. Forrester, A. Jordan, R. Kazman, G. Lewis, H. Lipson, N. Mead, E. Morris, L. O'Brien, J. Siviy, D. Smith, and C. Woody. "Results of SEI Independent Research and Development Projects and Report on Emerging Technologies and Technology Trends." SEI Technical Report CMU/SEI-2004-TR-018. Pittsburgh, PA: Carnegie Mellon University, 2004.

[Bider and Johannesson 05] Bider, Ilia, and Paul Johannesson. *Goal-Oriented Business Process Modeling*. Emerald Group Publishing, 2005.

♦ [Bramble 02] Bramble, Larry. "Lessons Learned from Merging Six Sigma and the CMM." European SEPG Conference, 2002.

[Breyfogle 02] Breyfogle, Forrest W. Keynote presentation at II Symposium on Six Sigma, sponsored by the Centro de Investigacion en Matematicas, Mexico, 2002.

[Breyfogle 03] Breyfogle, Forrest W. *Implementing Six Sigma: Smarter Solutions Using Statistical Methods*, 2nd ed. New York: Wiley, 2003.

[Bylinsky 98] Bylinsky, Gene. "How to Bring Out Better Products Faster." *Fortune*, November 23, 1998.

♦ [Byrnes and Vasques 07] Byrnes, Paul D., and Renato Chaves Vasques. "Integrated System Framework (ISF) for Excellence." Presentation to the Washington DC SPIN, March 7, 2007.

♦ [Carmody and Maher 07] Carmody, Christian, and John Maher. "One Size Fits All: Integrating SOX, CMMI, and ITIL for Enterprise-Wide Process Improvement." SEPG Conference, 2007.

♦ [Carter et al. 02] Carter, Lynn, Caroline Graettinger, Mac Patrick, Gian Wemyss, and Shelly Zasadni. "The Road to CMMI: Results of the First Technology Transition Workshop." SEI Technical Report CMU/SEI-2002-TR-007. Pittsburgh, PA: Carnegie Mellon University, 2002.

♦ [Chrissis et al. 07] Chrissis, Mary Beth, Mike Konrad, and Sandy Shrum. *CMMI: Guidelines for Process Integration and Product Improvement*, 2nd ed. Boston, MA: Addison-Wesley, 2007.

♦ [CMMI DEV v1.2] "CMMI for Development, Version 1.2." SEI Technical Report CMU/SEI-2006-TR-008. Pittsburgh, PA: Carnegie Mellon University, 2006.

[Creveling et al. 03] Creveling, Clyde, Jeff Slutsky, Dave Antis, and Jeffrey Lee Slutsky. *Design for Six Sigma in Technology and Product Development.* Upper Saddle River, NJ: Prentice Hall, 2003.

[Cusimano 06] Cusimano, Brian. "How Dealers Can Put TQM to Work." *Water Technology Magazine,* July 2006.

[Daniel 61] Daniel, D. Ronald. "Management Information Crisis." *Harvard Business Review,* September–October 1961.

[Davis 01] Davis, Rob. *Business Process Modeling with ARIS: A Practical Guide.* London: Springer, 2001.

◆ [Demery and Sturgeon 01] Demery, Chris, and Michael Sturgeon. "Six Sigma and CMM Implementation at a Global Corporation." SEPG Conference, 2001.

[Dettmer 97] Dettmer, H. William. *Goldratt's Theory of Constraints: A Systems Approach to Continuous Improvement.* Milwaukee, WI: ASQ Quality Press, 1997.

[DoD 04] Department of Defense. "Foreword." In *Defense Acquisition Guidebook.* December 20, 2004. https://akss.dau.mil/dag/DoD5000.asp?view=document (accessed October 2007).

◆ [Erwin 01] Erwin, Jane. "Flawless." *Quality World,* January 2001. www.thecqi.org/qualityworld/c4-1-38.shtml (accessed May 2007).

[Espejo and Harnden 89] Espejo, Raúl, and Roger Harnden. *The Viable System Model.* New York: Wiley, 1989.

◆ [Facemire and Silva 04] Facemire, Jeff, and Hortensia Silva. "Experiences with Leveraging Six Sigma to Implement CMMI Levels 4 and 5." SEPG Conference, 2004.

◆ [Florac 92] Florac, William. "Software Quality Measurement: A Framework for Counting Problems and Defects." SEI Technical Report CMU/SEI-92-TR-22. Pittsburgh, PA: Carnegie Mellon University, 1992.

[Forrester 03] Forrester, Eileen C. "A Life-Cycle Approach to Technology Transition." *News@SEI* 6, no. 3 (2003).

[Forrester n.d.] Forrester, Eileen. "Transition Basics." SEI Internal Training Materials, n.d.

◆ [Fowler and Levine 93a] Fowler, P., and L. Levine. "Technology Transition Push: A Case Study of Rate Monotonic Analysis (Part 1)." SEI Technical

Report CMU/SEI-93-TR-029. Pittsburgh, PA: Carnegie Mellon University, 1993.

♦ [Fowler and Levine 93b] Fowler, P., and L. Levine. "Technology Transition Push: A Case Study of Rate Monotonic Analysis (Part 2)." SEI Technical Report CMU/SEI-93-TR-030. Pittsburgh, PA: Carnegie Mellon University, 1993.

♦ [Fowler and Patrick 98] Fowler, P., and Malcolm Patrick. "Transition Packages for Expediting Technology Adoption: The Prototype Requirements Management Transition Package." SEI Technical Report CMU/SEI-98-TR-004. Pittsburgh, PA: Carnegie Mellon University, 1998.

♦ [Frost 03] Frost, Alison. "Metrics, Measurements and Mathematical Mayhem." SEPG Conference, 2003.

♦ [Garcia 02a] Garcia, Suzanne. "Are You Prepared for CMMI?" *CrossTalk*, March 2002. www.stsc.hill.af.mil/crosstalk/2002/03/garcia.html (accessed October 2007).

♦ [Garcia 02b] Garcia, Suzanne. "Accelerating CMMI Implementation with Technology Adoption Tools." *News@SEI* 5, no. 3 (2002). www.sei.cmu.edu/news-at-sei/features/2002/3q02/feature-1-3q02.htm (accessed May 2007).

♦ [Garcia and Turner 07] Garcia, Suzanne, and Richard Turner. *CMMI Survival Guide: Just Enough Process Improvement*. Boston, MA: Addison-Wesley, 2007.

[George 03] George, Michael L. *Lean Six Sigma for Service*. New York: McGraw-Hill, 2003.

♦ [Gibson et al. 06] Gibson, Diane L., Dennis R. Goldenson, and Keith Kost. "Performance Results of CMMI-Based Process Improvement." SEI Technical Report CMU/SEI-2006-TR-004. Pittsburgh, PA: Carnegie Mellon University, August 2006.

♦ [Goethert and Siviy 04] Goethert, W., and J. Siviy. "Applications of the Indicator Template for Measurement and Analysis." SEI Technical Note CMU/SEI-2004-TN-024. Pittsburgh, PA: Carnegie Mellon University, 2004.

[Goldratt 99] Goldratt, Eliyahu M. *Theory of Constraints*. Great Barrington, MA: North River Press, 1999.

[Gruber and Marquis 65] Gruber, William H., and Donald G. Marquis, eds. *Factors in the Transfer of Technology*. Cambridge, MA: MIT Press, 1965.

♦ [Hallowell 03] Hallowell, David L. "Understanding and Integrating the Voice of the Customer." Six Sigma for Software Conference, 2003.

♦ [Hallowell 04] Hallowell, David L. "A Six Sigma Case Study—Tutorial for IT Call Center, a Six-Part Case Study on Software (Part 1)." http://software.isixsigma.com/library/content/c040414b.asp (accessed May 2007). [Links to parts 2–6 are available from part 1.]

♦ [Hallowell and Siviy 05] Hallowell, David L., and Jeannine Siviy. "Bridging the Gap between CMMI and Six Sigma Training." SEPG Conference, 2005. [Slides available at www.sei.cmu.edu/sema/presentations.html.]

♦ [Halvorsen and Conradi 01] Halvorsen, Christian Printzell, and Reider Conradi. "A Taxonomy to Compare SPI Frameworks." *Lecture Notes in Computer Science* 2077 (Proceedings of the 8th European Workshop on Software Process Technology), 2001.

[Harrold 99a] Harrold, Dave. "Designing for Six Sigma Capability." *Control Engineering* 46, no. 1 (1999): 62–70.

[Harrold 99b] Harrold, Dave. "Optimize Existing Processes to Achieve Six Sigma Capability." *Control Engineering* 46, no. 3 (1999): 87–103.

[Harry 00] Harry, Mikel. *Six Sigma: The Breakthrough Management Strategy Revolutionizing the World's Top Corporations*. New York: Doubleday, 2000.

♦ [Hefner 04] Hefner, Rick. "Accelerating CMMI Adoption Using Six Sigma." CMMI Technology Conference and User Group, 2004.

♦ [Hefner and Caccavo 04] Hefner, Rick, and Dean Caccavo. "CMMI Benefits at Northrop Grumman Mission Systems." SEPG Conference, 2004.

♦ [Hefner and Sturgeon 02] Hefner, Rick, and Michael Sturgeon. "Optimize Your Solution: Integrating Six Sigma and CMM/CMMI-Based Process Improvement." Software Technology Conference, 2002.

♦ [Hefner and Ulrich 03] Hefner, Rick, and Ron Ulrich. "Minimizing SCAMPI Costs via Quantitative Methods." CMMI Technology Conference and User Group, 2003.

♦ Houston, Dan. "Why Software Inspections Are Essential to a DFSS Course." Six Sigma for Software Development Conference, October 2003.

[Huber and Launsby 02] Huber, Charles, and Robert Launsby. "Straight Talk on DFSS." *Six Sigma Forum Magazine* 1, no. 4 (August 2002).

♦ [Humphrey 95] Humphrey, Watts S. *A Discipline for Software Engineering*. Reading, MA: Addison-Wesley, 1995.

[ISO 9000:2000] ISO 9000:2000, Quality Management Systems—Fundamentals and Vocabulary, 2nd ed. December 15, 2000.

♦ [ISO/IEC 15939] ISO/IEC 15939:2007, Systems and Software Engineering: Measurement Process. 2007.

[J-STD 95] J-STD-016-1995, Trial-Use Standard for Information Technology, Software Life Cycle Processes, Software Development, Acquirer-Supplier Agreement. September 30, 1995.

♦ [Kasser 05] Kasser, Joseph E. "Introducing the Role of Process Architecting." Proceedings of the 15th INCOSE Annual International Symposium, 2005.

[Kawakita 91] Kawakita, Jiro. "The Original KJ Method." Kawakita Research Institute, 1991.

♦ [Kelliher et al. 00] Kelliher, Timothy P., Daniel J. Blezek, William E. Lorensen, and James V. Miller. "Six Sigma Meets Extreme Programming." General Electric Corporate R&D white paper, 2000.

♦ [Kirwan et al. 06] Kirwan, Patrick, Hans Sassenburg, and Urs Andelfinger. "Sustaining Results in Multimodel Environments." 28th International Conference on Software Engineering (ICSE), 2006.

♦ [Levine 93] Levine, L. "A Conceptual Framework for Software Technology Transition." SEI Technical Report CMU/SEI-93-TR-031. Pittsburgh, PA: Carnegie Mellon University, 2003.

[Marash 01] Marash, Stanley A. "21st Century Quality: Fusion Management, Part Four." *Quality Digest*, December 2001. www.qualitydigest.com/dec01/html/marash.html (accessed September 2007).

♦ [Mayor 03] Mayor, Tracy. "Six Sigma for Better IT Operations and Customer Satisfaction." *CIO Magazine*, December 1, 2003. www.cio.com/archive/120103/sigma.html (accessed September 2007).

♦ [McGarry et al. 02] McGarry, John, David Card, Cheryl Jones, Beth Layman, Elizabeth Clark, Joseph Dean, and Fred Hall. *Practical Software Measurement: Objective Information for Decision-Makers*. Boston, MA: Addison-Wesley, 2002.

♦ [Meyers 02] Meyers, Peter. "The Workaround: 32 Steps to Frustration." *New York Times*, April 25, 2002. www.nytimes.com/2002/04/25/technology/circuits/25WORK.html (accessed May 2007).

[Moore 91] Moore, Geoffrey. *Crossing the Chasm: Marketing and Selling Technology Products to Mainstream Customers*. New York: Harper Business, 1991.

[Moore 95] Moore, Geoffrey. *Inside the Tornado*. New York: Harper Perennial, 1995.

♦ [Murugappan and Keeni 03] Murugappan, Mala, and Gargi Keeni. "Blending CMM and Six Sigma to Meet Business Goals." *IEEE Software*, March 31, 2003.

♦[Musa 04] Musa, John D. *Software Reliability Engineering: More Reliable Software Faster and Cheaper*, 2nd ed. New York: Osborne/McGraw-Hill, 2004.

♦ [Mutafelija and Stromberg 06] Mutafelija, Boris, and Harvey Stromberg. "Architecting Standard Processes with SWEBOK and CMMI." SEPG Conference, 2006.

[Ould 05] Ould, Martyn. *Business Process Management: A Rigorous Approach*. Tampa, FL: Meghan-Kiffer Press, 2005.

♦ [Park et al. 96] Park, Robert E., Wolfhart B. Goethert, and William A. Florac. "Goal-Driven Software Measurement—A Guidebook." SEI Handbook CMU/SEI-96-HB-002, 1996. www.sei.cmu.edu/publications/documents/96.reports/96.hb.002.html (accessed May 2007).

[Patterson and Conner 82] Patterson, Robert W., and Darryl R. Conner. "Building Commitment to Organizational Change." *Training and Development Journal*, April 1982, 18–30.

♦ [Pavlik et al. 00] Pavlik, Rich, Cary Riall, and Steve Janiszewski. "Deploying PSP, TSP, and Six Sigma Plus at Honeywell." SEPG Conference, 2000.

♦ [Penn and Siviy 02] Penn, M. Lynn, and Jeannine Siviy. "Leveraging Six Sigma in Systems Engineering." INCOSE 2002 Symposium, 2002.

♦ [Penn and Siviy 03] Penn, M. Lynn, and Jeannine Siviy. "Integrating CMMI and Six Sigma in Software and Systems Engineering." SEPG Conference, 2003.

♦ [Prewitt 03] Prewitt, Edward. "Quality Methodology: Six Sigma Comes to IT." *CIO Magazine*, August 15, 2003. www.cio.com/article/29626/_Quality_Methodology_Six_Sigma_Comes_to_IT (accessed September 2007).

♦ [PSM 00] Practical Software and Systems Measurement Support Center. *Practical Software and Systems Measurement: A Foundation for Objective Project Management, Guidebook, Version 4.0b*. U.S. TRACOM-ARDEC, AMSTA-AR-QA-A. October 2000. www.psmsc.com (accessed May 2007).

[Pyzdek 01a] Pyzdek, Thomas. *The Six Sigma Handbook*. New York: McGraw-Hill, 2001.

[Pyzdek 01b] Pyzdek, Thomas. "Why Six Sigma Is Not TQM." *Quality Digest*, February 2001. www.qualitydigest.com/feb01/html/sixsigma.html (accessed May 2007).

[Recardo et al. 07] Recardo, Ronald, Kathleen Molloy, and James Pellegrino. "How the Learning Organization Manages Change." *National Productivity Review* 15, no. 1 (January 17, 2007): 7–13.

[Revere 03] Revere, Lee. "Integrating Six Sigma with Total Quality Management: A Case Example for Measuring Medication Errors." *The Journal of Healthcare Management*, November 2003.

[Rockart 86] Rockart, Jack F. "A Primer on Critical Success Factors." In *The Rise of Managerial Computing: The Best of the Center for Information Systems Research*, ed. with Christine V. Bullen. Homewood, IL: Dow Jones-Irwin, 1986.

[Rogers 03] Rogers, Everett. *Diffusion of Innovations*, 5th ed. New York: Free Press, 2003.

♦ [Rombach and Ulery 89] Rombach, H. Dieter, and Bradford T. Ulery. "Improving Software Maintenance Through Measurement." *Proceedings of the IEEE* 77, no. 4 (April 1989): 581–595.

[Scheer 00] Scheer, A. W. *ARIS—Business Process Frameworks*, 3rd ed. London: Springer, 2000.

[Schon 67] Schon, Donald A. *Technology and Change: The New Heraclitus*. New York: Delacorte Press, 1967.

♦ [SEI 07] Software Engineering Institute. "Improving Process Performance Using Six Sigma." SEI course, 2007 and ongoing. [Previously called "Measuring for Performance-Driven Improvement 1"; see www.sei.cmu.edu/products/courses/p49.html for additional course information.]

[Senge 90] Senge, Peter. *The Fifth Discipline: The Art and Practice of the Learning Organization*. New York: Doubleday, 1990.

[Senge 06] Senge, Peter. *The Fifth Discipline: The Art and Practice of the Learning Organization*, 2nd ed. New York: Currency, 2006.

[Senge et al. 94] Senge, P. M., A. Kleiner, C. Roberts, R. B. Ross, and B. J. Smith. *The Fifth Discipline Fieldbook: Strategies and Tools for Building a Learning Organization*. New York: Doubleday, 1994.

[Senge et al. 99] Senge, Peter M., Art Kleiner, Charlotte Roberts, George Roth, Rick Ross, and Bryan Smith. *The Dance of Change: The Challenges to Sustaining Momentum in Learning Organizations*. New York: Currency, 1999.

[Shiba et al. 93] Shiba, Shiji, et al. *New American TQM—Four Practical Revolutions in Management*. University Park, IL: Productivity Press, 1993.

[Simon 07] Simon, Kerri. "DMAIC versus DMADV." iSixSigma.com. www.isixsigma.com/library/content/c001211a.asp (accessed September 2007).

♦ [Siviy 04] Siviy, Jeannine. "Your Six Sigma Measurement Infrastructure and Beyond." Six Sigma for Software Development Conference, 2004.

♦ [Siviy and Forrester 04] Siviy, Jeannine, and Eileen Forrester. "Accelerating CMMI Adoption Using Six Sigma." CMMI Technology Conference and User Group, 2004.

♦ [Siviy and Hefner 06] Siviy, Jeannine, and Rick Hefner. "Six Sigma Tools for Early Adopters." SEPG Conference, 2006.

♦ [Siviy et al. 05] Siviy, Jeannine, M. Lynn Penn, and Erin Harper. "Relationships between CMMI and Six Sigma." SEI Technical Note CMU/SEI-2005-TN-005. Pittsburgh, PA: Carnegie Mellon University, 2005.

[Snee 01] Snee, Ronald D. "Dealing with the Achilles' Heel of Six Sigma Initiatives: Project Selection Is the Key to Success." *Quality Progress*, March 2001.

[Sorensen 96] Sorensen, Reed. "MIL-STD-498, J-STD-016, and the U.S. Commercial Standard." *CrossTalk*, June 1996.

♦ [Srivastava 06] Srivastava, Nidhi. "Harvesting CMMI Benefits—The Six Sigma Sickle." SEPG Conference, 2006.

♦ [StickyMinds.com 02] News articles from www.stickyminds.com News Center's 30-day rolling archive: "Californians' Direct Deposits to Bank of America Listed as Missing," March 17, 2002; "Travel Plans Thrown into Chaos," March 29, 2002; "Mizuho Accounts Erroneously Debited During ATM Malfunction," April 3, 2002; "RMIT (Royal Melbourne Institute of Technology) Software System Still Bug-Ridden," April 2, 2002; "Computer Glitch Caused Jet Scare," March 25, 2002.

♦ [Stoddard 02] Stoddard, Robert W. "Six Sigma for Software." 56th Annual ASQ Quality Congress, 2002.

♦ [Subramanyam et al. 04] Subramanyam, V., Sambuddha Deb, Priya Krishnaswamy, and Rituparna Ghosh, "An Integrated Approach to Software

Process Improvement at Wipro Technologies: veloci-Q." SEI Technical Report CMU/SEI-2004-TR-006. Pittsburgh, PA: Carnegie Mellon University, March 2004. www.sei.cmu.edu/publications/documents/04.reports/04tr006.html (accessed May 2007).

[Telelogic 07] Telelogic. "Department of Defense Architecture Framework (DoDAF, Formerly C4ISR)." 2007. www.telelogic.com/standards/dodaf.cfm (accessed October 2007).

[Tennant 02] Tennant, Geoff. *Design for Six Sigma: Launching New Products and Services without Failure*. Hampshire, UK: Gower Publishing Company, 2002.

[Thawani 02] Thawani, Sunil. "Six Sigma Quality—Linking Customers, Processes, and Financial Results." April 2002. www.onesixsigma.com/node/692 (accessed October 2007).

[Thawani 04] Thawani, Sunil. "Six Sigma—Strategy for Organizational Excellence." *Total Quality Management* 15, no. 5–6 (July/August 2004).

[Vickroy 03] Vickroy, Robert. Offered idea to strategically select MA, OPP, and QPM as first PAs in which to achieve capability level 5 at a CMMI course on January 17, 2003. The idea has evolved through several subsequent conversations as part of courses, conferences, and collaborations.

♦ [Westfall n.d.] Westfall, Linda. "Cause and Effect Diagrams." www.westfallteam.com/Papers/Cause&Effect_Diagrams.pdf (accessed October 2007).

♦ [Weszka 06] Weszka, Joan. "Honing the Right Process Architecture for the Enterprise." SEPG Conference, 2006.

[Womack and Jones 96] Womack, James, and Daniel T. Jones. *Lean Thinking*. New York: Simon & Schuster, 1996.

♦ [Zubrow 98] Zubrow, David. "Measurement with a Focus: Goal-Driven Software Measurement?" *CrossTalk* 11, no. 9 (September 1998): 24–26.

♦ [Zubrow 03] Zubrow, David. "Putting 'M' in the Model: Measurement and Capability Maturity Model Integration (CMMI)." International Conference on Software Quality, 2003.

Additional Resources

Following is a selection of online resources, books, and papers we would like to share with you. This list is by no means exhaustive (we have several hundred more papers in our personal files, and many more are available via conference proceedings, journals, and sponsored white papers). Rather, we have included some personal favorites, as well as papers covering a cross-section of topics—software, systems, and IT; different business sectors; integrated model implementation (we have included as many of these as we know); and so forth.

As such, this list is not intended to be a recommendation that you read every single item. Instead, we recommend scanning for your topics of interest and using this section to identify your starter reading list.

Notes:

- In general, references cited within the book are not repeated here.
- The listed Web sites and papers primarily focused on the implementation of CMMI and/or Six Sigma with each other or other models in the IT, software, or systems engineering domains.
- Only a few Web sites, papers, analyst reports, and so on have been included that are about software quality, measurement, and process improvement outside of multimodel or Six Sigma topics.

- The listed books focus on Six Sigma, Lean, systems thinking, and applied statistics—regardless of application domain. Essentially, they are our frequently used references from among the classics on these topics.
- This is by no means a complete bibliography on any of these topics.
- URLs are subject to change without notice.
- Resources and references specific to IT, software, and systems engineering are annotated with this symbol: ♦.

Online Resources

American Society for Quality Six Sigma Forum: www.sixsigmaforum.com/concepts/var/index.shtml

International Quality Federation: www.iqfnet.org (follow the Black Belt links)

iSixSigma: www.isixsigma.com

♦ SEI Software Technology Review, Six Sigma Description: www.sei.cmu.edu/str/descriptions/sigma6.html

Six Sigma Academy: www.6-sigma.com

Smarter Solutions: www.smartersolutions.com

Online statistics books:

- *Electronic Statistics Textbook*: www.statsoft.com/textbook/stathome.html
- *Engineering Statistics Handbook*: www.itl.nist.gov/div898/handbook/prc/section1/prc16.htm

♦ Discussion groups and repositories of examples, benefits:

- Six Sigma in Software and Systems Engineering: http://groups.yahoo.com/group/6S_SWSE
- iSixSigma's Software channel, including a Software Quality Discussion Forum: http://software.isixsigma.com

Books

♦ Ahern, Dennis M., Aaron Clouse, and Richard Turner. *CMMI Distilled: A Practical Introduction to Integrated Process Improvement*, 2nd ed. Boston, MA: Addison-Wesley, 2003.

AT&T/Western Electric Co. *Statistical Quality Control Handbook*. Charlotte, NC: Delmar Printing Company, 1956.

Automotive Industry Action Group. *Statistical Process Control (SPC)*. Version 2. Southfield, MI: AIAG, 2005.

Barney, Matt, and Tom McCarty. *The New Six Sigma: A Leader's Guide to Achieving Rapid Business Improvement and Sustainable Results*. Upper Saddle River, NJ: Prentice Hall, 2002.

Brassard, Michael, and Diane Ritter. *Sailing Through Six Sigma*. Powder Springs, GA: Brassard & Ritter LLC, 2002.

Creveling, C. M. *Six Sigma for Technical Processes: An Overview for R&D Executives, Technical Leaders, and Engineering Managers*. Upper Saddle River, NJ: Prentice Hall, 2006.

♦ Florac, William A., and Anita D. Carleton. *Measuring the Software Process*. Reading, MA: Addison-Wesley, 1999.

George, Michael L. *Lean Six Sigma*. New York: McGraw-Hill, 2002.

Goldratt, Eliyahu M. *The Goal*. Great Barrington, MA: North River Press, 1992.

Gonick, Larry, and Woollcott Smith. *The Cartoon Guide to Statistics*. New York: HarperPerennial, 1993.

Juran, J. M. *Juran's Quality Control Handbook*, 4th ed. New York: McGraw-Hill, 1988.

Kiemele, Mark J., Stephen R. Schmidt, and Ronald J. Berdine. *Basic Statistics Tools for Continuous Improvement*. Air Academy Press, 2000.

Memory Jogger books published by GOAL/QPC. [See www.goalqpc.com for the complete Memory Jogger series, ranging from Memory Jogger I and II for analytical methods to Lean to Black Belt.]

♦ Middleton, Peter, and James Sutton. *Lean Software Strategies*. University Park, IL: Productivity Press, 2005.

Musa, John D., Anthony Iannino, and Okumoto Kazuhira. *Software Reliability: Measurement, Prediction, Application*. New York: McGraw-Hill, 1990.

♦ Nord, W. R., and S. Tucker. *Implementing Routine and Radical Innovations*. Lexington, MA: Lexington Books, 1987.

♦ Persse, James. *Process Improvement Essentials: CMMI, ISO9001, Six Sigma*. Sebastopol, CA: O'Reilly, 2006.

♦ Poppendieck, Mary, and Tom Poppendieck. *Lean Software Development: An Agile Toolkit*. Boston, MA: Addison-Wesley, 2003.

♦ ———. *Implementing Lean Software Development*. Boston, MA: Addison-Wesley, 2006.

Snee, Ron D., and Roger W. Hoerl. *Six Sigma Beyond the Factory Floor*. Upper Saddle River, NJ: Prentice Hall, 2004.

Tornatzy, Louis. G., and Fleischer, Mitchell. *The Process of Technological Innovation*. Lexington, MA: Lexington Books, 1990.

Wheeler, Donald. *Understanding Variation—The Key to Managing Chaos*. Knoxville, TN: SPC Press, 1993.

Wheeler, Donald, and David S. Chambers. *Understanding Statistical Process Control*. Knoxville, TN: SPC Press, 1992.

Papers, Presentations, Journal Articles, and Technical Reports[1]

Adler, P. S., and A. Shenhar. "Adapting Your Technological Base: The Organizational Challenge." *Sloan Management Review* 32, no. 1 (1990): 25–37.

♦ Antony, Jiju, and Craig Fergusson. "Six Sigma in the Software Industry: Results from a Pilot Study." *Managerial Auditing Journal* 19, no. 8 (2004): 1025–1032.

♦ Ares, Juan, Rafael Garcia, Natalia Juristo, Marta Lopez, and Ana M. Moreno. "A More Rigorous and Comprehensive Approach to Software Process Assessment." *Software Process: Improvement and Practice*, 2000: 5–30.

Arndt, Michael. "Quality Isn't Just for Widgets." *Business Week*, July 22, 2002.

Arnheiter, Edward D., and John Maleyeff. "The Integration of Lean Management and Six Sigma." *The TQM Magazine* 17, no. 1 (2005).

♦ Arul, Krishna, and Harsh Kohli. "Six Sigma for Software Application of Hypothesis Tests to Software Data." *Software Quality Journal* 12, no. 1 (2004): 29–42.

♦ Atwood, Jonathon. "Maximizing IT: The Link Between Six Sigma, Information Technology and Business Strategy." *iSixSigma Magazine*, May/June 2006.

[1]Also see References.

Balestracci, Davis. "TQM, Six Sigma, Lean and Data?" *Quality Digest*, July 5, 2006.

♦ Banerjee, Preeti. "Integrating Lean and Six Sigma Methodology for Software Process Improvements." SEPG Conference, 2007.

Banoo, Sreerema. "Seagate's Sigma Approach to Quality." *Business Times—Malaysia*, March 28, 2000.

Banuelas, Ricardo, and Jiju Antony. "Six Sigma or Design for Six Sigma?" *The TQM Magazine* 16, no. 4 (2004).

Banuelas, Ricardo, Charles Tennant, Ian Tuersley, and Shao Tang. "Selection of Six Sigma Projects in the UK." *The TQM Magazine* 18, no. 5 (2006).

Basu, Ron. "Six Sigma to Operational Excellence: Role of Tools and Techniques." *International Journal of Six Sigma and Competitive Advantage* 1, no. 1 (2004): 44–54.

Bates, Christina M., and Francis R. Bates. "Sarbanes-Oxley and Six Sigma: Windfalls and Pitfalls." *Six Sigma Forum Magazine*, August 2006.

♦ Bates, Peter. "Dueling Initiatives—Lean Sigma and the SW-CMM at the Gates Rubber Company." SEPG Conference, 2003.

Bauer, Kent. "The CPM Dashboard Meets Six Sigma, Part 1." *DM Review* 13, no. 6 (June 2003).

———. "The CPM Dashboard Meets Six Sigma, Part 2." *DM Review* 13, no. 7 (July 2003).

Bendell, Tony. "A Review and Comparison of Six Sigma and the Lean Organizations." *The TQM Magazine* 18, no. 3 (2006).

Bertels, Thomas. "Six Sigma from the CEO Perspective: Achievements, Challenges, and the Future." Rath and Strong Management Consultants, 2002.

♦ Bessin, Geoff. "The Business Value of Software Quality." *The Rational Edge*, June 15, 2004. www.ibm.com/developerworks/rational/library/4995.html (accessed October 2007).

Bigio, David, Rick L. Edgeman, and Thomas Ferleman. "Six Sigma Availability Management of Information Technology in the Office of the Chief Technology Officer of Washington DC." *Total Quality Management* 15, no. 5–6 (July–August 2004).

♦ Binder, R. V. "Can a Manufacturing Quality Model Work for Software?" *IEEE Software* 14, no. 5 (1997): 101–105.

Biolos, Jim. "Six Sigma Meets the Service Economy." *Harvard Management Update* 7, no. 11 (November 2002).

Bisgaard, Soren, and Jeroen De Mast. "After Six Sigma—What's Next?" *Quality Progress*, January 2006.

Blakeslee, Jerome A., Jr. "Implementing the Six Sigma Solution." *Quality Progress*, July 1999.

♦ Blezek, Daniel J., Timothy P. Kelliher, William E. Lorensen, and James V. Miller. "GE Corporate Research and Development, Six Sigma Meets Extreme Programming: Changing the Way We Work." Quality Week Conference, 2001.

Blezek, Daniel J., William E. Lorensen, and Timothy P. Kelliher. "The Frost Extreme Testing Framework, GE Research and Development Center." Quality Week Conference, 2001.

Brady, James E., and Theodore T. Allen. "Six Sigma Literature: A Review and Agenda for Future Research." The Ohio State University, Industrial and Systems Engineering. www-iwse.eng.ohio-state.edu/ISEFaculty/allen/BradyAllenSSLitRev2006.pdf (accessed May 2007).

♦ Bratton, Janet. "Raytheon, Marrying High Maturity Processes to Six Sigma—From First Date to Happy Marriage." SEPG Conference, 2003.

♦ Caccovo, Dean, and Rick Hefner. "CMMI Benefits at Northrop Grumman Mission Systems." CMMI Technology and Conference User Group, November 17–20, 2003.

♦ Card, David. "Sorting Out Six Sigma and the CMM." *IEEE Software*, May/June 2000.

♦ ———. "Integrating Six Sigma and the CMMI." Software Technology Conference, April 29–May 2, 2002.

♦ ———. "Integrating Lean, Six Sigma and CMMI." PSM Users Group, 2005.

♦ Cechich, Alejandra, and Mario Piattini. "Managing COTS Components Using a Six Sigma Based Process." Proceedings of the 5th International Conference on Product Focused Software Process Improvement, PROFES, Springer-Verlag LNCS, Japan, 2004.

♦ Chandler, Doug, and Lionel Lamy. "Sun Sigma Helps Deliver Higher Service Levels to Customers, an IDC White Paper." August 2003. www.sun.com/software/sunone/boardroom/newsletter/0204sigmasun.pdf (accessed October 2007).

Chappell, Andrew, and Helen Peck. "Risk Management in Military Supply Chains: Is There a Role for Six Sigma?" *International Journal of Logistics: Research and Applications* 9, no. 3 (September 2006).

♦ Chillarege, Ram. "The Marriage of Business Dynamics and Software Engineering." *IEEE Software*, November/December 2002.

Choudri, Adi. "Design for Six Sigma for Aerospace Applications." Space 2004 Conference and Exhibit, 2004.

Connor, Gary. "Benefiting from Six Sigma: Does Your Company Have to Be Large to Benefit from Six Sigma?" *Manufacturing Engineering* 130, no. 2 (February 2003).

♦ Cool, Christopher B. "Lean and CMMI." CMMI Technology and User Group, 2001.

♦ Covatti, Andressa, and Renato Chaves Vasques. "Dell Case—Integrating Six Sigma and CMMI." SEPG Conference, 2007.

Davis, Arthur G. "Six Sigma for Small Companies: Implementing a Six Sigma Intervention Need Not Cost Millions." *Quality* 42, no. 11 (November 2003).

Davis III, Wallace. "Using Corrective Action to Make Matters Worse." *Quality Progress*, October 2000.

Dawne, Shand. "Six Sigma." *Computerworld*, March 5, 2001.

de Koning, Henk, and Jeroen de Mast. "A Rational Reconstruction of Six Sigma's Breakthrough Cookbook." *International Journal of Quality and Reliability Management* 23, no. 7 (2006).

Does, R., E. van den Heuvel, J. de Mast, and S. Bisgaard. "Quality Quandaries: Comparing Nonmanufacturing with Traditional Applications of Six Sigma." *Quality Engineering* 15, no. 1 (2003): 177–182.

Dusharme, Dirk. "Six Sigma Survey: Breaking Through the Six Sigma Hype." *Quality Digest*, November 2001. www.qualitydigest.com/nov01/html/sixsigmaarticle.html (accessed May 2007).

♦ Dutton, Jeffrey L., and Richard S. McCabe. "Agile/Lean Development and CMMI." SEPG Conference, 2006.

Ehie, Ike, and Chwen Sheu. "Integrating Six Sigma and Theory of Constraints for Continuous Improvement: A Case Study." *Journal of Manufacturing Technology Management* 16, no. 5 (2005).

♦ Eickelmann, Nancy. "Statistical Process Control for Software." Six Sigma for Software Development Conference, October 2003.

Fargher, John S. W. "The Roadmap from Lean to Six Sigma." IIE Annual Conference and Exhibition, 2004.

Ferrin, David M., and David Muthler. "Six Sigma and Simulation, So What's the Correlation?" Proceedings of the 2002 Winter Simulation Conference, Winter 2002.

Fitzpatrick, David, and Mike Looney. "A Roadmap to Greater Efficiency in Aerospace Operations Through the Application of Six Sigma and Lean Manufacturing Techniques." *Aircraft Engineering and Aerospace Technology* 75, no. 3 (June 2003).

♦ Fleischer, Nancy. "Raytheon's Six Sigma Process and Its Applications for CMMI." NDIA/SEI CMMI Technology Conference, November 17–20, 2003.

♦ Gack, Gary A. "Six Sigma for Software, CMMI Personal Software Process (PSP) and Team Software Process (TSP)." *Software Quality Professional* 5, no. 4 (September 2003): 5–13.

♦ ———. "Six Sigma Roadmaps: DFSS and DMAIC: Similarities and Distinctions." Six Sigma for Software Development Conference, October 2003.

♦ ———. "Connections Between Design for Six Sigma and CMMI." http://software.isixsigma.com/library/content/c050914b.asp (accessed September 2007).

♦ ———. "Six Sigma Applies to IT, as Evidenced by Success." http://software.isixsigma.com/library/content/c040121b.asp (accessed May 2007).

♦ Gack, Gary A., and Karl D. Williams. "Connecting Software Industry Standards and Best Practices: Lean Six Sigma and CMMI." *CrossTalk*, February 2007.

♦ George, Ellen, and Stephen Janiszewski. "Optimizing Software Inspections with Statistical Quality Techniques." *Software Quality Professional* 6, no. 1 (2003).

♦ ———. "Using Six Sigma to Drive Software CMM Based Process Improvement." ASQ Six Sigma Conference, January 31, 2004.

♦ Goh, G. N., and G. Y. Hong. "Six Sigma in Software Quality." *The TQM Magazine* 15, no. 6 (Fall 2003).

♦ Goldenson, Dennis R., and Diane L. Gibson. "Demonstrating the Impact and Benefits of CMMI: An Update and Preliminary Results." SEI Special Report CMU/SEI-2003-SR-009. Pittsburgh, PA: Carnegie Mellon University, 2003.

Green, Robert. "Reshaping Six Sigma at Honeywell: Dedicated Teams Successfully Merge Two Divergent Quality Systems." *Quality Digest*, December 2000.

♦ Hallowell, David L. "Software Design for Six Sigma: Assessing the Fit." SEPG Conference, 2004.

♦ ———. "Toward an Integrated Six Sigma Software Knowledge Base." 2004. http://software.isixsigma.com/library/content/c030416a.asp (accessed October 2007).

♦ ———. "Using Software CTQ Flowdown and Capability Prediction to Reduce Risk and Drive Results." Six Sigma Advantage, Inc.

♦ ———. "Design for Six Sigma Meets Agile—Exploring the Fit." SEPG Conference, 2007.

Hammer, Michael. "Process Management and the Future of Six Sigma." *MIT Sloan Management Review*, Winter 2002.

Harrington, H. James. "The Five Pillars of Organizational Excellence." *Quality Digest*, August 2006.

♦ Harrington, H. James, and Tom McNellis. "Six Sigma for Internet Application Development." *Software Quality Professional* 4, no. 1 (December 2001).

♦ Hayes, Bruce J. "Introduction to Six Sigma for Software: The Third Wave." Six Sigma for Software Development Conference, October 2003.

♦ ———. "Six Sigma Critical Success Factors." Six Sigma Software Conference, 2003.

♦ Hefner, Rick. "Accelerating CMMI Adoption Using Six Sigma." CMMI Technology Conference and User Group, 2004.

♦ ———. "Northrop Grumman Case Study: Integrating Quality Initiatives." Six Sigma for Software Development Conference, 2004.

♦ Hefner, Rick, and Leitha Purcell. "Merging Six Sigma with CMM/CMMI." SEPG Conference, 2002.

♦ Hefner, Rick, and Mike Sturgeon. "The Fundamentals of Six Sigma." Systems and Software Technology Conference, 2003.

♦ Hefner, Rick, and Charles Weber. "CMM/CMMI: Quantitative Measurement versus Quantitative Management." SEPG Conference, 2003.

Hensley, Rhonda L., and Kathryn Dobie. "Assessing Readiness for Six Sigma in a Service Setting." *Managing Service Quality* 15, no. 1 (2005).

♦ Ho, Linh C., and Richard Morgan. "Six Sigma for IT Service Management, an Enterprise Management Associates White Paper." Prepared for Proxima Technology, August 2003. www.sixsigmazone.com/assets/Article_-_Six_Sigma_for_IT_Management.pdf (accessed October 2007).

♦ Holmes, Jeffrey S. "Identifying Code-Inspection Improvements Using Statistical Black Belt Techniques." *Software Quality Professional* 6, no. 1 (2003).

♦ ———. "Optimizing the Software Life Cycle." *Software Quality Professional* 5, no. 4 (September 2003): 14–23.

♦ ———. "Software Measurement Using SCM." *Software Quality Professional* 7, no. 1 (2004).

♦ Hong, G. Y., and T. N. Goh. "Six Sigma in Software Quality." *The TQM Magazine* 15, no. 6 (2003).

♦ Houston, Dan. "The Value of a Good Checklist.doc." *Software Quality Professional* 6, no. 2 (March 2004): 17–26.

♦ Janiszewski, Steve. "Washington D.C., Six Sigma and Software Process Improvement." DC SPIN, March 3, 2004.

♦ ———. "Introducing Six Sigma to Software Development." PMI NYC Chapter, March 17, 2004.

♦ Janiszewski, Steve, and Ellen George. "Integrating PSP, TSP and Six Sigma." *Software Quality Professional* 6, no. 4 (September 2004).

♦ Jarvis, Bob. "Extreme Programming (XP), Six Sigma and CMMI: How They Can Work Together—A JP Morgan Chase Case Study." NYC SPIN, March 2002.

Keller, Paul, *Recent Trends in Six Sigma*, ASQ Annual Quality Conference, April 2001.

♦ Kovara, Joe, Jeffrey Elliott, and Rick DeCamp. "Security Kaizen: Security as a Dimension of Quality." SEPG Conference, 2006.

Kuchar, Norman R. "Implementing DFSS at GE: Challenges and Benefits." Design for Six Sigma Seminar, June 2000.

LaGrange, Christine. "Accelerating Six Sigma Rollout." *Quality Magazine*, June 2005.

Lahiri, Jaideep. "The Enigma of Six Sigma." The Net Business of the India Today Group. www.india-today.com/btoday/19990922/cover.html (accessed May 2007).

♦ Lane, Dianne. "Raytheon Six Sigma and Process Definition at Falls Church." SEPG Conference, 2004.

♦ Luttrell, Dan. "Energizing CMMI with Six Sigma." SEPG Conference, 2004.

♦ Mackertich, Neal. "Effectively Applying DFSS in Software Intensive Systems." ISSSP Changing the Practice of Product Development Symposium, January 2005.

♦ ———. "Raytheon Six Sigma: Approach, Results and Challenges." Second Annual Design for Six Sigma Conference, 2006.

♦ ———. "Why Is It That Every Time I Play Chess, the Pieces Keep Getting in the Way?" Systems and Software Technology Conference, 2006.

♦ Mahanti, Rupa. "Six Sigma for Software." *Software Quality Professional* 8, no. 1 (2005).

♦ Mahanti, Rupa, and J. Antony. "Confluence of Six Sigma, Simulation and Software Development." *Managerial Auditing Journal* 20, no. 7 (2005): 739–762.

Malin, Jane H., and Elaine Reichardt. "Strengthen the Six Sigma Portfolio." *Quality*, June 2005.

Martin, Dale R., Paul E. Juras, and George R. Adlhizer III. "Taming SOX Costs with Six Sigma." *Journal of Corporate Accounting and Finance* 17, no. 3 (2006): 13–22.

♦ Marx, Michael. "Information Technology and Six Sigma." *iSixSigma Magazine*, May/June 2005.

♦ Mayor, Tracy. "Six Sigma Comes to IT: Targeting Perfection." *CIO Magazine*, February 6, 2004.

McAdam, Rodney, Shirley-Ann Hazlett, and Joan Henderson. "A Critical Review of Six Sigma: Exploring the Dichotomies." *International Journal of Organizational Analysis* 13, no. 2 (2005).

McIllroy, Jay, and David Silverstein. "Six Sigma Deployment in One Aerospace Company, Northrop Grumman's Six Sigma Roadmap." Six Sigma Forum, 2002. www.asq.org/sixsigma/ (accessed May 2007).

◆ McLoone, Peter J., and Sharon L. Rohde. "Performance Outcomes of CMMI-Based Process Improvements." *DACS Software Tech News*, March 2007.

Mekki, Khalid S. "Robust Design Failure Mode and Effects Analysis in Designing for Six Sigma." *International Journal of Product Development* 3, no. 3/4 (2006).

◆ Middel, Christian. "Six Sigma Meets Personal and Team Software Processes." MKS white paper, June 2005.

◆ Moore, Dale L. "Naval Aviation Enterprise AIRSpeed: Leading a Consistent Approach for Success Across the Globe: The Naval Aviation Story." Eighth Annual Six Sigma Summit, January 2007.

Munro, Roderick A. "Linking Six Sigma with QS-9000." *Quality Progress*, May 2000.

Nee, Eric. "The Hottest CEO in Tech." *Business 2.0*, June 1, 2003.

◆ Null, Steven R. "Understanding and Applying DFSS to Software Design and Development." Six Sigma for Software Development Conference, October 2003.

◆ O'Donnell, Mary Ellen. "Applying Six Sigma to Areas Outside of Manufacturing in the Space Industry: Lessons Learned from Applying Raytheon Six Sigma to PATRIOT Missile Software and Systems Engineering." AIAA Space 2005 Conference and Exhibition, 2005.

◆ Oudrhiri, Radouane. "Six Sigma and DFSS for IT and Software Engineering." European Six Sigma Summit, April 2004.

◆ Park Ji-Hyub, Ki-Won Song, Kyung Whan Lee, and Sun-Myung Hwang. "Analyzing Relationships to the Quality Level between CMM and Six Sigma." *Lecture Notes in Computer Science* 3026 (2004).

Paul, Lauren Gibbons. "Practice Makes Perfect." *CIO Magazine*, January 15, 1999. www.cio.com/archive/enterprise/011599_process.html (accessed May 2007).

◆ Pavlik, Rich. "Deploying PSP, TSP, and Six Sigma Plus at Honeywell." SEPG Conference, 2001.

◆ ———. "Software Design for Six Sigma at Honeywell Aerospace." Six Sigma for Software Development Conference, October 2003.

◆ Pavlik, Rich, and Cary Riall. "Integrating PSP, TSP, and Six Sigma Plus at Honeywell." SEPG Conference, 2002.

Pfeifer, Tilo, Wolf Reissiger, and Claudia Canales. "Integrating Six Sigma with Quality Management Systems." *The TQM Magazine* 16, no. 4, 2004.

♦ Phadke, Madhav S. "Design of Experiment for Software Testing." 2003. www.isixsigma.com/library/content/c030106a.asp (accessed September 2007).

Pojasek, Robert B. "Lean, Six Sigma and the Systems Approach: Management Initiatives for Process Improvement." *Environmental Quality Management*, Winter 2003.

♦ Porter, Don. "Statistical Process Control (SPC) for Software Inspections." Motorola and the International Conference on Software Management, February 2001.

♦ Purcell, Leitha. "Experiences Using Six Sigma in a SW-CMM Based Process Improvement Program." SEPG Conference, 2001.

Pyzdek, Thomas. "Ignore Six Sigma at Your Peril." *Quality Digest*, April 2001. www.qualitydigest.com/april01/html/sixsigma.html (accessed May 2007).

———. "101 Things a Six Sigma Black Belt Should Know." 2003. http://www.pyzdek.com/101.htm (accessed October 2007).

Ramberg, John S. "Six Sigma: Fad or Fundamental?" *Quality Digest*, May 2000. www.qualitydigest.com/may00/html/sixsigmapro.html (accessed October 2007).

Robustelli, Pete. "Beyond Six Sigma." *Quality Digest*, September 2003.

♦ Rothman, Johanna. "Using Combinatorial Testing to Reduce Risk and Improve Product Quality." Six Sigma for Software Development Conference, October 2003.

Rowlands, Hiefin. "Six Sigma: A New Philosophy or Repackaging of Old Ideas?" *Engineering Management Journal* 13, no. 2 (April/May 2003).

♦ Saleh, Mohammad Saad, Abdualla Alrabiah, and Saad Haj Bakry. "Using ISO 17799:2005 Information Security Management: A STOPE View with Six Sigma Approach." *International Journal of Network Management* 17, no. 1 (2007): 85–97.

♦ Salviano, Clenio F., and Mario Jino. "Towards a {(Process Capability profile)_Driven (Process Engineering)} as an Evolution of Software Process Improvement." European Software Process Improvement, 2006.

Schein, Edgar. "The Three Cultures of Management: Implications for Organizational Learning." *Sloan Management Review* 38 (1996): 9–20.

♦ Serazio, Jim, and Charles Everett. "Leaning Out, the Often Overlooked 'Non-Manufacturing Environment.'" SEPG Conference, 2004.

♦ Sheard, Sarah A. "How Do I Make My Organization Comply with Yet Another New Model?" *CrossTalk*, February 2002.

♦ Shere, Kenneth D. "Comparing Lean Six Sigma to the Capability Maturity Model." *CrossTalk*, September 2003.

♦ Siviy, Jeannine. "Six Sigma and Software/Systems Process Improvement." IQPC, 2002.

Smith, Bonnie, and Emily Adams. "LeanSigma: Advanced Quality," ASQ Annual Quality Conference, April 2001.

Smith, Larry R. "Six Sigma and the Evolution of Quality in Product Development." *Six Sigma Forum Magazine*, November 2001.

Snee, Ronald D. "When Worlds Collide: Lean and Six Sigma." *Quality Progress*, September 2005.

♦ Software Engineering Institute. "Position Paper on Government Use of Lean Enterprise Self-Assessment Tool (LESAT) for Benchmarking (Comparison of LESAT and CMM/CMMI for Comparing Companies)." August 2001. www.sei.cmu.edu/cmmi/publications/comparison.doc (accessed May 2007).

♦ Srivastava, Nidhi. "Harvesting CMMI Benefits—The Six Sigma Sickle." SEPG Conference, 2006.

Stamatis, D. H. "Who Needs Six Sigma, Anyway?" *Quality Digest*, May 2000. www.qualitydigest.com/may00/html/sixsigmacon.html (accessed October 2007).

♦ Stoddard, Robert W. "Implementing Six Sigma in Software." Motorola, Inc., Software Engineering Symposium, 2000.

♦ Sturgeon, Mike, and Louise Mudd. "Strategies for Successfully Implementing CMMI and Six Sigma." NDIA CMMI Technology and User Group, 2002.

Su, Chao-Ton, Tai-Lin Chiang, and Che-Ming Chang. "Improving Service Quality by Capitalising on an Integrated Lean Six Sigma Methodology." *International Journal of Six Sigma and Competitive Advantage* 2, no. 1, 2006.

♦ Sutton, James. "Software and Lean: Like Chocolate and Cranberries." Systems and Software Technology Conference, 2005.

♦ Ward, Andrew. "Lean Thinking and Appropriate IT—Plus KPIs." *Manufacturing Computer Solutions*, January 2005. www.allbusiness.com/technology/977340-1.html (accessed October 2007).

♦ Watson, Gregory H. "Breakthrough in Delivering Software Quality: Capability Maturity Model and Six Sigma, Business Systems Solutions Inc." ECSQ 2002: 7th International Conference, Helsinki, Finland, June 9–13, 2002.

Waxer, Charles. "Six Sigma Costs and Savings." www.isixsigma.com/library/content/c020729a.asp (accessed May 2007).

Wessel, Godecke, and Peter Burcher. "Six Sigma for Small and Medium Sized Enterprises." *The TQM Magazine* 16, no. 4 (2004).

♦ Williams, Karl D. "CMMI or Six Sigma: Does It Matter Which Comes First?" http://software.isixsigma.com/library/content/c060524b.asp (accessed October 2007).

♦ Wilson, David. "CMMI and Six Sigma Synergy" SEPG Conference, 2005.

♦ Witkowski, Dorna, and M. Lynn Penn. "Use of SCAMPI C for Agile Methodology." NDIA CMMI Technology Conference and User Group, 2006.

♦ Young, Tim. "Merging Six Sigma and IT." *Six Sigma Forum Magazine*, February 2002.

Zmud, Robert W., and L. Eugene Apple. "Measuring Technology Incorporation/Infusion." *Journal of Product Innovation Management* 9 (1992): 148–155.

Zultner, Richard E. "QFD Schedule Deployment: Doing Development Faster with QFD." Transactions from the 10th Symposium on QFD, 1998.

Acronyms

This section of the book presents a list of relevant acronyms, followed by titles of and information about selected models and standards mentioned in this book.

ACWP	actual cost of work performed
ANOVA	analysis of variance
ARIS	Architecture of Integrated Information Systems
ASQ	American Society for Quality
AT&L	Acquisition, Technology, and Logistics
ATAM	Architecture Tradeoff Analysis Method
BB	Black Belt
BCWP	budgeted cost of work performed
BCWS	budgeted cost of work scheduled
CAR	Causal Analysis and Resolution (CMMI process area)
CASRE	Computer Aided Software Reliability Estimation
CBAM	cost/benefit analysis method
CDOV	Concept-Design-Optimize-Verify [Creveling et al. 03]
CEO	chief executive officer
CIG	Corporate Initiatives Group (Motorola case study)

CM	Configuration Management (CMMI process area)
CMMI	Capability Maturity Model Integration
COBIT	Control Objectives for Information and related Technology
COO	chief operating officer
COPQ	cost of poor quality
COQ	cost of quality
COTS	commercial off the shelf
CPM	critical parameter management
CTC	critical to customer
CTQ	critical to quality
CV	cost variance
DAR	Decision Analysis and Resolution (CMMI process area)
DCCDI	Define-Customer-Concept-Design-Implement [Tennant 02]
DFMEA	design failure modes and effects analysis
DFSS	Design for Six Sigma
DMADDD	Define-Measure-Analyze-Design-Digitize-Drawdown
DMAD(O)V	Define-Measure-Analyze-Design-(Optimize)-Validate
DMAIC	Define-Measure-Analyze-Improve-Control
DMEDI	Define-Measure-Explore-Develop-Implement
DoD	Department of Defense
DoDAF	DoD Architecture Framework
DOE	Design of Experiments
DPMO	defects per million opportunities
DPU	defects per unit
DSS	Digital Six Sigma (Motorola case study)
EAC	estimate at completion
EFQM	European Framework for Quality Management
EIA	Electronic Industries Alliance
EOL	end of life
EPIC	Evolutionary Process for Integrating COTS-Based Systems
EPSC	Executive Process Steering Committee (Lockheed Martin case study)
ETVX	Entry-Task-Verification-eXit
EV	earned value

FAST	Function Analysis Systems Technique
FMEA	failure modes and effects analysis
FOSS	free and open source software
GB	Green Belt
GDM	Goal-Driven Measurement
GEA	General Electric Aerospace (Lockheed Martin case retrospectives)
GOTS	government off the shelf
GP	generic practice
GQIM	Goal-Question-Indicator-Metric
GQM	Goal-Question-Metric
GSG	Global Software Group (Motorola case study)
HW	hardware
I2DOV	Invent/Innovate-Develop-Optimize-Verify [Creveling et al. 03]
ID(D)OV	Identify-Design-(Develop)-Optimize-Validate
IDEAL	Initiating-Diagnosing-Establishing-Acting-Learning
IEC	International Electrotechnical Commission
IEP	Integrated Enterprise Process (Lockheed Martin case study)
INCOSE	International Council on Systems Engineering
IPM	Integrated Project Management (CMMI process area)
IQR	interquartile range
IR&D	Independent Research & Development
IS&GS	Information Systems and Global Services (Lockheed Martin case study)
IS&S	Integrated Systems & Solutions
ISO	International Organization for Standardization
IT	information technology
ITIL	Information Technology Infrastructure Library
KC	key characteristic
KLOC	thousand lines of code
KPA	key process area (SW-CMM)
LCL	lower control limit
LMCO	Lockheed Martin Corporation

LOB	line of business
LOC	lines of code
M&DS	Management & Data Systems
MA	Measurement and Analysis (CMMI process area)
MBB	Master Black Belt
MBF	management by fact
MGates	Management Gates (Motorola case study)
MMC	Martin Marietta Corporation (Lockheed Martin case retrospectives)
MSA	measurement systems analysis
MSE	measurement systems evaluation
MTBF	mean time between failures
MTTD	mean time to detect
MTTR	mean time to repair
MU	Motorola University (Motorola case study)
MWG	measurement working group
NDIA	National Defense Industrial Association
NGC	Northrop Grumman Corporation
ODC	Orthogonal Defect Classification
OID	Organizational Innovation and Deployment (CMMI process area)
OPD	Organizational Process Definition (CMMI process area)
OPF	Organizational Process Focus (CMMI process area)
OPP	Organizational Process Performance (CMMI process area)
OT	Organizational Training (CMMI process area)
OUSD	Office of the Under Secretary of Defense
PA	process area
PAT	process action team
PCB	Process Control Board (Lockheed Martin case study)
PCM	Process Change Management (SW-CMM key process area)
PDP	Program Development Plan (Lockheed Martin case study)
PEP	Program Excellence Plan (Lockheed Martin case retrospectives)
PI	Product Integration (CMMI process area)

PIR	Process Improvement Recommendation (Lockheed Martin case study)
PM	project management
PMBOK	Project Management Body of Knowledge
PMC	Project Monitoring and Control (CMMI process area)
POC	point of contact
PP	Project Planning (CMMI process area)
ppm	parts per million
PPQA	Process and Product Quality Assurance (CMMI process area)
PPS	Program Process Standard (Lockheed Martin case study)
PrIME	Process Improvement in Multimodel Environments
PSM	Practical Software and Systems Measurement
PSP	Personal Software Process
QA	quality assurance
QAW	Quality Attribute Workshop
QFD	quality function deployment
QGates	Quality Gates (Motorola case study)
QMM	*Quantitative Measurement Manual* (Lockheed Martin case study)
QPM	Quantitative Project Management (CMMI process area)
QS&PM	Quality Systems and Process Management (Lockheed Martin case study)
R&D	research and development
RD	Requirements Development (CMMI process area)
RDP	required development process (Lockheed Martin case study)
REQM	Requirements Management (CMMI process area)
ROI	return on investment
RSKM	Risk Management (CMMI process area)
RSM	response surface methodology
RUP	Rational Unified Process
SA-CMM	Software Acquisition Capability Maturity Model
SAM	Supplier Agreement Management (CMMI process area)
SCAMPI	Standard CMMI Appraisal Method for Process Improvement

SCM	software configuration management
SDLC	software development lifecycle
SE-CMM	Systems Engineering Capability Maturity Model
SEI	Software Engineering Institute
SEMM	*Software Engineering and Management Manual* (Lockheed Martin case study)
SEPG	Software Engineering Process Group
SETA	Systems Engineering and Technical Assistance
SG	specific goal
SLOC	source lines of code
SMART	specific, measurable, attainable or agreed-upon, relevant or realistic, timely or timebound
SME	subject matter expert
SoS	system of systems
SOX	Sarbanes-Oxley Act
SPC	statistical process control
SPI	software process improvement
SSRI	Six Sigma Research Institute
SV	schedule variance
SW	software
SW-CMM	Software Capability Maturity Model
SWEBOK	Software Engineering Body of Knowledge
TCM	Technology Change Management (SW-CMM key process area)
TCMWG	Technology Change Management Working Group (Lockheed Martin case study)
TCS	Tata Consultancy Services
TDFSS	Technology Design for Six Sigma
TOC	theory of constraints
TQM	total quality management
TS	Technical Solution (CMMI process area)
TSP	Team Software Process
TWG	technology working group; or technical working group
UCL	upper control limit

UPIA	Unified Process Improvement Approach
VAL	Validation (CMMI process area)
VER	Verification (CMMI process area)
VOB	voice of the business
VOC	voice of the customer
VOM	voice of the market
VOP	voice of the process
VOT	voice of the technology
VP	vice president
VSM	value stream mapping
WIP	work in process

Following are titles and, in some cases, brief explanations of selected models and standards (other than the maturity models and Six Sigma).

Agile Software Development — While a spiral development approach focuses on using prototypes to mitigate high-priority risks, Agile provides working portions of systems that are demonstrated/delivered at the end of every 4- to 6-week iteration. Agile, with its focus on these short, time-boxed iterations, enables the earliest possible delivery of critical mission capabilities. At the end of each iteration, the customer can reprioritize needed capabilities and/or make equivalent scope changes to the product backlog as needs change. Continuous integration and testing supported by automated tools instill more and more quality and confidence in the product as it evolves. Planning for the next iteration/cycle/release is a continual activity throughout the development. As with most development methods, Agile provides various status measurements and indicators that, in addition to the working software, support the decision-making process. Through the iteration demonstrations, prioritization efforts, planning, and decision making, Agile not only encourages but also requires frequent customer interaction and the establishment of a strong, working customer/contractor team.

AS9100 — SAE AS9100 specifies requirements for a quality in the aerospace industry, inclusive of those requirements stated in ISO 9001:2000. Revision B was issued in January 2004. It was developed in the United States as AS9000 in 1997, expanded to address international aerospace requirements, and is now approved by aerospace companies in Asia and Europe as well.

British Standard 7799 — Part 1 was a standard originally published as BS 7799 by the British Standards Institute (BSI) in 1995. After several revisions, it was eventually adopted by ISO as ISO/IEC 17799, "Information Technology—

Code of practice for information security management" in 2000. ISO 17799 was most recently revised in June 2005 and was renamed ISO/IEC 27002 in July 2007. A second part to BS 7799 was first published by BSI in 1999, known as BS 7799 Part 2, titled "Information Security Management Systems—Specification with guidance for use." BS 7799-2 focused on how to implement an information security management system (ISMS), referring to the information security management structure and controls identified in ISO 17799. The 2002 version of BS 7799-2 introduced the Plan-Do-Check-Act (PDCA) (Deming quality assurance model), aligning it with quality standards such as ISO 9000. BS 7799 Part 2 was adopted by ISO as ISO/IEC 27001 in November 2005. BS 7799 Part 3 was published in 2005, covering risk analysis and management. It aligns with ISO 27001.

COBIT — Control Objectives for Information and related Technology (COBIT) provides a set of best practices whose purpose is to serve as a governance model that focuses on IT value and risk management, information and system integrity, and the bridging of gaps between business, oversight, and technical issues. COBIT was created in 1992 by the Information Systems Audit and Control Association (ISACA) and the IT Governance Institute (ITGI).

DoD 5000 — The Department of Defense (DoD) acquisition policy was contained in DoD Directive 5000.1. The guidance supplement is DoD Instruction 5000.2. This policy has been retired.

"The Defense Acquisition System exists to manage the Nation's investments in technologies, programs, and product support necessary to achieve the National Security Strategy and support the United States Armed Forces. In that context, our continued objective is to rapidly acquire quality products that satisfy user needs with measurable improvements to mission capability at a fair and reasonable price. The fundamental principles and procedures that the Department follows in achieving those objectives are described in DoD Directive 5000.1 and DoD Instruction 5000.2. The Defense Acquisition Guidebook is designed to complement those policy documents by providing the acquisition workforce with discretionary best practice that should be tailored to the needs of each program" [DoD 04].

DoDAF — "Agencies and suppliers of integrated defense systems require a common way of representing operational and systems architectures. The scale, complexity, and expense of defense systems mean that poor specification and design can significantly increase project cost.

"To overcome these challenges, defense procurement agencies have increasingly adopted standard frameworks to help evaluate the effectiveness of designs. With the U.S. Department of Defense mandating the use of its Department of Defense Architecture Framework (DoDAF, formerly C4ISR), and variants now being adopted around the world, suppliers of defense solutions must describe their offering in terms of an architectural framework" [Telelogic 07].

EFQM Excellence Framework	This is a framework for organizational management systems, promoted by the European Foundation for Quality Management (EFQM) and designed for helping organizations in their drive toward being more competitive.
EIA 632	This is an Electronics Industries Alliance (EIA) Standard: Processes for Engineering a System.
EIA 731	This is an Electronics Industries Alliance (EIA) Standard: Systems Engineering Capability Model.
IEEE 829	Also known as the 829 Standard for Software Test Documentation, IEEE 829 is an IEEE standard that specifies the form of a set of documents for use in eight defined stages of software testing.
IEEE 830	A fuller name for IEEE 830 is the Recommended Practice for Software Requirements Specifications.
IEEE 1471	This is the short name for a standard formally known as ANSI/IEEE 1471-2000, Recommended Practice for Architecture Description of Software-Intensive Systems.
ISO 9001	The ISO 9000 family of standards is primarily concerned with quality management. These standards provide an international consensus on good management practices, focusing on assurance of repeatable delivery of products or services that meet customer quality requirements as well as any regulatory requirements, all while enhancing customer satisfaction and improving performance. More information is available at www.iso.org.
ISO 12207	This standard is also known as ISO/IEC 12207: Information Technology—Software Life-Cycle Processes.
ISO 14000	The ISO 14000 family is primarily concerned with environmental management.
ISO 17666	This standard extends the requirements of ISO 14300-1, the principles and requirements for integrated risk management on a space project. It explains what is needed to implement a project-integrated risk management policy by any project actor, at any level (i.e., customer, first-level supplier, or lower-level suppliers).
ISO 20000	This is the first international standard for IT Service Management. It is based on and is intended to supersede the earlier British Standard, BS 15000.
ISO/IEC 15288	System Life Cycle Processes is the first ISO standard to deal with system lifecycle processes: hardware, software, and human interfaces.
ISO/IEC 15504	ISO/IEC 15504, also known as SPICE (Software Process Improvement and Capability Determination), is a standard for process assessment

developed by the Joint Technical Subcommittee between ISO and IEC. ISO/IEC 15504 derives from ISO 12207 and uses many of the ideas of CMMI.

ISO/IEC 15939 — This is another standard, Systems and Software Engineering: Measurement Process.

ITIL — The Information Technology Infrastructure Library (ITIL) offers a framework of best practice approaches focusing on high-quality IT services. It outlines a large set of management procedures for IT operations and infrastructure.

J-STD 016 — EIA/IEEE J-STD 016 is a trial-use standard for information technology, software lifecycle processes, software development, and acquirer-supplier agreement. It is a commercial version of MIL-STD-498 and "defines a set of software development activities and resulting software products. It provides a framework for software development planning and engineering" [J-STD 95, iv].

"It is applicable throughout the system life cycle. It establishes uniform requirements for acquiring, developing, modifying and documenting software. It defines standard terminology and establishes activities, tasks and products for a software development or maintenance project. It can be applied to any type of software" [J-STD 95, v].

The following comparisons with ISO 12207 have been noted: "The scope of ISO/IEC 12207 is broader than the scope of J-STD-016. J-STD-016-1995 focuses on the development process while ISO/IEC 12207 includes the acquisition, supply, operation, and maintenance processes. Consequently, the additional materials in US 12207-1996 focus on those areas where the two standards overlap, i.e., development and the supporting processes such as documentation, quality assurance, configuration management, and joint reviews" [Sorensen 96].

TL 9000 — This quality management system was developed for the telecommunications industry.

TSP — The Team Software Process (TSP) together with the prerequisite Personal Software Process (PSP) provide a process framework for high-performance software development teams—a framework with defined processes for creating quality software products within the planned schedule and cost estimates. PSP focuses on individuals and their processes for creating achievable schedule and effort estimates and reducing/managing defects in their products. Engineers trained in PSP use TSP to extend PSP principles to the team level and to apply integrated team management concepts when developing products.

About the Authors

Jeannine M. Siviy is the Deputy Director for the Dynamic Systems Program of the Software Engineering Institute (SEI) and is a leading researcher in the application of Six Sigma to software process improvement. She recently completed a two-year assignment as Technical Advisor to the CEO of the SEI. Previously, Jeannine was a member of the SEI's Software Engineering Measurement and Analysis (SEMA) initiative, where she explored and clarified relationships between Six Sigma and SEI technologies, architected a new measurement and analysis curriculum, and consulted with commercial and defense organizations to analyze data for process improvement. She supported the first software organization in the Department of Defense aviation community to achieve the Capability Maturity Model Integration (CMMI) Level 5.

Before joining the SEI, Jeannine worked for Eastman Kodak Company. Her work there included statistical software implementation for emissions monitoring and a leadership role in the conceptual design of a multimillion-dollar controls system for a new Kodak plant in China. Following ten years of primarily controls systems work, she broadened her experience with applied statistics work in a Kodak worldwide process development program, after which she led a globally dispersed team of engineers responsible for worldwide manufacturing reliability improvements.

Jeannine holds a B.S. in Chemical Engineering from Purdue University and an M.E. in Systems Engineering from Rochester Institute of Technology. She is a certified Six Sigma Quality Black Belt Practitioner and is a guest faculty member of Carnegie Mellon's Tepper School of Business, where she coteaches a Six Sigma course. She serves as cochair of the International Council on Systems Engineering (INCOSE) Measurement Working Group, is an Associate Editor for the American Society for Quality (ASQ) *Software Quality Professional* journal, and is on the editorial review board for the *International Journal of Six Sigma and Competitive Advantage.* She is a senior member of ASQ and a member of the International Society of Six Sigma Professionals (ISSSP), INCOSE, and the Institute of Electrical and Electronics Engineers (IEEE), and she has held several positions in conferences and local chapters. A Pittsburgh native, Jeannine enjoys gardening, reading, yoga, and frequent walks with her dog, Astro.

As Director of Process Management at Lockheed Martin Corporation, Information Systems & Global Services (IS&GS), **M. Lynn Penn** oversees policies and process command media, process compliance via audits, and process improvement activities. She develops and manages compliance to multiple standards and has coordinated the policy and process asset transition through multiple acquisitions. Lynn's previous experience includes serving as a Program Manager of two major Navy Software Development activities, and she was Director of Navy Business, which included six separate Navy Support contracts.

Lynn's involvement with the Capability Maturity Model (CMM) began with version 1.0 and has progressed to the current Capability Maturity Model Integration (CMMI) version 1.2. She has completed formal training in Understanding the SW CMM, SEI Statistical Process Control—Metrics Analysis, the conduct of Software Process Assessments (SPAs), and the CMM Based Appraisal for Internal Process Improvement (CBA IPI). She is currently listed as one of the early adopters of the CMMI, a CMMI Instructor and a SCAMPI B/C Team Lead, and an SEI Affiliate.

Lynn has a B.S. in Mathematics from Villanova University and has done graduate studies in Computer Science and Management Information Systems. She is a certified ISO 9000 internal auditor at IS&GS. She is also a Certified Green Belt and Black Belt in Six Sigma and Lean Techniques. Lynn enjoys quiet time with her husband, Steve, and daughter, Christie. They all enjoy attending Villanova football and basketball games. Go Cats!!

Robert W. Stoddard joined the SEI in 2005 as a Senior Member of Technical Staff. Within the SEI Software Engineering Measurement and Analysis team, he is responsible for training, coaching, and class development related to CMMI High Maturity and Six Sigma topics. Specifically, he completed development of two new SEI measurement courses, "Improving Process Performance Using Six Sigma" and "Designing Products and Processes Using Six Sigma" and made significant contributions to the new SEI "Understanding CMMI High Maturity Practices" course. He also serves as President and CEO of Six Sigma IDS, LLC.

Previously, Bob was both a Distinguished Member of Technical Staff within Motorola University and a Quality Director for Motorola's 3G cell phone business. He led the development of the first Software Design for Six Sigma curriculum at Motorola University, in addition to launching Motorola's first use of software fault-injection testing to help ensure robustness of cell phone products. Bob's Motorola experience was preceded by 14 years at Texas Instruments Defense Systems and Electronics Group as a site Software Quality Engineering manager leading 26 engineers.

He is a certified Motorola Six Sigma Master Black Belt and holds five American Society for Quality (ASQ) Certifications in Software Quality, Reliability, Quality Engineering, Six Sigma Black Belt, and Auditing. Bob is an active member of the IEEE Reliability Society as an elected member of the Adcom and the ASQ Software Division as the Council secretary. He holds a B.S. in Finance and Accounting from the University of Maine at Orono and an M.S. in

Systems Management from the University of Southern California, and he is in progress on a Ph.D. in Reliability Engineering at the University of Maryland at College Park. Bob spends his spare time with his family, including his wife, Heather, and children, Julie, David, and Michelle, and, not to be forgotten, the family pet wire fox terrier, Jeffrey.

SEI Credits

Special permission to reproduce portions of the following works is granted by the Software Engineering Institute.

Goethert, W. and Siviy, J. *Applications of the Indicator Template for Measurement and Analysis,* CMU/SEI-2004-TN-024

Bergey, J.; Dietrich, S.; Firesmith, D.; Forrester, E.; Jordan, A.; Kazman, R.; Lewis, G.; Lipson, H.; Mead, N.; Morris, E.; O'Brien, L.; Siviy, J.; Smith, D.; Woody, C. *Results of SEI Independent Research and Development Projects and Report on Emerging Technologies and Technology Trends,* CMU/SEI-2004-TR-018.

Siviy, Jeannine, Penn, M. Lynn, and Harper, Erin. *Relationships between CMMI and Six Sigma,* CMU/SEI-2005-TN-005.

Gibson, Diane L., Goldenson, Dennis R., and Kost, Keith. *Performance Results of CMMI-Based Process Improvement,* CMU/SEI-2006-TR-004.

Figures from the following presentations:

Siviy, Jeannine and Eileen Forrester, Accelerating CMMI Adoption Using Six Sigma, CMMI Users Group, 2004.

Siviy, Jeannine, Your Six Sigma Measurement Infrastructure and Beyond, Six Sigma for Software Development Conference, 200x.

Hallowell, Dave and Jeannine Siviy, *Bridging the Gap between CMMI and Six Sigma Training,* SEPG 2005.

Penn, M. Lynn and Jeannine Siviy, *Integrating CMMI and Six Sigma in Software and Systems Engineering,* SEPG 2003 (also presented in several other venues).

Siviy, Jeannine, Mission Success via Integrated Approaches to Six Sigma and Domain Practices, IQPC Six Sigma for IT and Software Conference, Chicago, 2006.

Siviy, Jeannine, Mission Success and Effective Multi-Model Process Improvement, III Symposium on Six Sigma Methodology, Guanajuato, Mexico, March 2007.

Florac, William and Jeannine Siviy, Data Analysis Dynamics, SEPG 2003.

Siviy, Jeannine, and Pat Kirwan, Process Improvement in a Multi-Model Environment: An Investigation, European SEPG 2007.

Figures from the course, SEMA Measuring for Performance Driven Improvement I, copyright 2005.

Index

The SEI Series in Software Engineering

ISBN 0-321-18613-3

ISBN 0-321-22876-6

ISBN 0-321-11886-3

ISBN 0-201-73723-X

ISBN 0-321-15495-9

ISBN 0-321-17935-8

ISBN 0-201-54664-7

ISBN 0-321-15496-7

ISBN 0-321-27967-0

ISBN 0-201-70372-6

ISBN 0-201-70482-X

ISBN 0-201-70332-7

ISBN 0-201-60445-0

ISBN 0-201-60444-2

ISBN 0-321-42277-5

ISBN 0-201-52577-1

ISBN 0-201-25592-8

ISBN 0-201-54597-7

ISBN 0-201-54809-7

ISBN 0-321-30549-3

ISBN 0-201-18095-2

ISBN 0-201-54610-8

ISBN 0-201-47719-X

ISBN 0-321-34962-8

ISBN 0-201-77639-1

ISBN 0-201-73-1134

ISBN 0-201-61626-2

ISBN 0-201-70454-4

ISBN 0-201-73409-5

ISBN 0-201-85-4805

ISBN 0-321-11884-7

ISBN 0-321-33572-4

ISBN 0-201-70312-2

ISBN 0-201-70-0646

ISBN 0-201-17782-X

Please see our web site at www.awprofessional.com for more information on these titles.

ESSENTIAL GUIDES TO CMMI

CMMI®, Second Edition: Guidelines for Process Integration and Product Improvement

Mary Beth Chrissis, Mike Konrad, and Sandy Shrum

0-321-27967-0

The definitive guide to CMMI—now updated for CMMI v1.2! Whether you are new to CMMI or already familiar with some version of it, this book is the essential resource for managers, practitioners, and process improvement team members who to need to understand, evaluate, and/or implement a CMMI model.

CMMI® Assessments: Motivating Positive Change

Marilyn Bush and Donna Dunaway

0-321-17935-8

Written for executives, managers, technical professionals, and assessors themselves, this book illuminates every phase of the assessment process, from planning through post-assessment follow-up.

CMMI® Survival Guide: Just Enough Process Improvement

Suzanne Garcia and Richard Turner

0-321-42277-5

Practical guidance for any organization, large or small, considering or undertaking process improvement, with particular advice for implementing CMMI successfully in resource-strapped environments.

CMMI® Distilled, Second Edition: A Practical Introduction to Integrated Process Improvement

Dennis M. Ahern, Aaron Clouse, and Richard Turner

0-321-18613-3

This book is a compact, informative guide to CMMI for practitioners, executives, and managers and includes expanded coverage of how process improvement can impact business goals, and how management can support CMMI adoption.

CMMI® for Outsourcing: Guidelines for Software, Systems, and IT Acquisition

Hubert F. Hofmann, Deborah K. Yedlin, Joseph Elm, John W. Mishler, and Susan Kushner

0-321-47717-0

Best practices for outsourcing and acquiring technology within the CMMI framework, reflecting initial results from a joint General Motors-Software Engineering Institute project, and written for both vendors and suppliers needing to improve their processes.

CMMI® SCAMPI Distilled: Appraisals for Process Improvement

Dennis M. Ahern, Jim Armstrong, Aaron Clouse, Jack R. Ferguson, Will Hayes, and Kenneth E. Nidiffer

0-321-22876-6

Offers concise, realistic guidance for every stage of the SCAMPI process, and demonstrates how to overcome the obstacles to a successful appraisal.

For more information on these and other books in The SEI Series in Software Engineering, please visit www.awprofessional.com/seiseries

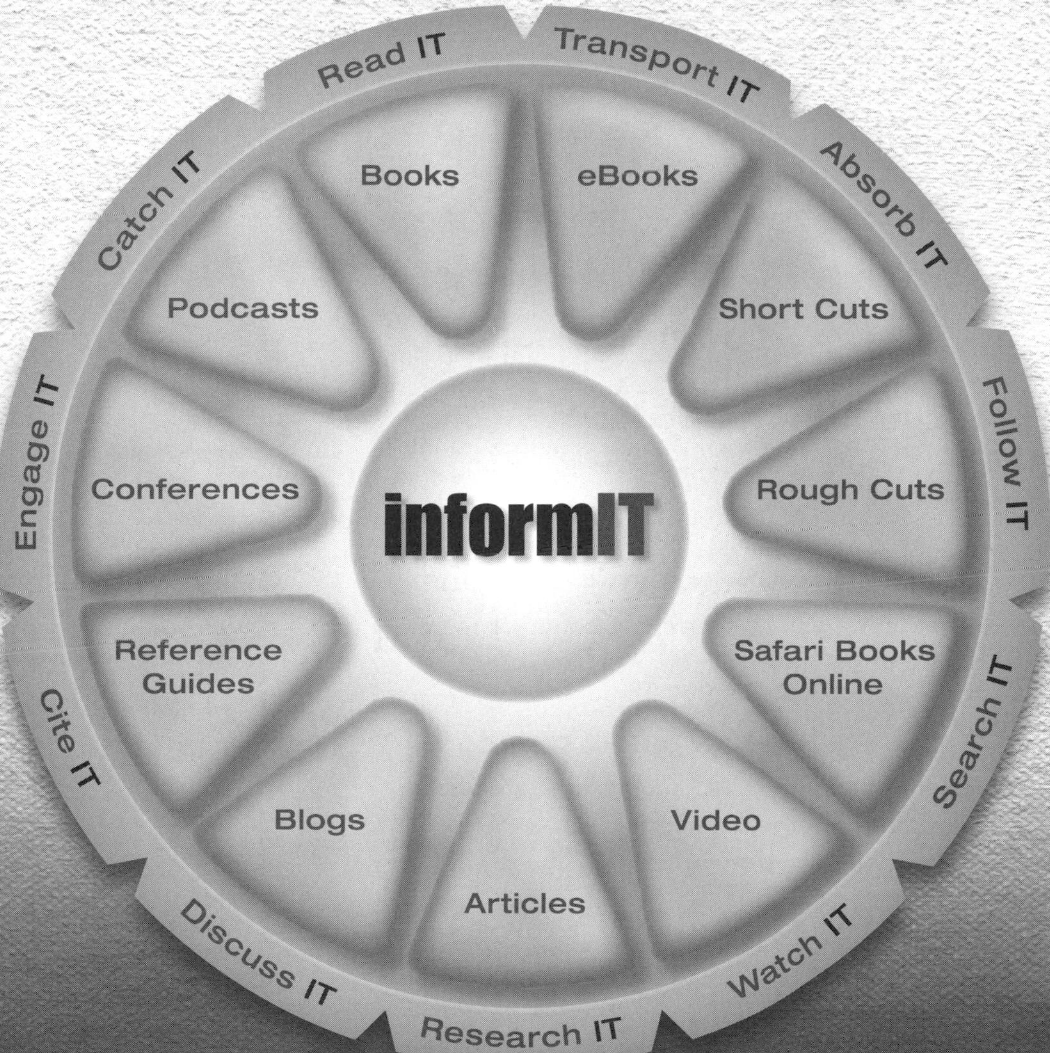